CHILDREN BEHIND BARS

The time is always ripe to do right.

Martin Luther King
('Letter from Birmingham City Jail', 1963)

CHILDREN BEHIND BARS

Why the abuse of
child imprisonment must end

Carolyne Willow

First published in Great Britain in 2015 by

Policy Press
University of Bristol
1-9 Old Park Hill
Bristol
BS2 8BB
UK
+44 (0)117 954 5940
pp-info@bristol.ac.uk
www.policypress.co.uk

North America office:
Policy Press
c/o The University of Chicago Press
1427 East 60th Street
Chicago, IL 60637, USA
t: +1 773 702 7700
f: +1 773 702 9756
sales@press.uchicago.edu
www.press.uchicago.edu

© Policy Press 2015

British Library Cataloguing in Publication Data
A catalogue record for this book is available from the British Library

Library of Congress Cataloging-in-Publication Data
A catalog record for this book has been requested

ISBN 978 1 44732 153 8 paperback
ISBN 978 1 44732 155 2 ePub
ISBN 978 1 44732 156 9 Kindle

The right of Carolyne Willow to be identified as author of this work has been
asserted by her in accordance with the Copyright, Designs and Patents Act 1988.

Cover design by Lyn Davies, www.lyndaviesdesign.com
Front cover image: Getty Images
Printed and bound in Great Britain by Hobbs, Southampton
Policy Press works with environmentally responsible print partners.

FSC
www.fsc.org
MIX
Paper from
responsible sources
FSC® C020438

Contents

List of tables

About the author

Carolyne Willow started her career in 1988 as a child protection social worker. Amidst widespread revelations of abuse in children's homes, she took up roles promoting and protecting the rights of children in care. Between 2000 and 2012, she was head of the Children's Rights Alliance for England, based in London, during which time she led the charity's successful fight for transparency in restraint techniques in G4S and Serco secure training centres and initiated legal action to force the government to notify former child prisoners they had been unlawfully restrained. Carolyne has written about and campaigned on many aspects of children's rights, always championing listening to children, and is proud to have drafted amendments to the law (passed by the UK Parliament in 2004) requiring child protection social workers to give due consideration to the child's wishes and feelings. She lives in Nottingham with her partner and two children.

Acknowledgements

I am very grateful to Tim Bateman, Camila Batmangelidjh, Chris Callender, Deborah Coles, Frances Crook, John Drew, Barry Goldson, Richard Hermer, Pam Hibbert, Frank Judd, Shauneen Lambe, Nick Lessof, Veronica Linklater, Juliet Lyon, Phillip Noyes, David Ramsbotham, Mark Scott, Vivien Stern, Malcolm Stevens and Ian Wise who gave full and stimulating interviews – as well as documents, coffee and the occasional meal.

My special gratitude goes to Yvonne Bailey, Liz Hardy, Carol Pounder and Pam Wilton who welcomed me into their homes and generously shared personal memories of their sons Joseph, Jake, Adam and Gareth respectively.

The Joseph Rowntree Charitable Trust kindly gave me a small grant to cover travel, transcription and other research costs – fantastic support that kept me writing full time.

Tim Bateman frequently acted as a hotline for youth justice queries (though he's not responsible for any mistakes I have made) and Helen Fair and Vivien Stern gave invaluable assistance as the work progressed. Others who promptly answered my calls for help included James Adeley, Eric Allison, Ian Cobain, Dexter Dias, Sue Minto, Joe Plomin, Clare Sambrook, Keith Smith and Thirza Smith.

My good friend and former social work manager Anna Sains carried some of the load of freedom of information (FOI) requests. It's been wonderful working together again after a gap of nearly 25 years, albeit hundreds of miles apart. Everyone at Policy Press has been very encouraging and supportive, and special thanks must go to Alison Shaw for being so enthusiastic from the start. I received very helpful feedback on earlier versions of the whole book, or individual chapters, from Yvonne Bailey, Tim Bateman, John Drew, Karon Monaghan, Phillip Noyes, Roger Smith and Ian Wise – thank you.

My biggest thanks is for my partner, Simon, for continuing to support me in every way possible, and Hambel and Jonah, our children, for showing just the right amount of curiosity about what I've been working on upstairs, and never failing to take my mind off the worst of it.

Preface

I became aware at a young age that children could be locked up. Two children living in opposite houses adjoining the entrance to my primary school were incarcerated. One popular teenager, whose father had died, was sent to borstal and we heard rumours that he had to scrub floors with a toothbrush. My mother felt sorry for him and told us we must treat him normally when he returned to the neighbourhood, despite his shaved head. Another child, who sits in the same line as me in our first infant school photograph, killed a psychiatric nurse. We lived on a council estate in South Shields, the northern town famous for being the birthplace of author Catherine Cookson, and for consistently returning a Labour MP since universal suffrage, but two imprisoned children in one cul-de-sac must still have been a record.

The strange world of institutions also struck me early as I had two long spells in a sanatorium on account of being severely asthmatic. I was aged four and five. Families were allowed to visit once a month. Being made to eat cheese pie, because my mother had forgotten to add it to the list of foods I didn't like, probably sowed the seed for my adult commitment to listening to children.

Then, in adulthood, I was the social worker of a young child who went through the worst of the care system before and after we met. By the time I sat in a courtroom watching him being given a custodial sentence, at the age of 16, we had been through a great deal together – abuse disclosures, foster placement breakdowns, adoption advertising (that led nowhere) and endless trips to a well-known burger outlet. When he was one of the children chosen to go on the stage during a pantomime scene change, we pretended I was his auntie: no child wants to publicly announce they are socialising with their social worker. I read him stories until he fell asleep crying on a camp bed in an emergency foster home, and babysat to try to ease things for other foster carers who still, in the end, 'sent him back'. This was a child I cared about being sent by a court to a place that instilled terror in him. The only other time we had both attended court was several years earlier when the subject of proceedings was the sexual assault he had suffered in his children's home. Now he was standing on his own in the dock, sobbing and powerless. There was no justice in what happened that day. Unlike parents, who are not allowed in court cells, I was able to see him downstairs afterwards and promised to visit him regularly. By then I wasn't his social worker, but social services gave me a letter that meant I could see him on the prison wing, as well as in the visitors' centre. I inevitably ended up visiting him in more than one prison (most children sent to custody reoffend on release).

There were other work-related contacts with prisons over the years, though it is clear that my interest began as a blend of personal and professional experience. The idea for this book came after I left the Children's Rights Alliance for England (CRAE), a London-based charity I ran for more than a decade. The tenth anniversaries of the outrageous deaths of 15-year-old Gareth Myatt and 14-year-old Adam Rickwood in Rainsbrook and Hassockfield secure training centres were approaching. I now had much more time to think, research and write.

One of the first projects I established at CRAE was an analysis of prison inspection reports published between 1998 and 2001, to put on record the disgraceful treatment of children in young offender institutions. Some years later, in 2005, I was invited to join the expert panel of Lord Carlile of Berriew QC's independent inquiry into the use of physical restraint, solitary confinement and forcible strip searching of children in penal custody. I visited two secure training centres and was shocked by what children told me. These newest child prisons had often been described by the state as purpose-built and, I suppose, I had naively expected to find places akin to secure children's homes. They weren't. It was during a visit to Hassockfield secure training centre in Durham that I learned of the nose, rib and thumb 'distractions'. These are restraint techniques that cause children severe pain – deliberately.

A large amount of my time over the next seven years was spent campaigning around various aspects of child incarceration and child protection, particularly the use of physical restraint in the secure training centres. I was lucky to be able to work with lots of energetic, passionate and tenacious people. And I turned to many of them to help me write this book.

Children behind bars presents a large body of knowledge about child prisons that is already in the public domain, though not always easy to locate. It includes information provided by ministers in response to parliamentary questions about different aspects of prison life for children. As there are many gaps in official publications, especially relating to child protection, children's complaints and staff misconduct, I have elicited extensive new data through hundreds of freedom of information (FOI) requests. I have also been lucky to have had access to some leaked documents. Interviews with leading experts, whose names are listed below, were crucial to my research. I sought to hear the views and experiences of individuals who know and care about the treatment and rights of imprisoned children. Each person shared crucial information and helped move along my thinking. The interviews had three broad themes: what is happening to children; why is it happening; and what would make it stop?

Throughout the book I use the term children to refer to people who are, mostly, aged between 14 and 17. I apologise if this causes offence to young people, but I needed to use this terminology to challenge those who claim child prisoners are not actually children. Yvonne Bailey, whose teenage son died in prison in 2002, gave the best rebuttal:

> 'There are some things that are just facts and that's a fact. Until you're 18, you're a child. And there's nothing in the European Convention that says you are a different child. You are just a child. So you're a child if you've got HIV; you're a child if you've got cancer; you're a child if you're perceived as good in society. You're a child.'

There are two types of child prison in England today. Young offender institutions are run by the prison service and hold the majority of child prisoners. Secure training centres are run by private contractors G4S and Serco and hold up to a quarter of child prisoners. Despite their names, both types of institution are listed in the Prison Act 1952. Inspection reports and other research generally show that secure training centres offer superior care and education to young offender institutions. My view is that the deaths of Gareth and Adam, and the history of illegality in the use of restraint, have tainted their reputation forever. Notwithstanding this, the two models differ in many respects and therefore general references to prisons throughout the book should be taken to mean young offender institutions. Discussion and data relating to secure training centres are highlighted separately. Some children remanded or convicted of crimes are held in secure children's homes run by local authorities and governed by the Children Act 1989 and childcare standards. As of July 2014, only 9% of detained children were held in secure children's homes. The Youth Justice Board (YJB) is the statutory body responsible for placing children in the different types of custody. One of its former chairs has said it 'operates something akin to a call centre'[1] to carry out this function.

The interviews that were the richest in experience and insight were also the most painful. These were the interviews with Yvonne Bailey, Liz Hardy, Carol Pounder and Pam Wilton, four mothers who lost their sons to child incarceration. I believe their reflections are the most powerful parts of the book.

Other people who shared their time and expertise were: Dr Tim Bateman, University of Bedfordshire; Camila Batmangelidjh, Kids Company founder and director; Chris Callender, solicitor and former legal director of the Howard League for Penal Reform; Deborah Coles, co-director of INQUEST; Frances Crook, chief executive of the Howard League for Penal Reform; John Drew, former YJB chief executive; Professor Barry Goldson, University of Liverpool; Richard Hermer QC, barrister, Matrix Chambers; Pam Hibbert OBE, chair of trustees, the National Association of Youth Justice; Lord Frank Judd, Labour peer; Shauneen Lambe, barrister and co-founder of Just for Kids Law; Dr Nick Lessof, consultant paediatrician, Great Ormond Street Hospital; Baroness Veronica Linklater, Liberal Democrat peer; Juliet Lyon, director of the Prison Reform Trust; Phillip Noyes, chief advisor on child protection at the National Society for the Prevention of Cruelty to Children; Lord David Ramsbotham, crossbench peer and former chief inspector of prisons; Mark Scott, partner, Bhatt Murphy Solicitors; Baroness Vivien Stern, crossbench peer; Malcolm Stevens, former director of three secure training centres and former government adviser on youth justice policy; and Ian Wise QC, barrister, Monckton Chambers.

None of the people I interviewed is responsible in any way for any factual or analytical errors I may have made. The views and conclusions expressed, unless stated otherwise, are my own.

It was difficult deciding to include very private information about children who have died in custody. Much of this is already in the public domain, but that is no excuse for me passing it around. In the end, I concluded that the more we can know about these children, the greater we can empathise. As the Norwegian sociologist Thomas Mathiesen has said, 'nearness makes for understanding'.[2] Spending so much time reading, thinking and writing about children's lives and suffering, while often incredibly sad, has definitely made me more determined to expose and oppose the harm.

My closing point is that I have not aimed, and do not claim, to have written a balanced book. One of my favourite children's quotes comes from a 15-year-old boy talking about social workers: 'I don't want any support from social workers. They're a load of shit. All they do is remind you of what you're like.'[3] *Children behind bars* originated from my work as a children's rights campaigner and it deliberately documents the worst elements of child prisons.

I finish the work feeling a combination of disappointment that I have been unable to dig as deeply as I wanted in some areas – I spent a lot of time playing 'cat and mouse' over the FOI requests and I didn't always get the cheese – and hopefulness that what I have brought together is enough to finally close the gates on child prisons.

Carolyne Willow
October 2014

Foreword

I was once a child prisoner. It was terrifying. I put up a front and I survived, but I know many children that didn't. This book tells our truth.

It speaks truth to power, and it speaks truth to all of us. The truth is that few people really understand the suffering of incarcerated children.

After reading these accounts I was angry. Then I was thoughtful. Then I stood up and said something must be done. I was both moved and inspired at the same time.

I have waited many years for a book like this to be published. Not only will it aid academics and students in their research, but, because it is written in a straightforward, uncomplicated way, it can be understood by dyslexic plebs like me.

This powerful collection of experiences and facts should serve to remind us all that we must never neglect the human rights of our children, regardless of where they are. It goes where others have not and will not. It shines a light on the dark areas of our 'civilisation'.

Carolyne Willow brings together a wealth of knowledge and research. She has created a very important book, but most importantly she has done this with genuine concern, compassion and understanding.

I'm not an academic, an intellectual, or professional book reviewer, but after my personal experiences as a child prisoner I cannot recommend this book highly enough.

It is a necessary reality check and I'm glad it's out there.

You need to read this.

Increase de peace.

Benjamin Zephaniah
October 2014

ONE

Introduction

The British abhor child abuse. The dam burst of disgust following the outing of Jimmy Savile as a prolific child sex offender, and the outpouring of sympathy for his victims, was testament to this. Maria Miller, then government minister responsible for the BBC, which employed Savile for 40 years, described his abuse as 'absolutely horrifying'.[1] The prime minister, David Cameron, said the nation was 'appalled' by the allegations about the deceased and knighted disc jockey and television presenter, adding that 'they seem to get worse by the day'.[2] Many separate inquiries were established into the conduct of the BBC, the Department of Health, individual hospitals, the police and the Crown Prosecution Service. As accusations resurfaced about abuse in children's homes in North Wales, which had been the subject of a public inquiry in the 1990s, the home secretary, Theresa May, announced another review and told parliament that 'child abuse is a hateful, abhorrent and disgusting crime'.[3] In January 2013, a joint report by the Metropolitan Police and the National Society for the Prevention of Cruelty to Children (NSPCC) quoted a supervisor on the charity's helpline:

> The whole thing … has brought child abuse to the fore…. Seeing people who are adults now talking about how nobody spoke up for them in the past, is a powerful motivator to speak up for children in the present.[4]

But there is one category of children for whom degrading and abusive treatment is more likely than a warm winter coat or a place at university. This is no secret within some parts of government: there

1

are enough official documents depicting children's suffering to supply an origami club with paper for the next 100 years.

There is a small group of children who have suffered the most horrendous hardships in their early lives – poverty, family breakdown, violence and bereavement to begin the list – for whom exile to prison is the sanctioned response to their troubled behaviour. Here they are exposed to environments and practices that in the community would entitle them to state intervention. Ninety years ago, the first international children's rights agreement declared 'the delinquent child must be reclaimed'.[5] Imprisonment is the epitome of physical and psychological exclusion.

Our apparent devotion to punishment has led to the surrendering of child protection norms for young offenders. What else could explain the lack of public outcry following an inspection report in March 2014 telling us a Staffordshire prison was locking children in cells that were 'the worst [inspectors] had seen for some time. Some cells were filthy, gloomy and covered in graffiti, and contained offensive material, heavily scaled toilets, damaged furniture and smashed observation panels'? Many of the cells holding children on their first night in the prison were said to be 'in an uninhabitable state'.[6] Three quarters of inmates at the time of the inspection were held in cells designed for single occupancy but holding two children, with inspectors reporting: 'Cells were cramped with not enough furniture and inadequate toilet screening.'[7] Another inspection report published that month tells of children in one part of the prison locked in cells so small they have to sleep 'in close proximity to the toilet'.[8] In a third report, released in August 2014, inspectors complain that children on the lowest level of the prison's punishment and rewards scheme spent a maximum of 135 minutes out of their cells at weekends. Boys sometimes had less than 15 minutes daily exercise in the open air.[9]

This book catalogues the mistreatment of vulnerable children who are hidden behind perimeter fences and banged up in cells for 14 or more hours a day,[10] miles from home.[11] These are children banished to young offender institutions that have a reputation for being violent and unsafe, and secure training centres found by the High Court to have been sites of 'widespread unlawful use of restraint' for probably a decade but possibly longer.[12] Let us be clear: nobody – child or adult – is ever sent to prison to be looked after, to be cared for and loved. Frances Crook has been chief executive of the Howard League for Penal Reform for nearly three decades. She summarises the effects of imprisonment on children as follows: "It's intellectually stultifying, it's emotionally inhibiting, it's sexually inhibiting, it's frightening, your educational opportunities are restricted. In every aspect it's negative." Former prison governor Andrew Coyle explains that 'prison is an abnormal institution'[13] that 'is by its very nature a debilitating experience'.[14] This is mostly describing the impact on grown adults, not growing children. Labour peer Lord Bradley was asked to investigate the treatment of children and adults with mental health problems and learning disabilities by the police, courts and prisons. His report observed: 'The prison environment, with its rules and regimes governing daily life, can be seriously detrimental to mental health.'[15] The Office of Children's Commissioner for England documented the case of a primary school girl who had suffered domestic violence and family breakdown. As a newly imprisoned teenager, she refused to leave her cell for the first six weeks.[16] Imagine the state sanctioning a child spending the whole of the school summer holidays locked in an austerely furnished room with a toilet, with parents delivering food trays to the door.

The experience of being sent to prison is deeply traumatic, as this boy explains: 'My first night in custody was the worst night of my life. I'd never been lonely before. I felt so lonely'.[17] Joseph Scholes left his parents a note before he hanged himself in prison a month after his 16th birthday: 'I'm sorry, I just can't cope.'

Barrister Shauneen Lambe is co-founder of Just for Kids Law, a specialist legal charity for children. She started her career representing people facing the death penalty in the US, and, during my research for this book, told me:

> 'The first time I went into Feltham [young offender institution], I was really disturbed by it and I'd come back from death row and it was more disturbing to me than death row. The reason was because they've got this kind of holding room, which is glass-walled, and then

there's the visits room there. There are some other private visit rooms there and I could see all these kids waiting, in a glass cage, and none of them were speaking to each other. And I thought how can they be so de-socialised that, when in a glass box, that we're all looking in, they're not even talking to each other? Normal kids would be messing around, wouldn't they? That really disturbed me.'

The public shows unconditional concern for those abused by Savile regardless of whether they were violated in a television studio, a hospital or an approved school. We stand shoulder to shoulder with child protection agencies in decrying child abuse; nearly £119 million was given to the child protection charity NSPCC in 2012-13[18] and tougher regulations were introduced for children's homes following public disclosures that vulnerable children are targeted for sexual exploitation (not news for anyone working in children's social care). It may be that child sexual abuse invites the greatest repulsion and resistance, and other forms of mistreatment are not as reviled. But have we really decided to turn our backs on children held in institutions where abuse and neglect is prevalent? I do not believe we have.

One of the challenges is that information about child prisons drips from different sources, with no single scandal unleashing a flood that cannot be ignored. There is a wealth of research and testimony published by campaign groups, human rights bodies and academics. Some of the most shocking evidence is in court reports and data and documents that take some tracking down. It is difficult to get the full picture. And officials rarely use the siren call of child abuse when it comes to prisons. 'Inappropriate' was the adjective chosen by the prisons inspectorate to describe the routine handcuffing and strip searching of vulnerable children brought to a specialist unit because they could not cope in an ordinary prison.[19] 'Significant weakness' was Ofsted's description for nurses usually being absent during the use of restraint in a secure training centre. Despite this contravening official policy,[20] inspectors gave G4S three months to rectify the breach.[21]

Former head of the prison service, Martin Narey, told parliamentarians of 'the possibility that the public greatly underestimates the full extent of the discomfort, pain and deprivation of liberty for anyone of any age. For a child it is particularly traumatic.'[22] Knowingly causing children discomfort, pain and trauma fits the definition of significant harm in the Children Act 1989 – the part of the law sending social workers to front doors.

Harm in the 1989 Act means ill treatment or the impairment of a child's health or development, including, for example, impairment suffered from seeing or hearing the ill treatment of others. Development encompasses a child's physical, intellectual, emotional, social or behavioural development. Health means physical or mental health; and ill treatment includes sexual abuse and other kinds of mistreatment that are not physical.[23] Chris Callender has worked for many years with children in prison, as a solicitor in law firms in Leeds and London and as the legal director of the Howard League for Penal Reform. In an interview for this book, I asked if any of his cases involved a child suffering significant harm in prison, and he replied as follows:

> 'Most of the cases are likely to be bullying or intimidation
> or risk from either other prisoners or officers within the
> context and confines of the imprisonment. I can't think
> of many cases where those young people were free from
> those issues. So I just think that incarceration in YOIs
> [young offender institutions], particularly YOIs, the risk
> of harm – whether through fights, through turf wars,
> through bullying, threats from officers to children, or
> children to children – is endemic.'

According to government child protection rules, physical abuse encompasses hitting, throwing and 'otherwise causing physical harm to a child'. Emotional abuse can include 'conveying to a child that they are worthless or unloved, inadequate, or valued insofar as they meet the needs of another person'. It may include silencing the child, belittling them and having inappropriate expectations. Serious bullying, and making children feel frightened and in danger a lot of the time, is a form of emotional abuse. Sexual abuse can include 'forcing or enticing a child to take part in sexual activities'. Neglect is the persistent failure to meet the child's most basic needs.[24]

Narey was not even referring to violations of children's rights exposed through freedom of information (FOI) probes, inquests and other legal proceedings. He was describing the effects of imprisonment when those in the system abide by the law. In July 2013, the chief inspector of prisons told BBC Radio 4's Today programme that parents would be 'terrified' were their child to be incarcerated in Feltham young offender institution in London. Had this been a statement from the head of the Care Quality Commission about an older people's home, or a hospital for people with learning disabilities, it is inconceivable that the establishment in question would not have been closed down. Prison service managers seem to have superhuman resilience to exposures that would topple other organisations. This is the same institution in which Zahid Mubarek was murdered in March 2000 by his profoundly disturbed teenage cellmate (Chapter Ten) and, nine years before that, 18-year-old Lee Waite was sexually assaulted with a broken snooker cue in a public part of the prison. Within hours, this asthmatic teenager hanged himself from his upturned bed. The prison service's first dedicated unit for dealing with bullies was, ironically, subsequently named after him.[25]

There were 181 boys in Feltham at the time of the 'terrified parents' inspection, and some of the inspectors' findings stand out as particularly grave – a segregation unit, also holding young adults, with 'ingrained dirt on floors and walls'; almost a third of children reporting victimisation by a member of staff; and 300 acts of violence perpetrated by children on each other in the six months preceding the inspection.[26] However, it was the intensity of violence and fear among children, and the scale of physical decay and squalor, that was untypical – not its existence.

The prisons inspectorate's survey of children held in 11 prisons the previous year found 32% of boys and 22% of girls had felt unsafe.[27] Almost a quarter of girls reported being subject to insulting remarks by prison staff (26% by other girls); and 4% said other girls had physically abused them. More than one in 10 boys reported insulting remarks by staff (16% cited other boys as perpetrators); physical abuse by staff was reported by 4% of the boys; and 10% said other boys had physically abused them. At least nine boys reported sexual abuse by staff and the same number said other boys had sexually abused them (in one prison unit staff sexual abuse was alleged by 6% of the boys). One in every 20 boys reported racial or ethnic abuse by staff (4% by other boys).[28] Nearly one tenth of children reported bullying by prison officers in another piece of research; child–on–child bullying was even higher.[29]

An FOI request I made to the prisons inspectorate revealed that, between July 2009 and March 2014, inspectors reported 130 child protection allegations from 112 children to prison child protection staff or managers following 30 routine inspections of young offender institutions and secure training centres in England.[30] Surveys in only two of the inspections resulted in no allegations of child abuse. Table 1.1 shows there were 87 allegations of physical abuse and 15 allegations of sexual abuse by prison staff, and 11 allegations each of physical and sexual abuse by other children. Six allegations were classified as 'other'. The inspectorate said safeguarding concerns – for example, when a child is threatening suicide or self-harm – are reported separately and physical abuse by child prisoners would ordinarily be dealt with through this route, 'hence the low numbers' here.[31] For reasons to be discussed later, surveys of children in unsafe surroundings are unlikely, on their own, to elicit the true level of abuse and other concerns (p 221).

Early in 2014, the National Offender Management Service (NOMS) disclosed that it had paid £252,370 in compensation over the past five years to individuals detained as children or young

Table 1.1: Child abuse allegations received by prisons inspectorate, July 2009 to March 2014 (30 routine inspections of English child prisons)

Type of abuse allegation	Number of allegations	% of total allegations
Physical abuse by staff	87	67
Physical abuse by other children	11	8
Sexual abuse by staff	15	12
Sexual abuse by other children	11	8
Other	6	5
Total	130	100

adults in 12 English prisons. Payouts in respect of two child prisons – Warren Hill and Hindley young offender institutions – amounted to £76,000 between 2008/09 and 2012/13. Officials refused to disclose the nature of the claims, supposedly to protect the identity of claimants. No data was provided for Ashfield young offender institution (which held children until 2013) as it is a private prison: 'While a contracted prison is required to provide NOMS with specified information as part of the contract, all other information will belong to the contractor.'[32] Private prisons are not covered by FOI legislation, which makes the failure of the state to collect this crucial information even more disgraceful.

State execution became unlawful for all children in the UK in 1933,[33] and judicial whipping was outlawed in 1948[34] (prison officers retained the right to flog until 1967), the same year the National Health Service was formed and the United Nations (UN) adopted the Universal Declaration of Human Rights.This means imprisonment is the worst sanction the state can impose. When I asked Labour peer Frank Judd what he would most fear if a child he cared about were sent to custody, he replied: "Finding out how far I was responsible."

In truth, we are all responsible for child incarceration. We vote in legislators and pay taxes that cover the cost of keeping up to around 1,100 children behind bars at any one time.[35] There has been a massive reduction in the number of detained children over the past five years (around 1,300 fewer children in custody in 2012/13 compared with 2008/09),[36] although the UK remains one of the chief child incarcerators in Europe. Latest results of the annual penal survey conducted by the Council of Europe reveals only two of 47 member states with more children in prison than the UK in September 2011 (Greece and Turkey, though the Russian Federation did not participate in the survey). Fewer than 10 children were imprisoned in 16 countries – including Denmark, Finland, Norway, Spain and Sweden.[37] Apart from Spain, which has more than eight million children, these countries have much smaller child populations than the UK. However, this data shows the UK operates far outside of European norms in its use of penal incarceration for children.

Imprisoning children involves substantially more than depriving them of their liberty. It squanders precious time that could be spent investigating what has gone wrong in their lives and changing it. Research on the factors affecting children in care's offending concludes there is 'a potential window of opportunity' all the way through to late adolescence. 'Highly targeted therapeutic and education support' is advocated for those whose behaviour remains problematic, alongside the warning that 'the prospects are likely to be bleak' if improvements do not occur before adulthood.[38] The juxtaposition of children 'killing time' in prison with the state fining parents for having holidays with their children during school term-time tells us something about the value ascribed to these contrasting childhoods (whether the wellbeing of children is best served by sanctioning parents for school absences is a different debate).

Adolescence is a period of massive transformation, when even teenagers who have not been 'dredged from the deepest reservoirs of structural neglect and institutionalised immiseration'[39] require very careful handling. Parents know too well the emotional landmines avoided and stepped on daily. This leads to my prime objection to the incarceration of children, and the motivation for this book: that, as well as being reckless (for the child and the taxpayer), imprisonment is deeply harmful.[40] Studies on the effects of incarceration have shown consistently that the pain spreads much further than the curtailment of freedom. Sixty years ago, the American sociologist Gresham Sykes researched the minutiae of life in a maximum security prison in the state of New Jersey and reported the following:

> The mere fact that the individual's movements are restricted, however, is far less serious than the fact that imprisonment means that the inmate is cut off from family, relatives, and friends, not in the self-isolation of the hermit or the misanthrope, but in the involuntary seclusion of the outlaw.... It is not difficult to see this isolation as painfully depriving or frustrating in terms of lost emotional relationships, of loneliness and boredom. But what makes this pain of imprisonment bite most deeply is the fact that the confinement of the criminal represents a deliberate, moral rejection of the criminal by the free community.[41]

Child prisoners rarely move from being fully included in society one day, to outsiders the next. Barrister and peer Lord Carlile conducted an inquiry into the treatment of child prisoners and later referred to the 'animalised [and] brutalised structure' of prison life that compounds what has been missing in the lives of these children.[42] One of the people I interviewed for this book said he would leave the country with his children were they to be sentenced to custody, adding quickly that this situation would never arise because "they are princesses". Our prisons are filled with the poorest, most disadvantaged children who often have considerable mental health and learning difficulties. Even before they begin the admissions process, which involves being given a number, removing clothes and answering questions about suicidal thoughts and substance misuse, the lives of most child prisoners will have told them they are worthless – certainly worth less than other children. Analysis of the forms completed when a child has contact with the criminal justice system shows more than a third of girls have been abused and many have endured significant bereavement or loss (29%) or witnessed family violence (24%). Only 17% live with both parents.[43]

Children learn in prison that suppressing their feelings and being outwardly tough is the best way to survive, although the chances are they believe this already. A sociology professor points to the 'sham veneer of machismo' children are forced to display in prison.[44] *Guardian* columnist and writer Erwin James, who started offending at the age of 10 and was incarcerated for 20 years as an adult, observes: 'Prisoners live at the mercy of those who are in charge, and of each other, and dignity is a scarce commodity.'[45]

Hunger is a common complaint of child inmates in our (still) rich country (Chapter Eight). In January 2014, prisons minister Jeremy Wright told parliament the prison service spent an average of £1.96 a day on prisoner meals in 2013/14, an 11% reduction on the previous year.[46] Hospitals spend three times this amount.[47] A 2013 inspection of Hassockfield secure training centre reported that the catering department was proposing to senior managers that children be given more fruit.[48] This was more than 13 years after the centre had opened (on the site of a derelict detention centre, where children had been raped and beaten in the 1970s and 1980s). By then the British taxpayer must have handed over circa £100 million to the private companies running the centre.[49] Children interviewed in a recent study of food in young offender institutions complained they 'were often left feeling hungry after meals'.[50] Only one of the nine prisons achieved the policy requirement of having no more than 14 hours between evening meal and breakfast.[51] In June 2014, children were served mouldy bread in Cookham Wood young offender institution – while inspectors were on the premises.[52]

Coroners and judges have ruled that unlawful restraint regimes continued unabated for many years in secure training centres; and human rights bodies have criticised the UK's idiosyncratic reliance on pain infliction as a tool of restraint (Chapters Five and Six). INQUEST, the charity that supports the bereaved families of children and adults who have died in police and prison custody, told the government in 2007 'that the violation of the rights of this large body of children goes worryingly beyond inhumane and humiliating treatment. It has been proved forensically that it presents a persistent risk of injury, suffering or death.'[53]

It is a matter of public record that large numbers of children have been injured, many very badly, following restraint in penal institutions over the past decade. In November 2011, parliament was told that 285 'exception reports' had been submitted to civil servants since 2006 by G4S and Serco in respect of the four secure training centres. The two companies are required to produce these reports whenever children's breathing has been compromised during restraint, or they have suffered serious injury requiring hospital treatment.[54] There are details that do not make their way to parliament, such as the five children who suffered six wrist fractures during restraint in Castington young offender institution between January 2007 and September 2008. A reply to a question in parliament in December 2007 reported that only one child had suffered such an injury after restraint in that prison that year.[55] Even the government's correction in September 2009 did not result in the true figure being recorded.[56] The internal report I obtained through an FOI request states that none of the five children was restrained because they were fighting and that most of the injuries were sustained in areas without CCTV (p 146). A separate internal prison review was undertaken after six incidents in which children were thought to have suffered a fractured or broken bone during restraint in Hindley young offender institution (one suspected fracture was later found to have been wrongly diagnosed). The injuries occurred between February 2009 and April 2011, and only one of the situations arose because a child was fighting. One boy made an official complaint to the Prisons and Probation Ombudsman after he was moved to another prison. It was upheld (p 150).

Information obtained from the Youth Justice Board (YJB) shows there was on average 84 self-harm incidents in young offender institutions, and 16 in secure training centres, every month throughout 2012 (Chapter Three). Between 2007/08 and 2011/12, 81 children in young offender institutions and 17 in secure training centres required hospital treatment following self-harm.[57] One teenage girl incarcerated in a women's prison in Wakefield self-harmed so badly she needed blood transfusions. She was passed back and forth between prison segregation and hospital until her lawyer at the Howard League for Penal Reform obtained a High Court injunction in 2005 preventing her return to prison (p 54).

Fifteen-year-old Alex Kelly had been in the care of Tower Hamlets council since he was six years old, after medical examinations found he had been raped 'over a substantial time'.[58] He hanged himself at Cookham Wood young offender institution in Kent in January 2012. The serious case review conducted after his death praises the 'considerable efforts' made by staff to support him, but observes that this was in tandem with Alex being subject to disciplinary charges, including for blocking the observation panel on his cell door.[59] It would appear from a review conducted by the Prisons and Probation Ombudsman that no one had considered leaving the child's cell door open.[60] Alex had been found on two occasions 'in the last few days of his life' with nooses made from trainer laces.[61]

As a child protection social worker, I worked with children who had been sexually assaulted in their own homes. Like other social workers, I spent a lot of time reassuring children they were not to blame and no-one had the right to hurt them. Some years later, during my work on Lord Carlile's inquiry (Chapter Four), I met children who had been strip searched in secure training centres. They said they felt embarrassed, degraded and uncomfortable. One girl told me about being strip searched during her period; she had to pass her sanitary towel to staff for inspection.[62] Had I still been a social worker and these children were telling me about their fathers, uncles or children's homes workers, they would have been officially classed as victims of child abuse. However, they were child prisoners and these routine attacks on their integrity were authorised by the state. Children in young offender institutions have reported being made to squat in front of officers without their underwear. Routine strip searching was banned for female prisoners several years before the same policy change for children.

Lord Carlile concluded that strip searching is not necessary to maintain good order and safety. The response of the YJB was to pledge a review and its then chair, Rod Morgan, wrote in *The Guardian* newspaper: 'Some young people arrive in custody with drugs or weapons hidden on their bodies and clothing. The consequences of drugs or knives inside a secure establishment are not hard to imagine, and every precaution, including searching, has been taken to stop this'.[63] It was reasonable to assume that Morgan's organisation possessed strong evidence making it resistant to change. Yet the YJB only began collecting strip searching data in 2011, five years after the Carlile Inquiry reported and 11 years after it was given legal responsibility for booking children into prisons.

This brings to mind Jerome Miller's toilet seat story. Miller was the psychiatric social worker responsible for closing down child prisons in Massachusetts in the US in the 1970s. When he questioned the absence of toilet seats in reform schools, Miller was told they were a security risk, as children could rip them off and use them as a weapon: 'The fact that a toilet seat attack hadn't occurred in the memory of any staff I asked was beside the point. A threatening new reality had been created.'[64] It is instructive that when he became head of the Department of Youth Services, Miller's goal was to humanise the state's reformatories. It was only when he realised he could not 'keep them caring and decent' that he set about their closure:

> [W]henever I thought we'd make progress, something
> happened – a beating, a kid in an isolation cell, an offhand
> remark by a [manager] that told me what I envisioned

would never be allowed. Reformers come and reformers go. State institutions carry on. Nothing in their history suggests that they can sustain reform, no matter what money, staff, and programs are pumped into them. The same crises that have plagued them for 150 years intrude today. Though the casts may change, the players go on producing failure.[65]

The lessons of abuse in children's residential care are still being learnt, not least because of the media and political attention given to two men, Jimmy Savile and the Liberal Democrat MP Cyril Smith, who died before being made to face up to their crimes against children. Not all of the abuse in children's homes was sexual and physical. One major inquiry concerned 'pindown', which operated in four Staffordshire children's homes between 1983 and 1989. The inquiry chairs concluded that 'not less than 132 children' suffered 'the worst elements of institutional control'.[66] One aspect of the abusive regime was to force children to remove their clothes and wear nightwear.

Young offender institutions do not make children dress in nightwear during the day, but they do compel them to wear prison clothes (including 'alternative clothing' – p 50). In June 2011, inspectors observed 'petty and restrictive' rules operating in Lancaster Farms young offender institution. Only children on the highest level of the behaviour management scheme could wear their own clothes and even this was restricted to their cells and during other very limited periods.[67] Earlier inspection reports showed this to be institutionally entrenched. Five months into the new millennium, inspectors found the prison was experiencing 'problems getting Prison Service clothes small enough for many of the residents' and recommended: 'Small clothing should be available from Central Prison Service Stores.'[68] This was five years after the NSPCC had published a report from survivors of abuse in care. One of the violations depicted in the report concerned the humiliation of being forced to wear communal clothing: 'If we did not achieve so many points we were not allowed to wear our own clothes.'[69]

The final inspection of Warren Hill young offender institution in Suffolk before it became an adult prison in April 2014 reported that children were made to wear prison clothes but could keep their own underwear and socks. The only washing facility for underwear and socks was cell basins, so 'many chose to wear prison-issue underclothes'.[70]

Cruelty lurks throughout the transfer process from court to prison, with some children even given plastic bags to urinate in (Chapter Nine). A children's charity was asked to review safeguarding in child prisons and its 2008 report observed the following:

> The escort arrangements operating to take young people to YOIs [young offender institutions] get them off to a frightening start. They often arrive late, after hours spent in a small, uncomfortable cubicle within a van, frightened not only about where they are being taken to but what will happen to them if the van crashes.[71]

We all know intuitively that prisons are treacherous places for children. They are up there with strangers loitering at school playgrounds, household fires and acrimonious divorces. Even with this awareness, it is shocking that 31 children have died in young offender institutions and two in secure training centres since 1990, the year the UK signed a children's rights agreement with the UN only to use detention as a measure of last resort. It is not that a child dying in the care of the state is rare. Fourteen-year-old Wayne Cann died in a secure children's home in Wales in January 1998[72] and 56 children looked after by English local authorities die on average every year.[73] Many of these deaths will have arisen from children having life-limiting conditions and health problems; a review found half of the 30 children who died in the care of Scottish local authorities between 2009 and 2011 fitted these two categories.[74] What makes child deaths in custody particularly distressing is that inquests have repeatedly uncovered children with mammoth-size needs held in squalid conditions with grossly substandard care. Deborah Coles is the co-director of INQUEST and has been working for the charity since before teenager Philip Knight hanged himself in an adult prison in Swansea in 1990 (pp 57 and 271) and during my research for this book told me:

'I didn't have children when I was involved with Philip
Knight, and 1994 was when [my son] was born and I do
think that, as my kids have grown up, and you see the
vulnerability of your own kids who are in supportive
environments with food on the table, have got a home,
are relatively stable or go to a nice school, and then you
look at these kids who are in prison, it just makes you ...
it hits you in a different way actually, it makes you even
more ashamed.'

Inquests recorded a verdict of suicide for 11 children's deaths in
penal custody, and accidental death for eight of the children. In
addition, there were four narrative verdicts,[75] five open verdicts,
three verdicts of misadventure and one unlawful killing. Accidental
death and misadventure are verdicts given when juries decide a death
was unintended; narrative verdicts are detailed statements of the
background issues surrounding a person's death; and an open verdict
means there was insufficient evidence to return another verdict.[76] At
the time of writing, an inquest into the death of 15-year-old Alex
Kelly had not been held.

All but four of the children whose deaths were judged to be suicide
were known to have self-harmed in the past or were being monitored
at the time of their death. It wouldn't take a child psychiatrist to
doubt whether the remaining four could withstand imprisonment.
One had developed serious alcohol problems after the death of his
mother from cancer on his 14th birthday; another had severe learning
difficulties and was worried about his parents who both had cancer;
a third child had endured chronic bullying and requested to be
placed in segregation for his own safety; and the parents of the fourth
child were very critical of the prison for not allowing their son his
medication for attention deficit hyperactivity disorder.

Two of the 33 children who died as prisoners, 15-year-old Gareth
Myatt and 14-year-old Adam Rickwood, were held in secure training
centres run by G4S and Serco respectively. These children died four
months apart, 10 years ago, after being subject to appalling forms
of restraint.

Before he lost consciousness, Gareth told the three guards holding him down that he could not breathe. The response was that if he could speak he could breathe. He died minutes later from positional asphyxia (Chapter Five). The YJB suspended the use of the seated double embrace, the authorised hold used on Gareth, two months later. Many other children's lives had been endangered.

Adam was subject to the 'nose distraction' – a prison restraining technique that involves a severe assault to the nose – hours before he was found hanging in his cell. Adam's nose bled for about an hour, and his request to go to hospital for an X-ray was refused. He left behind a note asking what gave staff the right to hit a child in the nose. Although this particular technique was eventually withdrawn by ministers, other forms of restraint that rely on the deliberate infliction of pain remain approved (Chapter Six).

None of the 33 child deaths in prison has been dignified with a public inquiry. A full and transparent investigation, involving a range of childcare and children's rights experts and seeking evidence of child-centred approaches in other countries, would allow lessons to be truly learnt about how we should be responding to child offenders. Grieving families may also see information or action hitherto denied. Adam Rickwood's mother told me she is still not certain what her son was wearing when he lost consciousness, as the prison mislaid some of his clothes.

The ordinary staffing ratio of prison officer to child in young offender institutions is 1:10[77] and is expected to deteriorate to 1:12.[78] Secure training centres have much higher ratios – between 2:5 and 3:8 per unit.[79] Neither institution matches the staffing levels of secure children's homes – between 1:2 and 6:8[80] – and special schools, which operate a 1:1 ratio.[81] John Drew, former head of the YJB, told me two members of staff would be necessary to look after every child in an establishment truly equipped to meet their needs.

There are people who believe it is only fair to refuse child offenders the care and treatment I advocate in this book. Some even deny they are children at all – a practice the historian Hugh Cunningham traces back to the 19th century, although at least the goal of the child rescuers of the time was to turn the 'delinquent' back into a child.[82] Michael Howard, the home secretary who signed the first contract for a secure training centre, famously said in 1993 that child offenders 'are adult in everything except years'.[83] Fifteen years later, Labour's secretary of state for justice, Jack Straw, was asked whether he would reverse the UK's standing in Europe as the greatest child incarcerator. His response was menacing: 'Most young people who are put into custody are aged 16 and 17 – they are not children; they are often large, unpleasant thugs, and they are frightening to the public.'[84] On that very day, Straw's prisons minister told parliament there were 458 children in young offender institutions and secure training centres who were known to be at risk of self-harm, 419 at known risk of drug dependency, 310 with known mental health problems and 91 at known risk of bullying. Nearly 400 children were in prison for the first time.[85] Furthermore, the justice secretary should have been aware that, of the 30 child deaths in custody there had been at the time of his speech, 24 were children aged 16 or 17. All 30 of the dead children were boys.

Parliament first legislated to protect children from maltreatment in 1889. It was after the Second World War, when the effects of evacuation became clear, that an evolutionary leap in the understanding of children's psychological needs was made. Knowledge of the risks of institutional care and the damage caused by applying criminal labels to children came later. Following widespread revelations of abuse in children's homes, in 1996 the Conservative government established a major review of safeguards for children living away from home, led by the former chief inspector of social services, Sir William Utting. He concluded that 'prison is no place for children'.[86] This was also the view of the then chief inspector of prisons, Sir David Ramsbotham, who around the same time published a review of the treatment of children and young people in prison. Ramsbotham said the prison service 'should relinquish responsibility for all children under the age of 18'.[87] Both reviews praised the work and dedication of prison staff and urged a radical change of direction that could be only ever achieved by ministers. A wide range of organisations continues to lobby government to remove children from penal institutions. This includes the Public and Commercial Services Union, which has more than 5,000 members working within NOMS in which the prison service is located.[88]

There was tremendous jubilation among penal reform and children's rights organisations when the Howard League for Penal Reform won its legal battle in 2002 confirming that the Children Act 1989 applies to child prisoners (Chapter Eleven). Prisons before this were seen to be child protection exclusion zones. I made FOI requests to every local authority in England to find out how they are implementing their duty to investigate suspicions of significant harm in prisons. The results are disturbing. Imprisoned children are also out of sight nationally. The independent review of child protection established by the incoming coalition government failed to consider child prisoners and, as of July 2013, not a single minister in the Department for Education, which leads child protection policy, had visited a child prison since coming into power.[89]

Young offender institutions and secure training centres were created in the late 1980s and 1990s respectively. The former replaced youth custody centres and detention centres and the latter were new constructions located adjacent to adult prisons or, in the case of Hassockfield secure training centre, on the site of a former detention centre. The invention of secure training centres marked a significant break with modern penal policy in locking up younger children, and the jailing of juveniles who have not committed serious offences. However, children have been imprisoned in a variety of penal institutions since the 1800s, before which prisons were holding places for capital punishment and banishment to the colonies. The first detention centre for under-21-year-olds was established in the village of Borstal in Kent in 1902 and Parkhurst prison on the Isle of Wight, which opened in 1838, was the first to have a dedicated juvenile wing for those awaiting transportation. As Professor Barry Goldson reminded me, "It is the locked institution that is the constant factor" – despite everything we now know about children and the damage done by incarceration. Surgeons operating on undeserving patients without the use of anaesthetic would be the medical equivalent of the cruel, dangerous and anachronistic practice of child imprisonment.

The mother of Adam Rickwood described the prison in which her child died as 'the scariest place I have ever witnessed'.[90] Adam himself referred to 'a 30-foot wall and cage all around me' in a letter home. The Prisons and Probation Ombudsman observed a 'prison-like' environment following his investigation into Adam's death:

> I was surprised at how austere and prison-like the centre was. Furnishings were sparse and unattractive and movement was impeded by an oppressive number of locked doors.[91]

The senior civil servant in the Home Office who had the task of designing secure training centres told a BBC reporter:

> 'My impression when I went into Hassockfield, when I looked at it, was that this was a category B prison, or a prison-looking building, which turned out to be a category B prison design. And not in keeping with what I'd put together whilst with the Home Office as a building fit for purpose of looking after children. It was pretty much a shock, to be honest with you.'[92]

A category B prison is one step down from a maximum-security prison. Some of our country's most infamous criminals have been held in category B prisons, including Fred and Rosemary West.

Between 56% and 79% of children released from penal institutions in 2011/12 were proven to have committed at least one other offence within a year (secure children's homes appear to have similarly high reoffending rates).[93] In other words, more than £200 million a year was given to the prison service and private companies[94] for an intervention that causes children to suffer greatly – and that does not work. Latest data shows a slight overall – 4% – reduction in proven reoffending from all forms of child custody, and the September 2012 rate is 9% lower than in 2000 (comparable records are not available before this),[95] but this cannot disguise the horrible reality. Politicians sometimes argue that at least incarceration stops people committing crimes while they are locked up. The high number of assaults in prison shows this to be delusional thinking (unless prisoner victimisation does not count as 'real crime'). Moreover, a parent who ties their child to a chair with a rope could proudly proclaim they had stopped them stealing from the biscuit tin, but how many of us would applaud their technique? The former chair of the YJB, Rod Morgan, in his resignation interview on BBC Newsnight, explained:

> 'I have to say to you that a custodial establishment, no matter how good we make them, is the worst conceivable environment within which to improve somebody's behaviour.'[96]

The resourcefulness of human beings means that some prisoners do thrive against the odds, just as plants grow through cracks in concrete. Prison for some people can be a refuge, providing them with the first real opportunity to feel safe and to learn. The following extract provides a good example of this; it is taken from a letter from Camila Batmangelidjh – the founder of Kids Company, a charity that provides support to vulnerable children – to Rocky, a boy with a desperately fractured childhood serving a nine-year prison sentence: 'You like prison. It is safe, it is better than home has ever been for you.'[97] These individual details must never obscure the larger canvas of penal harm. Many impoverished families enjoyed a balanced diet for the first time during Second World War rationing, although nobody advocates war as a public health strategy.

Child prisoners are easy prey for ministers keen to parade faux strength. The latest warrior is justice secretary Chris Grayling, who announced through a national newspaper that his department was reviewing the punishment and rewards scheme in child prisons: 'It seems ludicrous to me that we dole out privileges regardless of how children behave ... luxuries must be a reward for good behaviour not an automatic right.'[98] An international review of prison mother and baby units observed that girls in the G4S-run Rainsbrook secure training centre 'can even earn the privilege of putting posters on the walls'.[99] I have spoken with children who have had everything removed from their cells as a sanction, including photographs and education certificates from walls, and none has ever told me that this helped improve their behaviour. Without exception, they have communicated a profound sense of anger, bitterness and injustice. The minister's later announcement that child prisoners would 'face tough sanctions' for breaching a 10.30 pm lights and television curfew[100] was presumably aimed at portraying Grayling as a firm but fair patriarch. There are many reasons children come to rely on artificial light and television and radio into the early hours, including fear, loneliness and restlessness. Darkness does not take any of these away. The political benefits of talking and acting tough are obvious. It is intriguing that politicians seek such kudos. In the main these are adults who have enjoyed opportunities that child prisoners have only ever witnessed on television and computer screens. Most politicians espouse fair play, yet there is no equality of arms between ministers and child prisoners. When I asked Lord Judd, who held a number of ministerial positions in the 1970s, why he thought ministers felt the need to be tough with troubled, disadvantaged children, he mused:

> 'It's very interesting [and] certainly needs a lot of serious psychological analysis ... One thing I'm very certain about is that [ministers] do run scared of the media, they really are scared of the media; or scared is perhaps unkind for some. They really think the media can create havoc.... All politicians are human but it's the desire to prove they haven't gone soft: we're tough. And it's a complete misunderstanding of what toughness is. I mean, it's not tough, it's self-indulgent stupidity.'

I did not ask to visit prisons or seek to interview incarcerated children for this book because I wanted to bring together material already seen and collected by government. Extensive new information is included throughout – obtained through FOI requests and collated from parliamentary questions. This is new to us, the public, though not to government. I am not claiming all this data is lying dormant, wilfully unnoticed or disregarded by those working in and close to prisons. Neither am I denying the efforts and successes of people working in a variety of roles within the system. In highlighting the colossal harm done to children in penal institutions, it might appear at times that I downplay, or simply do not comprehend, the challenges inherent in looking after children who, for the most part, were failed catastrophically long before they were ever 'sent down'. This is not my intention. Another criticism might be that I do not, in this book, give enough attention to the damage done to children in other institutional settings. I agreed with Phillip Noyes, the NSPCC's chief advisor on child protection, when he told me "it's probably a fallacy to believe the prison service is worse in all things than other forms of institutional care", but this does not diminish the harm done to incarcerated children.

Past experience of residential care has taught us that banishing groups of children to large institutions far away from their families and public view, and casting them as unruly and untrustworthy, is fundamentally unsafe. It allows us to tolerate practices and treatment that would be unthinkable elsewhere, and tells would-be abusers these children stand alone and unguarded. Chapters Three to Ten consider particular aspects of children's experiences of incarceration, giving their own accounts when these are available. Before that, Chapter Two looks at the backgrounds and characteristics of the children we lock up. Chapter Eleven analyses the adequacy of systems and procedures established to detect and respond to child abuse and other concerns, and the concluding chapter calls for the complete abolition of penal custody for children.

TWO

'Things were not right at home'

King Charles II wanted to provide a loving home for veterans 'broken by age or war', and this led to the opening of the Royal Chelsea Hospital in 1692.[1] The Chelsea Pensioners, wearing their characteristic scarlet tunics and tricorne hats, are among the most venerated people in society. To find those shattered by age and circumstance, brought down in their own homes and communities, you would need to visit the small network of penal institutions run by the prison service and G4S and Serco. Here you will meet the veterans of child abuse, neglect, poverty, educational exclusion and health and wealth inequality. Not every child who is violated becomes embroiled in offending and the criminal justice system, or fails to get the help they need to stay on track, but it is exceptional to find a child prisoner whose biography is free of extreme suffering. As one child said during an investigation by the Office of Children's Commissioner for England into the wellbeing of young people in the youth justice system, 'I could write a whole book about the bad stuff that happened to me.'[2]

Baroness Vivien Stern has worked in the field of criminal justice since the late 1970s, and within the House of Lords is a vociferous champion of child prisoners. In a research interview, she told me that the 2011 summer riots may have led to a small number of children from nurturing backgrounds being incarcerated, but this was a 'special situation' because:

> 'The children we lock up in prison are a subsection of a subsection of children really. They constitute the most damaged and disadvantaged of a very damaged and

disadvantaged group of people. I would think myself that there's not a single child in custody who comes from what would be regarded as a normal background where the normal nurturing of upbringing goes on.'

Children in supportive homes and communities are usually diverted from prison, "so the institutions end up full of a real concentration of desperately deprived, unhappy, neglected children", says Stern. Professor Barry Goldson, a youth justice expert and former social worker, told me that children in prison are "a community of victims".

This is not to heap blame on the parents of child prisoners, as many will have made heroic attempts to access professional help. Most will have parented in the swamp of low income, substandard housing, closed doors and, increasingly, social stigma. Prisons are filled with people – adults and children – from very poor, working-class communities. Richard Wilkinson and Kate Picket's 'spirit level' study shows high levels of income inequality are correlated with high levels of imprisonment: 'more unequal societies are more punitive' and higher spending on imprisonment is associated with lower expenditure on welfare.[3] The most affluent in our society can delegate parenting tasks (though not parental love)[4] to live-in nannies, au pairs and boarding schools and still hold their heads high, whereas poor parents unable to cope have to fall back on cash-starved social services and charity handouts. There is also the matter of higher mortality rates in disadvantaged communities, which only those with hearts of stone would blame parents for. The Prison Reform Trust carried out an in-depth examination of the backgrounds of 200 children sentenced to custody in 2008, and found that those in this sample were three times more likely than children generally to have experienced the death of a parent or sibling.[5] Earlier research by crime reduction charity Nacro with persistent young offenders in a London borough (n=41) found 22% had suffered bereavement.[6] The Youth Justice Board's (YJB) own analysis of the backgrounds of 181 children in custody for serious offences found 20% were known to have experienced a significant bereavement, including the death of a parent, sibling or grandparent.[7]

Connections between income, wealth and child maltreatment are not the subject of this book. However, not acknowledging the pernicious effects of inequality is, to modify the Quaker edict 'speak truth to power', not speaking truth of the powerless. Deprivation makes parenting infinitely harder. It limits what parents can offer their children in the way of material comforts and it impinges on the psychological imperative of 'being there'. Only those with Herculean self-discipline could maintain a calm, child-focused and chirpy disposition while constantly fretting about paying the rent, delivering the next meal, feeding gas and electricity meters and negotiating with money lenders. That poverty, deprivation and stigma – like affluence, opportunity and status – tend to cloak the same families and localities means struggling parents were likely themselves to have gone without as children. Some will have been so injured by their own childhoods that their cavernous needs always prevail. But even in our wealthy country, with a child protection system emulated the world over, the vast majority of abused and neglected children are not taken under the wing of social services and neither do they perish at the hands of their parents. Most move through childhood without coming to the attention of criminal justice agencies. A small number of maltreated children becomes increasingly isolated and disconnected from the mainstream. Their inner turmoil shows in behaviour sometimes shocking and repulsive – not as a consequence of any intrinsic defection or difference but because these children have been wronged.

Take the case heard by the High Court in April 2012, concerning a young man whose first contact with psychiatric services was at the age of nine. He had two short stays in psychiatric hospitals, including a period after being detained under the Mental Health Act. From the age of 14, this boy was self-harming severely and often. The court was told this included 'breaking bones, lacerations, overdoses, cutting the tendons in his feet and inserting objects into his penile urethra leading to a number of operations' and suicide attempts. The child had been physically and sexually assaulted. One of his attackers was a man who held an axe to his throat and tried to rape him when he was 14. This was also the age at which he received his first custodial sentence for burglary, theft, handling stolen goods and criminal damage. Further imprisonment came at the age of 16, for similar offences, and was followed by adult incarceration. Now, aged 24 years, he was in court challenging his transfer from a medium- to high-security hospital.[8] Another case shows the depth of some children's suffering. This was a hearing about an imprisoned 16-year-old that was significant because it challenged the differential treatment of remanded boys and girls. The boy had been remanded to a young offender institution; had he been female, he would have been sent to a secure children's home run by social services. The court found parliament was entitled to make the 'invidious choice' to protect 15- and 16-year-old remanded girls from a prison environment but quashed the order sending the teenager to prison. What is pertinent to this discussion is the child's background. He had been in care from the age of five, after his mother was imprisoned for arson of a neighbour's house. It was believed he may have been physically and sexually abused by his father, who was also imprisoned after an incident where he dressed up as a Nazi and held the young child and his family hostage until armed police rescued them. The judge said the boy had had a 'wretched early childhood'. Once in care, he had been in numerous foster homes and children's homes and attended several special schools. By the time he was 16, he had not attended school for two or three years. His first experience of imprisonment was at the age of 14, when he was detained at Medway secure training centre in Kent. A consultant psychiatrist observed that this setting, like all of his previous social care placements, was neither appropriate nor helpful. The child was said to have high levels of psychological dysfunction and required a 'secure but therapeutic environment'.[9] This was not an exceptional case of child hardship. I interviewed the barrister who represented the boy in court, Ian Wise QC. He rattled off a long list of similarly vulnerable children he had worked for and said: "I could tell you horrific stories about children I've been to see in custody with one after another of them [in] desperate circumstances." John Drew, the former chief executive of the YJB, similarly reflected: "Very often when you visit a custodial establishment, prison officers will say to you, 'That child shouldn't be here.'"

Several years ago, Frances Crook, the chief executive of the Howard League for Penal Reform, published a report on the past abuse of children in custody. Having reviewed the available literature on the subject, the authors found that at least a third, but anywhere up to 92% of detained children, have suffered some form of physical or sexual abuse or neglect, concluding:

> [I]t is clear that the rates of maltreatment suffered by children held in custody, are very significantly higher, probably by a factor of several times, than those suffered by children in the general community.[10]

This disturbing finding also emerged in research undertaken by the Prison Reform Trust. The charity found children in custody were more than twice as likely to have experienced abuse in the family than children in the general population, and even this was an underestimate as full background information was not available for every child.[11] A different study carried out by children's charity Barnardo's discovered just under half of 12- to 14-year-olds sentenced to custody (n=214) had suffered abuse and 38% had witnessed violence within their home.[12] A survey for the Department of Health of 16- to 20-year-olds in prison found that 58% of males and 67% of females had run away from home.[13] All of these findings mirror research conducted by the Ministry of Justice revealing almost a third of adult prisoners had been subject to child abuse, and 41% had witnessed violence as children.[14] Of those who had been abused as children, 62% reported emotional abuse, 61% physical abuse and almost a third sexual abuse. A very high proportion of women prisoners violated as children – 67% – said this abuse was sexual.[15] A quarter of the total sample said they had spent some of their childhood in care, and the average age for first arrest for those in care was 13 years, compared with 16 for the general sample.[16] Latest government data shows that looked after children are four times more likely to be convicted or given a final warning or reprimand by the police than other children.[17]

What was extraordinary about the report published by Crook is that she had no role whatsoever in producing it. This was a study funded by the YJB and leaked to Crook, who published it on her charity's website. A task group of child psychiatrists, civil servants, charities and managers of prisons and secure children's homes was established to consider the past abuse of children entering custody. Barnardo's and Nacro, with support from the National Society for the Prevention of Cruelty to Children (NSPCC), carried out a literature review that was submitted to the YJB in November 2006. It was not released for another 18 months. The matter was raised in parliament in June 2007, with the response being that the government had no plan to publish the report.[18] Crook also made a freedom of information request that was refused. This period marked the start of the YJB being censured for placing children in inappropriate establishments and failing to protect children from dangerous and unlawful restraint (pp 107–44). The deaths of three extremely vulnerable children – Joseph Scholes, Gareth Myatt and Adam Rickwood – had revealed staggering levels of organisational incompetence. Perhaps it was thought to be a public relations disaster, amid all this criticism, to tell the public that a significant proportion, if not the majority, of child prisoners have been maltreated before they are ever put in a prison cell.

Another possible explanation is that the review's finding – presented in bold lettering in the leaked version – that child maltreatment, especially when inflicted at a very young age, 'should be regarded as a critical and primary pre-disposing risk factor in relation to offending behaviour'[19] would bring into question the very legitimacy of imprisonment. The report contains an overview of scientific research showing the effects of abuse on the development of children's brains, as well as their psychological wellbeing. The version published by the YJB points to studies examining the prevalence of post-traumatic stress disorder among detained children. Three separate studies in North America, Russia and Japan found that the rate of this incapacitating condition ranged from a quarter of child prisoners to 65%. The report also observes that dysfunctional behaviours are known to be coping mechanisms for overcoming 'the trauma of past experiences'.[20] Crook told the press that she could understand why the report was buried, because:

> They would have to treat these children as victims and the YJB would have to be disbanded and renamed the Youth Victims Board.[21]

Murder law has been reformed in recent years to recognise the debilitating effects of domestic violence. The new partial defence of loss of control can be invoked when the defendant was in fear of serious violence or subject to circumstances of an extremely grave character and had a justifiable sense of being seriously wronged.[22] It originates partly from a case where a 17-year-old girl, Emma Humphreys, was convicted of murder after stabbing a man who had repeatedly raped and emotionally abused her (he had nailed down the windows so she could not escape his house). Emma had been brought up in a very violent home, had spent periods in care and was abused through pornography and prostitution. The man she stabbed was twice her age when he first paid her to have sex with him, and he later offered her a home where more abuse followed. After 10 years in prison, Emma's conviction was quashed by the Court of Appeal on two grounds – cumulative provocation and the long-term impact of abuse on her personality and behaviour. She died in her sleep three years after release, having continued to struggle with anorexia and addiction.[23]

No legal defence exists for children who have endured a lifetime of maltreatment – the 'slow burn' of child abuse – or suffered such serious abuse that it has propelled them into a cycle of destructive behaviour. Child abuse encompasses many forms of deliberate harm and not every child feels or reacts in the same way. Abuse can evoke feelings within the child of terror, panic, shock, confusion and shame, as well as intense physical pain. Once the onslaught has ceased, children understandably are often afraid of repeat victimisation. They can burn with rage. One girl told UserVoice, an organisation run by ex-offenders, why she started offending:

> 'Things were not right at home. I was getting picked on by my step-dad. You have abuse happen to you and it doesn't feel like it was dealt with and you want to rebel in order to get away from the feeling.'[24]

A different study heard from a 16-year-old whose anger had dissipated after being given a loving foster mother:

'I wasn't a good child because my birth family never showed me any love…. I was always angry, all the time. And then my foster mother saw what was going on and she knew. So she gave me love and she gave me what every mother should give their daughter and I changed my ways and now I don't do drugs or anything bad like that.'[25]

It is the inner world of human beings that sets us apart from other animals. We ascribe great meaning to our relationships; we want to belong, to be loved and valued. Verbal and physical assaults from parents hold deep significance, as do sexual violations, which invade the core of children's integrity. Puberty and adolescence can bring new turmoil for children who have suffered earlier sexual assaults, as they begin to understand the gravity and depravity of what they have endured. A review of research published between 2006 and 2010 on the association of child abuse and neglect with mental disorders concluded 'children who are maltreated are at increased risk of developing depression, anxiety disorders, eating disorders, conduct disorders, substance use disorders, and suicidal ideation and attempts that continues throughout the lifespan'.[26] It is against this backdrop that the results of the Prison Reform Trust's detailed analysis fall into place: 20% of the children in custody studied had self-harmed; 17% had a formal diagnosis of emotional or mental disorder; and 11% had previously attempted suicide.[27] The Barnardo's study of 12- to 14-year-olds given custodial sentences found that 8% had attempted suicide at some point in their short lives.[28]

Some years ago I attended a lecture by a distinguished child psychiatrist who reported new research that shows abused children have a bias towards detecting anger in facial expressions. Children who had been subject to physical abuse were shown a variety of facial expressions and were much more likely than non-abused children to see anger in people's faces. Applying this to a prison environment, the consequences for children constantly on anger alert are potentially horrific.

If maltreatment is the root cause of even just a proportion of serious criminal behaviour by children, what justice is there in incarcerating them rather than providing therapeutic care? This is not about denying the capacity of children (however constrained) to make different choices. Indeed, it is organised, state punishment in the form of imprisonment that enables children to remain buried and unknown – and therefore ultimately unchallenged. Therapeutic interventions, by contrast, equip children to feel safe enough to face up to their own and others' suffering. Jerome Miller, the psychiatric social worker who set about closing reformatories in Massachusetts in the 1970s, has this to say about past abuse:

> Most people think an inmate who is being abused pines to tell others about it. Not so. Juvenile inmates hide their abuse and protect their abusers.... They hide the memories from themselves as well as from others, and the history of their being abused has to be dug out with the tenacity of a private investigator.... The idea of the delinquent wallowing in tales of his or her own abuse as an excuse for crime is another of the myths which nurture our misunderstanding of people who offend.[29]

A paragraph included in the 2006 version of the report, but omitted from the document published by the YJB in 2008, spells out the unfitness of prisons as destinations for abused children:

> Custodial institutions for children are generally not therapeutic institutions (although local authority secure children's homes seek to provide such an environment). But generally, custodial institutions have not been set up with the intention of addressing psychological problems, they are not staffed to do so, and the culture of the institutions is not geared to this way of thinking about children.[30]

An investigation that concluded paediatric surgeons were using procedures designed for adults, and dangerous to children, would presumably beckon the end of such surgery. Announcing that maltreatment is a common experience of those admitted to custody, at the same time as saying the majority of institutions are incapable of meeting children's needs, should have marked the demise of young offender institutions. This could explain why the paragraph was deleted. Even today, after a further six children have died and thousands more have been assaulted or self-harmed, the government's plan for a new type of prison – the 'secure college' – perpetuates the falsehood that only a minority of imprisoned children require 'a greater focus on therapeutic care'.[31] If the children we have in our prisons are not in need of such 'specialist provision',[32] why on earth are they in detention?

The findings of its own commissioned review of past abuse do not appear anywhere in the YJB's latest plans for children's custody. There is a small mention of abuse experienced by girls,[33] but the strategy for the 'secure estate' up to 2015 lacks any discussion of the maltreatment suffered by boys, who comprise 96% of children deprived of their liberty. Its corporate plan for 2014-17 commits to providing a 'more accessible service' (whatever that is) to children who sexually abuse, and says the YJB will issue guidance on the sexual exploitation of girls, but there is silence on the plight of violated boys.[34] When I interviewed child psychotherapist and founder of vulnerable children's support charity Kids Company, Camila Batmangelidjh, we talked about the ways in which children in conflict with the law are deliberately not understood. It is as if we approach child offenders like cryptic crosswords: we give up searching for answers after the first few difficult clues.

Blame and 'othering'[35] are the modus operandi of the criminal justice system, leading to a remarkable lack of intelligent enquiry about the origins of children's offending and how their behaviour might be changed. Batmangelidjh observes:

> 'No one needs to then reflect on what is it that we've done to this fundamentally good child for them to exhibit this sort of disturbed behaviour.'

In another interview, Liberal Democrat peer Baroness Linklater told me:

'We start from a very low base in terms of sympathetic understanding and I suppose that reflects the sort of reluctance, perhaps, to become more properly informed and humane. If we did become more informed, and we did allow ourselves to become more aware, then we would change things more than we do.'

The ministerial call for child prisoners to transform their lives through self-improvement (education) is the stuff of fairy tales, where downtrodden individuals move from rags to riches in 20 pages. The Prison Reform Trust's study found that half of the 200 children were living in a deprived household and/or unsuitable accommodation prior to incarceration, and that over a quarter had been in local authority care at some point.[36] Latest data from the prisons inspectorate shows local authorities had, at some point, looked after a third of imprisoned boys and 61% of imprisoned girls.[37] This is not to say young lives cannot be transformed, but change clearly requires a lot more than willpower. How many of us know adult acquaintances who have spent years trying to give up smoking or leave a violent relationship (the average period of detention was 77 days in 2011/12)?[38] Furthermore, this individualistic mindset is cruelly insensitive to the probability that most children living in abject circumstances will have spent a great deal of their conscious hours wishing for a better life.

Dr Tim Bateman, a former youth justice worker now lecturing at the University of Bedfordshire, told me that research shows "a massive concentration of adult prisoners within a very small number of postcodes", adding that "exactly the same would be true for children who are locked up". Data on the region of origin of children sent to custody in 2012/13 shows the three highest rates as London (1.04 per 1,000 children aged 10 to 17), Yorkshire (0.97 per 1,000 children) and the West Midlands (0.74 per 1,000 children), whereas the area with the lowest rate (0.31 per 1,000 children) is the South East.[39] Research undertaken for the Scottish prison service reported the overall imprisonment rate for men in Scotland to be 237 per 100,000, but this exploded to 3,427 per 100,000 for young men living in the 27 most deprived wards.[40]

What is also interesting is that the North East of England, not famed for ubiquitous affluence, has a comparatively low rate of child custody (0.64 per 1,000 children).[41] The Prison Reform Trust has criticised this 'justice by geography', noting the child prisoner rate in Manchester is approaching five times that of Newcastle's.[42] Courts in Newcastle are known to be less punitive than most, possibly because child deprivation runs through the North East like the River Tyne and officials are therefore hardwired with an understanding of the pressures facing local children. Analysis of court reports prepared by youth offending teams in six areas across England and Wales found that the homes of child offenders had been visited rarely (in only 18% of cases)[43] and the information being put to magistrates in youth courts had been discussed with children in just over a quarter of cases and hardly ever with parents or carers.[44] The majority of reports provided descriptions of offences, but no analysis, and safeguarding and matters relating to the child's vulnerability were dealt with adequately in less than half (42%) of the 115 assessed cases.[45] This makes it all the more important that individuals working in courts have their own appreciation of children's backgrounds.

Peter Townsend's 1979 definition of poverty survives because it continues to capture the material, social and psychological exclusion: 'the absence or inadequacy of those diets, amenities, standards, services and activities which are common or customary in society'.[46] Hunger; lack of or ill-fitting clothes and shoes; missing out on school trips; parents arguing about money; and feelings of shame and embarrassment – these were scenarios recounted to me and other charity workers by children living in deprived English communities at the turn of the millennium. Children said their hopes and dreams could be smashed by poverty, sometimes when they were as young as seven or eight. One 16-year-old girl explained: 'Everything that happens in your childhood, it has a really big effect on the way you live your life.... I find that if you haven't got a lot of money, things get you down a lot easier and you get quite depressed and you find the negative in everything.'[47] Government indicators of material deprivation in childhood include not having friends round for a snack or tea once a fortnight, children not having a warm winter coat and being unable to pursue a regular hobby or leisure activity. Child prisoners are among those anonymously filling these official charts. Acknowledging the harm deprivation causes is not making excuses for unacceptable behaviour, but it brings us closer to understanding the caustic effects of poverty. As the Social Mobility and Child Poverty Commission explains:

> ... child poverty and lack of social mobility cause suffering to those affected – cold, hunger and stigma in the present, unfulfilled potential in the future. This is both wrong and unfair. Children cannot choose the environment they are born into and have little power to adapt or leave the place in which they find themselves.[48]

Examining children's histories also signposts the challenges they are likely to face on release from prison. The economist Vicky Pryce, jailed for two months for illegally taking her then husband's speeding points, announced she had a publishing contract on the day her incarceration ended. Here she describes the weeks following her release:

> That evening [of my release] the whole family came for supper and it was glorious – I had been asked what I fancied and they all prepared food for me that was just amazing.... People would visit practically every night for eight weeks laden with food, puddings, drinks, flowers and the like – the house was continuously full of flowers after I returned home. Even the postman said it was good to have me back when he delivered the morning's mail.[49]

Without begrudging Pryce's homecoming, her memoir contrasts starkly with more than half the boys in young offender institutions last year predicting they would have difficulties getting a job and a quarter anticipating problems finding somewhere to live after release.[50] Over a third (39%) of imprisoned girls expected to have difficulty finding somewhere to live after release.[51] Children who had formerly been in care were significantly more worried about where they would live.[52] A separate prisons inspectorate review of resettlement, involving interviews with 61 boys in young offender institutions approaching their release date, found 72% of looked after children did not know where they would be living after prison (n=18).[53]

The impact of racial inequality on growing children must also be considered. It is a decade since Trevor Phillips, then chair of the Commission for Racial Equality, pointed out there were twice as many black people in prisons as attending university.[54] The ethnic composition of child custody remains alarming: 40% of those detained in July 2014 were from black and minority ethnic (BME) communities.[55] The 2011 census records the 10- to 17-year-old population as being 81% white,[56] meaning there are twice as many children from BME communities in custody as would be expected all things being equal. A two-year study by the Institute for Criminal Policy Research at King's College London found that black children are disproportionately remanded and this has a knock-on effect on later sentencing.[57] The inquiry into black children and the criminal justice system conducted by the House of Commons Home Affairs Committee highlighted that court sentences are likely to be 'more punitive' when meted out to children from BME communities.[58] Reasons behind the overrepresentation of black children in the wider criminal justice system – 'social exclusion, educational underachievement and school exclusion interact to form a web of disadvantage' – were the same as for their white counterparts.[59] Tense relationships between black communities and the police, as well as outright discrimination, were cited as additional contributory factors. This investigating group of MPs also suggested that missing fathers and the celebration of power and law breaking among some black children, and within wider popular culture and the media, is part of the landscape too.

Some inquiry witnesses raised the heinous effects of slavery,[60] although there was no discussion about how this might reveal itself within the criminal justice system. That black children, like their white contemporaries, address predominantly white prison officers as 'Boss' has always struck me as repugnant.

The appalling educational backgrounds of child inmates inevitably make them more vulnerable within the penal environment. At the conclusion of the inquest into Gareth Myatt's death, the coroner wrote to the secretary of state for justice, Jack Straw, recommending, among other things, that restraint incident reports should include a statement by the child, 'in their own hand where possible', and children should be given the opportunity to report any injuries.[61] Ministers gave their official response eight months later and said the low level of literacy among child prisoners meant the coroners' recommendation 'may not be the best way' to proceed. Instead, the YJB was to promote an 'emerging practice' used in Rainsbrook secure training centre – the place where Gareth had been restrained until death. This entailed officers who had restrained a child reviewing the incident with him or her, and a manager then checking the action plan with the child.[62] The government's claim that children would find writing their own accounts difficult was not deceitful. A study for the YJB found over half the children entering young offender institutions (n=1,454) had the literacy age of someone younger than 11 years and 19% were functioning at a literacy level of an average seven-year-old or younger.[63] A recent survey of more than 1,000 children in custody found one in five had learning difficulties.[64] Earlier research for the YJB discovered nearly a quarter of young offenders had an IQ score below 70 (the normal range is between 85 and 115) – indicated to be either the result of 'intrinsic learning difficulties' or poor or absent education.[65] The implications for children's ability to use formal complaints and abuse procedures, and follow the basic prison regime, are obvious.

Being able to read and write is no guarantee of justice. One of my saddest work memories surrounds a letter from an imprisoned boy telling me his foster father had raped him. I was a children's rights officer at the time and my job was to promote and protect the rights of children in care. I knew there would be looked after children in the local prison, so I sent some promotional leaflets to be distributed among the boys. Not long after, I received a handwritten letter from the boy telling me about the sexual abuse he had endured in his foster home. He gave more information when I visited him. This distraught child sat on a hard office chair in a dark, impersonal room and recounted what had been done to him. Prison must be one of the most undesirable locations for a child to remember abuse, although this boy was at least receiving support from a psychologist. There followed a number of encounters with social services and the police. In one particularly accusatory meeting, I was told the foster father had had a heart attack caused by the stressful investigation. This didn't faze me. I had been a child protection social worker and knew adults often have extreme reactions to abuse disclosures. What really upset me was a second letter from the boy. He told me he couldn't bear resurrecting the rape while he was locked up and asked for the investigation to be discontinued.

The Prison Reform Trust undertook research with prisoners identified by officers as possibly having learning disabilities and found they were greatly disadvantaged by not being able to read and write, as so many processes require a written 'application' (seeing the doctor, ordering from the prison shop and enrolling for education or work, for example). One young inmate had not received any visits in the period after admission because of not being able to fill in a visiting form.[66] In June 2014, inspectors came across a disabled boy with memory loss in Cookham Wood young offender institution who 'could not remember to complete applications or visits orders'.[67] In the latest inspection of Feltham young offender institution, which was condemned as violent and unsafe by inspectors, staff were praised for using photographs to advertise items in the prison shop: 'There was an excellent canteen list with photographs for young people who had difficulty reading.'[68]

What about the crimes committed by children which have led to their incarceration? In 2012/13, nearly a third of children were in custody because of robbery offences, and a further 16% were incarcerated for domestic burglary offences. Another 7% (an average of 115 per month) were in custody because they had breached rules imposed by the court.[69] These are children detained not because of their original offences, but because they have failed to follow court orders. Last year saw a 50% reduction in children locked up for breach (down from 14%) – around 160 fewer children in custody every month in 2012/13 compared with the year before[70] – which can be partly credited to work done by the YJB to change practice at a local level.[71] It is difficult, though, to understand why we are locking up any children for breach, when custody is meant to be a measure of last resort. An analysis of breach records by the Prison Reform Trust found younger children and girls were more likely to be sent to custody for contravening court-ordered rules than older children and boys respectively.[72] During a government inquiry into youth justice, a representative from the Howard League for Penal Reform recounted an incident of a boy who was sent to prison because he did not arrive promptly for court-ordered appointments. The child could not tell the time because he had learning difficulties.[73] In an interview for this book, Baroness Vivien Stern told me about a child she knew who failed to keep appointments because he was frightened of entering a particular area in south London where people were waiting to beat him up. He was imprisoned for a month as a result, the start of many more periods of incarceration. Stern remembers giving this frightened, vulnerable boy a radio to take into prison: "He's got to have a radio with a plug moulded into the flex, so I gave his mother our radio and said, 'Here you are, we've got one.'" Continuing the theme, Professor Barry Goldson had the following observation:

> 'I think the public, whoever the public is taken to be, would possibly be quite shocked if they knew that many of the young people locked up are actually not there for grave offences but there for persistent nuisance.'

Juliet Lyon is director of the Prison Reform Trust and was responsible, in a former role, for producing the first specialist training for prison officers working with children. In our interview, we discussed the backgrounds of children in young offender institutions and she reiterated:

> 'There isn't one big explosion of a terrible crime. It's getting into some trouble, nobody supporting or helping and then getting into more trouble and eventually having a peer group that is so tightly absorbed in offending. And they are the ones who the police will go to first, always, when there's trouble and, when you boil it down, that's who you have got in YOIs [young offender institutions].'

Less than a quarter of children entered custody in 2012/13 for crimes of violence against the person, and just 5% for sexual offences. During this same period, 13 children were, on average, detained for the offence of murder.[74] Notwithstanding their low numbers in our own prisons, it is sobering to learn that the first to benefit from Jerome Miller's decarceration programme in Massachusetts in the 1970s were children considered to be 'hard-core delinquents'.[75]

Baroness Veronica Linklater was a childcare officer (children's social worker) in the 1960s and has spent decades working in and around the criminal justice system. I asked her to describe the kinds of children held in our prisons today and she pointed to "a gap in perception between what people think or imagine they will find meeting people in custody" and their actual encounters:

> 'It is a cliché but what you'll find are children who are not demonstrably aggressive or violent, but who are very needy and sometimes indeed very disturbed.... Children who don't see much of their families when they're inside, or may indeed not have much in the way of families, especially if they have experienced care. So what you can extrapolate from that, although it won't be written on their arms or their foreheads, is that these are children who are lacking the kind of emotional support and infrastructure that you would hope for your own, and all, children.'

The vast majority of child prisoners are aged between 15 and 17, accounting for 96% of the child custody population in July 2014. Girls comprise just 4% of the detained child population[76] and the government announced in 2013 that it would stop sending them to prison service institutions.

There is no question that some children in custody are a grave danger to others, including to other children locked up with them. However, young offender institutions, which house the majority of young inmates, are not calm, therapeutic sanctuaries where violent children can learn to control destructive thoughts and feelings in conditions of security; they are not hives of educational expertise (children only receive an average of 12 hours' education a week);[77] they are not centres of mental health excellence; and they very often do not provide acceptable levels of basic care like food, warmth, access to fresh air and hygiene. One of the principal goals of the government's plan for a different type of child prison – the secure college – is to cut costs.[78] The other is to 'place education at the heart of detention'.[79] Providing education, training and work to child prisoners is a statutory requirement of young offender institutions.[80] Imagine the absurdity of, say, the Department of Health admitting the NHS has not properly cared for children with very complex health needs for many years and the solution it has come up with is – ta-da – a cheaper and even riskier version of the present model.

Pam Hibbert has been looking after other people's children for more than three decades, and was a manager in a large social services secure unit holding children who have murdered and committed other very grave offences. She believes there is no difference between the fundamental needs of locked-up children and those of other children. What differentiates these two groups is that incarcerated children have had the worst of everything: "We are talking about children who are poor, who have low skills, who are sad, who are abused and neglected."

The next chapter considers the preponderance of suicide, self-harm and other manifestations of childhood distress in prison.

THREE

'They just don't listen'

John Joseph Peter Scholes was born in Sale, Greater Manchester, on 20 February 1986, the day the Soviet Union launched the Mir Space Station. His mother told me Joseph was quite a large baby and "very, very beautiful". He grew into an extremely clever, enquiring child who loved nature and exploring National Trust buildings and museums; he was "interested in everything". Unlike his two older sisters, who would sit for hours adorning My Little Ponies, Joseph was always active. Yvonne Bailey recalled her son removing the limbs from his Action Man – not from anger or malevolence but sheer curiosity. He found great pleasure in pulling objects apart and rebuilding them. Joseph was also very humorous. He would wear his mother's hat and scarf and do "funny turns" when people came to the house. This fitted with his passion for the arts and music. At school, he was "sunny and popular".

Joseph hated losing at family board games. Sundays at his granny's house would see the whole family playing games like Monopoly and Frustration for hours. Yvonne said her mother "used to say she had repetitive strain because [games] would have to be played until Joseph had won". Joseph's granny "totally adored him".

One of four children, Joseph belonged to a close family that ate meals together around the kitchen table, had regular holidays and greatly enjoyed each others' company. One of his abiding loves was Lego and each Christmas he would ask for the biggest set, the castle or the pirate galleon, and devote the day to constructing his masterpiece with parental help. When I visited Yvonne at home she told me every year the family has recurring plans for what to do with Joseph's many childhood possessions, including his Lego sets, which are "all tucked away in plastic boxes with lids". Joseph died a month after his 16th birthday in a prison healthcare centre officially slated as 'wholly inadequate' less than a year before.[1]

The final year of Joseph's short life was the most difficult, Yvonne explained:

> 'Words could not describe how awful it was, how frustrated he became with us all. I have tears in my eyes now, thinking about it because you wish you could go back in time and deal with it better, or differently.... I would say there were real difficulties starting by, of course, his father and I splitting up in about '95, I think it was, so that would probably have been the start of the obvious difficulties. Before that, I would've viewed Joseph just as a usual boy. I would've done. Perhaps, looking back, there were little things, but a usual boy. Hard work, very physically hard work, but that was the beginning of the end for Joseph; that was the beginning of the end, definitely.'

This period is the most documented in newspaper and official reports, though it does not do justice to the child Joseph was prior to his very troubled adolescence (where earlier abuse and trauma typically reveal themselves). From what his mother told me, my impression of Joseph as a young child was completely wonderful, to which Yvonne replied:

> 'He was. I'd love people to realise that because, again, he's been dehumanised and the government are happy for that to happen. He's been dehumanised, even the memory of him has been dehumanised, you know, he is this Joseph Scholes who died in prison, but you know it was this Joseph who always had to win [the board game] Frustration.'

Joseph's parents married when he was two. Theirs was a "very turbulent relationship" and they separated by the time Joseph was nine. Like many children of divorcing parents, Joseph became embroiled in a hostile custody dispute and there was a lot of moving homes and schools. Social services were involved from the age of 12, following disclosures of physical and sexual abuse by someone outside the immediate family. Joseph was said to be young for his age: he still enjoyed climbing trees and building dens at 14 and 15 and was afraid of the dark. He continued to play Lego until just before he died. His self-harming began in his teenage years – Joseph would do things like push sharp objects into his toes – and he went from being obsessed about cleanliness to refusing to wash. He became aggressive towards his mother, stopped eating family meals and had many irrational fears, including of insects. When he was 15, Joseph jumped from a first floor window in a suspected suicide attempt. He was violent to ambulance staff and subsequently charged with affray. A psychiatrist carried out an assessment and concluded Joseph had a depressive conduct disorder. She said his response to the ambulance crew was self-preservation – though this did not stop him being treated as a criminal. The psychiatrist warned that Joseph's self-harming could escalate should he end up in custody.[2]

A few weeks before Christmas 2001, Joseph was taken into police protection and placed in a children's home. He had been missing for around a week and was found with another child staying in a deserted caravan on a car park. Yvonne told me she was sick with worry and each evening drove round the local area looking for him. Five days after being placed in the children's home, Joseph had peripheral involvement in three street robberies of mobile telephones with two boys from his children's home. (Policymakers and professionals have long been aware of the criminogenic effects of children's homes, though it was not until 2006 that the Crown Prosecution Service issued its first specialist guidance urging caution in prosecuting[3] – too late for Joseph).

Joseph was psychiatrically assessed a second time and reported to be in a 'fragile emotional state'.[4] The day after appearing in court for his involvement in the street robberies[5] he slashed his face more than 30 times. His bedroom in the children's home had to be repainted because the walls were splattered with blood.[6] On 15 March 2002, Joseph appeared in court for sentencing. In addition to the psychiatric assessments, a social worker wrote a letter to the court expressing concern about Joseph's safety given his propensity to self-harm when distressed. Although he ordered custody, the judge said in open court the authorities must be informed about Joseph's history of self-harm.[7] The Youth Justice Board (YJB) sent Joseph to Stoke Heath young offender institution in Shropshire. Placing officials should have known Joseph would be held in the prison's healthcare centre given the high risk of suicide and self-harm. The latest inspection report, drafted less than 10 months before Joseph was sent to the prison, had complained that children in the healthcare centre were being kept in cells for an average of 22½ hours a day; three inmates had been allowed access to fresh air 'lasting no more than 30 minutes during a 10-day period' and one child had not been outside at all; children ate all of their meals in their cells; there was no telephone in the healthcare centre so vulnerable children had to be escorted to one of the main prison wings to make phone calls; and the centre's bath and toilets were in 'poor condition'.[8] The inspection report from the previous year had discovered a 'horrendous' number of injuries caused through inmate violence – 717 in a space of eight months[9] – and expressed astonishment at the poor condition of the newly built healthcare centre:

> [T]he in-patients area failed to a spectacular degree to meet the standards established by the Prisons Board. Thus, a deprived environment for young, sick people was made worse by the complete absence of an area where patients could take outdoor exercise. It is hard to understand how the Prison Service came to build a Health Care Centre that failed to provide facilities, required by Prison Rules, for outdoor exercise.[10]

Those working within the system would have been cognisant of these deficiencies, but Joseph's mother had no idea what her son would be exposed to. Staff at the children's home told her Joseph was in the healthcare centre and Yvonne then spoke with a nurse on the telephone:

'I was told he was put in a safe cell, so it's again, it's this use of language … they should've said, "Yvonne, he's in a cell, he's stripped naked, he's got a horse blanket-like garment on, fastened with Velcro. It's filthy and squalid, I mean, the window's about two or three inches deep in dirt between the pane and the bars and the outer pane. He's on a concrete plinth with a thin plastic mat," that would've been the truth, but instead I was told he would come to no harm, he's in a safe cell, he's in safe clothing.'

When I asked Yvonne whether prison health staff ever asked for information about her son, for example whether he was afraid of the dark, she replied:

'No. I gave information. When I rang I tried to explain he was under two hospitals, he's tried to kill himself, he's been sexually abused, he's very vulnerable, we didn't think he'd be sentenced. You've got to remember that if I was having a conversation now, I'm clear-headed, I would say this, this, this, I would ask that, that, that … at that time, you see, everything, every answer they give you as a person with complete naivety, I just believed everything. So I came off the phone and told the girls, "He's in a safe cell, he's in safe clothing."'

Nine days after he was admitted to prison, and before his mother had the chance to make her first visit (it took nearly a week for a visiting order to arrive), a maintenance worker found Joseph hanging from the bars of his cell window in the healthcare centre where he was now being checked every 30 minutes. Joseph left a letter to his parents that included these words: 'I love you mum and dad. I'm sorry, I just can't cope. Don't be sad. It is no one's fault. I just can't go on. None of it was any of your fault, sorry. Love you and family, Joe. I tried telling them and they just don't listen.'

Joseph wasn't to know this country had made a legal undertaking with the UN in 1991 – when he was just five years old and John Major was prime minister – to uphold the rights of all children. One section of the United Nations Convention on the Rights of the Child gives children the right to have their views given importance. Another part of the children's rights treaty places duties on the authorities to treat children who have been abused, as Joseph had, in a manner that builds their health, self-respect and dignity.

The youth offending team social worker said at the inquest he had 'serious concerns about [Joseph's] welfare' and rang the prison to warn about self-harm.[11] Child prisoners have a suicide rate 18 times higher than children sleeping in their own beds, so prisons are probably used to telephone calls like these.[12] During his first four days in the healthcare centre, Joseph was placed in a garment described some years later by the European Court of Human Rights as a 'simple linen tunic, held together by adhesive strips under which he was naked'.[13] 'Horse blanket' and 'dehumanising' were two of the descriptions given at Joseph's inquest.[14] The author of the child protection report produced after Joseph's death said if the healthcare centre had been in a children's home he would have closed it down.[15] The institution's medical officer told the inquest Joseph had been 'deeply traumatised' by his treatment.[16] Two years before, the officer had written to the prisons minister, Paul Boateng, the chief inspector of prisons, David Ramsbotham, and the head of the prison service, Martin Narey, alerting them to unacceptable healthcare standards.[17] Two of these individuals – Boateng and Narey – had ultimate responsibility for the care of imprisoned children. To whom else could the medical officer have written? The Queen does not intervene to save vulnerable children from wretched prison conditions – as Yvonne Bailey found out when she wrote to Elizabeth II in December 2012. Her letter was passed to the justice secretary, Chris Grayling, and Yvonne was still waiting for a reply 18 months later.

The coroner presiding over Joseph's inquest took the highly unusual step of writing to the then home secretary, David Blunkett, asking that a public inquiry be established to consider the appropriateness of the custodial sentence Joseph received; the procedures that were meant to safeguard him once in custody; and the adequacy of secure accommodation to meet the needs of children. The government refused to follow the coroner's recommendation;[18] Joseph's mother unsuccessfully challenged this as far as the European Court of Human

Rights and, despite huge political and professional support, there has been no inquiry to date.

Parents tell their children that if they are ever lost or in trouble they should ask somebody wearing a uniform to help them – a police officer, traffic warden or shop assistant, for example. Prisons are overflowing with adults in uniform. Every prison governor has direct access to Whitehall. But these lines of command have not evolved to serve the interests of children. Furthermore, prisons are inherently conservative institutions, with an unhealthy reliance on the status quo. John Drew, who was chief executive of the YJB between 2009 and 2013, explains:

> 'We're expecting officers to operate in very highly charged and very difficult environments and therefore you interfere with the practical arrangements at your peril. That in a way, to my mind, is one of the critiques of prisons … it's another reason why an unmalleable organisation shouldn't come up against children.'

Individuals working within penal institutions can breach even basic codes of adult conduct. During my research for this book, Shauneen Lambe, co-founder of Just for Kids Law, told me about a child with learning difficulties in Feltham young offender institution who was astonished that officers refused to help when he vomited in his cell soon after admission:

> 'He'd been sick in there, vomiting, and he'd pressed his button [in his cell] to get some adult to help him and they'd laughed at him. And he'd never been in a situation where adults [had not helped]. He was a child and so he was used to when you ask an adult for help, they give you help.'

Joseph Scholes' faith in adults must have been shattered completely. The day before he hanged himself, he told his mother he would make a suicide attempt to force the authorities to move him from prison to a children's home. Yvonne told me she passed this information to the prison; the telephone call had, in any case, been routinely recorded.[19] Here was a child who had been sexually and physically abused, with a history of self-harm and substance abuse, pleading to be placed in a children's home. The only bargaining chip he had was his life. If listening to children is judged by actions, Joseph died willfully unheard.

Sixteen-year-old Kevin Jacobs was another child desperate to be admitted to a children's home, although, unlike Joseph, he was not begging for an immediate transfer. He simply wanted to know he could return to his children's home after release from Feltham young offender institution. The day before he was found hanging from the bars of his cell, on 29 September 2001, a social worker told Kevin that Lambeth social services would not be funding his return to the home. Kevin was subject to a care order, which meant the London Borough of Lambeth had parental responsibility for him. He had first entered care aged 18 months and had always lived in children's homes. At the age of six, he disclosed sexual abuse by a member of staff and another child in his children's home. His first arrest was at the age of 11 when he set fire to a barn (setting fires is a classic sign of child sexual abuse, particularly in boys). The 'home' Kevin wanted to return to on release from Feltham was the place in which he had spent the longest period of his childhood – 20 months. Like Joseph Scholes, Kevin was known to be a suicide risk. Two diligent prison officers had saved his life just two weeks previously. They had been preparing to leave the building after their shift ended but returned to tell the governor the boy needed medical attention for a self-harm injury inflicted earlier in the day and to recommend he be put into special clothing to stop him making a ligature. The officers found Kevin hanging unconscious in his cell.[20] The inquest jury examining his death found systematic neglect by the prison, the YJB and social services.[21] The campaign group INQUEST, which monitors deaths in custody, reported:

> Despite a wealth of information and evidence that was available to all concerned relating to his history of disturbed self-harming behaviour, Kevin was kept at

Feltham instead of being removed to local authority secure accommodation or hospital.[22]

There are no pauses in confinement for child prisoners in acute states of despair. Only those with very serious mental health disorders are moved to hospitals, but only after they are sectioned under the Mental Health Act and the approval of the secretary of state for justice – not the government minister with responsibility for health or for children – has been granted. The director of the Prison Reform Trust, Juliet Lyon, told me she ran an adolescent unit school in a psychiatric hospital earlier in her career and when, years later, she started visiting young offender institutions she "had expected to meet different young men to our young men in the unit. Really, palpably different somehow" but instead she "met boys like the boys we were working with, who, by a throw of the dice, had ended up going the [criminal] justice, rather than the health, route".

Research funded by the NHS found the waiting period for children and young people being transferred to hospital from one young offender institution was between eight and 155 days, with an average wait time of more than 51 days (the other four prisons in the study detained only adults).[23] A child incarcerated in Wetherby young offender institution in 2012 pleaded with the chief inspector of prisons to get him out of the prison:

> One boy in the segregation unit with a lifelong medical condition that would have been hard for any teenager to manage, and who had exhibited very disruptive behaviour, asked me tearfully if I could take him home to his mum.[24]

The child was moved to a secure medical facility. The inspection report does not say whether the transfer was planned or happened because the boy was in the wrong place at the right time when inspectors were visiting. In 2010, inspectors found two girls held in the adult segregation unit in Downview women's prison, under so-called 'GOOD' (good order or discipline) procedures. One child had been made to wear 'strip clothing' after trying to hang herself several times. Managers had contacted the YJB to have her moved to a more suitable place, but this 'had not been found and the young woman had remained inappropriately in the adult segregation unit before eventually being transferred to an adult medium secure psychiatric unit under section 47 of the Mental Health Act'.[25]

Children who end up in hospital are returned to prison once they have recovered. An official inquiry is still under way into a girl – known in official reports as 'SP' – who needed several blood transfusions after chronic self-harm and was held in prison isolation for months. She had endured severe physical and emotional abuse from her mentally ill mother from early childhood, been stopped from attending school and had started self-harming at the age of 11 or 12. She was only transferred to a high-security hospital, in 2005, after the Howard League for Penal Reform obtained a High Court injunction preventing her return to prison. Her barrister at the time, Ian Wise QC, explained:

'There were women prison officers who were trying to do the right thing for [the girl] I'm sure, but they were just totally out of their depth. I mean these people have got no training on mental health issues … she was self-harming, had to be taken to hospital for a blood transfusion, then back into prison and then self-harming again, back into hospital and so on … it was only at that point after I got the injunction and proceedings were issued that they realised she couldn't be kept safe; they couldn't actually protect her life in custody … I think there's a real chance that she'd have been dead if she'd gone back.'

If the authorities are hoping to 'learn lessons' from the prison service's treatment of this vulnerable girl, they have a funny way of showing it. Under threat of legal action by the Howard League for Penal Reform, the Ministry of Justice agreed to an inquiry in August 2006.[26] In January 2014, the government was asked in parliament about the inquiry's progress and the response was as follows:

The report from the first stage of the SP investigation will be published, alongside the second stage report, following the conclusion of the second stage of the investigation. The second stage of the investigation, which will include a public element, was commissioned by the Ministry of Justice on 22 March 2013 and is ongoing.[27]

Nearly a quarter of children in custody told charities in 2011 they had felt depressed or unhappy for long periods all or most of the time.[28] Liam McManus's first reaction to finding out he was to be sent to Lancaster Farms young offender institution was to threaten to refuse food. Prison records show the 15-year-old did stop eating for at least a day-and-a-half after admission.[29] Three weeks later, on 29 November 2007, he was found hanging in his cell, having received not a single visit from his local authority despite being a former child in care and suffering chronic mental health difficulties.[30] The Prisons and Probation Ombudsman observed Liam was a child who had 'suffered much unhappiness', including the death of his father when he was three years old after which, because of his mother's drug addiction, he moved to live with his grandmother who also died 'not long afterwards'.[31] Hilton Dawson, former social worker and Labour MP for the constituency in which Lancaster Farms is located, had this to say about the institution two years before:

> [Prison] is a horrible place to put a child. I thought that on my most recent visit ... 'What a horrible place for a child,' when I looked around at the walls, the wire, the uniforms, the keys and the disgusting little cells with their huge locked doors.[32]

During another of his visits, Dawson was told 'of a mentally ill, hallucinating and possibly psychotic child who had been refusing food. No one thought that he should be there – not the governor, the staff or anyone who was looking after him, and certainly not members of his family, who were visiting.'[33] During the inquest into the death of Gareth Price in 2005, a 16-year-old child who also hanged himself at Lancaster Farms young offender institution, a prison officer explained that low staffing numbers meant the best time to have a one-to-one conversation with a vulnerable inmate was on a weekend when children clean out their cells. Then a child and prison officer could speak for about 20 minutes – once a fortnight.[34]

Prisons have patrolling procedures and special tools for removing ligatures from children's necks and every cell has a bell that inmates can ring to gain the attention of officers. But these rudimentary safeguards cannot be relied on. More than half of boys and a quarter of girls surveyed by inspectors in 2012/2013 reported that their bells were not normally answered within five minutes.[35] The officer who found Sam Elphick hanging in his cell was not wearing a belt pack containing the tool for cutting ligatures or a radio to summon colleagues. He therefore had to hold up the boy as he rang the cell bell. The Prisons and Probation Ombudsman reported:

> But when the officer activated the alarm, nobody responded and he had no option but to lower the trainee back onto the ligature and run to the office for help.[36]

Misuse of the cell bell is a punishable offence. The inquest into the death in April 2011 of 17-year-old Ryan Clark at Wetherby young offender institution heard he had told a child in a nearby cell that he was going to 'string up' (prison slang for hang himself). Ryan had asked the boy to press his cell bell, but he had not done so because of previous warnings for misusing it. The prison's acting governor informed the inquest this would have been 'an appropriate use of a cell bell'.[37] The American criminologist Hans Toch refers to the 'Alice in Wonderland flavour' of individuals adapting to the prison environment.[38] There is much to be mystified about. Some years ago, I was told that 'at risk' children in a young offender institution were instructed to sleep with their head facing away from the wall, to make it easier for officers looking through cell hatches at night to check they were still breathing. In a debate in the House of Lords in 2004 about prison suicides, the crossbench peer Baroness Stern outlined the strategy adopted in response to a spate of child deaths in custody. Rather than commandeer appropriate care in adolescent psychiatric units, beds were screwed to the floor so desperate children could no longer upturn them and use them as hanging devices.[39]

In 1991, the year after 15-year-old Philip Knight hanged himself in Swansea prison, the helpline service the Samaritans launched the Listener scheme to train prisoners to support inmates in distress. Philip was another child from the care system: he had been adopted as a baby but was returned to local authority care as a teenager (two thirds of adoption disruptions occur from the age of 11 onwards).[40] He was a known suicide risk and, following public outcry after his death, the law was changed to stop children being remanded to adult prisons. Research on the impact of the Listener scheme among adult prisoners found it has a good reputation and is seen as trustworthy.[41] Children in young offender institutions have, since 2012, had access to an additional avenue of support through dedicated ChildLine telephones. Data shows that this service is well used, with over 7,000 calls across the first two years. Not all calls come from children in states of distress; many ring out of boredom or simply because the ChildLine telephones are available. Nevertheless, the main counselling themes – low mood/self-esteem, anger management, suicidal feelings and assaults and bullying – indicate this is a vital service. It is possibly significant that ChildLine's first dedicated service for children in care similarly received many calls about abuse and bullying, although suicidal feelings were very rarely the main reason behind children making contact.[42]

The risks inherent in being a prisoner are a combination of the vulnerabilities children carry with them into the prison, and the dangers imposed by the environment itself. The 1971 Stanford Prison experiment is famous for showing how behaviour can plummet when people are put into authority roles. Philip Zimbardo established a controlled experiment in the basement of Stanford psychology department in California after hearing his students had created a mock prison in their dormitory with very powerful results – including the end of some friendships. Around 100 answered the advert for male college students to join Zimbardo's experiment about prison life, and 24 were selected after screening. Twenty volunteers were then randomly assigned to the role of guard or prisoner. The experiment had to be stopped on the sixth day because of the sadistic behaviour of those 'acting' as prison guards. Prisoners who showed any form of defiance were harshly punished – through withdrawal of food, sleep and clothing, for example – and all inmates were subject to institutionalised degradation such as having to repeatedly shout out their number, sing demeaning songs or show false respect. Sexual humiliation occurred frequently and a culture of 'us and them' emerged within the first few hours. None of the guards had been trained in these systems of control. They had jointly constructed them once allocated their role; placed in a simulated prison with real cells; and given prisoners. Inmates mistreated their fellow captives too, for which they later expressed deep regret.

What is less often remembered about this social psychology experiment is that half of the students told to adopt the role of prisoner were released early because they showed signs of acute stress and depression. Each student had been subject to psychological assessments in advance of being accepted onto the study. After the experiment, all the participants were debriefed. Zimbardo writes:

> What was important about the extensive debriefing sessions was that they gave the participants a chance to openly express their strong feelings and to gain a new understanding of themselves and their unusual behaviour in a novel, alien setting.... I reminded them that they had been carefully selected, precisely because they were normal and healthy, and that they had been assigned randomly to one or the other of the two roles. They did not bring any pathology into the place; rather, the place elicited pathology of various kinds from them.[43]

'Psychic humiliations'[44] are part of the deliberate discomforts of prison life. Inmates, whether they are aged 16 or 60, suffer repeat attacks on their privacy, autonomy and individuality. Some longer-term effects of incarceration can be very subtle – finding ordinary cutlery heavy to handle, being overwhelmed by intimate relationships and avoiding eye contact lest it be misconstrued as an invitation to fight. The noise of a heavy door slamming shut can stay with a prisoner long after release, as this child's experience shows: 'If

someone shuts a door now I jump, right now I'm still paranoid....
I walk looking behind my back.'[45] These are all elements of the
'organised hurt' of child prisons.[46]

More than a decade ago, 19 boys held on remand were interviewed
by child psychiatrists and reported many adverse experiences,
including being 'banged up' in their cells for very long periods;
having to cope with shouting, name calling and noise from other
prisoners banging on pipes and windows; being deliberately wound
up by prison officers – by them, for instance, boasting about going
home or 'forgetting' to open up cells during association time; and
being subject to extortion by other prisoners. There were reports of
vicious abuse by prison officers in a segregation unit. Two boys gave
separate accounts of being forced to run along blue lines before being
allowed food and they were punched for not running fast enough or
if they veered off the designated markings (pp 214–17). The coping
strategies of the remanded boys in this study included: punching walls
and banging cell doors (both risking punishment); withdrawal from
leisure pursuits; thinking about their mothers and other loved ones,
even when they were not prominent in their lives; and fantasising
about finding happiness with girlfriends.[47]

A second study of prison life for children involved interviews
with 25 remanded boys and 20 prison staff. This looked in depth
at admission processes, particularly the methods used to identify
especially vulnerable children. Inspection reports today often praise
sensitive reception procedures, but the conclusion then was not
reassuring:

> The picture is clear. The reception, and so-called
> vulnerability assessment process is like a cattle market.
> Children are herded into crowded and unsuitable prison
> reception areas and processed with indecent haste. The
> circumstances do not allow for anything else. Despite
> the best individual efforts, late arrival, excessive numbers,
> limited space and institutional imperatives produce
> inhumane procedures.[48]

The cattle market analogy resembles a girl's description of being made to take off her knickers during a strip search on admission: 'You just feel like a catalogue delivery, like you're nothing. "Here's your delivery," that's it and you're just given a number.'[49]

There are a lot of numbers in Adam Rickwood's post-mortem report:

> The deceased was on remand for section 18 wounding and bail breech [sic]. His number was 923R and he was housed in block 2B room number 1.

Adam was a lively boy who loved being in the outdoors. His mother told me he enjoyed camping and rabbiting and on a Saturday would wash cars and help out at a local garage. He had ambitions to become a police officer, but then planned to set up a garage business because his friends said they could help get him started. Small for his age, Adam was a 'mummy's boy' whose behaviour changed when he was nine. Five family members died within a four-year period and these deaths, Carol Pounder told me, "played on Adam's head". He was constantly crying and upset, and would have angry outbursts:

> 'He wanted to know why people died. I tried to explain to him why people died, but he just couldn't understand it.'

Carol said she sought help from social services and her family doctor, who referred Adam to a psychiatric unit. She was "in and out of school" because of difficulties there. Eventually, in desperation, when Adam was 12, Carol left him at the social services office to force them to arrange some respite. The battle between the local education authority and social services over who should fund Adam's residential school placement, which his parents pushed for, is officially acknowledged in the serious case review.[50] Adam enjoyed his stay at a children's home in Blackpool, but became homesick and, after just six days, "ran away and came home to me", Carol explained.

Adam was arrested twice when he was 14, once for having a penknife and another time for possessing cannabis. This was during a very difficult two-year period, when he was admitted to hospital seven times following overdoses of alcohol and drugs.[51] Then he was charged with wounding a man and was subject to a court-ordered secure remand. An investigation by the Prisons and Probation Ombudsman after Adam died refers to him telling the police and a member of staff at Hassockfield secure training centre that he had stabbed the man because he sexually abused him ('touched him up').[52] In a therapeutic setting, such information would be seen as highly significant, potentially offering further clues to Adam's self-destructive behaviour. It would also reinforce the necessity of providing a safe, caring environment. However, these two separate disclosures were not recorded in Adam's 'risk profile' at Hassockfield.[53]

A place in a locked establishment was not immediately available so Adam spent a short period in a local (privately run) children's home where he settled well. When staff told Adam he was going to be moved to Hassockfield secure training centre, some 150 miles from where he lived, he panicked and ran home. He was arrested, held in the cells at the police station and escorted by police officers to the Serco prison, arriving after midnight on 10 July 2004. Two days later, one of the principal witnesses retracted his police statement – an event that should have given Adam's lawyer the grounds she needed to appeal for bail.[54]

On arrival at Hassockfield, Adam was assessed as being high risk and monitored every five minutes. Carol was allowed to speak with him on the telephone five days later, and attended a meeting eight days after Adam was admitted. She told me she found her son deeply distressed:

'Adam was sat there, he were crying his eyes out. He had snot dripping off his face, he were shaking. He didn't even hardly speak throughout the meeting. His hand was all swollen and bandaged up so I asked what he'd done. Adam wouldn't even tell me. They'd said he'd punched a wall.'

Adam saw his mother in private after the meeting and told her he "would do himself in" if he was not moved. Carol passed on this information to a female member of staff:

> 'Her words to me were, "We've never had a death here yet, and we're not about to have one." And then 12 days later my child was dead. It's not as though they didn't know.'

Close monitoring continued and a transfer request was made, though Carol told me this did not highlight Adam's vulnerabilities, his self-harming, poor mental health state or the prohibitive distance from home. The last letter Adam posted to his mother laid bare his misery: 'I need to be at home with you. I need to be at home in my own bed or my head will crack up. I will probably try to kill myself and I will probably succeed this time. I can't stay in here.' He also wrote a letter to the judge pleading for bail, paraphrased here by the Prisons and Probation Ombudsman:

> [T]he boy wrote a letter addressed 'Dear Judge'. In this, he said he had learned his lesson and intended to stay out of trouble in the future. He said that, if he was granted bail, he knew he had 'to stick to it and I will for definite' because a friend had offered him a job. He said he had stopped smoking and would not smoke cannabis again. He said he wanted to change his life and start again. He asked the Judge to take into account how he was feeling about things and said he was 'really upset and distressed'. He asked for the chance to prove that what he was saying was true.[55]

On 7 August, Adam was visited by family members and punished afterwards for having contraband. Officers had observed the security breach during the visit but elected to 'discover' the items in a search after the boy's family had left the prison. Adam was placed on the lowest level of the punishment and rewards scheme and his television was removed from his cell. He became angry that evening after learning he was not allowed to earn any points for the day because of the contraband. He threw a plastic cup at a table which bounced and hit an officer on the arm before landing on the floor. Adam immediately apologised and went to his cell himself. Nevertheless, he was locked in for around 20 minutes as punishment.[56] This 14-year-old child had accrued three separate punishments in about seven hours – relegation to the institution's lowest privilege level, which included the removal of his television; not being able to accrue any points; and 'time out' – all originating from him accepting seven matches and two cigarettes from a family visitor. The Prisons and Probation Ombudsman observed:

> There can be little doubt of the effect this affair had on the boy – evidenced by the cup-throwing incident. He felt it was unfair (given that it was his family who brought in the cigarettes) and he would have felt the loss of points and privileges (and especially the loss of his television and CD at the weekend) keenly. He had quickly achieved Championship status and would have been proud of that (he said on one occasion on receiving ten points for the day that he was 'King of the world'). He may also have felt there was no escaping trouble no matter how hard he tried. It is perhaps pertinent here to recall his judgement that, whilst luck was responsible for the good things that happened to him, he believed he alone was responsible for the bad things.[57]

The following day, a Sunday, Adam and another child were in the association area of their unit. A child with special educational needs was on 'time out' and passed a note to Adam to give to another child. His mother told me a female officer instructed Adam to hand over the note, which he did. The officer did not approve of what was written in the note and ordered Adam into his cell. Adam asked what he had done wrong a couple of times and the officer then tried to drag him into his cell. Adam pulled away and went to sit down at one of the unit's fixed table and benches. The officer then activated the 'first response' restraint procedure and four officers came running into the unit, grabbed hold of Adam and carried him, face down, into his cell. Adam struggled against this unlawful assault and was inflicted with a 'nose distraction' (pp 128–38). Carol recounted that, during the inquest hearing, one of those who had carried out the restraint conceded that, when the officers ran into the area, Adam was quite calm and even tried to defuse the situation himself. Hours later, this 14-year-old boy was found hanging in his cell. He left a letter for his family, which opened with three words: 'Sorry! Sorry! Sorry!' The letter was found in the side pocket of Adam's sports bag some days after his death. The bag had sat in the office for a week, packed by Adam in preparation for a transfer to a children's home. He had asked for it back the night he died, apparently resigned to not getting bail (he rang his solicitor about his bail application every day until 5 August, three days before he died).

The manner in which Adam died is heartbreaking and should serve as an epitaph for the suffering of children in prison. This 14-year-old child wrapped a shoelace around his neck, used an Elastoplast to secure the shoelace onto the end of a curtain rail and, sitting on a bench facing the cell door, tugged at the shoelace until he lost consciousness. In his final letter to his family, Adam promised to look after his deceased grandparents, and asked to be buried with his grandfather. His mother Carol observed: "Within two days that cell that my child died in was being occupied by other kids."

There is nothing unusual about teenagers feeling overwhelmed. The physiological changes in the human body during puberty and adolescence are immense. But angry and agitated children in prison are unable to temporarily leave the field of battle. They cannot hammer across an open field, seek the safe company of friends or knock on the door of a trusted adult. Arguing their point risks adjudication and punishment (perversely called 'awards'), whereas in supportive families adults often show their love and maturity by giving way. Ordinary expressions of teenage frustration – shouting, swearing, banging doors, disobedience – all count as behaviour management problems in prison. The same penal tools used against recalcitrant adults are used against children – physical restraint, loss of privileges (which includes wearing their own clothes), segregation, restricted visits and telephone calls, cell clearances and strip searching.

The Howard League for Penal Reform found a child who had been put in segregation as a sanction that had been given nothing but word puzzles to alleviate boredom – despite being unable to read or write.[58]

Data obtained from the YJB shows that there were 973 self-harming incidents in young offender institutions during 2013, amounting to 19 incidents every week. Self-cutting accounted for more than half the incidents, followed by head butting and punching cell doors, walls or other parts of the prison (21% of incidents) and asphyxiation (14% of incidents). During the same period, there were 82 self-harming incidents in the four secure training centres, with self-cutting accounting for nearly three-quarters of incidents.[59]

Between 2007/08 and 2011/12, a five-year period, children required hospital treatment 81 times following self-harm in young offender institutions. A further 17 children were hospitalised from secure training centres. Official reasons for hospital visits include 'serious cuts, fractures, loss of consciousness, damage to internal organs and poisoning' and requiring medical intervention that 'may include stitches, re-setting bones, operations and providing overnight observation'.[60] Data obtained from the National Offender Management Service shows that 330 children were found trying to hang themselves between 2004 and 2012, an average of 37 children a year. In a study on the mental health needs of young offenders, a prison officer told researchers of the impact of finding a child who had killed himself:

> If it ever happens again, I'm not coming back to my job, because that was horrific – you're not supposed to be pally with the inmates, but you interact with them all every day and you do get to like them.[61]

A year after Kirk Edwards died in Wetherby young offender institution, the cellmate who had found him hanging was himself on suicide watch in the same prison. The 17-year-old boy was returned to the prison for burglary and other theft offences, although magistrates had reduced the length of incarceration because of his 'extremely sad background'. Two family members had recently killed themselves and the boy was addicted to heroin.[62]

Between December 2013 and February 2014, ChildLine and other charities surveyed young people about self-harm. When asked about the feelings that first led them to self-harm, 61% responded they had felt 'alone'; nearly half (46%) reported feeling 'numb/empty'; 41% 'sad'; 36% 'angry'; and 34% 'out of control'.[63] A team from the Centre for Mental Health interviewed inmates and staff and made their own observations in five prisons in the West Midlands in 2006, one of which had a juvenile unit. Self-harming by child prisoners, the researchers concluded, 'increased the likelihood of having a member of staff to talk to and at the very least got them more attention'.[64]

Children's goal to summon kindly treatment through self-harming was noted during the investigation into the death of 17-year-old Sam Elphick at Hindley young offender institution in September 2005. Such behaviour could backfire. Sam had been found with nooses the previous evening and had told a doctor less than 12 hours before his fatal hanging to 'just watch me tonight':[65]

> Staff described a 'noose culture' at Hindley, where young prisoners would sometimes fashion nooses in order to gain special consideration, for example, to be given back privileges, which had been removed on disciplinary grounds. As a result, staff experienced difficulty in determining which incidents of self-harm were genuine and which were not.[66]

During a parliamentary inquiry, the Howard League for Penal Reform reported that 'some prison officers take as a starting point the notion that the people in their custody are troublemakers and not to be trusted. This can lead them to interpret self-harming behaviour as manipulative, designed to procure a benefit for the prisoner, to annoy staff or to get attention'. Citing the case of 'SP' (discussed earlier), the charity said prison officers often interpret mental health disorders as matters of discipline and control.[67]

A national inquiry into self-harming among young people[68] explained that 'self-harm is often a way of releasing feelings of self-hatred, anger, sadness and depression'.[69] Shame and guilt is omnipresent. The inquiry urged professionals working with young people to 're-connect to their core professional skills and values: empathy, understanding, non-judgemental listening, and respect for individuals'.[70] Only malfunctioning computer software or a jobcentre trickster would recommend a career in the prison service to individuals looking for empathetic, caring and listening roles.

The recent deaths of three children are shameful reminders of the incapability of the prison service to provide consistent care to vulnerable children. Ryan Clark, aged 17, was found hanging in his cell at 7.51 am on 18 April 2011 while on remand at Wetherby young offender institution. Jake Hardy, also aged 17, was found hanging in his cell at Hindley young offender institution at 11.45 pm on 20 January 2012 while serving a six-month sentence for affray and assault. He was pronounced dead in hospital four days later. Inquests into the deaths of both boys found they had been seriously bullied (Chapter Ten). Alex Kelly, aged 15, was found unconscious in his cell at Cookham Wood young offender institution in Kent at approximately 8.30 pm on 24 January 2012, and was pronounced dead in hospital the following evening. He was in prison for burglary and theft from a vehicle, and the night he hanged himself had told a prison officer about the sexual abuse he had suffered as a young child.[71]

The Prisons and Probation Ombudsman analysed the backgrounds and prison treatment of the three boys and concluded that they were all 'extremely vulnerable'.[72] Two were in the care of local authorities and the other had a statement of special educational needs; two had diagnoses of attention deficit hyperactivity disorder, with prescribed medication; and the third boy was a known cannabis user and had suffered a recent family bereavement. The normal prison environment was acknowledged to be too much to bear for two of the children. There were places available in specialist units but these were not used. Youth offending teams had recommended alternative accommodation. The reasons given for one of the children needing a transfer from prison included 'learning difficulties, bullying and thoughts of suicide while he had been held in the [young offender institution] before sentencing'.[73]

Before they died, two of the children were subject to the prison monitoring procedure for people at risk of serious self-harm or suicide.[74] The third child became extremely aggressive to staff and damaged his cell. This was his first time in custody; the Ombudsman says this incident should have led to an assessment of the child's mental health, a conclusion likely to be reached by any compassionate onlooker.

All three children misbehaved in prison. Their behaviour was generally treated as a disciplinary matter, rather than as indicative of extreme stress. They were put through adjudications, and given punishments, and none had the assistance of an advocate during these processes. They were entirely alone, in other words. Each boy had difficulties maintaining family contact and the Ombudsman noted one was distressed about lack of contact with his mother on Mother's Day.[75] INQUEST reports that two weeks before he hanged himself, 17-year-old Ryan Clark:

> … became aggressive towards a prison officer, saying he was upset because [he] couldn't contact his mum on Mother's day and believed the officer insulted his mother. The incident was adjudicated and he lost his privileges for 7 days and was moved to a different wing.[76]

Bereavement and loss punctuated the final days of other children who have died in prison. Fifteen-year-old Jeffrey Horler, who hanged himself in Feltham young offender institution on 22 September 1991, was not allowed to attend his grandmother's funeral. A prison officer told the child's inquest he had found him sobbing in his cell after hearing of his grandmother's death.[77] A senior prison officer from Feltham contacted social services to say an exception to prison rules would be made, allowing Jeffrey to attend the funeral, if they organised his transport and escort. Social services decided 'missing the funeral would not have a very great effect on him' and were also deterred by the cost and journey length: Jeffrey had been imprisoned nearly 200 miles from home. The child was dead three weeks later.[78]

Seventeen-year-old Kevin Henson also hanged himself at Feltham. His mother had died from cancer on his 14th birthday and he had since developed severe alcohol problems. He was desperate for bail and anxious that he would not be able to visit his mother's grave on her birthday. His sister told BBC's Panorama programme that seeing Kevin in prison was awful, as the visiting room was full of boys crying.[79] The morning after Kevin had attended court and been refused bail, he was found hanging in his cell. He left behind a note explaining, 'Dear family, I'm sorry for doing this to you but I can't ride this amount of time in here without seeing Mum's grave.'[80]

Kirk Edwards, aged 17, was found hanging in his cell at Wetherby young offender institution on 26 May 1999 and died in hospital four days later. A boy with severe learning difficulties, Kirk had survived just two days in prison. He told a prison nurse he felt guilty about being unable to help his parents, who both had cancer. A fellow inmate told the inquest into Kirk's death that he had been locked in his cell for 23 hours since arriving at the prison and had no books or television in his cell. He said prison officers had placed books in Kirk's cell after he was taken to hospital to make his family feel better.[81]

The day before Gareth Price was found with a torn bed sheet around his neck he had been given an 'award' of loss of television for refusing to leave the education room three days earlier. After this, he threw some cold water in the face of an officer and set fire to his bedding. This led to him being removed from his cell through control and restraint and taken to another wing where he was strip searched for weapons. Later that afternoon, Gareth wrote some graffiti over the walls of the cell with a pencil. He chose to clean it off rather than receive another punishment. However, while standing on the sink he accidentally broke a tap and was moved again. That evening, Gareth rang his cell bell and asked for some tobacco, saying he had not had any all day. When he was told some would be given the following day, he twisted the taps off the sink and flooded his cell. He was moved again. The next morning, 19 January 2005, Gareth was allowed to mop out the cell he had damaged the evening before. He then attended an adjudication hearing for the taps damage and throwing cold water at an officer. He was given seven days' segregation as punishment; in addition, the fire damage to his bedding was referred to the police. He asked several officers throughout the morning for his belongings, which had remained on his former wing. When they were finally given to him, Gareth became emotional and started throwing his possessions around the cell because a photograph of his dead brother was missing. Three years previously, when Gareth was just 12, he had gone to a barn with his father and found his older brother hanging. Gareth himself was found hanging less than two hours after his belongings were returned without his brother's photograph. These final, erratic two days of Gareth's life occurred around the second anniversary of his best friend dying in a car crash. Gareth had been driving the car and lost control, and was referred by his GP to a clinical psychologist because he had 'developed traumatic symptoms, namely poor sleep patterns, flashbacks, nightmares and withdrawal'.[82] He had been known to self-harm since he was 13 and had been monitored as a suicide risk within the prison.[83]

There had been three prior ligature 'incidents' before 16-year-old Anthony Redding was found hanged in his cell at Brinsford young offender institution on 14 February 2001. Less than a week earlier, during a visit, Anthony had told his mother he was hearing his deceased grandmother's voice telling him to 'come to her'.[84]

One of the catalysts for Gareth Myatt's distress, ahead of him being fatally restrained by three G4S officers, was the removal of everything from his cell, including a piece of paper containing his mother's new mobile number. Pam Wilton told me she had passed the piece of paper to Gareth's solicitor in the courtroom after he was given a custodial sentence (p 109).

In a parliamentary question, Baroness Stern asked the Ministry of Justice how child prisons mark events like birthdays, Mother's Day and Christmas Day. She was told in relation to young offender institutions:

> Whilst there is no policy to govern arrangements for young people's birthdays, mother's day and father's day, each under 18 Young Offenders Institution has arrangements in place to appropriately observe culturally significant events.[85]

The same neglect emerged for secure training centres, those purportedly purpose-built institutions for children as young as 12, as the following response shows: 'The Youth Justice Board does not issue any specific policy instruction or guidance'.[86]

Being receptive to children's anguish is a highly skilled and demanding job. Child psychiatrists train for a minimum of 13 years, social workers and mental health nurses for three years. In 2004, a specialist course was introduced for officers working in juvenile prisons[87] but the programme lasts just seven days.[88] It is unclear whether recent revisions have extended the period of study.[89] Even if working in prisons were a graduate profession, and officers were given excellent training and intensive supervision and support, they would still be located in buildings and working for an organisation without the expertise to look after children. As a lawyer who has dealt with a large number of inquests into the deaths of child prisoners, a major concern of Mark Scott's is the safety of cells that house vulnerable children, because "a lot of the YOI [young offender institution] cells are fundamentally unsafe, in terms of ligature points. But that's a massive, massive multimillion pound issue." Liz Hardy told me she could not understand why suicidal children like her son could be given sheets in their cells that can be ripped into hanging strips. How can money be put before children's lives, she asked.

We should not imagine children's suffering ends when their property is returned and they are freed at the prison gate. Of the 38 young people aged between 18 and 21 years who died in custody between 2008 and 2012, more than a third (37%) had been imprisoned as children.[90]

FOUR

'I think it's quite like rape'

The National Society for the Prevention of Cruelty to Children (NSPCC) launched a national campaign in the summer of 2013 urging parents to teach their children the 'underwear rule', which is that no-one should be able to touch or look at a child without his or her underwear against the child's wishes.[1] Until very recently, thousands of children entering and leaving young offender institutions every year were systematically forced to take off their underwear and endure additional 'random' searches. The sociologist Erving Goffman referred to these kinds of institutional practices as 'will-breaking ceremonies'.[2] In an interview for this book, the former head of the Youth Justice Board (YJB), John Drew, voiced the potent message given to individual children when strip searching was rife: "'You're mine, I can do anything I like with you.'"

The routine strip searching of female prisoners ended in 2008,[3] and girls held in women's prisons benefited from this, but it took until 2011 for risk assessments to replace institutionalised undressing in secure training centres and 2014 for the same limitations to be applied to all young offender institutions.[4] As with 'stop and search' police practices, close monitoring will be necessary to detect any discrimination in its continued use. But these latest developments should not detract attention from the abhorrent nature of the procedure itself, whether undertaken systematically or after a prison risk assessment. The law prohibits headteachers (or other authorised persons) from requiring a student to remove anything other than outer clothing when searching for offensive weapons.[5] Prison rules allow officers to use force to remove children's clothes – bizarrely, they are instructed to do this without causing the prisoner stress[6]

– and 'safety scissors' remain an authorised strip searching tool.[7] At its least ugliest, children are made to stand in front of officers exposing the top and then the bottom half of their naked bodies while handing over their underwear for inspection. It can get much worse than this, however.

A decade before the launch of the NSPCC campaign, the then chief inspector of prisons gave a lecture on the role of inspection in protecting human rights, noting:

> 'We have reported to at least two governors that, without their knowledge and against prison service orders, incoming prisoners were routinely squat-searched while stripped naked for strip-searching: and that included children.'[8]

It's safe to assume the practice continued. Jake Hardy was admitted to Hindley young offender institution in December 2011 and told his mother he was made to squat down and bend over during his strip search.[9] Children held at Castington young offender institution told inspectors in 2009 they were made to squat during strip searches on admission.[10] Squatting was also recorded at an inspection of Feltham in 2011: one child 'had been strip searched three times within a very short period and it had been recorded that this was because he would not squat properly'.[11]

When Lord Carlile's independent inquiry concluded strip searching was not necessary for good order and security, the YJB responded by promising a review, despite the wealth of disturbing testimony from children, including this from a 17-year-old boy in a young offender institution:

> David explained that he was expected 'to get fully naked – the order is to take off your trousers, top, boxers and then you are asked to squat then you are passed back your boxers and trousers'. No one explained what was going to happen. He told us that the officers always shouted their orders at the boys.

> David also talked to us about being forcibly strip searched while he was already being held on the segregation unit. He told us he was banging on his cell door. He was bored and upset. Staff told him to stop but he didn't. He said that the next thing he knew was a group of officers wearing full riot gear and carrying plastic shields were bearing down on him. He told us that he saw seven or eight men storming into his cell. They pushed him up to the window using their shields. David was then restrained and taken down to the floor. He said he felt angry. The officers held him face down on the stone floor and controlled his arms. His clothes were taken off by force so that he was naked.[12]

Three months after the publication of Lord Carlile's report, inspectors visiting Huntercombe young offender institution in Oxfordshire found four children had alleged abuse after being strip searched during the previous six months. The clothes of two of these children had been forcibly removed. Inspectors recommended strip searching should never be undertaken using force and noted 'staff in the establishment had mixed views about its efficacy'.[13] A year after Lord Carlile's report was published, inspectors observed that some children in Brinsford young offender institution in Wolverhampton had been forcibly strip searched after a restraint incident 'without any clear authorisation or risk assessment'.[14] Had this been a theatre performance, this grand finale of nakedness would have provided audiences with a sickening portrayal of utterly powerless children. When prison inspectors visited Werrington young offender institution in Stoke-on-Trent in April 2007, they found evidence of two children having their clothes cut off during a forcible strip search. The inspection team was 'appalled by a video recording of the strip-searching by force of a refractory young person, which included cutting off his clothing, even though at various times he said that he was willing to comply'.[15] The previous month, inspectors complained that no separate records were kept showing how often children in Wetherby young offender institution had their clothes forcibly removed.[16] In July 2007, inspectors found 31 instances of children being strip searched 'under restraint' in the preceding 12 months in Warren Hill young offender institution in Suffolk, yet there was no evidence that full assessments had been carried out to ascertain whether strip searches were even necessary.[17] An inspection of Huntercombe young offender institution in Oxfordshire in December 2008 discovered a child had been forcibly strip searched the previous year and this was being investigated internally (managers were said to be discouraging the practice).[18] In February 2009, inspectors found children admitted to Cookham Wood young offender institution in Kent were routinely strip searched in a 'crowded property store which added a further indignity'[19] and:

> There was a notice in reception warning young people that they would be strip-searched using force if they refused to cooperate.[20]

Inspectors reported that the notice 'was removed by the governor during the inspection'.[21] In the summer of 2009, inspectors reported that two children held in Werrington young offender institution had been subject to 'forcible strip-searching' during the previous six months.[22] An 'extremely vulnerable' girl was found by inspectors visiting Downview women's prison in Surrey in December 2010 to have been subject to a forcible strip search.[23] In the summer of 2013, more than seven years after the Carlile Inquiry recommended the end of strip-searching, inspectors visiting the specialist unit in Wetherby young offender institution found that force had been used sometimes to remove children's clothes.[24] Keppel Unit holds some of the country's most vulnerable child prisoners. At the time of its inspection, 47% of children detained there had been in care and 56% were disabled.[25]

During autumn 2013, inspectors uncovered 'at least four incidents of young people being strip-searched under restraint and not as a last resort' in Werrington young offender institution. The inspection report recommends the cessation of strip searching under restraint, although it fails to question the legality of the officers' actions.[26] During the March 2014 inspection of Hindley young offender institution, three children were found to have been strip searched while being restrained. This is 'a practice which should never be carried out on a child' concluded the inspection team, who also pointed to 'the potential for abuse'. Only one of the incidents was referred by the prison to the local authority – following a child protection allegation – though 'a decision was made not to proceed with a detailed investigation'.[27] None of the incidents of boys being searched under restraint in Cookham Wood young offender institution had been referred to the local authority for investigation, according to the October 2014 inspection report. Inadequate recording meant inspectors were unable to 'ascertain the level of searches carried out'.[28]

In September 2014, Ofsted reported two children had been strip searched in Hassockfield secure training centre after a pair of scissors went missing in a classroom. There is no discussion in the inspection report about alternative means of finding scissors assumed to be hidden on a child. Inspectors say the scissors 'were subsequently discovered' but do not specify whether this was achieved through making children undress.[29]

As a member of the Carlile Inquiry expert panel, I made three visits to two secure training centres and asked children about their experiences of strip searching. Even talking about such practices felt intrusive at times: when a 17-year-old boy told us he felt 'a bit degraded' and looked to the side awkwardly, we moved on to another subject. In former child protection roles, I had listened to many children recount horrific violations and frequently probed even when they were in obvious discomfort. But then I was expected to take action to stop the abuse – measures that would also protect other children. This inquiry process was far more sedentary and I could only hope that, once their words reached the pages of Lord Carlile's report, the authorities would realise the extent of children's suffering. Who, after all, could defend officers wearing latex gloves and inspecting children's underwear and worn sanitary pads, or making girls stand with their arms outstretched exposing their breasts?

During the Inquiry, one 16-year-old girl told me, "For people who've been abused it's not very nice," a conclusion also reached by Labour peer Baroness Jean Corston, who, a month after the Carlile Inquiry was published, was asked by ministers to review the treatment of vulnerable women within the criminal justice system.[30] Nearly a third of females and at least 3% of males reported being victims of sexual abuse in an official survey of imprisoned 16- to 20-year-olds[31] – figures we should take as underestimates, given the context of the research, and the difficulties boys especially have in disclosing such crimes. Another 16-year-old girl in a different secure training centre said, "The more you do, the less embarrassing it gets." She was to be released in two weeks' time and wondered if she should ask for one of the six staff who had already seen her naked to undertake her final strip search: "I could ask for one of them. It's not nice for the whole centre to see you in the nude." That this child had logged in her mind the officers who had seen her naked body is a powerful rebuke to those who dismiss its significance. Neither should we assume these procedures have been undertaken by a system oblivious to children's backgrounds. Inspectors visiting Wetherby young offender institution in the summer of 2008 reported being 'told that even if it was known that a young person had been the victim of abuse previously, the requirements of security took precedence'.[32] As recently as December 2012, inspectors criticised Rainsbrook secure training centre for making children undress in front of staff:

> The lack of a screen in the searching room fails to allow young people to remove their clothes and put on a dressing gown with the required level of privacy as described in the centre's own searching policy which states 'this (removal of clothing) will be out of sight of staff, either in the search room, bathroom or a separate room allocated for the purpose'. In reality, young people undressed in front of staff.[33]

Baroness Corston's report was published in March 2007 and recommended strip searching be reduced to an absolute minimum for women, given its 'dreadful invasion of privacy':

> There is one particular aspect of entrenched prison routine that I consider wholly unacceptable for women.... This is the regular, repetitive, unnecessary

use of strip-searching. Strip-searching is humiliating, degrading and undignified for a woman and a dreadful invasion of privacy. For women who have suffered past abuse, particularly sexual abuse, it is an appalling introduction to prison life and an unwelcome reminder of previous victimisation.[34]

Women's prisons began piloting risk-based strip searching that year, followed by a full ban on routine strip searching. This is why economist Vicky Pryce was able to report in 2013:

I must confess that my arrival at Holloway was smooth, humane and expertly carried out. Quick fingerprinting and BOSS chair (Body Orifice Security Scanner, essentially a metal detector). No strip search.[35]

This contrasts unacceptably with a girl's experience in a secure training centre:

When I had my first full search I was 14, it was horrible as I have been sexually abused and I didn't feel comfortable showing my body as this brought back memories. They told me if I didn't take my clothes off they would do it when they got permission [to use force].[36]

The year before Corston was invited to review the plight of women prisoners, Feltham young offender institution asked prison service headquarters if it could carry out strip searches on children only after a risk assessment 'but had been told that all children must routinely undergo this procedure'.[37] The success of Wetherby young offender institution in introducing risk-based searching seems to have also been thwarted by central policy.[38] Some months after the women's ban, the report of the European Committee for the Prevention of Torture and Inhuman and Degrading Treatment or Punishment was published and said the routine strip searching of child prisoners was 'a disproportionate measure, which could be considered as degrading'. The Committee recommended 'a strict policy of risk-assessed strip searches only'.[39] The Labour government, which had introduced risk-assessed searching for women prisoners, said it had 'no current plans' to make the same change for children. It claimed routine strip searching was not disproportionate, while, at the same time, highlighting the YJB review being undertaken 'to ensure that practice is proportionate and appropriate'.[40]

Nearly five years after it promised to establish a review of strip searching in child custody,[41] the YJB published its findings and action plan in March 2011, and also recommended an end to routine strip searching.[42] This was the first public sign of a change in official thinking. Twelve establishments were visited as part of the review between October and November 2008 (this included four secure children's homes run by local authorities).[43] In young offender institutions, boys were routinely strip searched on admission and discharge, including when making court appearances. Other strip searches occurred as part of random cell searching, after temporary release from the prison, following drug testing and when children were placed in segregation.[44] All four of the secure training centres were, at that time, routinely strip searching on admission and some also on release. Additional strip searching occurred when seen to be necessary. Financial penalties (called 'performance awards') incurred by G4S and Serco for contraband discoveries were seen to encourage strip searching.[45] If these were the mandatory reasons for strip searching, until recently, what exactly is the official procedure? The extract below depicts the authorised steps for strip searching boys in young offender institutions (it also applies to staff and visitors). I have not included the description for females as girls were removed from prison service establishments in 2013.[46]

The YJB found that split-site prisons – those holding children in one part of the institution, and young adults in another – tended to use the same reception areas for all age groups. This meant children were being subject to admission processes in close proximity to adult prisoners 'including when being full searched'.[47]

The United Nations Convention on the Rights of the Child requires that imprisoned children be always separated from adults. The UK ratified the convention in December 1991, although it took

Table 4.1: Prison service procedure for searching boys and men

Officer 1	Officer 2
The officer in charge of the search. He is responsible for controlling the search. He will normally observe the subject from the front.	*Responsible for receiving clothing and other items from the subject and searching them. He must return the clothing and other items back to the subject at the direction of Officer 1. Observes the prisoner throughout the search, normally from back or side. Remains vigilant to potential risks and remains alert throughout the search.*
Ask the subject if he has anything on him he is not authorised to have. Ask him to empty his pockets and remove any jewellery [and other items].	Search the contents of the pockets and the jewellery and place them to one side. Search any bags or other items.
Search his head either by running your fingers through his hair and around the back of his ears, or ask him to shake out his hair and run his fingers through it.	
Look around and inside his ears, nose and mouth. You may ask him to raise his tongue so that you can look under it.	
Ask him to remove the clothing from the top half of his body and pass it to Officer 2.	Search the clothing.
Ask him to hold his arms up and turn around whilst you observe his upper body. Check his hands.	Return the clothing.
Allow him time to put on clothing.	
Ask him to remove his shoes and socks and pass to Officer 2.	Search the shoes and socks and then place them to one side.
Ask him to lift each foot so the soles can be checked.	
Ask him to remove his trousers and underpants and pass to Officer 2.	Search trousers and underpants and place to one side.

Continued.../

... continued

Officer 1	Officer 2
Once the clothing has been searched ask him to raise the upper body clothing to his waist.	
Observe the lower half of his body. He must stand with his legs apart while the lower half of his body is observed.	
Look at the area around him for anything he may have dropped before or during the search.	
Ask him to step to one side to ensure he is not standing on anything he has dropped before or during the search.	Return the clothing, unless search is to continue.
Most searches will end here. However, if a closer inspection of the anal or, exceptionally, the genital area is justified ... advise him of this and ask him to bend over or squat.	Use mirrors to view these areas better.
Ask him to step to one side to ensure he is not standing on anything he has dropped before or during this additional procedure.	Return the clothing.
Allow him time to put on his clothing.	

Source: NOMS (2011) National security framework. Ref: NSF 3.1. Searching of the person. PSI 67/2011, London: Ministry of Justice, pp 26–8.

until November 2008 for its reservation to this part of the treaty to be lifted. (Anyone who considers holding children and adults in the same prison to be uncontroversial should picture the merger of children's and old people's homes, or paediatric and adult hospital wards, or letting keen adults enrol at secondary school.) The practice of making children remove their clothes in the presence of adult prisoners, however rare, would clearly be a very serious breach of the requirement for separate facilities, as well as violating the child's right to privacy and exposing him or her to inhuman and degrading treatment.

Contraband was mostly detected during the routine procedure but only ever between 1% and 3% of the time. Nearly all of the contraband was cigarettes or small amounts of cannabis. The YJB review team considered the use of technology and other ways of maintaining security without routine strip searching, but feared tiny items might go unnoticed:

> Findings suggest that there is no single body-scanning technology that is able to reliably detect and identify all concealed items within clothing, on the body or within the body.... very small items, such as a matchstick head, strands of tobacco, or a small quantity of milk powder, which could be useful components in lighting a fire, can only be found by, for example, asking the young person to empty their pockets or by conducting a full body search....[48]

With a penal mindset, this explanation for rejecting humane replacements to strip searching probably appears incontrovertible. From the outside, it smacks of paranoia and is a classic form of institutionalisation, best described by Goffman in the 1950s:

> The admission procedure can be characterized as a leaving off and a taking on, with the midpoint marked by physical nakedness.[49]

About a million visitors enter the Houses of Parliament each year without being subject to full body searches, and the presence of concrete posts and armed officers show security is no small concern there either. There is no discussion in the YJB's report of the proportionality of making children strip off their clothes in the hope of finding a strand of tobacco. Indeed, there is no exploration of the UK's human rights obligations, which is a significant omission, especially as the European Court of Human Rights had found breaches in a case involving prison strip searching some years before (*Wainwright v United Kingdom*).[50] A woman and her disabled son were making their first visit to her other son in a Leeds prison when they were made to undergo strip searches. This was in accordance with a governor's ruling that all of her son's visitors must be strip searched because he was suspected to be dealing drugs within the prison. The middle-aged woman and her adult son who has 'cerebral palsy and severe arrested social and intellectual development'[51] acquiesced to the searches as they were told they would be refused their visit if they did not comply. They suffered serious mental anguish as a result. The mother was so badly affected she did not return to the prison for another four months. The court found a breach of article 8 of the European Convention on Human Rights, which includes the right to bodily integrity, and article 13, the right to an effective remedy (the UK courts had found that a legal wrong had been committed only in the case of the young man whose penis had been lifted up and foreskin pulled back during the search; his mother had not been touched). A separate case brought by an adult French prisoner who was forced to undergo full searches, including anal inspections, was also found by the Strasbourg Court to have amounted to degrading treatment (*Frérot v France*).[52]

When the YJB published its review, the first line of its press release declared in bold lettering: 'The routine use of full searches will stop across the secure estate'.[53] The organisation announced it would start temporarily collecting data on the use of strip searches, observing that no government department was undertaking any kind of monitoring.[54] This was in March 2011, more than a decade since the board was given the statutory role of placing children in custodial establishments.[55] I subsequently learned from John Drew, the former chief executive of theYJB, that he had tried unsuccessfully in 2009 to persuade the head of the prison service to move to a risk-based system:

'In late 2009, I had a meeting with Phil Wheatley as the director general of the prison service and I told Phil that was where I wished the prison service to go [and] there were voices within the prison service who said they could operate on that basis ... I was left with the strongest impression that Phil viewed me as a "do-gooder" who didn't understand the reality of operating a prison.... So then it's just been a long process of whittling away the opposition, talking to governing governors, building support amongst them so that there's pressure within NOMS [the National Offender Management Service] around it; finding practical examples of how you can make a risk-based approach work.'

In January 2013, I asked the YJB to provide data on the use of strip searching in child custody. This revealed there were 1,699 strip searches of children in the four secure training centres in the 21 months up to December 2012. This is more than double the number of Members of Parliament elected in 2010, so enough naked children to fill the Commons chamber twice over. Twenty-six of the children were aged 13. Contraband was found just three times and consisted of tobacco; a mobile phone, charger or sim card; and some unauthorised medication. There was a substantial decrease in strip searching from April 2012, with 36 procedures in nine months compared with an average 35 searches every month in each of the institutions in 2011/12.

There were a further 41,321 strip searches in young offender institutions between April/May 2011 and December 2012. Each of the nine young offender institutions run by the prison service conducted 174 child strip searches on average a month; and the one each run by Serco and G4S (in England and Wales respectively) carried out a monthly average of 238 child strip searches. Only 315 items of contraband were discovered. By far the most common item found was tobacco, seized 70 times; followed by 29 'other weapons' (no guns, knives or explosives were found); 18 disallowed substances; 14 drug finds; 10 mobile phones, chargers or sim cards; and one item of unauthorised medication.

The two privately run young offender institutions reported reductions in the use of strip searches from April 2012, although the rate of contraband discovery remained below 2%. The nine young offender institutions run by the state reduced strip searches from around 194 each month in each prison in 2011/12, to an average 150 from April 2012. However, the rate of contraband finds had not changed from half a percentage point. In other words, an unauthorised item was discovered just once every 200 times a child was forced to undress before watching officers. Data from an inspection of Ashfield young offender institution in 2013 gives an even bleaker picture. Children were made to remove their clothes entering or leaving the prison during the previous year on 3,773 occasions. Only one item was found; it was recorded as 'other contraband', so presumably harmless.[56]

The response to my data request showed physical force was used 50 times to remove children's clothes, 34 of these in Wetherby young offender institution. These would have been situations where children refused to comply with an order to undress. In all likelihood, these boys would have been held face down to the floor struggling and their clothes wrenched off; they may have also been subject to wrist or thumb locks. I asked consultant paediatrician Nick Lessof, who is the safeguarding lead at Great Ormond Street Hospital, whether doctors ever use force to remove a child's clothes. His response was both quick and graphic: "If they've been under a bus." He continued:

'You know, we do undress children all the time, but in deference to the child, and maintaining the child's sense of autonomy. Having a complete loss of personal autonomy is very degrading.'

The YJB and the Office of Children's Commissioner for England commissioned research into children's experiences of strip searching, published at the same time as the promise to move to a risk-based policy. One imprisoned girl explained:

> They look at you like you're a dog, making you strip is bang out of order, it proper makes me angry, it really does.[57]

A boy expressed similar feelings: 'I was angry, I didn't want to strip in front of two men.'[58] Another girl explained: 'I think it's quite like rape me, getting forced to take all your clothes off.'[59] This child is not alone in equating strip searching with rape. I asked psychotherapist Camila Batmangelidjh, the founder-director of the vulnerable children's support charity Kids Company, how a child might feel being threatened with segregation or restraint, or even having their clothes cut off during a strip search. Batmangelidjh was unequivocal: "It's tantamount to being raped for a child." She described what children might go through during this mortifying treatment:

> 'I think children who comply achieve it by disassociating often, so they leave their own bodies, because it's a very difficult thing to do. They either, if you like, in a way trash themselves. They think there's nothing to preserve so you might as well have this one as well. Have my body as well.… Or they leave their bodies and disconnect completely. Children who fight have still got a sense of wanting to preserve something, but of course they're going to get disempowered. And look at what happens. You've got a naked child being disempowered by clothed adults who are using force. This kind of memory doesn't go away. Children hold on to these traumatic memories.'

Gareth Myatt was a child who refused to comply with a strip search on prison admission. Weighing a mere six-and-a-half stone and standing just four foot 10 inches tall, it is not difficult to imagine why this 15-year-old would be reluctant to remove his clothes. I agreed with his mother when she told me: "Nobody would want to be strip searched, but especially a teenager who's little for his age." Gareth was taken to his cell under restraint as a consequence: a nurse told the inquest he had been 'bent over with his head below his groin'.[60] In February 2013, the Prisons and Probation Ombudsman published a document on sexual abuse in prisons, noting that the organisation had dealt with a number of allegations of sexual assault by officers during strip searching. The Ombudsman's findings confirm the extraordinary culture of prisons:

> Not infrequently, the Ombudsman found that the perceived sexual assault was an inherent and lawful aspect of the search.[61]

Strip searching may well be intrinsic to the role of prison officers, and in this sense regular and routine, but to those having their clothes removed it feels like an assault. As well as words like rape and sexual abuse, children reported during the YJB review that strip searching made them feel humiliated, embarrassed, intimidated, paranoid, dirty, strange, stressed, vulnerable, scared, violated and weird.[62] I heard children using very similar words when I was a child protection social worker interviewing them about sexual abuse. Those children also told me about threats. It is clear that strip searching provokes the same devastating feelings among children as other forms of sexual abuse. From this perspective, it is shocking to read of the 'head of safeguarding' in one young offender institution who said during the YJB review:

> To be honest, I've never thought of this as a safeguarding issue – it's always been a security issue first and foremost.[63]

A review established after the death of 16-year-old Joseph Scholes (p 45) examined the advice given to prison staff about routine strip searching on admission. David Lambert, asked by the prisons minister to conduct the review, chaired a local authority child protection committee; was a former social services inspector; and had managed children's homes earlier in his career. Even this professional background did not serve as a reality check, as Lambert concluded:

> If [the prison service's] advice is followed and such full
> searching is conducted with due sensitivity then young
> people should not experience the practice as abusive or
> invasive. It has to be recognised that there are genuine
> security issues to deal with here, including the illicit
> concealment of drugs or potential weapons, all informed
> by wider issues of trainee safety and security.[64]

There is a disturbing race dimension to the practice of strip searching
because the vast majority of prison officers are white and children
being forced to remove their clothes are disproportionately from black
and minority ethnic communities. The strip searching data provided
to me showed that, in 2011/12, 48% of children being made to
remove their clothes in secure training centres were from black and
minority ethnic communities (this decreased to 28% the following
year). In the two privately run young offender institutions, 52% of
children strip searched in 2011/12 were from black and minority
ethnic communities (this increased to 53% the following year). Almost
half of those strip searched in the public young offender institutions
in 2011/12 were from black and minority ethnic communities (this
decreased to 41% the following year). The YJB's review of strip
searching practices in eight establishments noted: 'Approaches to full-
searching did not always appear to be culturally specific. There may
well be instances in which a young person's culture or religion has an
impact on complying with full-searching procedures'. It concluded,
vaguely, that more research might be necessary, but opted 'in the first
instance' to simply collect data on the ethnicity of children being
strip searched.[65] The Carlile Inquiry had reported five years earlier
the experience of a circumcised boy:

> Having been told about the rules of the establishment
> [the boy] was then informed that he would be strip-
> searched. Not having ever experienced anything like this
> before Karim questioned why he was to be strip searched
> and what would happen if he failed to comply. He told us
> that he was informed that if he did not voluntarily strip
> he would be forcibly stripped. Feeling that there was no

alternative Karim removed all his clothing and when he attempted to cover himself with his hands he was told to put his hands by his side. Karim told us that although he is circumcised he had been asked to retract his foreskin. Reflecting on his experience of strip searching he told us of his feelings of 'loss of dignity', 'embarrassment', and being 'shocked'.[66]

Forcing children to strip off their clothes was a feature of the abusive 'pindown' regime in four Staffordshire children's homes in the 1980s. In October 1989, a 15-year-old girl reported to her solicitor that she had been in pindown at her children's home in Staffordshire. The solicitor was acting for the girl in care proceedings and contacted the local authority, after which the director of social services issued an instruction ending the regime. The solicitor obtained injunctions in respect of two more children to protect them from pindown. Local and national media became involved and, in June 1990, Allan Levy QC and Barbara Kahan were appointed to conduct an independent inquiry into the treatment of children in children's homes and other settings in Staffordshire.

Michael was first placed in pindown in 1984, at the age of 11, and at least another 12 times over the next four years. His first experience of pindown is described in the inquiry report:

> Michael told the Inquiry that he was taken up to the back Pindown room and told to remove his clothes. He refused to do so. He was then held down on a bed in the room and stripped. He was made to have a bath and given a pair of pyjamas to wear....[67]

Sophie, aged 13, was admitted to pindown in the same way: her clothes were removed and she was given a nightdress to wear. The children's home log book recorded another child, 15-year-old Sheraz, putting up resistance to pindown:

> Physically and verbally abusive to staff – had to be escorted by several staff to bathroom, where she was

stripped of clothing and placed into the bath – kicking, screaming and lashing out at staff.... Eventually got into pyjamas.[68]

There was a great deal more to pindown than forcing children to remove their clothes and wear nightwear during the day, but this was fundamental to 'breaking them down' and having control. Levy and Kahan concluded:

> Pindown, in our view, falls decisively outside anything that could properly be considered as good child care practice. It was in all its manifestations intrinsically unethical, unprofessional and unacceptable.[69]

Regulations governing children's homes subsequently prohibited any intimate physical examinations of children.[70] The statutory guidance noted: 'Intimate physical searches are totally unacceptable.'[71] This was later amended to a ban on intimate searches as a disciplinary measure;[72] nevertheless, the law still gives much greater protection to children detained in secure children's homes than those held in penal custody.

I asked Yvonne Bailey, the mother of Joseph Scholes, whether her son had been strip searched. Joseph was terrified throughout his incarceration and died in the most atrocious conditions. Any parent would understand the answer Yvonne gave:

> 'I actually don't ask some of these questions because, one, I probably know the answer to it in that it'll be "yes" and, two, I don't want to hear any more.'

There is no escaping the haunting truth that prison officers based in young offender institutions later convicted of sexual offences against children would have had, as part of their regular role, opportunities to make children remove their clothes. Furthermore, the safeguarding report jointly published by inspection bodies in 2008 warned that many prison officers were not even subject to basic criminal checks:

> While all inspected youth [sic] offender institutions were checking new staff, the HM Prison Service (HMPS) did not require the checking of existing staff and only one establishment was carrying out retrospective checks. Only six out of the 14 establishments had 90% or more of their staff CRB [Criminal Records Bureau] cleared for working with young people. Three establishments only had around half of their staff CRB cleared. This is of particular concern in closed institutions where staff who may not have been vetted are permitted to carry out procedures such as strip-searching...[73]

Data protection exclusions in the Freedom of Information (FOI) Act 2000 have prevented me from checking the prisons in which convicted sex offenders worked prior to conviction. Enquiries with the Ministry of Justice were not productive. Officers frequently transfer between prisons as their career progresses, and cross-deployment on split sites is common, so it is a reasonable assumption that many (if not all) of the following individuals worked at least some of the time with child prisoners.

This could include men like John Cornwell who, in May 2013, was found guilty of four charges of sexual assault of children, four charges of indecent assault of children, and two charges of engaging in sexual activity in the presence of a child. The offences dated back to the 1990s. After his conviction, Cornwell was sacked from his support worker job at Northallerton young offender institution,[74] which had detained children until 1998.

In August 2012, the Ministry of Justice agreed to pay compensation to a former child prisoner who had been sexually assaulted on more than one occasion by a prison officer while detained at a young offender institution in Oxfordshire two years previously.[75]

John Maber had been a prison officer for 18 years[76] when the Crown Prosecution Service announced in July 2012 he had been handed a life sentence 'after pleading guilty to 27 offences of child sexual abuse including the rape of a baby girl aged just four months'.[77] The police investigation found he was at the centre of a paedophile ring and 15 other arrests were made after evidence was found on his laptop, hard drive and mobile phone.[78] At the time of his arrest, Maber was a senior officer at the adult prison Pentonville.[79]

Acting prison governor Russell Thorne was jailed in July 2011 for five years for misconduct in a public office between 2006 and 2010 after coercing a young female prisoner to engage in sexual acts with him.[80] Allegations of sexual abuse were made about other prison officers at Downview,[81] which had a dedicated unit for girls, and a prison service review was established in 2012.[82] Surrey police established a special investigation, called Operation Daimler, which involved interviews with over 200 past and present prisoners. I asked the force how many girls were seen during this investigation and was appalled to learn that not a single child was interviewed. After being instructed by the Information Commissioner to release the information, the Ministry of Justice confirmed in May 2014 that four officers working at Downview prison had been suspended, dismissed or convicted between January 2009 and October 2013 'as a result of a sexually inappropriate behaviour with women prisoners or a young offender'. The Information Commissioner did not support disclosure of the report from the internal prison service investigation, stating it 'could potentially cause unnecessary and unjustified distress'[83] to the prison officers discussed within it, so this remains buried. A separate FOI request I made to Surrey County Council revealed that 'less than 10' girls in Downview prison made sexual abuse allegations against staff in the five years to March 2013 (p 239). I was told that these, and other allegations from girls, were either investigated internally by the prison, or no further action was taken. Had a statutory child protection investigation been undertaken by the local authority following any of the sexual abuse referrals, one obvious consideration would have been the role of strip searching in facilitating abuse.

Another prison governor, Barry Cummings, was given a four-year custodial sentence in June 2011 after being convicted of three charges of sexually touching a girl under the age of 13 some years ago. Cummings had worked at Low Newton prison, which formerly detained children.[84]

In May 2011, retired prison officer Christopher Pearce was given a 12-year custodial sentence for raping and indecently assaulting a young girl over a period of five to six years. The child was six when Pearce first began indecently assaulting her, and 10 when he started raping her. The court heard Pearce had raped the young child up to 200 times. The offences were committed around 20 years ago.[85] Acklington prison in Northumberland was one of the institutions Pearce had worked in. It had a dedicated wing for children until 1986 and specialised in the incarceration of sex offenders.

A court sent Leslie Winnard to prison for two years in November 2010 for possessing and distributing indecent images of children. Winnard had been a prison officer for over 30 years. Of the 1,567 indecent images stored on his computer, 11 were level five (child sexual abuse involving an animal) and 257 were level four.[86] He may have had regular sight of children's naked bodies as a routine part of his employment, as could retired prison officer Andrew Burns, who, in August 2010, was convicted of possessing indecent images of children, including seven of the most serious type. He was given a three-year community order and banned from having any unsupervised contact with a child aged under 16.[87]

A former Royal Marine and prison officer at Warren Hill young offender institution was sent to custody for three years in May 2010 after sexually abusing a 17-year-old prisoner, both inside the prison and after release. The boy was being treated for depression. Prosecuting counsel told the court that William John Payne was able to abuse the boy 'at every opportunity'. Payne would have also been able, as part of his official role, to conduct strip searches of his 17-year-old victim as well as other children. He had been a prison officer for 30 years.[88]

In February 2010, Francis Hart was sent to prison for 14 months for possessing and distributing indecent images of children. Hart pleaded guilty to possessing 245 level-four indecent images (depicting penetrative sexual activity involving a child or children, or both children and adults) and more than 1,000 level-one to level-three images. Having served in the army for 15 years, Hart worked as a prison officer in Portland young offender institution at the time of his arrest in 2007.[89] It is possible he would have undertaken strip searches of children.

A 53-year-old prison officer worked at Deerbolt young offender institution when he downloaded images of child pornography and distributed them to paedophiles. He boasted to online acquaintances that he had had sex with two girls, aged seven and 10, and that he had sexually assaulted a four-year-old girl. A court ordered David Lamb's name be placed on the sex offenders' register in October 2009, and bailed him pending sentencing. As well as admitting he distributed images to paedophiles, Lamb pleaded guilty to making indecent photographs and having 565 indecent images on his camera at home.[90] Deerbolt young offender institution had a dedicated juvenile unit in the 1990s, and was formerly a borstal.

In 2012, *The Guardian* newspaper reported the case of Neville Husband, a prison officer who managed to get away with abusing boys in penal institutions for decades. This included a period at Deerbolt young offender institution, a posting he requested. The newspaper reports that the police charged Husband with importing sado-masochistic images involving teenage boys in 1969 (these charges were later dropped) and, when he worked at Medomsley detention centre (pp 245–6) in the 1980s, pornographic material and sex aids were found in his drawers and locker. After 27 years as a prison officer, the prison service discharged him on medical grounds in 1990.[91] Thirteen years later, he was convicted of sexual offences against nine child prisoners, four of whom came forward after media reporting of the initial trial.[92]

Ronald Hollier was convicted of child rape and sentenced to seven years' imprisonment at Guildford Crown Court in August 2006. He had been a prison officer at Feltham young offender institution, which holds juveniles as well as young adults.[93]

Prison officer John David Hall was given a life sentence in May 2006 for sexual offences against girls and young women in West Yorkshire.[94] He was found to have indecently assaulted two girls aged 12 and 13 and tried to attack three others aged 13, 14 and 15. Hall wore his uniform off duty, pretending to be a police officer before kidnapping his victims. He had been a prison officer for 15 years; one of his workplaces was Wetherby young offender institution,[95] where his job would have probably included strip searching children.

In November 2002, the press indicated that 'a long-serving prison officer in Lancaster' had been cautioned for internet child pornography after information was passed from US investigators.[96] Lancaster Farms young offender institution held children from April 2000[97] until 2008/09.

The prison service would have been aware of many of these cases (and presumably others not reported by the media) when, in 2007, it began eliminating routine strip searching in women's prisons but left the policy intact for children; when it rejected the European anti-torture committee's recommendation the following year; and when the YJB finally lobbied for change in 2009. The policy document issued in May 2014 still empowers governors to introduce routine strip searching across whole prisons for designated periods and routine strip searching remains mandatory for child prisoners assessed to be a serious security risk.[98] Assessments of risk and decision making about strip searching are made entirely within the walls of the prison, with no independent, external oversight. The barbaric practice of cutting off children's clothes under restraint is still allowed, even within the new, supposedly child-centred, behaviour management system:

> The option of cutting off the clothing using safety scissors must be considered only where necessary and must be balanced against the risk of prolonged use of restraint and the consequent psychological impact on the young person and staff. (The cost of replacement clothing is irrelevant in such circumstances.) The young person must be provided with alternative clothing during the search.[99]

While recent policy changes should continue to reduce the frequency of strip searching, the abusive practice of forcing an isolated and powerless child to undergo bodily and underwear inspection survives. There is no formal recognition of the safeguarding risks of strip searching in the main or addendum policies. For that we have to look to the National Crime Agency's report on institutional child sexual abuse published in the aftermath of the Savile case. It includes a case study of the abuse of children in a locked setting (not a penal institution) and carries this warning: 'Poor procedures can facilitate abuse ... creating supposedly legitimate reasons for offenders to conduct strip searches.'[100] In that scenario, men had been authorised to strip search girls, although the lessons are as plain as day for boys as well.

FIVE

'I can't breathe'

Public disclosure of the child abuse perpetrated by former disc jockey and television presenter Jimmy Savile has led to wider questions about the treatment of vulnerable children living away from home. BBC Newsnight, pilloried for dropping an investigation into Savile, interviewed an adult who alleged a former senior politician had sexually abused him when he was a child in Bryn Estyn children's home in North Wales. This was subsequently retracted, although, for a short period, the media held its gaze on the past abuse of children in North Wales' children's homes. A BBC journalist made a freedom of information request for the 1996 report that had never been made public for fear of compensation claims.[1] The six councils that replaced Clwyd County Council published the Jillings report in July 2013. It starts with a review of the changes in children's residential care across the 1970s and '80s:

> Indeed, the whole concept of aggregating deprived, disturbed and delinquent young people into large residential establishments, often remotely located in rural areas, came to be seen as inappropriate.[2]

The closure of community homes with education, which, like Bryn Estyn, had formerly been approved schools run by the Home Office, represented a major shift in professional thinking about the care and containment of vulnerable children. The report continues: 'Eventually Bryn Estyn, too, closed its doors as part of society's long overdue shift in thinking away from large institutions.'[3]

Contrary to John Jillings' analysis 20 years ago, vast, impersonal establishments are still in use. The capacity of children's homes has contracted enormously, frequently accommodating fewer children than the average foster family. However, young offender institutions, where the majority of detained children are held, have residential units (or 'blocks') holding between 30 and 60 children[4] and sometimes over 90.[5] Europe's largest child prison – Hindley young offender institution in Wigan – can hold 440 children, 100 more than Great Ormond Street Hospital. In the latest inspection report on this institution, the chief inspector of prisons expresses alarm at the proposal to close one of its smallest units (holding up to 13 children with the most complex needs), stating this 'would be a reckless and dangerous development'.[6] In January 2014, the coalition government announced that its first secure college would be located on the site of an existing prison in Leicestershire and hold 320 children aged between 12 and 17 years.[7] Given that a third of imprisoned boys and 61% of imprisoned girls have previously been looked after by local authorities, it is clearly not the case that large institutions have been abandoned for this constituency of children.[8]

The prisons inspectorate analysed its data on 17 prisons holding juveniles and concluded that institutions with 173 or fewer children are 24.5 times more likely to perform within the top 50% of the healthy prison assessment.[9] It is to be assumed the justice secretary Chris Grayling was ignorant of this when he wrote to the parliamentary human rights committee in March 2014:

> ...neither the Government nor the YJB [Youth Justice Board] are aware of any studies that have directly looked at the links between the size of an establishment or unit and the impact on safety....[10]

Furthermore, a review of safeguarding commissioned by the YJB in 2007 concluded that the size of units was one of the main factors affecting children's perceptions of safety:

> [H]aving more staff was cited by the young people as the single most significant factor in keeping them safer.

There were clear differences within the smaller units, particularly the girls' units, where the size, design and higher staffing ratios made the young people feel much safer.[11]

Attempts have been made to reduce the size of prison accommodation blocks; for example, Cookham Wood young offender institution in Kent has 'a more modern 17 cell unit which incorporates the first night centre [holding] up to eight young people. The other nine cells are for enhanced young people and young people employed as orderlies.'[12] 'Enhanced young people' are those who have worked their way up the prison privilege levels, and 'orderlies' are children who have earned prized jobs giving them more time out of their cells – mopping floors or serving food, for example. Inspectors recently praised Serco's Hassockfield secure training centre for its 'creativity' in placing newly admitted children onto units 'which are populated by the best behaved young people who have achieved the highest level on the incentive scheme'.[13] The idea is that newly admitted children will see immediately what is to be gained from good behaviour. The inspection report fails to explore what happens when children are relegated to a lower level of the punishment and rewards scheme, although the implication is that they will be relocated. The latest inspection of Hassockfield, conducted in July 2014, found a reduction in the use of restraint on recently admitted children. Research carried out by the centre attributes this to the superior conditions offered to new inmates. Inspectors describe this as 'highly innovative practice' but still do not explore the impact on children who are sanctioned and presumably have to move cells. They also appear to accept uncritically the centre's concern that it cannot apply the same policy to girls because there are not enough of them 'to create a separate enhanced regime'. There were 12 girls 'in residence' at the time of the inspection.[14]

Inspectors criticised as 'inappropriate in the absence of an individual risk assessment' the system operating in Medway secure training centre, run by G4S, in November 2012 whereby:

... all new arrivals are locked in for the night in rooms without access to a television, radio, books or magazines. Neither are they permitted to retain any personal possessions, including letters, until they progress to the next stage of the incentive scheme.[15]

Improvements had occurred by the time of the next inspection, in June 2013. Children are now placed on arrival on the silver level of the incentive scheme, as opposed to the bronze level, and they are allowed a radio on their first night 'unless it is assessed that it might be misused for self-harm'.[16] Does this mean children deemed likely to smash a radio into pieces for self-mutilation are left without any means of contact with the outside world? The latest report on Oakhill secure training centre, also run by G4S, observes: 'A range of items are *considered* for young people to have in their rooms on their first night, including magazines, books, posters and a radio' [emphasis added]. No information is given as to the circumstances in which children might be deemed unsuitable for a book or radio. More positively, inspectors highlight that 'the same quality of accommodation' is provided across the establishment and children are allocated 'irrespective of their incentives level or behaviour'.[17]

The prisons inspectorate expects children to be out of their cells in young offender institutions for at least 10 hours every day.[18] If this were achieved, children would still be spending 58% of the week locked in a cell the size of a small box room (20 years ago, prisoners in open young offender institutions spent 44% of weekdays locked up).[19] Besides, few prisons holding boys actually achieve this 'unlock' target.[20] Two inspections of young offender institutions carried out in autumn 2013 show that some children have as little as one hour a day out of their cells at weekends;[21] and all children are locked in their cells from 5.30 pm[22] or 5.25 pm[23] on Saturdays and Sundays. A third inspection, undertaken in March 2014, found that children in Hindley young offender institution's segregation unit 'spent much of their time locked in their cells' which were dirty and damaged by graffiti. The observation panels of two cell doors in the unit contained broken glass, an obvious hazard for one of the boys who was being monitored for self-harm and suicide.[24] Only 37% of boys in Cookham

Wood young offender institution reported being able to have daily 'association' (prison term for the period when inmates can socialise with one another, make telephone calls and have a shower) when inspectors visited in June 2014. More than a quarter of prison officer posts were unfilled: there were 135 boys held there at the time.[25]

In March 2013, inspectors found that most children held at Warren Hill young offender institution in Suffolk 'achieved' over nine hours out of their cell each day during the week; less at weekends. Some children in the segregation unit spent more than 21 hours a day in their cell and 'lock up' for all children was 5.15 pm at weekends.[26] At Feltham young offender institution in January 2013, inspectors were told that children had an average of six hours a day unlock time, although some 'potentially spent 22 hours locked up'.[27] The Independent Monitoring Board's latest published annual report on this prison states: 'There have been confirmed instances of at least one boy on single unlock being denied his entitlement of 30 min daily fresh air exercise'.[28] Single unlock is where a child is only allowed to come out of his cell on his own.

The 2013 annual report of the Independent Monitoring Board attached to Downview women's prison in Surrey found that girls were held in their cells for longer than 13 hours a day. Clearly in sympathy with the prison, the board complained that the dedicated children's unit had been 'running at much higher occupancy levels … with an average of 13 young women out of a possible 17' and blamed 'current staff profiles' for the institution's failure to meet the YJB's target of 11 hours unlock daily.[29] The half-page report on the children's unit ends enthusiastically:

> We are pleased to note that a new core day has now been introduced with appropriate staff profiles which will permit unlock hours of 11.25 [hours] during the week and 10.5 [hours] at the weekend.[30]

By this time, the unit was holding an average of just five girls, although they were still spending more time locked in than out of their cells. In July 2013, the YJB announced that girls would be moved out of the prison because of low numbers.[31]

Prison cells can be as small as 5.5 square metres and, since slopping out ended, contain a toilet and sink, sometimes a shower. The former Children's Commissioner for England, appointed in 2005 to promote the views and interests of children, wrote about a visit he made to a young offender institution where he found a child who 'slept with his head three feet away from an open, filthy, stinking lavatory'.[32] The mother of Joseph Scholes, Yvonne Bailey, recalled the disgust she felt on seeing the small area attached to Stoke Heath young offender institution's healthcare centre, in which her son and other children were expected to take exercise:

> 'I was horrified because [the prison] built a new play area or exercise area that you wouldn't even put a polar bear in, in the zoo. There was no shade, there was no seating so how is it acceptable for teenagers to be sent to have exercise in it? You wouldn't put an animal in there.'

That space and the physical environment have a profound effect on human beings is not a modern discovery. Holes in the ground, castle dungeons, and prison hulks are part of Britain's history, as are stately homes with their expansive grounds. When the social research company MORI asked people to indicate the types of accommodation in which they would most like to live, not a single respondent chose a tower block.[33] First-class train and air travel passengers enjoy bigger seats and extra legroom not because they have unusually large backsides or extra-long limbs but because they pay for physical comfort. Parents know the benefits to family life, and their own sanity, of children being able to let off steam outdoors. It should come as no surprise, then, that the chief inspector of prisons told a parliamentary hearing in 2011 that: 'Insufficient time out of cells, a lack of access to the open air and to exercise and inadequate education and training provision leaves young people restless and bored, and more likely to display challenging behaviour.'[34] In the previous year, only 11% of boys had been able to access the gym five times a week, despite this being a favourite activity for many.[35] (This later dropped to 9%).[36] State-run young offender institutions are contractually obliged to provide each incarcerated child with just 30 minutes in the open air each day.[37] During my research for this book, Juliet Lyon, director of the Prison Reform Trust, told me about taking officials from a funding body round a juvenile prison and one of them remarking that he had never before heard teenage boys talking so intensely about fresh air. The boys were exchanging information about how much fresh air they had had that day. Lyon explained: "They were all pale and ill looking, and shut in, and it was this glorious day, and this desire to be outside in the air was so overwhelming."

Mental anguish is a known consequence of confinement for all ages. The preponderance of violence in child prisons (pp 212–13) points to this age group externalising their pain and frustration much more than adults. Prison chiefs should be aware that the Department of Health has issued guidelines on the physical exercise of five- to 18-year-olds, recommending a daily minimum of 60 minutes' moderate to vigorous activity plus up to several hours of physical activity. There is 'strong and expanding' evidence that this amount of regular exercise is associated with a variety of health benefits, including 'enhanced psychological well-being' for this age group.[38] When the justice secretary, Chris Grayling, announced plans for secure colleges, he observed that some custodial places cost five times more than the fees charged for the country's top private schools.[39] Above and beyond its academic reputation, the minister may have been alluding to the games facilities of institutions like Eton College, which requires its boys to choose a major sport each term, with between two and four choices. Minor sports are offered throughout the year and include 'aikido, archery, badminton, basketball, beagling, canoeing, chess, clay-pigeon shooting, croquet, cross-country, eventing, fencing, fives, golf, gymnastics, judo, karate, lacrosse, mountaineering, polo, rackets, sailing, sevens, shooting, squash, sub-aqua, swimming, table tennis, tai chi, volleyball, water-polo, windsurfing, and the Wall Game'.[40]

Retired army general David Ramsbotham was the chief inspector of prisons who threatened to take the government to court for not applying the Children Act 1989 to young offender institutions (pp 237–9). I asked him if he thought the experience of imprisonment is different for children and adults, to which he responded:

'You need to remember that [children are] growing and they need proper access to the fresh air. They don't just need to put weights up, they need to get out there and play things. They need to have time to let off steam. And they need time with adults, just time to talk to them, time to establish a relationship – that's the difference.'

Physical restraint has historically been the staple method of managing difficult behaviour in prison, for all age groups. A commission of inquiry on violence in child penal institutions more than 20 years ago observed that control and restraint training was 'a key part' of prison officer basic training, reflecting 'the emphasis on security and physical control implicit in the concept of imprisonment'.[41] Since 2003, when staff development was delegated to prison governors, control and restraint has been the only ongoing mandatory training for prison officers.[42] Ramsbotham conducted the inspectorate's first (and only) thematic review of the treatment of young prisoners, looking at children as well as adults up to the age of 21. He reported that the use of control and restraint in some establishments 'filled me with concern' and observed, 'It is no coincidence that those young offender institutions with the poorest regimes appeared to have the highest incidence of the use of control and restraint.'[43] By 'poorest regimes', the chief inspector meant prisons that kept children locked in their cells most of the day, offered little in the way of education or purposeful activity, were often overcrowded and lacked key services such as drugs treatment. Ramsbotham was clear that 'one of the primary tasks, for custodial authorities, is to provide an environment in which young people are not abused by their peers or by staff'. He and his inspectors had found recognition in every prison that there was a problem of bullying between prisoners, but 'less acknowledgement of unprofessional behaviour, bullying, inappropriate sanctions and poor attitudes by some members of staff'.[44] A decade later, an independent review of restraint conducted by two former heads of social services reported:

> ... it is at least arguable that C&R [control and restraint – the prison service's system of restraint], with its emphasis

on coercion and pain compliance, itself reinforces the
very culture of danger and violence in YOIs [young
offender institutions] in which it operates. C&R displays
for young people an example in which overwhelming
force is sanctioned by authority and in which 'might' is
perceived to be 'right'. It does little to break the cycle
of violence which many young people in custody have
known for much of their lives.[45]

Some years after the ex-directors of social services completed their
review, the ringleader of the abusive restraint and other cruelty of
adults with learning disabilities at Winterbourne View Hospital told a
BBC Panorama undercover reporter of his time working in a young
offender institution:

In my other place [with] young offenders we were
allowed to fire them up and you were allowed to go
into them and get them into like kicking off. Not like
all the time but if you could see there was going to be a
flash-point better off getting the manpower in place ...
[and] getting it over and done with ...[46]

The producer of the Panorama programme observed that Wayne
Rogers, who was jailed for two years in 2012, had been 'literally
advocating winding-up vulnerable children then and later vulnerable
adults in 2011'.[47]

The restraint review had been established by former Labour
ministers in response to widespread alarm about the mistreatment
of imprisoned children. Substantial evidence of unlawful assaults
had been dragged into public view after the deaths of Gareth Myatt
and Adam Rickwood. Specific restraint techniques were found to
be extremely dangerous – constricting children's breathing, causing
them to vomit and generating terror and panic. It was not inspectors,
YJB monitors, child protection agencies or independent advocates
who exposed this abuse. It was the deaths of two children and the
tenacity of their mothers – and the fact that their lawyer, Mark Scott,
recognised the restraints they suffered were unlawful – that brought

this out into the open. Fifteen-year-old Gareth was the first to die in the most horrific circumstances, on the evening of 19 April 2004.

Gareth's mother told me he was a loving and kind child, who was always keen to help others. He was funny and quick-witted and enjoyed watching South Park and the Simpsons on television. Being outside on his bike was a favourite pastime throughout Gareth's childhood and, as he got older, he enjoyed tinkering with cars and hoped one day to qualify as a mechanic or engineer. He started playing chess with friends and family from around the age of 12; his board and pieces were still set up in the corner of the living room when I visited the family home. Official reports say he was 'academically very able' but point to a range of difficulties at home and school.[48] Having spent a lot of his early childhood in the care of his grandparents, between the ages of 11 and 14 Gareth was looked after by social services on five separate occasions and he also had a period in private foster care (this is where families, rather than social workers, make arrangements for the child). A mixed-race child, Gareth was said by his mother to have endured racist abuse from primary school onwards and had struggled with his identity.[49] Gareth was sent to Rainsbrook secure training centre for stealing a bottle of beer, assaulting a member of staff in his children's home (his mother told me he was cornered by staff and pushed past to get away) and not complying fully with the non-custodial programme ordered after previous convictions for petty offending. His youth offending team worker recommended a custodial sentence, even though just two months before he had told the court he 'would be very concerned should Gareth receive a custodial sentence [because] I believe he is a vulnerable young man because of his size, low self-esteem, and also his confusion over his ethnic identity'.[50]

I asked his mother, Pam, whether she was worried about Gareth being sent to a penal institution and she said she wasn't because Rainsbrook's name has 'secure' in it and she assumed the establishment would be like the secure children's homes he had been in before. Pam had spoken with Gareth on the telephone on the night of his admission, and was aware he had been restrained for refusing to take off his clothes (pp 87–8). She advised him to "just keep his head down" and they arranged for her to bring some clothes and money when visiting the following week. They were to have two more telephone calls before the police knocked on Pam's door at 5 am one morning to tell her Gareth was dead.

At around 9 o'clock on a Monday evening Gareth had refused to clean a sandwich toaster after eating a toasted cheese sandwich. He was not the only child to have used it. Another child volunteered to do the chore and this should have been the end of the matter. However, an officer called David Beadnall ordered Gareth to his cell. Gareth obeyed this order calmly. Beadnall and another officer, Diana Smith, then entered Gareth's cell and began removing items – a magazine, papers and pencils. Beadnall picked up a piece of paper with Gareth's mother's new mobile phone number on it and, in a judge's words, 'his other links with the outside world'.[51] Gareth became distressed and, according to the inquest testimony of the three officers (there is no CCTV in cells), raised his fist at Beadnall, who reacted by 'enveloping' and pushing him on to the bed. At 14 stone, this grown man was more than double Gareth's weight, and he stood six feet tall.

After Gareth resisted and struggled, a third officer, David Bailey, joined Beadnall and Smith and they applied a restraint technique called the seated double embrace. This was a Home Office-approved restraint method for children as young as 12, in use since the first secure training centre opened in 1998. The director of the G4S prison was later to admit that his officers would 'jump' to use this particular form of restraint. A police investigation pointed to 'a worrying disposition of staff to [use it] as the default method of restraint'.[52] Lady Justice Hallett in the High Court explained what was done to Gareth:

> [The seated double embrace restraint] involves bending the child forward while in a seated position, securing both arms to the child's side, preventing movement of the legs and securing the child's head by means of holding the chin and the back of the head and neck.[53]

The YJB gave this description in separate legal proceedings:

Gareth Myatt was held ... in a position where his upper body was bent over at an acute angle so that his head and chest was too close to his thighs and knees which resulted in his respiratory system being prevented from functioning properly.

[The child] was restrained for an excessive period of time, notwithstanding that he was small in stature and was easily overpowered by three adults ... he said he couldn't breathe; he said that he was going to shit himself; he defecated; he became motionless, irresponsive, unable to support his own body weight and was supported with his eyes shut, but [the officers] continued to restrain him....
To this it should be added that the boy had become very red in the face – a further recognised sign of distress.[54]

Gareth was 'unconscious and inert' at the end of this ordeal, which lasted between six and seven minutes. Although he still had a pulse, and was given the wrong first aid (the ambulance crew could not at first get into the prison), the pathologist at the boy's inquest said that Gareth was essentially dead when the three officers had finished restraining him. In the Court of Appeal judgment dealing with the former Labour government's attempt to legitimise unlawful restraint, set out in the following chapter, Lord Justice Buxton referred to a parliamentary report summarising Gareth's death, adding: 'If that account is true (and it has not been suggested to us that it is not) it demonstrates an outrageous attitude on the officers' part.'[55] The inquest was shown CCTV footage of Beadnall continuing to remove items from Gareth's cell even after the child had been sick.

The macho culture of this G4S-run prison was exposed at the inquest. Training supervisor Leanne Clay had provided a restraint refresher session to Beadnall, Smith and Bailey a few months before Gareth's death. She was apparently known within the staff group as Clubber Clay. A training document issued by Clay to staff reveals a selection of other restraint instructor nicknames, including Crusher, Mauler, Muncher, Rowdy, Lightning and Breaker.[56] Internal reports on the use of restraint described children who had been subject to the most restraints as 'winners'. One document I have seen, dated

October 2003, refers jokingly to a member of staff returning to 'active duty' through being involved in a restraint – under the heading 'TRIVIAL FACTS'. This section also recounts 'the most experienced PCC [physical control in care – the system of restraint then in use at Rainsbrook] ever' – an incident of a girl being restrained by five officers 'plus two other mere beginners! That equates to four Unit Managers and one Supervisor/PCC Instructor. Heavy, or what?'[57] This was six months before Gareth Myatt's death.

The inquest heard that David Beadnall had been investigated along with two other officers in 2003 when a boy had to attend hospital after beginning to choke during restraint. Beadnall's use of 'distraction techniques' – authorised methods of restraint that deliberately cause children sharp bursts of severe pain – had also aroused concern.[58] A number of statutory bodies were told that children held in this institution were complaining about being unable to breathe, vomiting and suffering injuries (including burst blood vessels) from restraint up to two years before Gareth's death.[59]

Gareth was pronounced dead on arrival at Walsgrave Hospital in Coventry. The YJB suspended the restraint method used on him two months later on the recommendation of Northamptonshire Police, which was conducting a criminal investigation.[60] The inquest commenced in February 2007. Proceedings were suspended the following month while lawyers acting for Gareth's mother argued in the High Court that the coroner should allow the jury the option of a gross negligence manslaughter verdict. This could have led to the former chief executive of the YJB, Mark Perfect, being held to account for the boy's death. The legal challenge was unsuccessful because so many within and close to government had failed to recognise the risks of the seated double embrace, thus making it impossible to find evidence of gross negligence on the part of Perfect (who, in legal terms, was the 'directing mind' of the YJB for the period under consideration). Lady Justice Hallett explained:

> The restraint experts did not foresee the risk of death. Practitioners did not see the risk of death. The monitor, Mr Tuck, did not foresee the risk of death [although he did alert senior managers to his grave concerns]. The

independent Social Services Inspectorate did not appear to have expressed concerns about the risk of death. Even medical experts [who had first reviewed the techniques], for example Dr Susan Bailey, who was aware of previous deaths from positional asphyxia in the prone position and very experienced in the field of physical restraint of children, did not foresee the risk of death from the seated double embrace.[61]

The inquest jury returned a verdict of accidental death, to which Gareth's mother responded: 'At the end of all of this he is still dead and no-one has been held accountable.'[62] When I interviewed Pam some years later, she told me the inquest process was "soul destroying, that's the only word I can think of, because that was the end. I never got justice for him. At the end of the day he deserved justice." A damning list of failures by the government, the YJB and G4S was produced. The coroner wrote to the then justice secretary, Jack Straw, urging 34 separate actions. He noted the independent review of restraint already announced by ministers, but stressed:

> It would be a wholly unforgivable and a double tragedy, would it not, if the holding of this 'joint review' was to obscure the clear and urgent issues raised by Gareth Myatt's death, or was to lead to any delay in learning from and acting on the lessons that result from his death?[63]

Asked whether an inadequate assessment of the safety of restraint methods, and a failure to conduct a medical review, had caused or contributed to Gareth's death, the inquest jury replied 'yes'. There was no-one at the YJB with specific management responsibility for the safety of restraint in secure training centres, and this was determined by the jury to have caused or contributed to Gareth's death. The jury was asked whether any inadequacy in the YJB's response to a report on restraint it had commissioned in 2003 had caused or contributed to Gareth's death: it answered 'yes'. (The report, produced by the National Children's Bureau, had said there was 'urgent need' to collect evidence on the safety, psychological and emotional impact and effectiveness of restraint techniques. [64]) The failure of YJB managers to respond to concerns expressed by one of their monitors also caused or contributed to Gareth's death, as did the organisation's inadequate monitoring. When asked whether any inadequacy in the monitoring of restraint by Rebound (now G4S) had caused or contributed to the 15-year-old's death, the jury replied 'yes'.[65] It emerged during the inquest proceedings that the director of the G4S prison, John Parker, had not even read the restraint manual.[66] Turning away briefly from these findings of monumental institutional neglect, there is the desperate reality that three custody officers chose to use two of the most lethal penal interventions available to them – full cell clearance and a physical hold that, at best, removed the child's ability to control his head – because of low-level teenage defiance.

In his introductory remarks at the start of the inquest, the coroner told the jury that Gareth was 'sent to the smaller institution because he was a smaller boy and was seen to be vulnerable'.[67] Gareth's MP was later to say: 'He was so small that he hardly existed.'[68] The Crown Prosecution Service announced there was 'insufficient evidence for a realistic prospect of conviction against any individual or organisation' in December 2005.[69] My understanding is that the police officers investigating the case were deeply disappointed that prosecutions did not follow.

At least one of the custody officers has not kept a low public profile. Diana Smith has made damages claims in both the High Court and the Court of Appeal against the YJB and the Ministry of Justice for the post-traumatic stress disorder she has suffered as a result of using a restraint technique not subject to medical review. She is the officer who said at the inquest into Gareth's death that 'I should never have PCCd ['PCCd' means using the physical control in care system of restraint]; he was half my size. It was rather like having run over a cat and then thinking ... if I hadn't gone down that street, it wouldn't have happened.'[70] The Court of Appeal refused Smith's claim for damages, with Lord Justice Sedley observing:

> If the officers had been dealing with a large and violent youth whose release, if he was not in truth in distress, might have enabled him to attack them, one could at

least have understood their reluctance to release him. But this was an undersized, underweight 15-year-old who had done no more than show his fist to an officer twice his size – an officer who, moreover, had provoked him into doing it by a pointless and insensitive act. When one recalls the clear advice in the [restraint] manual to release the hold if it became unsafe for the trainee, the repeated ignoring or misreading of his signs of distress becomes inexcusable. As the appellant herself said in evidence, for those seven minutes common sense went out of the window. There were perfectly safe ways of controlling Gareth, assuming that control was still needed, which did not involve [the seated double embrace].[71]

Some years before Smith sought compensation, the director of children's services at Rainsbrook secure training centre was reported in a social work magazine as saying: 'It was a shock to find that a restraint hold considered to be safe turned out to be unsafe. This was as much a tragedy for the staff as for Gareth's family'.[72] The Home Office invited G4S to devise and deliver training on keeping children safe in immigration detention three years after Gareth's death.[73] David Beadnall, the officer who first ordered Gareth into his cell and took the leading role in his restraint, has stayed with G4S children's services and been promoted to safety, health and environmental manager. A G4S spokesperson told a journalist that this role does not involve any direct contact with children.[74]

Many other children came close to death after being restrained in the G4S prison. The three judges considering Diana Smith's claim in the Court of Appeal were told that, in the 12 months before Gareth's fatal restraint, there were 369 incidents of children being held down using exactly the same technique. In about 10% of these cases, children suffered life-threatening harm.[75] A separate examination of 52 uses of restraint in Rainsbrook between April 2003 and March 2004 concluded that there were 'clear signs of potentially lethal events' 65% of the time (34 cases). The consultant in emergency medicine who read the medical notes of children who had been subject to the seated double embrace said the 'potentially lethal effects' included 'vomiting, airway compromise, interference with the mechanics of breathing, neck injury, vagal stimulation [which slows down the heart], reported difficulty in breathing and restriction of the blood flow from the head and neck'.[76]

Gareth's inquest heard that the YJB's monitor had written a letter to managers in June 2002 expressing concern that children were vomiting during restraint and complaining they could not breathe. He wrote again the following year saying children had told him their heads were being pushed so far forward during restraint that their air supply was being restricted.[77] According to Diana Smith's counsel, as reported by Lord Justice Sedley, 'it was a common fallacy that if a trainee could say I can't breathe he must in fact be able to breathe; it was perfectly possibly that a trainee would not only threaten to soil himself but would actually do so in order to get released ... and [Gareth] slumping forward could well have been another subterfuge'.[78] Ironically, this mentality of disbelieving children's motives operated during a period of intense national policy activity on listening to children. Indeed, less than three weeks before Gareth's death, a Bill began its passage through parliament that would establish a children's commissioner to give 'a clear voice for children and young people'.[79] Among the many causes of Gareth losing his life is the indecent truth that the last words he uttered were not believed. A special code word was later discovered to be in use in staff training exercises:

> Instructors will ensure pupils are not using excessive force when practising Physical Control in Care techniques and that if they hear the word **'OXO'** everyone must stop and release any holds immediately.[80] (emphasis in original)

During interviews with children detained at Rainsbrook secure training centre, one girl told me she had been unable to breathe while being restrained. She informed officers many times that she was struggling to breathe and they responded, "If you can't breathe, why are you speaking?" When her head was held down, a member of staff told her: "We are the boss, we have control. When they send you here you have no control." When the girl repeated these words, she started to sob. This was in May 2005, a year after Gareth's death, and I was in the prison as part of Lord Carlile's independent inquiry. The inquiry reported the following year and recommended the development of a single 'certified physical intervention technique that is safe for children' in all custodial settings.[81] The YJB rejected the recommendation claiming that 'the age, size, and strength of the children concerned are so widely divergent, as well as staff ratios and the physical environment that apply in the different sectors of the estate'.[82] More than two years later, the government announced it had asked the National Offender Management Service to develop a new system of restraint for use in young offender institutions and secure training centres.[83] If this was a sign of contrition, it had been a long time coming: Gareth Myatt had been dead for 56 months.

It remains the case that the only legislative action by ministers following Gareth's terrifying death was to amend the rules governing secure training centres to permit restraint for good order and discipline. Far from making restraint safer, this gave officers the legal power to restrain children who simply disobeyed orders. This is what officers in secure training centres had been doing – unlawfully – since 1998 (p 143). The amendment rules were rushed through Parliament in 2007. At least one official in the YJB had predicted two years before that the move would be criticised. An email from a YJB senior manager to Home Office lawyers in June 2005 explains:

> We believe that such an amendment [to the secure training centre rules] should be presented as a 'clarification' of the existing legislation rather than as a change to its intent. However, this is likely to attract attention, and perhaps opposition, from various bodies which have childcare as their central focus.... Before we put a submission to Ministers, it would be helpful to have legal advice as to whether, in presenting such an amendment as a clarification ... we are likely to be safe from a successful challenge that this must mean that the legislation as presently drafted does not permit the use of physical restraint to enforce compliance with instructions, and that such use to date must therefore have been unlawful.[84]

The Home Office's senior legal adviser was unable to give the YJB the reassurance it sought, but advised it not to 'lead with the chin by proclaiming the rules change as a clarification of the law – simply make the change alongside the other changes, perhaps saying in an explanatory memorandum that the new rule is consistent with [the powers in the Criminal Justice and Public Order Act 1994]'.[85]

The next chapter tells the dishonourable story of how former Labour ministers and the YJB changed the law to cover the backs of those who had unlawfully restrained children. In pushing for legal powers allowing officers to restrain disobedient children, the board contradicted its own code of practice issued in 2006, itself a recommendation from the Commission for Social Care Inspection, Ofsted and other inspectorates.[86] The code stressed that restraint must never be used simply to secure compliance from a child.[87] Facing strident opposition to the new restraint powers, the interim chair of the YJB at the time, Graham Robb, wrote a letter to a national newspaper criticising what he called 'the hysterical nature of the debate'.[88] The deaths of two children and hundreds, possibly thousands, of others suffering unlawful assault, degrading treatment and injuries had led to emotional outpourings – unnerving perhaps for civil servants, but a healthy human response. The following year, in December 2008, the government published the restraint review it had commissioned. Children in young offender institutions, secure training centres and secure children's homes were interviewed as part of the review and 'breathlessness' appeared in their accounts of restraint:

> [Children] described the intense pain of wrists being bent as though their bones were about to break, of shooting pains and numbness, of breathlessness from frontal holds on the floor and facial friction burns and of being held in head locks by staff. Bruises can last for days if not weeks and experiences of pain in joints the day after being restrained was not uncommon.[89]

A few years after the restraint review was published, Baroness Stern asked ministers for information on restraint causing serious harm to children. She was told that the two multinationals running secure training centres had sent 285 separate reports to the YJB of children's lives being endangered or children suffering serious injury following restraint between 2006 and 2011. Lord McNally, the justice minister at the time (he became Chair of the YJB in March 2014), explained the circumstances in which these 'exception reports' must be produced:

> The list of warning signs are as follows: struggling to breathe; complainant unable to breathe; nausea; vomiting; swelling to face or neck; abnormal redness to face; blood spots on face or neck; limp or unresponsive; change in degree of agitation; respiratory arrest; and cardiac arrest. The category of 'serious injury requiring hospital treatment' includes: serious cut; fractures; concussion, loss of consciousness, and damage to internal organs.[90]

Not only had no-one been held to account for the death of Gareth Myatt, but this data also indicated that, several years later, the lives and wellbeing of children in secure training centres were still being endangered during restraint.

So where are we now? Recent years have seen a concerted policy emphasis on de-escalation and minimising the use of force, and children's views and experiences have been integrated into a new behaviour management system[91] that, at the time of writing, three secure training centres and two young offender institutions are following.[92] A new policy document on the use of force in young offender institutions stresses that imprisoned children have the same rights to protection as those in the community, and makes clear their welfare 'is of paramount importance'.[93] All children are apparently offered the support of an advocate in debriefing sessions following restraint. But none of these measures deals with the fault lines. The physical and cultural environment of prison continues to fundamentally threaten children's welfare; staffing levels in young offender institutions remain appallingly low; and most officers are professionally untrained for this kind of work. With these conditions, even Pollyanna would struggle to believe restraint could become a genuine last resort. Secrecy reigns over authorised techniques and plans to give custody officers in the new secure colleges wide restraint powers show a deep-seated inability to move on. Added to this is a disturbing penal attachment to the deliberate infliction of severe pain as a form of restraint, a practice rejected outright in childcare settings and criticised by the UN anti-torture committee, the UN Human Rights Council, the European anti-torture committee, the Council of Europe's Human Rights Commissioner, the Association of Directors of Children's Services, the prisons inspectorate, the Equality and Human Rights Commission, the NSPCC, the Royal College of Paediatrics and Child Health, the Secure Accommodation Network and all four of the UK's children's commissioners.

Opposition to the deliberate infliction of pain during restraint is not a new phenomenon. In 1993, social services inspectors highlighted continuing concerns about restraint methods 'which depend on the application of pain to joints for their effectiveness and are derived from those originally devised for use with adults in different circumstances'.[94] The inspectors had conducted an independent investigation into a secure children's home in Durham after a television documentary alleged that at least six children had suffered broken bones during restraint. One immediate consequence of the exposé was that Durham County Council banned staff from using techniques taught to them by prison officers: this included the arm and wrist locks and 'decking' (using force to get children onto the floor).[95] Government gave no such protection to child prisoners, however, and the next chapter shows that restraint abuses are far from over.

SIX

'What gives them the right to hit a child in the nose?'

In June 2007, statutory rules were laid before parliament massively increasing restraint powers in secure training centres.[1] The minister's written statement eight days later began:

> The recent inquest into the death in 2004 of Adam Rickwood has drawn attention to a lack of clarity as to the powers of custody officers in secure training centres to restrain trainees, where it is necessary to do so. We have been asked by the coroner to rectify the position and clarify the rules.[2]

Two inquests were held into the prison death of 14-year-old Adam Rickwood, in 2007 and 2011. The second took place after his mother, Carol Pounder, brought a successful judicial review which ordered that jury members should be given guidance on the lawfulness of the restraint used on her son hours before he hanged himself. The coroner presiding over the first inquest had recommended 'an urgent review' of the law relating to restraint in secure training centres[3] following claims by the Youth Justice Board (YJB) and Serco that officers were legally permitted to use restraint to secure good order and discipline, as had been done to Adam. Lawyers acting for Carol Pounder were alerted to the forthcoming change in the law through their correspondence with the YJB and Serco and, alongside campaigners, had been keeping track of new statutory instruments. Going on past form, there was little expectation among campaigners

121

that any revisions to the law would be announced in a fanfare of publicity. It was clearly implausible that the discovered amendment rules originated from the coroner's advice, as they appeared only a week after ministers received his written recommendations.[4] In any case, the coroner had pressed for a review, not a change in the law. Besides, at the end of the previous month, before the inquest into Adam's death had concluded, the then chief executive of the YJB, Ellie Roy, wrote a letter to the G4S and Serco directors of secure training centres:

> I want to reassure you that the YJB has been working closely with the Ministry of Justice and previously the Home Office to amend the secure training centre rules in line with previous consultation with yourselves. I am advised that changes are imminent. In the meantime, it is your responsibility to ensure that the use of force within your establishment is being carried out lawfully.[5]

The strengthened restraint powers appeared in parliament a month ahead of ministers announcing an independent review of restraint, although it was to be a further 82 days before the joint review chairs were appointed. Gareth Myatt had, by then, been dead for more than 41 months, and Adam Rickwood for 38 months. There was more time between these two children's deaths and the independent review of restraint commencing, than between the twin towers falling and the invasion of Iraq.

There was plenty of activity behind closed doors. Since the two boys' deaths, three reports on the use of restraint were produced for the YJB, one by ex-prison governor David Waplington; a second by trauma consultant Dr Anthony Bleetman and former police officer Peter Boatman (the man found dead soon after the government revoked his Taser firm's licence in the wake of Raoul Moat's death);[6] and a third by secure training centre directors. A fourth review was of the holds themselves, conducted by medical and other experts. The Waplington behaviour management report to the YJB in October 2004 – two months after Adam died – indicated that every one of the four secure training centres 'routinely' used restraint to secure compliance and this 'was probably one of the main reasons for its use'.[7] Bleetman and Boatman reported in June or July 2005 that physical control in care (PCC), the system of restraint used in secure training centres, was being widely used for non-compliance:

> Another issue is that PCC skills are deployed against trainees for non-compliance, as well as for violent behaviour. For instance, PCC is used to overcome resistance when trainees refuse to attend education, move location, or go to bed. Data from the reporting process at one STC show that over a quarter of PCC was undertaken to overcome non-compliance. Further data showed that, in one month, a third of PCC was undertaken to overcome non-compliance, while around a fifth of all PCC skill was undertaken to overcome non-compliance.[8]

Against this backdrop, and with the deaths of Gareth and Adam inviting intense criticism, ministers and the YJB had two choices: to admit the scale of unlawful restraint that was now as obvious as a full moon, or to seek to convince everyone that G4S and Serco custody officers had been acting lawfully all along. They chose the latter strategy. And to bolster their position, they changed the legal rules governing restraint in secure training centres. The change was made through a statutory instrument requiring no parliamentary debate. The new rules came into force on 6 July, a few days before G4S was made to replace the director of one of the four secure training centres[9] amid grave concerns about high levels of restraint. The YJB actively championed the new restraint powers and even indicated that they would protect visitors as well as staff and children within the secure training centres.[10] Without providing any supportive data, the board claimed children in secure training centres were becoming more out of control:

> We already have reports of an increase in indiscipline since the lack of clarity in the law became highlighted

during the inquest into the death of Adam Rickwood at Hassockfield.[11]

In a case led by solicitor Mark Scott, the Court of Appeal was later to quash the amendment rules, and ministers failed in their attempts to appeal the judgment in the House of Lords. The government presented the appeal court with only two pieces of 'evidence'. One was a statement from the Serco director of Hassockfield secure training centre, Trevor Wilson-Smith, and the other was the draft explanatory notes accompanying the amendment rules. Lord Justice Buxton dismissed both as 'pure assertion'[12] and reminded the court that the serious case review established after Adam's death had reported:

> Adam Rickwood was a model trainee and ... the incident just prior to his death was his first episode of non-compliance and his first experience of being restrained. He was reported to have acted aggressively thereby evoking the ultimate restraint response. However, there was some video evidence that [sic] suggesting he did not respond in an overly aggressive manner.[13]

The amendment rules were found to be in breach of article 3 of the European Convention on Human Rights, which protects individuals from torture and inhuman or degrading treatment or punishment, as well as article 8, which safeguards mental and physical integrity.[14] The court referred to 'a history in the life of [secure training centres] of disobedience to legal and contractual requirements' and agreed the new rules 'were introduced to legitimate practices that up to then were illegal and in breach of the operators' contracts'.[15] By the time they were quashed, the strengthened restraint powers had been in force for one year and 22 days.

The YJB only started collecting data on restraint in secure training centres in April 2008 – four years after the deaths of Gareth and Adam; eight years after the board took on legal responsibility for placing children in custodial establishments; and nine months after G4S and Serco custody officers were given additional restraint powers. A question in parliament revealed that there had been 16 occasions when children had been restrained to ensure good order and discipline from the time central restraint records began until July 2008.[16] It is likely that these restraints were unlawful. Furthermore, leaked spreadsheets have come to my attention, indicating children were possibly being restrained for good order and discipline in one of the four secure training centres until January 2010 (the data ends the following month). This includes incidents where children were restrained for having arguments with each other; for involving themselves in the restraint of another child; for spitting at a teacher; for throwing drinks around the dining hall; for attempting to take staff keys; for kicking doors and windows; and for throwing books. At least two other incidents in the months following the quashing of the new restraint powers raise obvious child protection questions: the case of a girl restrained after tying ligatures around her neck; and a boy who was restrained for being aggressive to staff after receiving bad news. None of these incidents appears trivial, and staff intervention was obviously necessary. But was there really no alternative means of dealing with these situations than subjecting children to restraint?

Unlawful restraint may also have continued in another of the four establishments. Three restraint review reports obtained from Durham safeguarding children board (the statutory body bringing together local agencies to coordinate child protection in the area) show there were at least 35 separate instances of children being injured following restraint for 'concerted indiscipline' in Hassockfield secure training centre between August 2009 and March 2012.[17] The safeguarding board raised questions in its 2011 report to the YJB:

> The LSCB [local safeguarding children board] have concerns about the use of 'concerted indiscipline' as a criterion for restraint and would welcome clarification of the YJB's views on the matter of continuing to use the criterion in question, and on the difference between 'ensuring good order and discipline' and 'concerted indiscipline', given the recent inquest findings.[18]

More questions were raised in 2012:

Restraining for the purposes of 'good order and discipline' is not included as a reason for restraint and would therefore be unlawful. A 'concerted indiscipline' involves two or more young people acting together with the intention of disrupting the regime of the centre, however, the STC Rule 38 criteria would still need to be met in order for a young person to be restrained.[19]

When I made a freedom of information (FOI) request to the YJB for data on concerted indiscipline in Hassockfield, it replied that establishments are not permitted to restrain for such reasons. I probed further, explaining I knew that Durham safeguarding children board had raised the matter. The YJB told me that the incidents had been 'looked into at the time' and were found to be incorrectly categorised:

> The reference to concerted indiscipline in the original incident reports from the establishment were actually a description of the overall incident under which the permitted restraints had occurred.[20]

No explanation was given for why other incidents listed in the Durham safeguarding children board report, depicting assaults and damage to property as the reasons for restraint, did not also fall within an 'overall incident' of concerted indiscipline. The YJB refused to conduct a review to establish whether it had, indeed, been made aware of alleged restraint episodes for good order and discipline outside its formal restraint reporting procedure, stating that 'there is nothing to suggest that had we carried out a review of such material ... our answer will have been any different'. It continued:

> Of course, I could only give an absolute assurance on that point if we were to actually undertake an exercise of identifying, retrieving and reviewing every potential such item. However, the likelihood of us being able to do so within the FOI costs limit of £600 is highly unlikely....[21]

Given the difficulties I had had with accessing other information, and the obvious limitations of the YJB reviewing itself, I decided not to pursue this particular request.

Had the Court of Appeal not quashed the restraint amendment rules, all four of the secure training centres could have carried on restraining for good order and discipline. The long list of opponents included the Children's Rights Alliance for England, the National Society for the Prevention of Cruelty to Children (NSPCC), the justice campaigning charity INQUEST, the Howard League for Penal Reform, the Office of Children's Commissioner for England and the Equality and Human Rights Commission. In submissions to the parliamentary human rights select committee, the Royal College of Psychiatrists expressed 'serious concerns',[22] and the Commission for Racial Equality said it feared the new rules could 'impact disproportionately on ethnic minority children, who are already over-represented in the youth justice system'.[23] It further argued the new restraint powers 'legitimise the use of violence against vulnerable children who should be regarded as children first and offenders second'.[24]

That there was no public consultation, but the YJB had been quietly seeking the views of G4S and Serco managers about changing the law, was one reason many children's rights campaigners felt so outraged. There was tremendous activity over many months by a small group of dedicated parliamentarians opposed to the changes. Former Labour MP Sally Keeble led the opposition in the House of Commons, and 56 of her colleagues added their signatures to her early day motion calling for the rules to be withdrawn.[25] The House of Lords put up the strongest attack, and looked set to 'pray against' the amendment rules. Lord Carlile headed the debate, describing the use of restraint in the G4S and Serco prisons as 'an unpleasant secret'.[26] Lord Elstyan-Morgan condemned the infliction of severe pain to maintain good order and discipline:

> The idea that you should be allowed to use substantial force and pain as an instrument is quite wrong. Would you use pain to train a dog or horse? Why should you use pain to train a child?[27]

The Lord Bishop of Worcester said attempts to pass off the legal change as simply clarification was 'positively Orwellian'.[28] Baroness Stern said the debate was 'a sad occasion' and noted that the minister, Lord Hunt of Kings Heath, newly in post, had been given 'the task of defending the indefensible and supporting the insupportable'.[29] Of 15 peers speaking in the two-hour debate, only one other than the minister defended the restraint changes. This was Lord Warner, who had been chair of the YJB from its inception in 1998 until he was made a Labour health minister in 2003. In March 2008, before the rules had been quashed, the parliamentary human rights select committee announced 'the use of force in such widened circumstances is unacceptable and unlawful'.[30] The chief catalyst driving opposition to the rules was the deaths of Gareth and Adam in scandalous conditions and the state now appearing to act to protect its own interests, and those of the two multinationals, rather than vulnerable children.

The CCTV film of the final restraint of 14-year-old Adam Rickwood in Serco's Hassockfield secure training centre was presumably available to ministers and the YJB immediately after his death, but it was not until his first inquest in 2007 that his mother saw what her child went through. During my research for this book, Carol Pounder told me:

> 'Basically, they beat him up and they took him to his cell and left him. They beat Adam up in the association area. They carried him like a dead animal, face down. And what they said was the reason why they carried him face down was because his nose was bleeding so badly they didn't want him to choke to death on his blood. That's exactly what they said.... On the CCTV evidence that I've seen, they throw Adam in his cell like a dog, and then they go and jump on him again.... The way they were carrying my son, I actually thought he was dead. And he was in his socks. He didn't even have shoes on his feet. And then they threw Adam in the cell, and then they all jumped on him again ... I think the lightest one was 13-and-a-half stone, and you see him pushing on to

the top of Adam, and you could tell they get a kick out of it. I mean, if we'd done that to a kid, well…. Then they all came running out that room, out of the cell…. When they came running out you can actually see the smirks on their faces.'

In addition to the letter he left behind for his family (p 64), Adam wrote a statement for his solicitor:

> When the other staff came they all jumped on me and started to put my arms up my back and hitting me in the nose. I then tried to bite one of the staff because they were really hurting my nose. My nose started bleeding and swelled up and it didn't stop bleeding for about one hour and afterwards it was really sore. When I calmed down I asked them why they hit me in the nose and jumped on me. They said it was because I wouldn't go in my room so I said what gives them the right to hit a 14-year-old child in the nose and they said it was restraint.[31]

Carol Pounder had to go to the High Court to get an honest answer to her son's question. 'There was no right to hurt such a child in these circumstances,' responded Mr Justice Blake.[32] Wider admissions of abusive treatment came only with the second inquest, which concluded in January 2011. All parties to the inquest, including Serco and the YJB agreed that the removal of Adam to his cell had been unlawful; the use of restraint to move Adam to his cell was unlawful; the use of the nose distraction on Adam was unlawful; and restraint 'was regularly used' unlawfully at Hassockfield secure training centre before and at the time of Adam's death.[33] In addition, the inquest jury found that Hassockfield was running an unlawful regime and there was serious system failure within the YJB in not preventing the regular and unlawful use of restraint in the Serco prison. The jury agreed that several factors had contributed to Adam taking his own life: being in a secure training centre approximately 150 miles from home; the news that a bail application was not being pursued; the unlawful use of restraint; the unlawful use of the nose distraction; and his intrinsic vulnerability.[34] In light of this damning verdict, Carol Pounder's legal team wrote to the Director of Public Prosecutions asking him to institute proceedings against the four individuals who had unlawfully restrained Adam, and the director of the Serco prison, Trevor Wilson-Smith. At the end of April 2013, the Crown Prosecution Service notified Carol's lawyers that no prosecutions would be brought as, principally, a court would be likely to find that the suspects had a genuine and reasonable belief that the methods in which they had been trained to restrain children were lawful. I asked Carol's barrister, Richard Hermer QC, what impact the case had on him personally. He explained:

'I think different aspects of the case engaged different aspects of me. Obviously, on a human level, Adam's story was just deeply tragic. This small child, who was clearly bright, able and insightful, met a tragic death alone in a cell. As a lawyer, the thing that stays with me about that case is what we discovered – namely, a detention system in which for years those responsible for the care and welfare of children were breaking the law and assaulting the children with impunity. What perhaps struck me most was the response of the YJB to the discovery of the unlawful system. Their reaction was, firstly, to try and sweep the discovery of the illegality under the carpet by arguing at the initial inquest that the matter should not be even mentioned to the jury. Thereafter the YJB and the government attempted to change the law to render restraints for GOAD [good order and discipline] lawful without, it seemed, any consideration as to the impact it would have on children, let alone any attempt to seek to learn lessons from what had just been discovered about unlawful practices in institutions for which they were responsible. As a lawyer, I found that a remarkably shoddy response from government. The response from the private company running the STC [secure training centre] was even worse: they actually sought to argue that the restraints were lawful. These were arguments that were rightly treated with some contempt by the High Court and Court of Appeal. How much better it would have been if the response of both government and Serco had been not to seek to justify the unjustifiable but to say, "Look, we have really messed up. What lessons can we learn? How can we make sure that this isn't done again?" What does it tell us about the way that we treat children?'

Being aware of some of Richard's other cases, I asked him whether he was being naïve in expecting the various bodies to hold up their hands:

'I don't think its naivety to expect that. That's pretty fundamental if you've got a job with children. It is also an important aspect of the rule of law. Whether you are dealing with a case that concerns a death in custody in an STC or in a British Army camp in Iraq, the response of government to such incidents should be to ensure that they are investigated impartially and with a willingness to learn lessons and, where appropriate, take responsibility and make amends.'

When the Home Affairs Select Committee conducted its inquiry into the rules governing enforced removals, prompted by the restraint death of Jimmy Mubenga (whose inquest found unlawful killing, prompting the Crown Prosecution Service to prosecute three G4S custody officers for manslaughter),[35] the group managing director of G4S's Care and Justice Services, David Banks, gave this description of the nose distraction: 'That involves a very short chop up on the nose to distract the individual.'[36] The YJB rejected this description some years before:

There is no such thing as a 'karate chop to the nose'. However, there are allowed, as a last resort, three 'distraction' techniques that can be used to inflict a brief, sharp burst of pain to the nose, thumb or rib. They absolutely must be used as a last resort, as a 'breakaway' technique, after other attempts to control the young person have failed, and only where there would be a material impact on the running of the centre.[37]

The YJB's protestations did not reflect what was actually happening to children, as reported by the Carlile Inquiry a year earlier. During interviews for the inquiry with children in two of the four secure training centres, one girl told me:

> I got PCCd [subject to the physical control in care system of restraint] from education because I would not go to a tutorial. I really liked the lesson I was already in and I didn't want to go. I was PCCd by a female and male staff member. The man got my head down and pushed me against the wall. Two people on response were holding my arms. The man had my head and pushed my nose up and it was bleeding. The woman was saying, 'Again Martha, this is stupid.' I got walked from education to the [residential] unit. My trousers were half way down. My knickers were showing. I asked the female staff member to pull up my trousers and she said 'no'. Nothing happened about the nosebleed. I didn't see the nurse. I never see her because I'm always angry. They push your nose right up here. I put in a complaint but they are allowed to use force.[38]

Another girl reported:

> Sometimes it depends on your size. To start off, there'll be two [staff restraining you]. They'll just hold your arms. They try not to hurt your arms. They take off your shoes and hold down your head. Sometimes if there's too much pressure you get blood shot eyes and little red marks on your cheek. They do a little distraction like a thumb

distraction and they swipe your nose. They push it in and then up. It's like a distraction to help calm you down.[39]

When asked if the distraction succeeded in calming her down, the girl replied:

> No it made me more angry. It hurts so you want them to stop it.... Some of the staff get abusive towards you, like say, 'Shut the fuck up,' and 'You're making a prat of yourself you little shit.' Others calm you down.[40]

One boy told a member of the inquiry team that staff could become:

> ... quite rough, like in the stairwells where there are no cameras; they would be quite rough there. Like the pressure points for quick release, when they bend your thumb and things like that ... when they take you back to your cell they pull your nose back and hold your head down to stop you spitting. They can be a bit rough.[41]

Subsequent research by children's charities elicited similar accounts, as this description of the nose distraction reveals:

> The [supervising officer] was on my head to restrain my head – his legs were on the side and [he] used his fingers to push up my nose. It started to bleed quite badly and I still have a bruise. It made me angry. I asked him to stop pushing my nose or I would bite him. He laughed and said, 'It's a fight' so I gave him a little nip. He let go of my head and gave it to someone else to restrain and then I was taken down to the block [segregation].[42]

The NSPCC uncovered similar incidents:

> [T]hey would put their fingers up your nose and pull tightly. It would feel like they were going to pull your nose clean off.[43]

[Y]ou feel funny, dizzy, feel like your arm's breaking, blood goes to your head, your arm stings for about 10 or 20 minutes afterwards, [they're] numb and you feel sick with the nose one.[44]

The child protection charity launched a campaign for a ban on distraction techniques[45] and 5,000 of its supporters wrote to their MPs demanding change. As well as the nose 'chop up', two other pain infliction techniques were authorised for use on children in secure training centres. These were the thumb and rib distraction. To be lawful, the distractions should have been used only in situations of dire emergency. The deputy president of the UK Supreme Court, Baroness Hale, has observed that these techniques are 'obviously capable of being perceived as physical punishment'.[46] Corporal punishment in prisons was prohibited in 1967.[47] Two decades later, torture became a criminal offence in the UK, its legal definition being the intentional infliction of severe pain or suffering by a public official or individual acting in an official capacity.[48] I made an FOI request to the YJB for data on the three distraction techniques in the year to November 2005, and was told they had been used a total of 768 times. This amounts to each of the four secure training centres using a form of restraint designed for life-threatening situations four times a week. There were 51 injuries recorded on children following the use of this radical form of restraint in the 12-month period. It was the YJB that gave me this data, so it must have been aware then, at least, that this extreme technique appeared in restraint statistics so frequently. The most common means of 'distracting' children in the four private prisons was the infliction of severe pain to the nose, used 449 times. The training manual for this technique contains the following instructions:

The number one of the team will move the hand on the trainee's chin to a position to just underneath the nose and above the top lip. The fingers stay taut with the index finger making contact with the trainee's face. The opposite hand acts as a counter pressure on the back of the head. The number one will direct pressure at an angle of 45 degrees toward the back of the trainee's head. Once used the hand moves back onto the trainee's chin in the head support position.[49]

The thumb distraction, where the child's thumb is yanked back, was used 287 times. Officers were warned during training that children's arms 'may react quickly to this technique' and they should therefore protect themselves from 'flaying arms'.[50] The rib distraction was to be applied by the officer using both hands to take hold of the child's clothing around the rib cage. The officer was then to 'drive sharply inward and upward' with an inverted middle finger.[51] In 2004/05, it was used 32 times. Several years ahead of the rib distraction being used in any secure training centre, the inquiry into Frank Beck's sexual and physical abuse of children in Leicestershire's children's homes opened with the account of the woman whose disclosures in 1989 finally led to the man's arrest and prosecution:

> The hell started on the day I walked into the place. I had just left home and was naturally upset. I was quiet and tearful. Although I must have been there for a long time it just seemed like minutes later that they got hold of me. Accusing me of chucking out angry feelings, of hating my mothers and sisters. When I tried to explain that I missed my mother they trapped me between their legs and dug their fingers into my ribs and made me scream and cry out in pain.[52]

Another FOI request the following year revealed that the techniques were used 121 times in the four G4S and Serco child prisons between February and August 2006. There were 26 recorded child injuries following the use of the nose distraction in Serco's Hassockfield secure training centre in the 12 months preceding Adam's death. Children suffered nose bleeds on 19 separate occasions.[53] A High Court judge said of the use of restraint (including the so-called distractions) for good order and discipline:

This was not a one-off error of understanding but a persistent practice, duly recorded, in dealing with children in detention in breach of the law, the rules, the STC contract and the training manual as well as the in-house rules. Astonishingly, none of this seems to have aroused any query or concern by the YJB who had an officer monitoring the returns....[54]

Use of the techniques was very rare by 2009.[55] Had Adam not left a note criticising the officers who hit him on the nose – and his mother, parliamentarians and campaign groups not generated a media storm – it is highly likely they would have remained in common use. In a particularly scathing comment on child protection failures in the secure training centres, Lord Justice Buxton observed in the Court of Appeal proceedings in July 2008:

> We were told that the hold used on Gareth Myatt was no longer approved [p 17]; and that the nose distraction technique used on Adam Rickwood had also been withdrawn. I will be forgiven for wondering whether there are any other techniques awaiting withdrawal only when something goes wrong.[56]

It was more than three years after Adam's death when ministers suspended the use of the nose distraction in secure training centres (it was permanently withdrawn the following year). Prison officers in young offender institutions were allowed to continue using the brutal technique. In December 2008, ministers accepted the recommendation from the independent restraint review that the 'nose control' in young offender institutions should also be banned. A 'safer alternative' was promised 'within the next six months'.[57] A delegation from the European anti-torture committee had recently visited the UK and it had also recommended a complete ban. Baroness Stern was not alone in believing pressure from European anti-torture experts to be the real reason for the ministerial prohibition:

> I never thought that I would see the day when the
> European Committee for Prevention of Torture, which
> among other things concerns itself with prison conditions
> in Russia and what happens in police stations in Turkey,
> came here and told Her Majesty's Government that it
> was not acceptable in children's prisons to hit children on
> the nose until they felt pain to make them do what they
> were told. I assume that that is what happened as, soon
> after the committee's visit, the Government announced
> that this practice was to be discontinued.[58]

One of the Prisons and Probation Ombudsman's investigations in
2009/10 concerned a boy who suffered a broken nose during restraint
in a young offender institution. The boy had been misbehaving
with other children in an education session and was told to leave
the area. A prison officer accompanied the child on each side,
and a third walked behind him. The boy alleged that one of the
officers 'prodded him in the back several times. He said that, when
he turned to protest, one officer held his nose and face, pushing
his head to the floor, while the others held his arms and legs.'[59]
The independent investigation found that the distraction technique
'is indeed an extremely painful procedure', but there was no evidence
on the CCTV footage of an officer prodding the child in the back.
The three officers told the investigator the boy had been 'surly and
argumentative'. (Restraint is meant to be a last resort in any setting
otherwise it is an unlawful assault. Restraining a teenager because he
is being 'surly and argumentative' sounds to me like restraining an
elderly man because he is being forgetful, or a toddler because she
is being intransigent). As there was no corroborative evidence, the
Ombudsman said it could not fully uphold the complaint, adding:

> But to say the least, any situation in which a boy has his
> nose broken as a result of being restrained by three adult
> prison staff must be a cause for great concern – all the
> more so when, as in Mr Z's case, there was no violent
> struggle prior to the injury and no previous history of
> violence.[60]

Somewhere between August 2010 and January 2011, hitting children on the nose as a form of behaviour management ended for all child prisoners.[61] However, prison officers in young offender institutions were given the mandibular angle technique in exchange. A panel of specialists 'provisionally recommended' the technique be authorised for use on children 'conditional on legal advice to the effect that the use of a pain-inducing technique for restraint is lawful in England and Wales'.[62] In responses to my FOI requests, Ministry of Justice officials have refused to disclose the date they asked for and received such legal advice, and have predictably failed to release the advice itself (assuming it exists). The precise details of the mandibular angle technique have also been kept secret, but what limited information is in the public domain shows that it has been authorised for use on a child who is standing or lying face down on the floor, face up from the floor or on their side.[63] And that it works by the infliction of pain through driving the tip of a finger or thumb or a knuckle into an area just below the child's ear at a 45 degree angle.[64]

The same technique was used on a 39-year-old man, Habib Ullah, in a High Wycombe car park in July 2008, during a routine stop and search by four police officers.[65] The man collapsed and died while being restrained. In February 2014, the Independent Police Complaints Commission (IPCC) completed its investigation into the conduct of the four officers – which included 'seeking further opinion from restraint experts and doctors' – and referred the case to the Crown Prosecution Service (CPS).[66] The IPCC refused my request for sight of the expert advice it received on the mandibular angle technique during consideration of the case, on the grounds that this could jeopardise 'the decision making process and any prosecution that may follow'[67] (less than four months later the CPS announced there would be no further action in the case[68]). It is to be hoped the IPCC has shared with the prison service, the YJB and child protection agencies any information it has obtained on the health risks of the mandibular angle technique.

Following an FOI request, the Ministry of Justice disclosed to me that the mandibular angle technique had been used 156 times in 10 young offender institutions in the 12 months to August 2011.[69] There were 111 incidents, meaning this grave technique was used on a child more than once in close succession. The report containing the data, produced by the Restraint Advisory Board, is phlegmatic on this point:

> From the monthly reports there is no suggestion of protracted use of the technique beyond 5 seconds. Repeated application however is sometimes required.[70]

Several minor injuries were recorded – scratches to a child's ear or neck, swelling to the ear, bruising and redness. One child complained of feeling dizzy. After an incident in Hindley young offender institution in Wigan, officers recorded the 'young person's pain threshold was high so the technique had no effect'.[71] Generally, however, there was little evidence of children being debriefed after use of the technique, apparently because children elected not to participate in this process.[72] But this was not the only paperwork missing:

> Various parts of the quality assurance programme did not occur as planned for operational reasons e.g., sickness, holiday period or competing priorities. This suggests that as yet these are not yet completely embedded in every day practice.[73]

One institution was found to use the technique frequently – it was applied on children 28 times in 11 months[74] – seemingly a symptom of its change from a women's to a juvenile prison more than two years previously.[75]

In March 2013, prison inspectors found that Warren Hill young offender institution in Suffolk had used the mandibular angle technique 26 times on children in 2012, and three times in 2013. They said this was 'inappropriate' and reported that the governor planned to review its use.[76] An inspection of Wetherby young offender institution in October 2013 found that the technique had been used during 11 incidents in the previous six months; again, this was said to be 'inappropriate'.[77] Another inspection that month found it was being used in Werrington young offender institution in Stoke-on-Trent.[78] In January 2014, the Prisons and Probation Ombudsman reported the case of a 17-year-old boy who refused to go into his cell. He became aggressive and prison officers kitted out in riot gear restrained him. One of the officers subjected the boy to the mandibular angle technique. His statement after the event gave 'virtually no explanation for its use' and most of the other officers' write-ups did not mention that the child had been deliberately hurt. The Ombudsman concluded that the child's actions had presented 'minimal' risk of serious physical harm and he was not satisfied the use of the technique 'was either necessary or proportionate'.[79]

Custody officers in the secure training centres have also been authorised to use the technique as part of a new system of restraint. Only one secure training centre was using the new system during the first data collection period and no 'pain-inducing techniques' were recorded during those six months.[80] It is notable that the new system does not extend to secure children's homes, where the YJB also places children who have been charged or convicted of criminal offences. When I asked John Drew, chief executive of the YJB between 2009 and 2012, whether the rumours were true that the Prison Officers' Association had refused to countenance losing the power to use arm, wrist and thumb locks on children, he replied as follows:

'[I]t is a fact that the Prison Officers' Association is still very powerful ... I well remember a discussion I had at the time that we were selling the introduction of the new arrangements for restraint and we had a big stakeholders meeting at which, amongst others, three senior national officials of the Prison Officers' Association were there and one of them, in lots of other ways a reasonable man, said to me, "We can't have a different system for restraint for children than for adults." And I said, "Well, why not?" And he said, "It would be too complex for my members."'

Prison officers are not recruited to work exclusively with children. Long careers in the prison service frequently see individuals moving between different types of establishment. I believe this is why challenges to practices in the children's 'secure estate' are often received as wider attacks on the prison service. The three-year campaign for publication of the training manual governing restraint in the secure training centres was illustrative of this. In 2007, the YJB refused my request on behalf of the Children's Rights Alliance for England for a copy of the complete document – I was sent a heavily redacted version – so we complained to the Information Commissioner, who ordered full disclosure on public interest grounds. The YJB appealed the ruling on the flaky grounds that children would develop countermeasures; there would be security risks in adult prisons; and, most bizarrely, members of the public could endanger themselves and others by use of the restraint techniques. We suspected that the prison service was behind the blockage as it was the organisation's riot squad that had developed the document. We learned later that this was the first time the state had been forced to reveal prison restraint techniques. Less than a week before the tribunal hearing, the YJB withdrew its appeal. We received the document by courier two weeks later.

Another two years had passed when the then justice secretary, Kenneth Clarke, announced a new system of restraint for child prisons – called 'minimising and managing physical restraint' (MMPR).[81] A 28-page document published jointly by the Ministry of Justice and the YJB sets out the various roles of statutory and voluntary agencies in implementing and monitoring the new scheme,[82] yet omits to explain how social workers, independent advocates, inspectors and children's rights organisations can fulfil their duties while ignorant of many of the new restraint techniques. Large sections of the MMPR manual are redacted, making it impossible to see what techniques have been approved. My FOI request to the National Offender Management Service (NOMS) for a full copy of the new manual was rejected. Exactly the same reasons for non-disclosure were given as for the YJB's refusal five years earlier. The Information Commissioner's Office has inexplicably supported secrecy this time, so the case is going to tribunal. In June 2014, NOMS also refused an FOI request for a copy of the companion manual containing personal safety techniques for use in child prisons as part of the MMPR system. The document is under review pending publication alongside other restraint manuals in spring 2015, came the response.

Transparency about the frequency and methods of restraint used within institutions is an obvious form of child protection, and here there has been steady progress over recent years. MMPR data is published regularly, and open invitations to training sessions have been advertised to, among others, penal reformers and children's rights campaigners. However, such progress is hindered by the failure of the state to acknowledge the scale of past restraint-related child abuse, and to proactively provide redress for those who suffered.

Early in 2011, the Children's Rights Alliance for England began legal proceedings to seek an order that would require the government to examine G4S and Serco restraint records to identify potential victims of unlawful restraint. The alliance wanted these individuals to be contacted by the state and given information about how they might challenge any unlawful treatment. A former senior civil servant who supported what the organisation was trying to achieve told me ministers would "die in a ditch" rather than agree to such action. I remained optimistic: surely it was obvious that if institutions had for years acted as if they were entitled to use physical restraint to secure compliance, and no outside inspectors, monitors or advocates had challenged them, vulnerable children could not have been expected to know they were being unlawfully assaulted.

As a former child protection social worker, I knew children could endure the most awful abuse and blame themselves, or expect no one to believe and take them seriously – something we have all been reminded of in the Savile case. I also knew the authorities had made proactive attempts in the past to trace victims of abuse in children's homes.

The two-year police investigation of abuse in Leicestershire children's homes involved taking statements from nearly 400 former residents now living in four continents. Their identities were found after police searched for files held in the archives of County Hall; at the time, officers were working on abuse allegations from just two adults.[83] A parliamentary inquiry reported in 2002 that 34 of 43 police forces in England and Wales had investigated abuse in children's homes and other institutions in the preceding five years.[84] This invariably involved seeking out former residents.

After two days of sitting in the Royal Courts of Justice in London, listening to counsel for the Ministry of Justice and G4S and Serco argue that children had plenty of opportunity to complain about unlawful treatment, I watched the chief executive of British Gas announce on BBC's Newsnight programme that his company was to send a letter to each of its seven million customers telling them about its new tariffs, introduced because of public concern over the price of domestic fuel.[85] Meanwhile, the two firms responsible for running secure training centres were in court protesting about the work involved in contacting individuals who were unlawfully assaulted as children in prison. (I learnt later that Lord Justice Woolf and the then chief inspector of prisons, Judge Stephen Tumim, had written to every single prisoner during the Woolf Inquiry).[86] Ministry of Justice officials had calculated they would need to review in excess of 27,000 restraint incidents – a process they complained could take many months. It was also said that making contact with former child prisoners could breach data protection rules and risked rekindling unpleasant memories. Notwithstanding these arguments, counsel for the Ministry of Justice told the court that the government and the two multinationals would not stand in the way of my charity, the Children's Rights Alliance for England, making a public appeal, perhaps by way of a newspaper advert. G4S Group and Serco reported pre-tax profits of £279 million[87] and £238 million[88] respectively in 2011 – enough combined funds to keep the small charity operating comfortably for hundreds of years. Above all, this misunderstood the purpose of the legal challenge, which was to make the state itself take responsibility for contacting former child prisoners.

The judge agreed that the children concerned were very vulnerable, by virtue of their backgrounds and through being imprisoned, and that widespread unlawful restraint had probably occurred for at least a decade. These were children sent to secure training centres, Mr Justice Foskett explained, 'because they had acted unlawfully and to learn to obey the law, yet many of them were subject to unlawful actions during their detention. I need, I think, say no more.'[89] Mark Scott, representing the Children's Rights Alliance for England in the case, told me during an interview for this book that one of the things that most shocked him from all the restraint discoveries was the failure of the Commission for Social Care Inspection (since merged with Ofsted) to take action. To its credit, the organisation had realised during an inspection that children were being unlawfully restrained, but then amended its draft report after intervention from the YJB:[90]

> 'They completely watered down their findings and so, actually, they had an opportunity to stop it years before, and they did nothing about it. You've got to question the whole independence and effectiveness of an inspection body that's prepared to change its findings [as a result of] pressure from the state.'

In the High Court, Mr Justice Foskett said there was no legal basis for ordering the identification and notification of victims. Further legal proceedings proved similarly unsuccessful. Cases involving such serious human rights abuses would ordinarily make their way to Strasbourg. The European Court of Human Rights is only available to victims, so a legal challenge about locating victims has nowhere left to go. There is a new mechanism for children's rights abuses allowing third parties to submit complaints to the UN Committee on the Rights of the Child in Geneva, but the UK has not signed up to it. However, the judge did point to there being a strong moral case for some form of government action:

> Merely because the action of disseminating the relevant information is not required by the law does not mean that there is no obligation to consider whether some action is necessary if only as a matter of good and fair administration. The fact that those potentially affected were vulnerable children and young persons would, in my judgment, at least dictate the need for the Defendant to consider whether something ought to be done.[91]

No remedial action of the kind sought by the Children's Rights Alliance for England was ever taken. This compares conspicuously with the duty of candour to be imposed on health and social care services registered with the Care Quality Commission.

Recommended by the public inquiry into the 'appalling suffering of many patients'[92] in the care of the Mid Staffordshire NHS Foundation Trust, the duty is expected to require health providers and managers to notify a service user (or those acting on their behalf – a parent or social worker, for example) when they have suffered a 'safety incident' resulting in moderate or severe harm. The notification must be in writing, give a truthful account and include an apology.[93] The NHS is the fifth largest employer in the world, with vast scope for mistakes and malpractice, yet, in introducing this duty, ministers have shown impressive commitment to transparency and accountability. What more would have had to happen to vulnerable children in the care of G4S and Serco to have secured a political response equivalent to that in the Mid Staffordshire case? And how safe are children today from unlawful restraint?

A question in parliament in 2010 established that 14 officers in the four G4S and Serco secure training centres had been disciplined following a restraint incident; a further 13 had been suspended; and one officer had been sacked between 2006 and 2010.[94] The information was incomplete, but it points to problems persisting after Gareth and Adam's deaths. A more positive outlook would be that this shows a willingness by the companies involved to act to protect children. Less reassuring, however, is the data released to parliament in October 2013 showing that children in the four secure training centres had made 332 separate complaints about the use of physical restraint between 2008 and 2012.[95] A spin-doctor might exclaim, "Look, this is proof children can speak out," but this wouldn't wash if the institutions were boarding schools or hospitals. During this same period, 47 children required hospital treatment for a serious injury following restraint in young offender institutions.[96] Latest data shows that injuries following restraint have fallen in the past year, but so have the numbers of children in custody. Between 2008/09 and 2012/13, 725 children in young offender institutions and 346 in secure training centres suffered injuries during restraint.[97] Some of these would have been children held in Castington young offender institution in Northumberland.

The prisons inspectorate reported in June 2009 that 'a large number' of prisoners at Castington had suffered broken bones following restraint,[98] and the head of the prison service responded by saying an investigation had been commissioned.[99] A copy of the investigation report obtained through an FOI request shows that five children suffered wrist fractures between January 2007 and September 2008. One child suffered two fractured wrists. The investigation found that none of the injuries occurred in situations where a child was fighting; there was no evidence of any attempts at de-escalation; and officers were mostly in control of the situations making it 'questionable if force was really necessary in all cases'.[100] Most of the injuries were sustained in the child's cell or in interview situations with no CCTV cameras. Health staff within the prison, as well as the local hospital, had raised no concerns about children's injuries. There was no evidence of a formal investigation in three of the cases; in the fourth, the police advised the child that there was not enough evidence to pursue an investigation; and in the fifth there was an internal review. Independent advocates were not involved in any of the cases. A sixth person held in the juvenile part of the prison, but recorded as aged 18, sustained a fractured arm in May 2009 after a drugs find.[101] This could have been the same incident that led to a prison officer being dismissed in February 2011. An employment tribunal was told a juvenile's arm had been broken during restraint in May 2009. After an internal investigation, prison managers charged the officer with using unreasonable force and giving false information.[102] The police had earlier investigated but took no further action.[103]

Six adults, aged between 18 and 21 years, also suffered wrist fractures, and one a fractured knee. All of these injuries occurred between March 2005 and May 2009. The investigation report was dated February 2010. On 22 February 2010, the YJB issued a statement indicating that children would no longer be placed at Castington because 'there is considerable spare capacity'. There was no mention of the fractures.[104]

Another two Castington officers took their cases to an employment tribunal, after being sacked for gross misconduct for causing a 21-year-old prisoner to suffer two broken wrists in March 2007. They were also charged with causing grievous bodily harm, although their criminal trial was halted because the prison CCTV footage was not kept. Their successful claim of unfair dismissal was overturned on appeal in August 2012 (the outcome of the fresh tribunal is unknown at the time of writing). The governor's rationale for determining that the officers had deliberately intended to cause harm to the young prisoner included the following:

> [M]edical evidence indicated that the force used must have been considerable. I also took account of the rationale as to why one medical practitioner believed that it was unlikely that officers applying wrist locks could have caused the injury. That was not because it would have been impossible to do so, but because the pain to the prisoner would have been so severe that he believed officers acting properly would have been aware of it and not have proceeded further.[105]

The lack of external investigation into children's injuries following restraint was highlighted in a June 2013 inspection report about Ashfield young offender institution in Bristol. Two children suffered broken bones in 2012 following the use of force. Although both incidents were referred to social services and the police, only internal investigations were undertaken. Also in 2012, an officer had been dismissed for inappropriate use of force on children. None of the sample restraint documentation examined by inspectors showed that the child had been asked to give his version of events.[106] Eliciting the child's perspective on restraint was one of the recommendations made by the coroner presiding over the inquest into the death of Gareth Myatt (p 39). The Ministry of Justice and the YJB announced in January 2013 that children would no longer be placed in this prison.[107]

Leaked documents in my possession reveal the circumstances of a child suffering a broken wrist during restraint in Hindley young offender institution in Wigan in March 2011. An investigation by the Prisons and Probation Ombudsman reported CCTV film showing that the child was standing in his cell doorway, an officer was leaning into the cell and both he and the child appeared 'to be propelled away

from the door, both landing on the floor almost under the stairs'.[108]
The report continues:

> [The child] fell with his arms under his body and [the
> officer's] weight on top of him. Both officers say that
> [the child] screamed when he hit the floor. [The officer
> assisting the restraint] says he heard a noise like a pencil
> snapping and he thinks this is when the wrist was broken.
> [The child] is not sure when the injury occurred. He
> has said both that he thinks it happened when [the
> main restraining officer] fell on top of him and that it
> happened when [the main restraining officer] bent his
> arm back.... Not only did [the child] scream in pain,
> but both officers say he identified the pain as being in
> his wrist. I am, therefore, very concerned that [the main
> restraining officer] proceeded to pull [the child's] arm
> out from under his body and place it in a back hammer
> when he had already heard [the child] scream. He went
> on to say that, as he managed 'to take control of [the
> child's] left arm, he again screamed as I placed it in the
> back hammer'.[109]

Details of the 'back hammer' prison restraint technique were redacted
when the training manual governing the use of restraint in adult
prisons, young offender institutions and immigration deportations
was made public in 2011, after the death of Jimmy Mubenga. The
relevant section, dealing with prisoners who are non-compliant and
cannot be moved in a standing position, reads:

> This section has been redacted. It describes the technique
> to be used by a three officer C&R (control and restraint)
> team to apply 'back hammers' (a type of wrist lock to
> enable safe withdrawal of C&R team members from the
> cell) to a prisoner following relocation.[110]

Baroness Stern asked a parliamentary question about the circumstances
in which the back hammer can be used on children. The minister

replying, Lord McNally, omitted to mention that the method involves the deliberate infliction of pain:

> The back hammer restraint is an approved technique for use in National Offender Management Service [adult and child] establishments involving holding of the arm behind the back. It is used to ensure the safe relocation within the prison of a violent and non-compliant prisoner in order to minimise the risk of harm to both the prisoner and staff. The technique enables the safe withdrawal of staff from an area such as a cell where the prisoner is threatening staff.[111]

The prison officer leading the back hammer restraint of the child in Hindley young offender institution was more than six feet tall and weighed 19 stone. A prison nurse examined the boy after the restraint and found he had a bleeding mouth, severe swelling and deformity of his left wrist, loss of movement and pins and needles.[112] When he was taken to hospital, his wrist joint had to be manipulated back into position under anaesthetic.[113] The Prisons and Probation Ombudsman expressed alarm that the boy was placed back in his cell and left without any supervision until the nurse appeared, despite being in excruciating pain:

> I am also concerned that, when the officers let [the boy] up and put him back into his room, no one remained at the door to check whether he was alright. [The supporting officer] said that [the boy] had completely calmed down and was giving no resistance by this point. He also said that he could see [the child] was in pain and had tears in his eyes, that he kept complaining that his wrist was broken and that his wrist had a big lump on it. Both officers said that when [the boy] was placed behind his door, he kept shouting that he was in agony and also that he hit the room door with something hard. [The supporting officer] called a nurse to attend, but no one checked [the boy's] condition until the nurse

arrived. I do not consider this to be safe treatment of a young person who is in pain and who has been subject to the use of force.[114]

Prior to the March 2011 restraint incident, there had been five separate complaints from children, and one mother of an imprisoned child, about the officer who used the back hammer. A further nine complaints were made about the officer to the prison between March 2011 and May 2012. All of the allegations related to him threatening, frightening, bullying or assaulting children.[115] An internal prison investigation of the March 2011 incident concluded the boy had been restrained appropriately and it was difficult to see how the incident could have been dealt with differently. The child, the report observes, was 'the author of this incident' and there was no evidence the injury occurred as a direct result of the restraint.[116] Had this child not complained to the Ombudsman, this could have been the end of the matter for the prison. His earlier complaint to the Independent Monitoring Board of Ashfield young offender institution, made just days after he was moved to that prison, resulted in him receiving a reply from a governor at Hindley rejecting his account of the incident. The matter had been reviewed by an independent panel, the prison's safeguarding department, the police and social services and 'there were no concerns raised by them and no findings of wrong doing', the governor said.[117] Two officers from Hindley even visited the boy in his new prison to try to get him to sign some paperwork about the restraint (he refused).[118] The child's persistence brought justice. The Ombudsman upheld his complaint and instructed the prison to apologise to him for the 'inappropriate use of force' and the 'insufficiently robust' investigation into his complaint. The prison and social services were also ordered to produce a joint action plan after a child protection meeting had failed to ask probing questions.[119] The independent investigator was alarmed by the CCTV footage of the lead prison officer leaving the child's cell:

> Finally, I do not know what construction to put on [the main restraining officer's] behaviour after the incident when he hit his fist into his open palm more than once

while walking away from [the boy's] room. It makes disturbing viewing. The Governor has suggested that [name of officer] may have hurt his hand in the fall and that he may have been rubbing it. I have to say, this is [sic] does not seem to me to be the most obvious interpretation.[120]

The Guardian newspaper's prisons correspondent Eric Allison asked NOMS in September 2013 if the officer was still working with children at Hindley young offender institution, and whether the organisation considered him a fit person to work with children. The response – 'It would be inappropriate to comment at this time' – illustrates the low level of accountability the prison service is accustomed to.[121] Persistent attempts by theYJB to obtain the CCTV footage of the March 2011 restraint incident, appear to have been unsuccessful, despite the following ministerial assertion:

CCTV footage is not routinely made available to the Youth Justice Board or Local Authority where restraint has resulted in a serious injury but is made available to them upon request, where available.[122]

The March 2011 incident was one of six separate restraints that led to a child suffering a fracture or broken bone in Hindley young offender institution between February 2009 and April 2011 (one fracture was later found to have been misdiagnosed). Given the preponderance of serious injuries, a team of NOMS officials reviewed each restraint and produced a 13-page report with 10 recommendations, including that 'young people should never be taken to the ground in straight arm locks' and governors should specify which wrist can be handcuffed by escorts taking children to accident and emergency with suspected wrist fractures following restraint.[123] This latter recommendation arose from an incident in April 2011 where a child's fractured wrist was handcuffed as he was taken for emergency hospital treatment (this was the same child who had suffered the back hammer, discussed above).[124]

The internal report highlighted that nearly all of the children who suffered injuries 'had a mental health history and/or learning disability'.[125] A child was fighting in only one of the six restraint incidents. In three of the incidents, 'controlling locks' were used to move children from the education or association area of the prison or to 'take them to the floor'; and in the fourth incident back hammers were used on a child with a speech and language learning disability who was smashing up his cell. This was a 'planned cell intervention' to take the child 'to a more robust room'.[126] There was no medical assessment and cameras were not used, in breach of policy. The internal prison investigators said officers had put themselves at risk of harm by not wearing full personal protective equipment when moving the disabled boy. Such equipment includes a riot helmet, flame-retardant overalls, gloves, belt, side arm baton and holder, shin guards, elbow protectors, boots, flame-retardant balaclava and a shield cover.[127]

Inspectors visiting Wetherby young offender institution in October 2013 said they had seen CCTV films of two instances of planned restraint where fully compliant children 'were handcuffed with wrist locks applied and were required to walk bent over to the separation and care unit, which was excessive'.[128] Abusive and unlawful could be two other descriptions. In June 2014, inspectors visiting Cookham Wood young offender institution found that officers had deliberately inflicted pain on children to get them to comply with orders. They also reported the case of a boy who was 'fully restrained' because he 'refused to give his name and prison number when he returned from court to reception'. Officers were said to know the boy well.[129]

Unlawful use of physical restraint is an assault and therefore a criminal offence. It falls within the statutory definition of physical abuse. It took close to five months for the Ministry of Justice to release data, following an FOI request, on the number of prison officers disciplined for physically abusing children between April 2009 and December 2013. Eventually, I was told that 26 prison staff were disciplined under the category of 'assault/unnecessary use of force on a prisoner' across nine establishments holding juveniles (p 245). These must have been particularly grave incidents to result in disciplinary action. Given the immense difficulties children in closed institutions have in making complaints and being believed, and the hideously secret nature of prisons, it is also reasonable to fear that this is the tip of the iceberg.

SEVEN

'We should be able to hug our families'

One of the enduring lessons I learned from my time as a young social worker was the tremendous capacity of children to excuse their parents' failings. This was matched by a striking optimism in so many children that one day their mothers and fathers would give them the love and attention they rightly yearned. Supporting children in these circumstances was often painful and frustrating, as they frequently reproached themselves for being in care. (Children have a remarkable capacity for taking responsibility for catastrophes way beyond their control.) Connected to this self-blame was the misery and mayhem caused by angry and frightened children convinced that their new carers were destined to join their scrapbook of rejecters. I discovered early on that being able to appease foster carers, in the hope of averting more crushing loss for children, is a primary social work skill. As one child offender reported during a study into the wellbeing of young people in the youth justice system:

> I went through 11 foster carers in four years. That was not social services' doing. It was my own doing. I could have been with the first foster carer I was with but I just ruined it because I thought if my mum doesn't want us then no-one wants us![1]

Into their teenage years, the children on my caseload would often undertake their own detective work as a precursor to a happy family reunion that mostly never happened. I had studied child attachment and the effects of separation, but it was only through working with

155

children in care that I came to understand the glowing torch many of them carry for their imperfect parents.

Neither the prison service nor the Youth Justice Board (YJB) held any central records on the number of children in custody who were subject to care orders or had been formerly looked after by local authorities when the prisons inspectorate conducted a review of this constituency in 2010.[2] The inspectorate estimated that at any one time there are around 400 children in prison who have been in care.[3] Its latest annual survey of children in prison found a third of boys and 61% of girls had spent time in care.[4] Four in every 10 of the boys in a specialist unit for especially vulnerable children in Wetherby young offender institution had been in care.[5] By any reckoning, these are children who require skilled assistance in their relationships with parents, even if they will never again live together. When return home is possible, intensive family work is necessary to ensure parents are getting the right support to meet their child's needs and to prevent further offending.

The importance of social workers and other official visitors cannot be overstated for children who have lost all contact with parents. Without visits, letters and gifts through the post, children are bound to feel agonisingly alone in prison. If the image of social workers sending mail to child prisoners sounds fantastical, it is worth remembering that 'corporate parents', as councils who have legal responsibility for the upbringing of a child are called, are meant to treat children as any good parent would. Twenty years have passed but I can still vividly remember the words of a 13-year-old boy who lived in a children's home in the West Midlands. We were discussing the offer of a media interview on the rights of children in care. I asked him whether he ought to discuss the matter with his parents or any other family members, in case they had concerns about protecting his (and their) privacy. Looking me straight in the eye, this child replied: "I am on my own, I have no-one."

The tragedy of elderly people living their final years without the love of family or friends is at least in the public's consciousness, if not driving our actions. Unless they are an abandoned newborn, or a young child perishing under the noses of teachers, doctors and social workers, the plight of isolated children receives little public attention. Being alone in the first decades of life must be at least as devastating as in old age. It goes against the natural order of things, for every child is meant to have somebody ready to pull them from a raging fire, to stage a hospital vigil for them in times of ill health and to keep their face clean.

Liberal Democrat peer Baroness Linklater told me during research for this book about her former work in a prison visitors' centre, where families had different reactions to the incarceration of loved ones:

> 'The ripple effect on families of children in custody of any kind is very often absolutely huge, and there are people who can't face coming to visit. There are other people who move heaven and earth to get there, whether it's to see a child or a spouse. And sometimes they have all thought that it's too traumatic and difficult.'

There were many heart-wrenching moments when I used to make weekly prison visits to a former child in care but some of the most poignant involved witnessing the disappointment of the children who received no visitors. These spruced-up adolescents would sit waiting at bare tables, repeatedly switching their gaze from the visiting hall entrance to the tabletop. After the final visitors had walked through, and it became clear that no one was coming to see these boys, the prison officers would escort them back to their wing – a process called the 'walk of shame'.[6] The kind words and gestures of the officers in these situations, as well as the solidarity shown by the relieved boys whose visitors had arrived, were totems of compassion. Former prison governor Andrew Coyle speaks of how, in prison, 'the veneer of politeness which covers most human relationships is stripped away to be replaced by a naked clarity which goes right to the heart of how each of us feels about our fellow human beings'.[7] How prison officers deal with children's separation from their parents, and the hurt pride of those who receive no visits at all, is but one example of the humanity of individuals defying a system unworthy of children. A particularly moving anecdote appeared in a newspaper article several months after the horrific racist murder of Zahid Mubarek in Feltham young offender institution (pp 217–18):

I remember once a colleague said to me one Saturday, 'Have you noticed Williams? Every weekend he's all tidy, his shoes are polished up and he's in his best gear. What's that all about?' It turned out every weekend he was waiting for a visit from his parents that never came. They used to visit but then they stopped. I looked into it and it turned out his parents had moved but the visiting orders were still being sent to the old address. We got them sent to the new address and they started visiting again. Things like that used to make the job worthwhile. The way we're going now we don't even have the time to realise we have got a fucking neo-Nazi thug in the same cell as an Asian lad.[8]

Prison officers cannot be expected to compensate for the failures of others. Alex Kelly, who was in the care of Tower Hamlets local authority from the age of six, had been incarcerated for less than four months when he hanged himself in his cell. For most of this period, Alex had no allocated social worker and council managers argued with each other about their responsibilities to him. The local authority failed to respond to requests from the prison for contact with the child's grandmother and other family members.[9]

Kevin Jacobs, in care since he was a toddler, was found hanging just hours after his social worker had visited and confirmed that the local authority would not be funding his return to his children's home and that there were no other plans for where he would live on release (p 272). Two nights earlier, prison staff had checked the boy every 15 minutes such was the level of concern.[10]

Children consulted about violence in custody in 2012 said that family contact helped reduce stress and frustration,[11] although other research carried out by the Howard League for Penal Reform found that some children chose not to have any family visits 'as they found the experience of their families leaving afterwards too distressing'.[12]

At the time of writing, five inspection reports of young offender institutions in England had been published in 2014. Around a third of the boys held in Cookham Wood young offender institution in June 2014 told inspectors they had no visitors.[13] At Werrington young offender institution, over a quarter of boys received no visits;[14] and at Wetherby,[15] Hindley[16] and the specialist Keppel Unit,[17] a fifth of boys received no visits.

In June 2013, inspectors reported a 2012 internal prison survey showing over a quarter of children in Ashfield young offender institution in Bristol did not receive any visits; 12% received just one visit a month; and one in 10 children received a visit between every three to six months.[18] Other inspection reports reveal similarly high levels of child isolation. Almost one in every five boys held in Feltham young offender institution in January 2013 reported having no visits from family or friends;[19] 20% of boys held at Warren Hill young offender institution in March 2013 received no visits;[20] and over a quarter of children imprisoned in Cookham Wood young offender institution in May 2013 had no visits.[21] Hassockfield secure training centre in Durham was said to host about 12 weekly family visits early in 2013, yet there were 33 children detained at the time of the inspection.[22] A fifth of children in Medway secure training centre in Kent told inspectors it is not easy to keep in contact with family and friends.[23] The 2013 inspection of Oakhill secure training centre found around half of the 66 boys detained there received no visits from their families.[24] By the time of the next inspection, this had improved to between one quarter and a third of children not receiving at least one visit a month – still painfully high.[25]

When local authorities are looking after a child, they are legally required to keep under review the need for an independent visitor who will visit, advise and befriend the child. The role was created over 30 years ago for children on care orders placed in community homes with education (the institutions that replaced approved schools). Subsequent legislation extended the duty to provide independent visitors to any looked after child who has infrequent parental contact or whenever it would be in the child's interests to have such a befriender.[26] There is no equivalent duty on local authorities, the prison service or the YJB to provide independent visitors to children in young offender institutions, but the heads of the four secure training centres are required to appoint independent persons to visit and befriend children in their care who do not have family contact. An answer to a parliamentary question in October 2013 indicates that this is not being implemented:

> Since 2002, the Youth Justice Board has awarded contracts for Independent Advocacy services in Secure Training Centres (STCs) to ensure that each child has regular and frequent access to an independent person throughout their period in custody to assist and support them with issues relating to their well being and care. This service aims to meet the intention of Rule 29(4) of the STC Rules. The service is measured through indicators such as contact hours rather than individual appointments so it is not possible to specify how many independent persons have been appointed as part of past and current advocacy contracts.[27]

This disingenuous response sidesteps the legal duty of directors to appoint a befriender to individual children – a completely different role from that of an advocate, as government guidance makes clear.[28] It is therefore to be expected that the service specifications (advocacy in penal institutions is provided by Barnardo's) do not include befriending children who have no family contact.[29]

With the exception of the debtors' prisons, which were common in the UK in the mid-19th century and permitted families to be housed together (the author Charles Dickens' parents and younger siblings were imprisoned together in Southwark's Marshalsea prison),[30] prisons have always removed the wrongdoer from society. This physical and psychological distancing remains as strong as ever, and penal norms governing family contact are virtually identical for adults and children. During my research for this book, Yvonne Bailey, the mother of Joseph Scholes, told me how powerless she felt when her son was taken to Stoke Heath young offender institution in Shropshire:

> 'You are entirely helpless. You've no power whatsoever. It's the most awful feeling. You're absolutely powerless. You go from being their mother with complete control,

and even when Joseph was in voluntary care at the children's home, I could ring, I could've said "no" or "yes" or Joseph probably could've said he wanted to leave there.... You have no control whatsoever. Your child is taken from you; you have no say in anything, nothing at all.'

Sam Elphick's mother bought her son new trainers after receiving permission from the prison to do so. When she arrived at Hindley young offender institution with the new shoes, officers refused to accept them.[31] It could have been that the officers were mechanically 'carrying out orders', rather than setting out to be insensitive; I once had a postal order I sent to a child in prison returned because I hadn't specified the recipient's prison number, only his name.

Whatever the reason Sam was not permitted the trainers, his mother's experiences of the prison were only sought because her son never left Hindley. Having been held in 17 different cells in a six-month period,[32] Sam hanged himself from the pole of the so-called privacy screen surrounding his cell toilet, aged 17. An independent investigation was then undertaken, which led to the trainer incident being officially noted. The minutia of most children's prison experience, however, remains undocumented.

When Adam Rickwood was told he was to be moved from a children's home in which he felt settled to a prison in County Durham, his mother told me "he panicked and he came straight home to me" (p 61). He was arrested by the police for breaching his bail conditions and taken to Burnley police station. His mother was frantic with worry:

'Nobody, nobody whatsoever had the decency to contact me. I kept ringing Burnley police station because obviously I knew that's where Adam had been taken to, to find out what was going on, and then a police officer from Burnley police station he phoned me back. He said, "Carol, Adam's been taken to a place called Hassockfield secure training centre." I said, "I've never heard of it, where is it?" ... Now, I've got to give that police officer

100%, he got the details and he rang me back, and he told me it's in County Durham. I said, "Where's County Durham?" So he explained to me where County Durham was. I said, "It's over 150 miles away.'"

Adam's mother contacted Hassockfield to ask how her son was. She was told he was very frightened and subdued. The Prisons and Probation Ombudsman has cited the prison's recording that Adam was 'morose and uncommunicative' on admission, and 'did not want to phone his mother'.[33] This is strongly contested by his mother, who says Adam was prevented from ringing home. Carol recalls ringing the prison numerous times and finally threatening to contact the police if she was not allowed to speak with her son. Four days passed before she spoke with Adam:

> 'Later on that day, Adam rang me, and I said to him, "Adam why haven't you rung me? I've been worried sick, love." He said, "I wasn't allowed, I've been asking to ring you mum and they wouldn't let me." ... He said, "Mum, I've been asking them to ring you, to ring you up. Please come and see me." I said, "I will come and see you." I said, "They told me I need a visiting order." And Adam said, "I wrote to you. Have you not got my letter?" I said, "I've got nothing love."'

One two-hour visit or two one-hour visits a week were offered to Adam's mother, an arrangement criticised by the Ombudsman, who observed that adult remand prisoners are allowed daily visits. He recommended a strengthening of the rules governing visiting in the secure training centres,[34] which has not happened. Carol chose the two visits, on Wednesdays and Saturdays, despite being reliant on public transport and having limited income. It took four hours to reach the prison on the first visit; once Adam's family was familiar with the route, it was a six-hour round trip.

Yvonne Bailey never got to see her son in prison. She received her first visiting order just three days before Joseph hanged himself in prison, and was planning the journey from North Wales to

Shropshire when a police officer knocked at her door. Sandwiches were already packed for the next day's visit. She ended up visiting her child in a hospital resuscitation area where she was told not to touch him because his body had become evidence. Here she recounts her reaction:

'[T]hey had covered him over nicely and they'd put a Bible next to him, so actually there was a little glimmer of compassion. But then we were told you mustn't touch him. His body is now evidence.... [If it was now] I would just gather him up and kiss him.... But I never touched him again after, never, never.... Can you imagine that? Can you imagine your dead child? I don't want you to, but you know, a dead relative in front of you and you aren't allowed to touch him because they've become evidence?....A mother with my dead son in front of me and I couldn't touch him.'

The variety of schemes in young offender institutions aimed at supporting family relationships, many of them highly praised by inspectors, is testament to the care and concern of prison officers and managers. These include the 'email a prisoner' project and family fun days operating in many prisons and family town visits[35] and monthly reports to parents/carers[36] in individual institutions. However, none of these positive initiatives can compensate for children being held in captivity miles from home. Moreover, as we have seen, humane strategies to keep children in contact with their families sit alongside cruel practices that drive a wedge between child and parent. These include linking the duration of family contact with a child's behaviour[37] and restricting parental access to only a tiny part of the prison building. (During one of the tours of a secure training centre I undertook as part of the Carlile Inquiry, areas closed off to children were said to be 'sterile'). The YJB's rewards and sanctions guidance meekly proposes that children be allowed to see their families on the prison wing or unit in return for good behaviour.[38]

Five children have died in Hindley young offender institution in Wigan in the past 15 years. Seventeen-year-old Jake Hardy was the most recent child to hang himself, in January 2012, after being subject to chronic bullying (p 281). There has been no independent investigation to consider any similarities between the children's backgrounds and needs, and the care and treatment they received before they died. Nevertheless, given the inquests and reviews undertaken in response to each child's death, this prison has been subject to more than usual scrutiny. It would be reasonable to conclude it has been allowed to continue detaining children because the quality of its care reaches acceptable standards. Hindley's 2013 inspection report, however, points to a 'pretty bleak, prison-like environment'.[39] Inspectors complained that family visits for children on the lowest level of the incentive scheme were half as long as for other children (one hour instead of two). They described this as 'unnecessarily harsh and work[ing] against the promotion of family links', and reported that these same children were unlocked from their cells for just three or four hours a day at weekends.[40]

When Hindley was inspected in 2014, time out of cell for children placed at the bottom of the prison's behaviour management system had reduced further (p 102) and they were still receiving only one-hour visits.[41] Seven children who completed the inspectorate's November 2012 survey said they had been sexually abused in the prison – four by other prisoners, and three by prison staff.[42] A further 13 said they had been physically abused (hit, kicked or assaulted) – nine by other prisoners and four by staff.[43] Inspectors said they 'heard persistent, consistent and credible complaints about the abusive behaviour of a small number of officers', which, although being dealt with by the governor of the prison,[44] would inevitably cause great concern among parents. Jake Hardy's mother told me she knew nothing about prisons before her son's incarceration in Hindley and would now tell people that children are "treated like cattle". Several times throughout our interview she said she did not expect her son to be pampered, but she did think he would be looked after:

'When I gave my son, who was a child at the time, to the prison, you expect them to be looked after – not pampered, to be looked after. To keep them safe, warm and fed, that's all you expect.'

Family contact is a known protector. It helps children feel loved and wanted, and it gives them a vital outlet for sharing concerns. The High Court ruled in 2013 that 17-year-olds should have the same safeguards as other children arrested and detained in police stations, compatible with the United Nations Convention on the Rights of the Child and the European Convention on Human Rights. Lord Justice Moses explained:

> It is difficult to imagine a more striking case where the rights of both child and parent under Article 8 are engaged than when a child is in custody on suspicion of committing a serious offence and needs help from someone with whom he is familiar and whom he trusts, in redressing the imbalance between child and authority. The wish of a 17 year-old in trouble to seek the support of a parent and of a parent to be available to give that help must surely lie at the heart of family life which, quite apart from Article 8, the government seeks to maintain and encourage.[45]

Even with regular visiting, the powerlessness implicit in being an inmate of a closed institution means children can be too afraid of repercussions and either omit to disclose their worries, or beg their families not to 'rock the boat'. This was the experience of Mark Johnson, a former prison inmate who now runs a charity working to reform the criminal justice system and reduce offending. When he was detained in Portland young offender institution in Dorset, Mark was savagely mistreated in prison segregation (pp 216–17). Here he recounts a visit from his mother and sister:

> My mother visits with Bethany. I've barely seen them since I left home but since I'm in the Block, we're not allowed more than fifteen minutes together. Mum and Bethany have a one-thousand-mile round trip from the Lakes to Portland and they're given fifteen minutes with me.... Mum and Bethany stare at my cuts and bruises and black eye. They start to cry. I try to explain about

the Block…. My mum says, through her tears, that she's going to write to the Prime Minister, Mrs Thatcher. I ask her not to, as it would make things even worse for me.[46]

One in every 20 boys[47] surveyed by the prisons inspectorate in 2012/13 (n=942) and 6% of girls[48] (n=16) said staff in young offender institutions had victimised them for making a complaint. The situation was significantly better in secure training centres, where only 1% of children reported staff victimisation relating to complaints (n=148).[49] Direct contact is the only means by which parents can try to reassure themselves that their child is safe. Liz Hardy visited Jake as often as she could when he was remanded in Hindley young offender institution. She never got to see him again after he was sentenced, as Jake was dead within days. The last words she mouthed to him across the courtroom were, "Don't cry, duck" (parents are not allowed to visit their child in court cells – p 198).

Parents are now valued for the unique role they have in comforting sick children while doctors and nurses carry out frightening medical procedures, and for providing basic care during their child's hospital stay. Within prisons, even those held in 'gated observation cells' – with the barred doors we are used to seeing in films and documentaries – are kept apart from their parents. This is the penal equivalent of a child lying alone in a hospital intensive care unit, although, unlike a patient attached to a ventilator or other life-saving equipment, the prisoner is fully conscious. During research by the Howard League for Penal Reform into the experiences of boys in prison, participants reported that 'on the block you just have a mattress on a concrete slab', with 'no education, no canteen, no tv, no association' and 'you just get one hour a day outdoors on your own'.[50] During the Carlile Inquiry, investigators visited a young offender institution that was using an isolation cell in which to detain children in the segregation block. Children held in this bare cell had to sleep on a 'raised concrete plinth'. In a separate prison, the segregation block was housed in the healthcare unit and held up to five children during the week (less at weekends, presumably because of lower staffing). Children could stay in this 'bleak and dilapidated cell [with] an old and rusty metal bed frame' for up to 14 days. Children were said to be held for up to a quarter of an hour in 'a stone room with only a blanket on the floor with no washing facilities or toilet'.[51] Inspectors visiting a children's prison in May 2013 reported that inmates were being held in the same unit for segregation purposes and because of complex needs. One child had been there for 80 days. The inspection report observed: 'The unit was clean but shabby and lacked natural light. Many cells contained graffiti and dirty toilets.' Some children could spend as much as 92% of each 24-hour period locked alone in their cell.[52] One boy was held in a 'stark' and gated cell 'for several days ... and did not have his personal possessions with him'. There was no sense that this child was being provided with high-quality care:

> Supervision was undertaken by nurses, often agency staff, who did not carry keys and could not enter the cell immediately if the young person was attempting suicide or self-harm. Nurses had limited knowledge of the boys they were observing and we saw minimal engagement.[53]

Inspectors praised the 'patiently and kindly' approach of officers on this unit,[54] although this is clearly no substitute for children being looked after in humane conditions by trained staff and with parents close at hand.

The families of especially vulnerable children must go through hell imagining what is happening to them in prison. The Prison Reform Trust found prisoners with learning disabilities or difficulties were more than three times as likely to have spent time in segregation.[55]

Only parents whose children have died in prison get to see where their child was sleeping. The mother of Philip Griffin, who hanged himself in Wetherby young offender institution in 2000, visited her child's cell the day after his funeral. The poster of a silver Ferrari was still on the noticeboard; her son had hoped one day to own a sports car.[56] Kirk Edwards' parents said they only discovered their son left a suicide note after they visited the prison to collect his clothes the week after he died (the prison had said none existed).[57]

That children arrive at the prison gates without a parent, or a social services carer, is a telling symbol of the institutional cruelty reserved for this group of children. Nobody expects teenagers to attend hospitals for major surgery on their own, or to have a brace fitted by an orthodontist without moral support. Few undergraduates travel to their first university digs without a mother or father (or both) by their side. Yet we admit thousands of children to prison every year in states of acute detachment.

Frances Crook, the chief executive of Howard League for Penal Reform, told me she would "be camping outside" if her daughter was incarcerated and said it is "ridiculous" that parents are cut off from their children's care in prison:

> 'If a child goes into hospital, the parents are going to be there for them, they're going to be part of that. They may not be there every night if it's a long stay – you know, cancer treatment or something – but they're part of the whole system.'

Hospitals have not always been so child-centred. Only about a quarter allowed daily visiting by parents 60 years ago[58] and thousands of disabled children were, at that time, permanently placed in long-stay hospitals, often in remote geographical settings, with very limited parental contact. Two years after the NHS was born, a government minister issued an edict that all hospitals must make arrangements for parents to visit their children. This had little effect, so a committee chaired by Sir Harry Platt was established in 1956 to examine the welfare of children in hospital. The Platt Report was published three years later and opened with commentary on changing attitudes towards children:

> During the past 50 years or so profound changes have taken place in the lives of children, at home and at school. The child of today is better housed, better clothed and better nourished than at any time in our history. His individuality is recognised and appreciated both at home and in school and there is a growing readiness to understand and care for his emotional needs.[59]

Children should have unrestricted visits from parents, the report recommended. The needs of adolescents were considered in addition to infants and young children, and the message was clear that restricted parental contact harmed children:

> When a child is in hospital he is in danger of losing contact with the outside world, which has been up to that time the background of his development. If he is not kept in touch with the life that is familiar to him, he will suffer emotionally and mentally and his normal development will be retarded. It is vital that while he is in hospital he should be visited frequently so that he does not feel that hospital life is divorced from everything that he knows.[60]

A pioneering study of children in eight long-stay hospitals in 1975 found that, of 185 children, 18% had no family contact at all and a further 22% were visited very infrequently.[61] There were an estimated 4,500 children in mental handicap hospitals around that time,[62] the majority of whom would spend their whole childhood in these large, impersonal institutions. The 1980s and 1990s saw most of these establishments closed down in favour of 'care in the community', and local authorities now have a myriad of duties to support the upbringing of disabled children within their families. Irrespective of parental contact, since April 2011, any child spending three or more consecutive months in a care home or independent hospital must be visited by the local authority at least twice a year.[63]

In June 2011, the coalition government announced that all remanded children would be given looked after status,[64] a safeguard advocated by many children's and penal reform charities. The measure came into force 18 months later.[65] Every child in prison who is subject to a care order, or was looked after by a local authority on a voluntary basis prior to their detention, and now this group of remanded children, must be visited regularly by a social worker. Local authorities are under a statutory duty to promote and safeguard the welfare of each of these children. However, the majority of child prisoners have no official visitor checking their individual treatment and welfare. The prisons inspectorate is highly respected for its surveys and interviews with prisoners, but it has no mandate to intervene to protect individual children. Animal welfare inspectors, by contrast, have the legal authority to take immediate action to alleviate the suffering of an animal.[66]

Neither government nor the YJB has issued any guidance to prisons on facilitating contact between children and their families.[67] The prison service instruction on visiting, issued by the Ministry of Justice in 2011, only discusses the value of parental contact from the perspective of the 'offending parent', that is prisoners who are parents. There is nothing in this 56-page document stressing the importance to children of visits from their parents and other family members. Even the section on 'reasonable physical contact' omits to mention the particular needs of child prisoners:

> Reasonable physical contact between prisoner and visitors should be permitted, subject to security considerations and any public protection measures that may be in place. Prisoners should be allowed to embrace their visitor at least at the beginning and at the end of the visit, unless they are on closed visits or subject to other restrictions.[68]

Representatives from the Office of Children's Commissioner for England made several visits to prisons in 2010/11, leading to the end of the 'no hugging rule' in one prison.[69] A separate report published by the same organisation and the YJB in 2011 gives children's views on complaints, searches, helplines and segregation. Several children raised concerns about family contact. One girl held in a secure training centre explained:

> I think we should be able to hug our families when they come and visit us because it is bad enough being away from them for a year and a half. It's awful.[70]

When inspectors visited Werrington young offender institution in the autumn of 2013, they found 10% of children (12 in all) on closed visits (where a screen or other barrier separates prisoner and visitor, or officers strictly supervise non-contact). Inspectors observed: 'Records showed that closed visits did not always arise from inappropriate behaviour or incidents relating to visits',[71] which could indicate breaches of children's right to family contact under article 8 of the European Convention on Human Rights. The prohibition on children hugging their parents is not a new phenomenon in secure training centres; a review of the first centre highlighted this very issue. In an evaluation of Medway secure training centre, researchers selected 13-year-old Thomas as a case study. He had 'spent his childhood in various children's homes and with different foster carers'.[72] Like so many other incarcerated children, Thomas had suffered a family bereavement early in life (his father had died). His mother and other family members visited the centre fortnightly on account of the long distance. They told researchers they wished they could be alone, and regretted not being allowed to physically embrace Thomas:

> The family reported that they talked with Thomas about family, friends, wishes for the future, but they sometimes wished they could be alone so that they could be emotional with him. '[I wanted to] cuddle him but I couldn't.'[73]

Thomas would have been in his twenties by the time children in secure training centres were asked by the YJB to make recommendations about improving custody and one child suggested 'more time outside and [to] be able to hug your parents'.[74] Others requested more telephone contact and for the duration of visits to be longer.

Following inspections undertaken between March and November 2013, two of the four secure training centres were told to improve access to enhanced family visits. The scheme in Hassockfield secure training centre 'allows young people and their families to spend time together in a less formal setting than the visitors' room and engage in normal family activities such as eating a meal together, playing games or watching TV together'.[75] Only eight children had been granted an enhanced visit in the three months before the inspectors' visit.

An inspection six months later, in September 2013, illustrates both institutional inertia and the patience of some inspectors:

> The centre has amended its eligibility criteria for enhanced visits in line with a recommendation at the last inspection but this has not yet led to an increase on the numbers accessing these, although it is early days.[76]

The earlier 2013 inspection praised the fact that 'visitors who travel long distances may accumulate their weekly visits allowance to increase the standard visiting time of two hours'.[77] This implies that children are going without visits because of prohibitive travelling times, and that parents or family members, like Carol Pounder 10 years ago, may have to make onerous journeys for visits that allow only enough time to watch a film or enjoy a short walk with their child, were either of these activities to be permitted.

Inspectors reported in 2013 that Oakhill secure training centre in Milton Keynes allowed children who lived more than a 50-mile radius from the centre an extra 30 minutes to their one-hour visit entitlement each week.[78] This centre also allowed enhanced visits, whereby children and families could eat a meal together or 'play games as a family in relative privacy'; in the month before the inspection, only four children had received such visits. The highest number of enhanced visits noted by inspectors in any one month was 18, occurring in December 2012[79] (from a population of more than 60 children). By the next inspection, in February 2014, these enhanced visits had been replaced by 'engagement visits', said to be available to all children. Yet inspectors reported that the number 'remains similar to the previous number of enhanced visits'.[80] More positively, families were complimentary about how they were treated during visits and praised the centre's care of their children.[81] The later 2013 Hassockfield inspection report quotes a parent delighted to receive a pamphlet explaining how children are looked after and highlighting the flat in which parents can stay overnight.[82] Very positive feedback from parents about the importance given to contact appeared again in the centre's September 2014 inspection report, which also pointed to the 'hospitality suite' being 'well used' (though no data is provided).[83] In a similar vein, following an inspection in December 2013, inspectors highly praised Rainsbrook secure training centre for its work in maintaining family links. This includes children being able to have daily telephone contact, privately in their rooms.[84]

Malcolm Stevens was the Home Office civil servant given the task of drafting the regulations governing the secure training centres after the primary legislation was passed in 1994. There was widespread opprobrium among children's and penal reform charities in response to the Conservative government's plans to send 12-year-olds to penal institutions. With support from several prominent children's charities, the Howard League for Penal Reform threatened legal action. The Labour Party also opposed the centres, championing instead secure children's homes run by local authorities. One major advantage of local provision is that work can be done with families, argued Labour's shadow home secretary Alun Michael before he and more than 200 colleagues voted against the secure training centres in April 1994.[85]

Within a few years, Labour ministers presided over the opening of all four institutions. Civil servants apparently expected the incoming Labour government to terminate the procurement process started by the Conservatives but the new home secretary, Jack Straw, pressed ahead with implementing a policy he had voted against and thus reneging on an 'absolute promise' he had given the Howard League for Penal Reform that he would not proceed if none of the new child prisons had been built prior to him coming into office.[86] In a research interview, Stevens told me that the then home secretary Kenneth Clarke – who, rumour has it, came up with the idea of mini-borstals for young children while chatting to a neighbour in his local public house – was well aware that "you will find yourself in all sorts of shit if you turn these things into the jails everybody's calling them, and let the prison service have anything to do with them". So the prison service was not allowed to tender and Stevens "sat down with the children's home regulations and transposed all the principles of children's homes regulations into two things – the STC [secure training centre] rules and the STC contracts themselves, and all the bids that came in were judged from the point of view of ability to look after children from the principles of the Children Act".

The rules governing secure training centres do require governors to ensure that special attention is given to the child's relationship with his or her parents, although the fight not to turn these centres into jails may well have been lost much earlier. No expressions of interest, or subsequent bids, were received from local authorities or children's charities. Local authorities then, as now, had an ambivalent attitude towards locking up children, and the country's largest children's charities had declared publicly that they would have nothing to do with the centres. Of the 19 companies, organised into nine consortia, invited to bid to run the centres, only one ran a residential home for children and another a school, whereas six specialised in detention and correctional facilities and the others were mostly building firms.[87] In June 1999, Premier Prison Services was awarded the contract to run Hassockfield secure training centre amid concerns of abuse scandals in US child prisons run by its parent company, Wackenhut.[88] Less than six months after Hassockfield opened, the US Department of Justice completed its investigation into the Jena Juvenile Justice Centre in the state of Louisiana,[89] and subsequently took legal action against Wackenhut, its owners and operators, alleging 'excessive abuse and neglect' of children.[90] Soon after, CBS News reported 12 lawsuits from girls alleging sexual assault in a Wackenhut prison in the state of Texas.[91] These serious violations apparently did not prevent the multinational from profiting from the incarceration of UK children.

Around 30% of staff working directly with children in the first secure training centre had relevant professional experience, and the first Home Office official with statutory responsibility for monitoring the care and treatment of children in the institution had no prior experience of working with children in institutional settings.[92] By November 2013, two of the four YJB monitors had a social work qualification and all had previously worked with children in institutional settings.[93] That same month, between 2% and 4% of staff in the secure training centres were reported to be qualified social workers.[94]

More than one in 10 children held in young offender institutions are themselves parents.[95] Infants and young children need their parents like nobody else. No matter how well equipped they are, prison visitors' centres cannot begin to remedy the missing weeks, months and sometimes years of bonding and relationship building between parents and children. Then there is the profound emotional distress caused to both sets of children, particularly infants and their mothers, by successive separations. A review of women in the criminal justice system reported the effects on children of incarcerating mothers as 'so often nothing short of catastrophic',[96] and it is known that having a family member in prison as a child is a strong predictor of future imprisonment. The latest research shows almost a third of adults entering prison have childhood experience of a family member being imprisoned.[97]

During one of my visits to Rainsbrook secure training centre, as part of the Carlile Inquiry, I interviewed a girl who was tearful throughout our time together. She recounted some awful experiences within Rainsbrook, although the hardest for me to hear was that she had given birth six months previously and her baby was now in foster care. The plan was for mother and baby to be reunited on release. I sat looking at this girl, incredulous that our sophisticated welfare system was incapable of keeping together two minors who were, as the hands on a clock turn, being robbed of an utterly irreplaceable period in both of their lives. The following year, I heard that G4S had opened a three-bedroomed mother-and-baby unit in the centre, so girls and their babies could now be jointly incarcerated, and pregnant girls could be held in the final stages of pregnancy. The YJB's annual report for 2006/07 announces jovially:

> Look through any dictionary and you won't find a single definition of custody that mentions the detention of a baby. So what happens when a pregnant young woman ends up in a secure establishment? Until recently, mother-and-baby units existed only within adult prisons – an environment that we think is inappropriate. But now – with the opening of new, YJB-funded mother-and-baby units, that situation has changed.[98]

The unit at Rainsbrook cost £4.5 million[99] – another substantial sum poured into penal incarceration. By January 2008, the Office of Children's Commissioner for England reported that five girls had given birth in this prison unit since it opened over a year before, and another six had been held there. Home for these girls was, on average, 76 miles from the prison, being 'likely to have serious consequences as to the level of support the young mothers receive from their friends and family'.[100] An international study of mother and baby units, published in 2012, reveals that babies are only allowed in Rainsbrook if their mothers meet certain criteria, including that they pose no risk to any other child and they are highly likely to look after their own child on release. This instantly cancels out any preconception that these young mothers must be a danger to themselves or others. The report notes:

> The facility goes to considerable effort to ensure that babies experience all the normal noises they would expect to hear if they were in the community, which includes visits to animal parks, rides on buses, cafés, supermarkets, swimming etc.[101]

Mothers and babies do not share these pleasurable experiences: staff take babies off the premises while girls attend the prison school. Each secure training centre place costs the taxpayer an average of £178,000 per year – easily enough to fund intensive social work support for mother and baby, childcare and remedial education and mental health provision where this is required. Are we really so hardwired to child punishment that we prefer to support the prison expansionism of multinational companies rather than invest in local interventions that would allow young mothers and their babies to, among other things, enjoy time together in the fresh air? As secure colleges legislation progressed through the Commons, the Labour amendment aimed at halting their creation fell by 99 votes and the minister responsible, Jeremy Wright, struggled to answer many of MPs' concerns. He did, however, find time to say this about the incarceration of girls with babies:

> The one question I can answer immediately relates to care for young mothers. There is currently a mother and

baby unit at the Rainsbrook secure training centre. If that
is not to continue, we must make provision elsewhere.[102]

When the Bill reached the Lords, an amendment banning the
placement of girls (and boys under the age of 15) in secure colleges
was carried by a single vote.[103] Its return to the Commons will reveal
just how desperate ministers are to incarcerate teenage mothers and
their babies in these newest of child prisons.

EIGHT

'Every night I'm starving'

We all use food to demonstrate how we feel about others, whether this is splashing out on celebratory meals, preparing family feasts or sneaking treats into children's lunchboxes. Camila Batmanghelidjh, founder and director of the vulnerable children's support charity Kids Company, writes about the importance of giving 'fantastic food' to children: 'The offer of a free meal, with no strings attached, is often the first indication the agency cares.'[1] Batmanghelidjh has many stand-out virtues, but her understanding of the power of food is not unique. While most of us can reminisce about lumpy mash and runny custard, or, indeed, runny mash and lumpy custard, there are some foodstuffs only some of us will encounter. Fortnum & Mason hampers, food-bank offerings and prison meals are minority culinary experiences. As well as serving the physiological functions of keeping minds and bodies working, each emits signals about social worth. Unlike the lavish hamper and the charity hand-out, which, in different ways, communicate that their recipients matter, the prison meal has few affirmative qualities. It lacks generosity in style and substance, and maintains children in a state of hunger and neglect. There is no sense that children in receipt of prison meals are held in high esteem. Recent research for the Youth Justice Board (YJB) found that the governors of all nine young offender institutions visited thought 'the food provision budget was inadequate to meet the nutritional requirements of their young people'.[2] Some children bought their own salt, condiments and drinks from the prison shop and 'items such as instant noodles and porridge to provide sustenance in the period between the evening meal and breakfast'.[3]

The immense parental satisfaction derived from seeing your child wolf down a favourite meal is an early casualty of imprisonment. Young prisoners complain repeatedly of feeling hungry and mothers and fathers are powerless to do anything about it. In our research interview, Yvonne Bailey, the mother of Joseph Scholes, told me about a vigil she and other bereaved parents held outside Lancaster Farms young offender institution. One of the topics of conversation incensing these mothers was the failure of the prison to provide children with warm food at weekends. The new 'core day' in young offender institutions prescribes that children must be served a cold lunch inside their cell, following the pattern of 'breakfast out, lunch in, evening meal out'.[4] Children always ate their lunch locked inside their cell in four of the nine prisons surveyed, and only two gave children the choice of a hot or cold meal.[5] When healthcare teams in these institutions were asked about the new core day, 'they felt it was more about reducing staff numbers and less about young people's welfare and the benefits that would be gained by eating in a more social environment'.[6]

Parents of children in one prison were asked by researchers to make suggestions for improving mealtimes. The requests, coming soon after the then secretary of state for children, schools and families, Ed Balls, announced the government's goal to make the UK the best place in the world for children to grow up,[7] were pragmatic and completely achievable in a wealthy nation like ours. These parents asked for their boys to be given:

> [P]roper seats to sit on, to eat at tables rather than in their cells, to have longer time to eat their food, and for less delay in getting the food they had requested on the menu sheets.[8]

It is surely no coincidence that Batmanghelidjh, a psychotherapist, places enormous emphasis on feeding children well (Christmas lunch for thousands of children costs her charity £100,000) – her life's work has been to make children feel whole. Clare Hobbs from Wessex Dance Academy, a partnership between Hampshire County Council and Dance United, told a parliamentary inquiry on youth justice of the impact of their 12-week dance programme, where breakfast and 'wonderful lunches' are served:

> We nourish all of them over time; we nourish their physicality, because their bodies are changing. We nourish them inside because we are feeding them proper food.[9]

Lack of food causes children to feel empty, it hurts physically and it affects their mood and behaviour. It would be a cruel set of parents that had the knowledge and resources to feed children, but kept them hungry. Indeed, failure to provide children with adequate food can constitute neglect and lead to prosecution under child cruelty legislation. The desire to feed children is primeval. How many of us remember the stories of four-year-old Daniel Pelka, a victim of appalling abuse by his mother and her partner, rummaging in school bins for food, compared with the broken arm he suffered the year before?[10] Social workers know deprived children entering care often put on weight. Both of the boys convicted of the murder of James Bulger increased in weight after their arrest, Jon Venables over two stone[11] – a result no doubt of limited opportunity for ordinary childhood exercise but also the new experience of regular nourishment. It was shocking to hear from his mother that Jake Hardy lost two stone in weight in just 46 days at Hindley young offender institution between December 2011 and January 2012.

The Howard League for Penal Reform published a report in 2010 of discussions with 55 teenagers with experience of imprisonment. On food, the charity reported that child prisoners were 'frequently hungry':

> Many young people told us that they were served the same food each day, particularly rice; bread was stale; food was cold; there were not enough multicultural options; and they did not get enough hot meals.[12]

Another consultation the following year found that children had a 'predominantly negative' view of food in custody; that some children remained hungry after meals; and others were never actually full up.[13] This was a flashback to discussions I had with a group of child prisoners over a decade ago, in preparation for a report to the UN. One imprisoned boy told me, 'Every night I'm starving,' and others said they woke up hungry 'all the time'.[14] The prisons inspectorate told a parliamentary committee in 2012 that children had told inspectors the quality of food in young offenders institutions had deteriorated from the previous year and many 'often felt hungry'.[15] In a separate review, the organisation reported the case of a looked-after child who was using the money he earned from attending educational sessions to buy extra food. This meant he had no money left to make phone calls.[16] Frances Crook, the chief executive of the Howard League for Penal Reform, has reported the case of a hungry boy in prison who was put in solitary confinement for being found with 10 slices of white bread. The organisation's legal team successfully had the boy's adjudication (formal punishment) quashed, although Crook notes that 'it was too late to prevent the time in solitary'.[17]

Only one of 13 English prison surveys published between February 2013 and October 2014 shows a higher proportion of children rating food more favourably than unfavourably: 35% of children in Serco-run Ashfield young offender institution, in Bristol, said prison food was good or very good, compared with 32% who said it was bad or very bad.[18] In all other young offender institutions, negative assessments far outweighed positive ones. The worst division was in the girls' unit in Eastwood Park women's prison where none of the inmates reported the food being good and 84% said it was bad or very bad.[19] In Cookham Wood young offender institution in Kent, in May 2013, fewer than one in 10 children reported the food being good and 70% said it was bad or very bad.[20] Inspectors found some food to be 'tepid and unappetising' and agreed with children that having a cold lunch issued at their cell doors was 'disrespectful'.[21] About 20 children were forced to eat all of their meals in their cells at the time of the inspection, presumably as a form of punishment. As if this were not sanction enough, these children 'were served last and the quality of hot food had deteriorated by the time they received it'.[22] By the time of the next inspection, 18 boys were eating all of their meals alone in their cells. Inspectors noted they were being served first at dinner, 'an improvement since the previous year'.[23]

The latest inspection of Werrington young offender institution near Stoke-on-Trent found 'a considerable number' of children subject to loss of privileges or on the lowest level of the rewards and sanction scheme being served their meals at their cell doors.[24]

A 2013 inspection revealed the existence of a young people's council in Cookham Wood young offender institution. Children often raised food as an issue of concern, but no catering staff ever attended the meetings. Inspectors said a child had attended the catering meeting 'but records indicated that his contribution was minimal and no action had been taken on points he had raised'.[25] The Independent Monitoring Board had noted children's frequent complaints about the quantity and quality of food in the prison's segregation unit the year before these criticisms from the prisons inspectorate. Although board members were satisfied themselves with the meals given to children, they conceded that portions could 'appear less when covered and compressed for transport from the kitchen'.[26]

The latest inspection of Feltham young offender institution found that the evening meal was served at 4.45 pm, and hot meals were provided just once daily during the week and twice daily at weekends. Children ate out of their cells in only one of the prison's eight units.[27]

Two of three secure training centre inspection reports published between July 2013 and January 2014 show significantly higher levels of satisfaction with food than in young offender institutions: half the children in Hassockfield secure training centre[28] and 36% of children in Rainsbrook secure training centre rated the food as good or very good.[29] Only 16% of children in Medway secure training centre were as complimentary.[30]

Children's homes, including those providing secure care, are legally required to serve food in adequate quantities and at appropriate intervals. Food must be properly prepared, wholesome and nutritious; suitable for children's needs; sufficiently varied; and meet children's reasonable preferences. There must also be access to fresh drinking water at all times. Homes are under a duty to meet the special dietary needs of children arising from their health, religious persuasion, racial origin or cultural background.[31] Secure training centres are bound by similar legislation specifying that, so far as practicable, the governor must ensure that meals are provided three times a day at regular intervals and there is a choice for each course at each main meal. One of the day's main meals must be hot.[32] In a similar vein, the law states that food provided in young offender institutions must be wholesome, nutritious, well prepared and served, reasonably varied and sufficient in quantity.[33]

These shiny laws did not blind torture experts visiting UK prisons at the end of 2008. Representatives of the European anti-torture committee heard a variety of food-related complaints from children detained in Huntercombe young offender institution in Oxfordshire and recommended reviews of the provision of breakfast packs and baguette lunches. They also asked that children be allowed to eat their meals communally rather than alone in their cells.[34] At the time of the visit, there were 309 children incarcerated in this prison. The government's response, published a year later, said prison governors had enjoyed control over their catering budgets since 1994 and claimed efficiency savings had not affected the quality of prisoner meals. Displaying classic civil service emotional detachment, the official response continued:

> Some governors choose to give food a higher priority than other areas of spend, while others have more pressing concerns and choose to spend less.[35]

The UK's own prison inspectors went into the young offender institution the week after the delegation left, and received 'numerous complaints' from children that they were still hungry after eating their breakfast packs. Inspectors repeated the recommendation they had made in 2006 that children 'should be given a substantial breakfast that is adequate to meet the needs of growing adolescents'.[36] At that previous inspection, more than two years before the European Committee for the Prevention of Torture and Inhuman or Degrading Treatment or Punishment found hungry children in Huntercombe, breakfast packs were found to be 'inadequate'.[37] Research for the Department of Health referred the following year to the 'counterproductive practice' of distributing breakfast bags the afternoon before children are meant to eat them.[38]

In 2010/11, representatives of the Office of Children's Commissioner for England visited children in young offender institutions, secure training centres and secure children's homes. After visits to five young offender institutions, the office reported that in some of these prisons children:

> ... have their last meal of the day between 5.00 pm and 6.00 pm; they are then given a breakfast pack when they are locked up for the night at 7.30 pm.... Lunch in some units was only a baguette with a bag of crisps and a drink. Complaints about being hungry were common as were complaints about the quality of the food. In some places only one hot meal per day was provided.[39]

The delivery of breakfast packs before evening lockup is an inevitable byproduct of staffing shortages, although the practice may be disappearing; only one of nine prisons visited by researchers between November 2012 and January 2013 handed out bagged breakfast packs the previous evening.[40] It does not take a childcare expert to work out that hungry and bored children, confined in cells from early evening, will soon eat their way through the contents of a small food bag intended for the next day's breakfast. After the prison evening meal – which can be officially served as early as 5pm – there is nothing else before morning besides a small supper (a biscuit or two, packet of crisps or a small cake).

Moreover, the centerpiece of the next meal, as the European anti-torture watchdog and the Office of Children's Commissioner discovered, could be a single baguette. Research for the YJB found:

> A typical cold bagged lunch included a sandwich, baguette or bap (filled with cold meat or meat product, cheese, peanut butter), and other items such as a small packet of crisps, a pot of yoghurt, a chocolate biscuit bar, a piece of fruit, a carton of fruit juice (not all of these items were provided every day).[41]

The pioneering work of American sociologist Gresham M. Sykes, who first looked at the harmful effects on prisoners of incarceration, comes to mind:

> The prisoner is supposed to live in poverty as a matter of public policy ... the physical conditions of life in prison would seem to reflect a sort of half-hearted or indecisive punishment, the imposition of deprivation by indifference or forgetfulness rather than by intent.[42]

Concern about breakfast packs was conspicuously not dealt with in the government's response to the European anti-torture committee in December 2009. However, two years later, officials sought to justify breakfast packs to the Office of Children's Commissioner for England. In some prisons, it was said:

> ... breakfast packs are routinely provided in the evening to young people who are scheduled to attend court the following day. The timing of court appearances means that it is often not possible to serve breakfast to those young people at the same time as the rest of the establishment. Breakfast packs are therefore useful for providing an early meal to young people who may have lengthy journeys to court.[43]

The deputy children's commissioner published a letter to ministers announcing that the office was 'truly pleased' with the government's response to its report (which dealt with many aspects of children's treatment in custody), and looked forward to 'the cessation of the use of breakfast packs on a routine basis'.[44] This seemed to imply that handing out breakfast packs half a day too early is an acceptable practice, as long as it is not a regular occurrence. Would it be legitimate for children's homes staff to dole out breakfast packs to children attending court or a hospital appointment the next morning? Or acceptable for hospitals to deliver breakfast packs with the supper trolley?

Could it be that those who oversee prisons are oblivious to the pains of childhood hunger? The prison service may point to the larger food budget of child prisons compared with adult institutions, but this is a meaningless comparison. The marker of meals, snacks and drinks for children in captivity should be children's homes, hospitals and the best boarding schools. It is illuminating that no child-specific catering guidance has ever been issued to young offender institutions, and that five of nine child establishments do not have their own kitchen; meals are prepared and transported from the adult part of these prisons.[45]

I remember attending a meeting at the YJB when I was managing the Children's Rights Alliance for England and senior officials reported back on a consultation undertaken by two children's charities. Unsurprising to anyone who has ever read an inspection report or spent time with children in captivity, food was a main concern. One of the officials told us action was being taken to remedy the situation. He said this was a positive example of the organisation's commitment to children's participation (the catch-all term used in charity and government circles to denote children being listened to). I found it incredible that being receptive to children's pleas to be properly fed was seen as some kind of progressive commitment to children's rights, and grumpily communicated this to the bemused line of officials. Frances Crook of the Howard League for Penal Reform also expressed exasperation and said she had for many years been trying to interest civil servants in feeding children adequately in prison. Even this belated announcement turned out to be over-optimistic. When the board's plans for the secure estate were published in April 2012, there was no evidence of anything having changed.

Three separate reviews were promised: a review by the YJB of its service-level agreement with the National Offender Management Service, particularly looking at catering arrangements; a review of 'the whole-day experience' of children in prison, including an assessment of breakfast packs; and a review with a food charity 'to explore potential initiatives to enhance food provision'. The document thanks the 678 children 'who so openly shared their views',[46] but fails to explain why change could not happen immediately. Comparing the service-level agreements between the two organisations for the past two years, it is reassuring to see that the latest version, agreed in June 2013, includes the following 'outcome indicator': young offender institutions 'provide a healthy, balanced diet for young people. The types, amounts and variety of food provided meet the dietary, cultural and religious needs of young people.'[47] Less comforting is the lack of any detail in the written agreement about how implementation will be recorded and verified – none of the 50 monitoring specifications relates to food.[48]

The YJB's plan for the secure estate until 2015 includes a set of principles, the first of which states that establishments holding children 'should be distinct from adult provision'.[49] Yet the catering norms of young offender institutions are identical to those in adult prisons – be this prisoners eating in locked cells, the use of plastic utensils or the ban on visitors bringing in any kind of food. When I used to visit a former child in care in prison, the only items I could offer this hungry adolescent were chocolate bars and fizzy drinks from a vending machine. Even the tray on which food is served is the same in both types of institution. I once observed a child who appeared to have cerebral palsy struggling to balance food on his tray as he walked back to his cell. Had he been able to dine at a table close to the serving hatch, he may have not lost so much of his meal.

One element of the notorious pindown regime in Staffordshire children's homes (p 14) in the 1980s was forcing children to eat in their rooms. The log entry for the youngest child to be placed into pindown, nine-year-old Simon, reads as follows:

> ... a totally negative approach to be adopted ... plenty of stern looks and tellings off to make him glad to go home.... He will be based in the back pindown room and will eat in there....[50]

Statutory rules for children's homes subsequently prohibited the deprivation of food or drink as a disciplinary measure, and government guidance explained:

> It is well established that the enjoyment of eating and drinking is fundamental to a child's healthy physical and

emotional development. Meal times are an important social occasion in the life of a child and it would be quite inappropriate for a child to be refused meals. Deprivation of food and drink should be taken to include the denial of access to the amounts and range of foods and drink normally available to children in the home....[51]

A case was heard in the High Court in December 2012 concerning the segregation of seven boys in Ashfield young offender institution in Bristol. They had been part of a disturbance on a sports pitch, sparked off after the prison had removed toilet seats from a residential living block. The judge ruled that five of the boys had been unlawfully held in 'a shadow segregation scheme' for three days, only being allowed out for half an hour in each 24-hour period. The boys were said to have given 'persuasive' accounts of their time in solitude, which included reports of having to eat alone in their cells:

> ... they were alone and confined to their cell save for showers, phone calls and exercise. When released from his cell each claimant would be alone in performing any of the identified activities. There was no association or mingling, meals were eaten alone in the cell.[52]

Less than a month after the court hearing, the government announced that Ashfield was now a 'surplus young offenders institution' that would be converted to an adult prison.[53] Figures released to parliament soon after Mrs Justice Nicola Davies said the five boys had been unlawfully segregated showed that there had been 1,651 uses of segregation in this one prison between 2006 and 2012. Children had been kept in these extremely isolated conditions for longer than 28 days on 111 occasions across this same time period[54] – presumably eating all of their meals alone in their locked cell.

If children are eating their meals in cells with unscreened toilets, they are 'effectively eating in their toilets', observed the Office of Children's Commissioner for England in 2011.[55] Inadequate toilet screening and children eating next to uncovered toilets was criticised in three of four young offender institution inspection reports published in 2014.[56]

Goffman's classic 1950s study of total institutions concluded that they trade in 'abasements, degradations, humiliations and profanations of self'.[57] Such behaviour has not necessarily died out, as the following self-congratulatory reference to meeting the basic needs of incarcerated boys (described as 'young men') shows. Most professionals outside the prison service would surely not need to attend a conference to be apprised of a fundamental human right such as access to drinking water. It is difficult to imagine a health visitor or social worker heaping praise on a parent sharing a similar revelation:

> A Good Practice conference had highlighted the need and the advantages of access to drinking water in the day, not just in hot weather. At Wetherby YOI [young offender institution], young men [15- to 17-year-olds] did not have access to water unless they happened to be near a tap or fountain and had no means of carrying water with them within the prison. The Leeds PCT [primary care trust] public health department was persuaded to fund the provision of sport drinking bottles bearing the PCT and YOI logos. Each new entrant is given one so that they can fill it up during the day and take it with them as they work in the garden, visit the gym and or undertake building work and other active training exercises.[58]

In one of my research interviews, a former manager in a secure children's unit, Pam Hibbert, told me she could not think of any large children's charity currently raising public awareness of the needs of children in custody. After mentioning the successful Full Stop Campaign, run by the National Society for the Prevention of Cruelty to Children and featuring images of wide-eyed young children suffering cruelty and neglect, she observed:

'Nobody does a 15-year-old behind the cell bars saying, Henry will go to bed hungry tonight and wake up hungry in the morning. Nobody does that. It's too tough.'

NINE

Children were 'given bags to urinate in'

Probably the most iconographic footage associated with children in custody vehicles dates from 1993, when Robert Thompson and Jon Venables made their first appearance at South Sefton magistrates' court after being charged with the murder of two-year-old James Bulger. The blue police vans these two young children were thought to be travelling in were attacked with eggs, bottles, stones and fists, and some in the baying crowd screamed for their necks to be snapped. The author Blake Morrison reflects on news clippings from that day over 20 years ago:

> The men in the photograph had come wanting to kill the kids who'd killed the kid, because there's nothing worse than killing a kid.[1]

It turned out that the primary school boys had been led away from the court in cars, and the vans had been decoys, such was the level of public vitriol. No child transported to or from an English court has since attracted so much interest, although there is plenty to be troubled about.

A few years after the police vans were attacked in Merseyside, the then chief inspector of prisons, David Ramsbotham, undertook a review of the treatment of young prisoners. He reported that the prison transportation of children had been recently contracted out to companies with vehicles containing inbuilt cells, and that this had been done 'in the interests of improved security'.[2] He goes on to describe the conditions in these vehicles:

Each cubicle in these vehicles is about the size of a telephone box and contains nothing more than a bench seat and a small window. My team found many examples of children and young adults locked in these cramped conditions for hours while awaiting delivery to the establishment to which they are being sent.[3]

During 2009/10, researchers from the Howard League for Penal Reform discussed prison life with 55 teenagers. The journey from court to prison was particularly grueling. The charity's subsequent report explains why vehicles transporting prisoners are known as 'sweatboxes':

[This nickname] reflects the conditions: they are in a cramped space, caged by wire; with heating always at extremes; they're dirty; and they 'stink'.[4]

One boy described feeling as if prisoners in security vans were treated 'like animals'.[5] This child probably did not realise it is an offence to transport animals in a way that causes, or is likely to cause, injury or unnecessary suffering.[6] European law requires that member states provide this protection for vertebrate animals transported as part of an economic activity. There is no specific European or domestic law preventing the suffering of children (and adults) in prison vehicles.

However, UK legislation requires officers escorting prisoners to attend to their wellbeing[7] and, in the specific case of child prisoners travelling to and from secure training centres, they must at all times take into account the child's physical and mental health. The child's religion must also be catered for and officers must provide 'adequate supplies of food, of a suitable, wholesome and nutritious nature, and drink'.[8] Furthermore, the European Convention on Human Rights gives protection from inhuman and degrading treatment and punishment, and guards escorting child prisoners are presumably not exempt from domestic child cruelty legislation.

The pains of imprisonment start the moment a custodial sentence is passed and the child becomes the property of the state. The transfer of the boy or girl from the courtroom to a cell below ground, out of sight of parents and the public at large, is the first of many procedures designed by our ancestors to inflict shock and fear. In July 2013, a regional newspaper reported cells being flood-damaged in Newton Aycliffe magistrates' court. Defendants sentenced to custody were asked to wait in the reception area for the arrival of prison escort staff. The previous week, a 17-year-old boy was made to sit in the court foyer for over an hour before he was collected and transported to prison. A magistrate complained that the use of the foyer was undermining the spectacle of punishment:

> When you send someone to custody obviously it is partly to rehabilitate them but it is also a punishment and part of that punishment is to be handcuffed in front of the magistrates and led away to the cells. They shouldn't be sat in the foyer with their friends and family having a cup of tea.[9]

Once those fateful sentencing words are pronounced in court, children and adults alike are handcuffed and led downstairs, searched and locked in a cell to await transportation to an institution likely to be tens or sometimes hundreds of miles from home. The waiting period may last several hours, passed sitting on a wooden or plastic bench, with little for children to do except eavesdrop or read magazines if any are available – and if the child can understand them. One assessment of child prisoners found that 62% had a literacy level below the age of 11.[10] Only rarely is the child allowed to see or speak to family members. When Adam Rickwood was remanded into local authority custody at the age of 14, his mother was not able to see her son after he was taken downstairs to the court cells. She had to go home without saying goodbye and her son was transferred from court to the local police station to await an establishment being found. A youth offending team worker turned up at the family home to collect a bag of clothes – a task Adam's mother was more than capable of undertaking.

In a 2013 report on custody facilitites in Cleveland, Durham and Northumbria, inspectors found that many custody suites prohibited family visits even when recommended by judges.[11] Tim Bateman is an academic specialising in youth justice who has many years' experience of working with children charged and convicted of offences. In a research interview for this book, he told me:

> '... kids just disappear out of the court and even if they're sitting with their family, their parents effectively will just be pulled apart, and I'm sure you've seen it: you've been in court where incredibly distressed parents and children are forcibly pulled apart, and normally they just don't know where they're going, they don't know how long it's going to be, they've got no idea what it's going to be like for them.'

There cannot be many professionals who have worked in criminal courts who have not seen the faces and legs of children collapse on being given a custodial sentence; who, in the lead up to sentencing, have not witnessed and felt the sickening dread of incarceration. Former inmate Erwin James said he 'felt a ball of fire ignite in my stomach' as he was led back to the court to hear the jury's verdict that was sure to send him down.[12] Although some children do later report that the reality was not as awful as they had imagined, the terror of imprisonment is entirely rational: it is meant to hurt. The 'custody-free zones' of the 1980s – local authorities like Northamptonshire that excelled in protecting children from incarceration – survive as historical evidence that imprisonment was once officially recognised as causing great harm to children. Bateman has written about the 'vociferous practitioner lobby' campaigning against child custody during this period.[13] Moreover, parliament passed a law in 1982 prohibiting courts from sending any person under the age of 21 to custody unless the court believed he or she would not respond to non-custodial penalties; a custodial sentence was necessary to protect the public; or custody was the only justifiable sentence given the seriousness of the offence.[14] The late Baroness Lucy Faithfull, a former social worker and tireless campaigner for children, proposed the restrictions, hoping they would lead to 'a shift from custodial to non-custodial care'.[15] The first part of the triad was repealed in 1991 and it was, in any case, criticised widely because it carried the risk of repeat offending while serving a community penalty being seen as *a priori* evidence that the child 'needed' to be locked up. Faithfull's amendment was proven to be successful overall: a former Home Office minister reported that it was 'effective, with the support of many agencies in the voluntary and other sectors, in reducing the custodial detention of young people'.[16]

Today, the law on sending people to custody remains the same for all age groups and includes only the third element contained in the 1982 Act – that the seriousness of the offence or offences warrants incarceration.[17] In addition, there are a number of crimes where a custodial sentence is mandatory, irrespective of the age and circumstances of the defendant. The current sentencing framework disastrously forces the focus away from what could be achieved with children in their families and communities and is mechanically geared to punishing individual acts rather than understanding and dealing intelligently with the whole child. A new duty on the court to explain why a sentence consisting of (or including) a youth rehabilitation order with intensive supervision and surveillance or fostering cannot be justified[18] is a measly concession to the UK's obligation under international law to make custody a last resort. Furthermore, it will not make any dent on the harmful procedures the child is forced to endure once a custodial sentence has been passed.

I asked Bateman why, given the high level of distress displayed, the practice of separating child and parent in the courtroom continues. It is obviously harmful, and not a procedure that would happen in any other children's setting. He replied as follows:

'I think it's about a particular population of kids who don't matter so much. I think there is, too, the fact that, because it's within a criminal justice process, there is an element of punishment attached to it, that's part of the purpose … if the child goes into hospital, clearly the purpose isn't to punish them. If they go into a children's home, even though they may experience it as being punitive, the intention isn't to punish them. If they go into a secure children's home through the welfare route, the intention isn't to punish them, again, even if that's the way that it may be experienced.... So there is a difference in terms of hospitals and prisons because the latter is intended to be a punitive environment.'

There was something else Bateman said that I found more troubling: that severe separation in the managed environment of the courtroom may actually make the emotional task of incarcerating children bearable:

> 'Locking children up is a hard process, and if you think about it too much, it becomes increasingly distressing … if you had loads of wailing parents down there, as well, it would make the job much messier, much harder … and it might make it even worse for the kids, you know, because they've been separated in the court, then they've been separated in the cells. How far do you take it, how many times do you separate them?'

Not all children appear in court with parents alongside them. The Prison Reform Trust found in some areas up to half of children living at home turned up at court without a parent, even though the law requires such attendance for under-16s.[19] Physical presence is no guarantee of support, however. Breakthrough moments of warmth and affection seldom occur in courts. Parents and family members with long histories of neglecting children often fail them again within the walls of these austere buildings. In a review on violence and trauma in young people's lives, one young prisoner, who had committed murder at the age of 14, recounts:

> They ask you to stand before they give the verdict. When they said 'guilty' my knees went weak and then I had to hold myself up but no-one really said anything. And [one of my relatives in the dock] didn't say anything to me when I walked past him, he didn't say anything when I was convicted, and neither did anyone who was up in the gallery, none of my family who were up in the gallery. It was kind of like, 'Oh well'.[20]

It is understandable that even a child with experience of chronic emotional deprivation would hope for familial comfort during these terrifying moments. This optimism is not naïve or foolish; the survival of the human species depends on parents looking after their young. Children's fiction never leaves young characters alone on the final page. Someone or something always emerges to love, befriend and understand them.

It is too simplistic to write off as callous family members who stare blankly at their young relatives. Unlike school theatre productions and musical concerts, parents are not welcomed at the courtroom door, shown to their seat and offered refreshments. Nobody in the building is celebrating their children, or encouraging expressions of love and pride. Suffering and solemnity is intrinsic to the civilian experience of criminal courts, so frozen exchanges, while crushing for children, are par for the course.

That the harm caused to children by imprisonment is not accidental was stressed by many of the people I interviewed, including Professor Barry Goldson, who has studied child prisons and written extensively about the deaths and despair of incarcerated children. He warned: "We must not lose sight of the fact that children aren't put in prisons as a courtesy to them; they're put in prison as a punishment; I mean it's meant to be unpleasant."

The prisons inspectorate began inspecting court custodial facilities in August 2012 and its first six inspections show systemic child neglect. Court custody staff in Norfolk and Suffolk told inspectors children could wait in cells for 'several hours' while the Youth Justice Board (YJB) allocated a place;[21] in Lancashire and Cumbria the process could take up to five hours.[22] None of the custody facilities inspected in that area had any children's reading material, and no other time-filling activities were noted. Children being sent to Wetherby young offender institution from Peterborough magistrates' court – a three-hour drive – often did not start their journey until early evening, 'sometimes as late as 8pm'.[23] Inspectors found that all courts in the Cambridgeshire and Essex region gave prisoners a hot microwave meal if they were still in the cells at 4 pm 'as it was likely that they would miss their evening meal in prison'.[24]

The inspection of court custody facilities in Merseyside and Cheshire found three instances of children having to wait in cells for several hours, from 8.30 in the morning. As in Lancashire and Cumbria, nothing was available to help these children pass the time:

> At Liverpool Youth Court, we were told that there had previously been a budget for magazines and comics, which had been effective in helping to keep young people occupied. Since the budget had been withdrawn, staff had resorted to bringing in their own magazines for detainees, but they were mainly of appeal only to adults.[25]

Most courts inspected in the Lancashire and Cumbria area had a designated cell for children (the one in Burnley court 'was in particularly poor condition, with soggy toilet paper stuck to the ceiling'),[26] but these were not positioned in a different part of the building from adult cells. Separation of adult and child detainees in the court custody facilities inspected in Cleveland, Durham and Northumbria was 'limited by the layout of the cell corridors'; the only apparent physical safeguard was the positioning of children in cells closest to the desk of custody staff.[27]

In May 2013, the High Court found a breach of 1933 legislation requiring the separation of children from adults in police detention, and during escort to and from court.[28] The case concerned a 13-year-old boy who had breached the terms of his curfew order and accordingly reported to the police. He was arrested, handcuffed and taken to a cell. The private contractor GeoAmey escorted him to Birmingham magistrates' court, where he was detained in a cell. When the boy's solicitor arrived to interview him, the child was taken in handcuffs to an interview room. He had to pass adult prisoners and a series of cells holding adults and was exposed to loud shouting. The child's lawyer told the court he had been very distressed, scared and intimidated. This was no doubt exacerbated by his difficulties; the child has special educational needs and, according to a report prepared by a consultant clinical psychologist from Great Ormond Street Hospital, severe impairment of intellectual functioning. As well as finding the child had been treated unlawfully under domestic law, the judges rejected the government's contention that the United Nations Convention on the Rights of the Child applies only to prisons, and not to courts or escorts: 'In our view these international instruments cannot be given so narrow an interpretation.'[29]

The inspection of court custody facilities in Merseyside and Cheshire found that children and adults were held in cells on separate corridors 'where possible', but that this was not always 'practicable because of their design'.[30] In Nottinghamshire and Derbyshire, inspectors found 'little specific provision' for child detainees.[31] This widespread practice of mixing child and adult detainees in court custody is in clear contravention of article 37(c) of the United Nations Convention on the Rights of the Child, which requires separate detention, and diminishes attempts above ground to distance young and old defendants.

Cellular vehicles were found to be dirty in two of the six inspections. Concerns about court cells included: dirt and graffiti (a large swastika was daubed on a wall of the juvenile cell at Hartlepool magistrates court);[32] substandard toilet facilities; poor ventilation; and inadequate heating. Staff in a number of courts had painted and cleaned cells themselves. The cells in the oldest of two Newcastle Crown Courts, which are still used for overflow cases, date back to the 18th century. Inspectors omitted to mention whether any children are still tried in this court, but the description rekindles past brutality:

> The cells at Newcastle Crown Court Moot Hall were ancient and dungeon-like, with stone arches. There were shackles in the cell corridors, to which detainees being transported to Australia in the 18th century had been chained. The cells were used sporadically but sometimes held up to six detainees at a time. They were dirty and contained a small amount of graffiti. Staff told us that there was no effective heating.[33]

Moot Hall was the site of the notorious murder trial of 11-year-old Mary Flora Bell (and her teenage co-defendant, who was acquitted) in December 1968. The journalist Gitta Sereny covered the proceedings and observed a last-minute alteration in the courtroom used, so there was a waiting room and toilet close by and it 'would be easier to take proper care of the children'.[34] The court custody inspections between August 2012 and January 2014 unearthed little evidence of the particular needs of children being cared for. None of the staff in the six regions had received training in child protection, there were no named staff members assigned to individual children (escort staff used to stay with children in court, but the funding for this was withdrawn by the YJB) and children were usually treated the same as adults. The latest inspection report, for Cambridgeshire and Essex, observed that, 'Neither HMCTS [Her Majesty's Courts and Tribunal Service] nor Serco Wincanton had a safeguarding policy.'[35] In Blackpool, inspectors found a 16-year-old boy who had been escorted to court by Serco:

> The escorting staff confirmed that, following changes introduced by the YJB, they were no longer responsible for the care of the detainee once they had lodged them at the court custody suite. Responsibility for looking after him subsequently rested with the member of staff assigned to cell observations and visits that day, who treated him no differently to any adult detainees in the suite.[36]

Unlike adult prisons, which operate a 'lockout' policy whereby prisoners are not accepted after a certain time and must be held overnight in police cells, child prisons admit throughout the day and night (children used to be detained in police stations like adults).[37] These are not accident and emergency departments or psychiatric hospitals with children arriving in ambulances with blue lights flashing. Every act of child imprisonment is the result of a court process and a placement decision by the YJB. Each child comes from a local authority area containing a vast number and range of professionals with experience of caring for troubled and traumatised children. From a childcare perspective, it is incomprehensible that placement in locked establishments happens so abruptly. On arrival at Portland young offender institution in Dorset, Ben Grimes was made to wait in a prison escort van while prison officers finished a meeting. Only then was his transfer from Feltham young offender institution completed. Ben had opposed the move to Dorset, as he was close to his family in Feltham; he was found hanging after only three nights. This young person had turned 18 just six weeks before incarceration. The report written for his court hearing explained he had 'severe special education needs and diagnoses of attachment disorder, possible attention deficit and hyperactivity disorder and conduct disorder'.[38] Sixteen year-old Anthony Redding tried to hang himself with his shoelaces in an escort vehicle. His penal journey continued and three weeks later he died in prison, having been moved from the healthcare unit where he was on suicide watch.[39]

The NHS would collapse should every person requiring in-patient care be transferred immediately from GP practice to hospital regardless of level of need and urgency. The International Centre for Prison Studies reports convicted individuals in Iceland being put on a prison waiting list; if their sentence expires before a place becomes available, they no longer get sent to prison.[40] This classic form of rationing has been used for decades in our own health and social care services. Within the penal context, however, children are never turned away or told to join a queue. They are frequently sent to institutions miles from home where meaningful contact with families and agencies with legal obligations to provide, among other things, special educational needs support, mental health services and social work is virtually impossible.

When the YJB was given responsibility for placing children, more than a decade ago, it set a target of 90% being held within 50 miles from home. This target was never achieved and, in 2012, the Ministry of Justice and the board declared 'it is unrealistic and inappropriate to continue to make this commitment', noting that the board 'has not included it in its corporate targets for a number of years'.[41] Latest published figures show nearly a third of imprisoned children are held over 50 miles from home; one in 10 of these are held more than 100 miles away.[42] I have information on all but one of the 16 children who died in prison since the YJB took over the allocation function and calculate that 47% were detained in institutions more than 50 miles from their home area. In September 2013, the then secretary of state for education, Michael Gove, said it was 'indefensible' that over a third of children in care are placed more than 20 miles from home.[43] A report published by the Department for Education the same day listed the 'extra challenges' faced by local authorities when looked-after children are placed over 20 miles from home: not having local knowledge and intelligence about the quality of homes; social workers finding it more difficult to oversee children's care and treatment; and a negative impact on family contact and the ability of professionals to work with families.[44] Every one of these impediments applies to incarcerated children, many of whom were formerly in the care of local authorities, but the government has been silent about their transportation to counties far from home.

Nobody in central government keeps track of the times children arrive at young offender institutions, although Independent Monitoring Boards (IMBs) often include information in their annual reports on individual prisons. Of nine IMB reports sent to the government in 2012, six raise concerns about children arriving late. In 2011/12, 295 children arrived at Ashfield young offender institution, in Bristol, after 8 pm and 27 after midnight. Three children arrived between three and four in the morning.[45] These frightened boys would have been held in escort vehicles for several hours after leaving court, an excruciatingly long period, only to be followed by prison 'processing'. Many could have been transported with adult prisoners despite ministerial assurances a decade ago that this would stop.[46] The chief inspector of prisons' annual report for this same period noted that new prison escort contracts had been agreed in August 2011, with Serco Wincanton and GeoAmey, with no requirement to transport children and adults separately:

> We were particularly concerned that the new contracts permitted women and children under the age of 18 to be transported in the same vehicles as adult men. Protocols to separate them within vehicles appeared underdeveloped.... Removable partitions that could be used to divide vehicles into separate compartments for men, women and children were not effective and hampered the ability of staff to supervise all prisoners.[47]

At the time of writing, five IMB annual reports for 2012/13 were published and three of these complain of children arriving late, although the situation was said to be improving in Feltham young offender institution.[48] An inspection of court custody facilities in Nottinghamshire and Derbyshire in July 2013 found several instances of children being taken on extremely lengthy, circuitous routes to and from court, presumably as a cost-saving measure.[49] It is not just the length of these journeys that is uncivilised; it is also the conditions in which children are held. One child wrote on a prison inspection survey some years ago: 'Felt like I couldn't breathe in a small cabin and the chair felt like I was sitting on the floor.' Another reported: 'I felt sick from the heat and when I said this to the guards they laughed.'[50] The IMB for Warren Hill young offender institution in Suffolk reported a boy attending court daily, leaving the prison at half past seven in the morning and sometimes not returning until 11 pm. The board commented: 'This is neither humane treatment nor a good use of resources.'[51] More than two years later, in May 2014, it 'remained extremely concerned at the continued number of late arrivals' to the prison.[52]

The shameful practice of escort staff giving children plastic property bags in which to urinate during their long journeys was condemned in a series of prison inspection reports over a decade ago, and cited in the landmark Children Act case brought by the Howard League for Penal Reform (pp 237–8).[53] This particular form of mistreatment was reported by inspectors as recently as March 2014:

> Gel bags were carried for young people who needed to go to the toilet en route. (Werrington young offender institution in Stoke-on-Trent, inspected September/October 2013)[54]

> [Children] had been provided with bags if they needed to urinate during the journey. (Brinsford young offender institution in Wolverhampton, inspected November/December 2009)[55]

Some juveniles who arrived on transfer during the inspection had to use plastic bags in which to urinate. (Castington young offender institution in Northumberland, inspected January 2009)[56]

One young person in a focus group indicated that he had asked for a comfort break, but this was refused and he had been given a bag to urinate in. (Stoke Heath young offender institution in Shropshire, inspected October 2008)[57]

Some young people said they had been refused comfort breaks and given bags to urinate in instead. (Ashfield young offender institution in Bristol, inspected August 2008)[58]

In a research interview for this book, Malcolm Stevens described cellular vehicles as "disgusting" and recounted his reaction to hearing, during his time as director of two of the country's four secure training centres, of the YJB's cost-cutting plan to stop using family saloon vehicles to carry children to and from these institutions. This would have allied the transportation of children in young offender institutions and secure training centres, with children held in secure children's homes being the only ones protected from sweatboxes. Stevens arranged for three or four YJB officials to be placed in a cellular vehicle and taken for a journey "round the roundabouts of Milton Keynes" to experience for themselves what these children have to endure. His clever tactic succeeded up to a point as it prevented a change in escort vehicle for children in secure training centres. However, the individuals thrown around the prison van clearly did not experience a full epiphany, as cellular vehicles have continued to be used for children in young offender institutions.

When inspectors checked to see if 10-hour round trips had ceased in Nottinghamshire and Derbyshire, they discovered that children were being held temporarily at another prison to break up their journeys.[59] Presumably children were subject to the usual admission procedures, including strip searching, on arrival at these stopgap prisons. No criticism was made of this particular practice, although inspectors were not satisfied that the wider issue had been resolved:

> These [temporary prison] placements were arranged on an individual basis by the Youth Justice Board, and we were not convinced that a permanent arrangement had been made to prevent such unreasonably long journeys being experienced again.[60]

Every inspection report of young offender institutions visited between January 2013 and June 2014 confirms that children continue to be transported to prison with adults or a mixture of males and females. This applied to a quarter of children travelling to Warren Hill, in Suffolk;[61] a third of those travelling to Hindley in Wigan;[62] and to over half the children taken to Feltham, in the London borough of Hounslow.[63] Ten per cent of children admitted to this prison in the last three months of 2012 arrived after 8 pm.[64] Inspectors reported the case of one child held in Warren Hill young offender institution in Suffolk whose hearing was over by 12.30 pm but who did not leave the court building until 8.42 pm. He eventually arrived at the prison at 10.46 pm.[65] Another child arrived at 9.30 pm after a four-hour wait at the court – after the YJB had issued the placement order.[66] On average, half of all the children surveyed by inspectors in this young offender institution had not been offered a toilet break during their journey, and over a third were not offered anything to eat or drink. One child had arrived at prison at 10 pm, his court case having finished at midday. There was no record of him being provided with any food throughout this time.[67] A former child prisoner recalled that the first thing he saw on arrival at Feltham young offender institution was the prison's graveyard.[68]

Suicide prevention is the official reason for the absence of seatbelts in prison escort vehicles; the other is that prisoners may use them as a weapon.[69] The Howard League for Penal Reform reported the case of a child who had fallen asleep in a prison van and 'awoke when the sweatbox took a corner sharply and he smashed his head against the side of the van'.[70] Superficially, the prison service's explanation for rejecting seatbelts sounds reasonable. It would be a cold-hearted system that put prisoners' lives at risk, and who could argue with protecting custody officers from seatbelt attacks? As someone who has spent years going head-to-head in media interviews with advocates of smacking, I am well acquainted with the well of human ingenuity when it comes to defending the status quo. I have been warned that the number of children electrocuting themselves will soar if we stop slapping them as they toddle towards electricity sockets; that young children must be hit to keep their blood circulating; and, the most frequent claim, that a slap is not actually a form of assault but rather a 'tap'. My ultimate comeback is that thousands of parents in this country – and whole countries across Europe and the rest of the world – have committed to violence-free parenting. Faced with this truth, the hard-line smacker has two choices: to espouse wacky theories about smacking or admit that they do not want to give it up. I believe the same applies to seatbelts in prison vans, and all other entrenched practices where money and punishment comes before the interests of children.

The multinational Serco was the 'winning bidder' of the latest contract – worth over £9 million over a four-year period – for transporting children to and from secure training centres and secure children's homes.[71] These are the establishments in which the YJB says it places the youngest and most vulnerable children. Between 30 August 2012 and 6 June 2013, 146 children arrived at these places between 9 pm and midnight; and a further 14 children arrived between midnight and 2.59 am.[72] The latest inspection report on Hassockfield secure training centre in Durham observes that, between March and July 2014, 44% of children arrived at the prison after 9 pm.[73]

Serco's duties include taking children to hospital appointments where its escort custody officers are permitted to attach chains to handcuffed children 'for reasons of comfort or decency during a bed watch'.[74] The latest inspection report of Oakhill secure training centre commends 'a significant reduction' in the use of handcuffs, with decisions now being made on the basis of risk rather than habit.

Inspectors observed occasions when the use of handcuffs was refused. Data is not provided on the frequency of use, although the report suggests that children are still being handcuffed when attending hospital appointments and funerals:

> Thoughtful discretion is evidenced by instances seen where the request for handcuff use was turned down because of insufficient justification. This means that when young people leave the centre to attend, for example, hospital or a funeral, handcuffs are only used if there is an identified need, and for the minimum time necessary.... Young people's welfare is further assured by a nurse always seeing them upon their return to the centre.[75]

In March 2013, the Howard League for Penal Reform submitted a complaint to the UN Committee on the Elimination of Discrimination Against Women after a pregnant girl was handcuffed when attending hospital appointments and subject to strip searches.[76] Outcry at pregnant prisoners being chained to their beds led the then home secretary, Michael Howard, to introduce a ban in 1996.[77] The new chief inspector of prisons had suspended his inspection of Holloway prison after finding repugnant building design and unacceptable treatment almost everywhere he looked. Ramsbotham's shock at finding women chained during labour was palpable: 'nothing prepared me for [that]'.[78] Jack Straw, then shadow home secretary, complained of the government's 'inhumanity'[79] towards women prisoners. He became home secretary himself the following year, and was four years in post, but he failed to prohibit the shackling of child prisoners, including pregnant girls.

Data is not collected centrally on the number of children attending hospital from young offender institutions, although a year-long audit to April 2006 revealed that there were 993 separate hospital escorts and 'bedwatches' of juveniles.[80] Child prisoners who are critically ill are also kept under hospital bedwatch. Sixteen-year-old Gareth Price was found hanging in his prison cell in January 2005, and was rushed to hospital. Two prison officers travelled with him in the ambulance. He was placed on a life support machine. When the prison was told 'there was a strong possibility [Gareth] had suffered brain damage', his escort was reduced to one officer.[81]

In a research interview for this book, Liz Hardy told me when her son Jake was rushed to intensive care after being found hanging in his cell, she automatically asked for permission to visit him in hospital. She was still in the mindset of her child being a prisoner. There can be few more powerful illustrations of prison's brutal separation of child and parent.

TEN

'The violence is unbelievable'

Enter a primary school playground and you are bound to encounter human aeroplanes with outstretched limbs taking their pilots sky high; child-sized spinning tops with wild hair and scuffed shoes; and the classic caped crusader, free at last of zips, toggles and Velcro. Finding a safe space to stand, you may spy a few dishevelled children propping up walls, alone, and others with hands clasped to adult protectors. There will always be uncomfortable sights, but the prevailing atmosphere of a children's play area is happy and inviting. Go into a child prison and you will find miserable, frightened children making desperate attempts to hide their frailty. This is not about the different demeanours of those inhabiting the early years and adolescence. It is prison – an utterly perverse setting in which to find the young. Whenever I was escorted on to a wing for visits with a former child in care (p xiii), the experience felt like entering a building after someone – everyone – had been given devastating news.

Ryan Clark was found hanging in his cell in Wetherby young offender institution in April 2011. One of his older brothers said at the subsequent inquest that Ryan was 'scared to death' about being imprisoned.[1] This was a child who had been in care since he was a toddler, and was now in custody for the first time. He was right to be afraid. During my research for this book, youth justice expert Pam Hibbert told me about a boy she had interviewed in prison who, unusually, had previously lived in a boarding school. For him, being admitted to prison:

'... was akin to his first day at private school: he was scared of the staff, he was scared of the boys, he knew that something horrible was going to happen fairly soon'.

211

In his memoir on life inside, ex-prisoner Erwin James explains that there is 'a frightening precariousness to prison life' and runs through an exhausting list of peer cruelty:

> The cell doors were opened only briefly at mealtimes, but long enough for the almost daily incidents of violence to take place. The violence appeared to erupt over arguments which had started during the shouting out of cell windows or, more often, it involved ambushes of suspected sex offenders or attacks on former acquaintances who had turned informers.... But violent incidents could also occur spontaneously. Bumping into someone on the landing, catching the eye of someone who didn't appreciate being 'looked at' or simply appearing vulnerable could be enough to unleash the pent-up frustrations that so much bang-up generates.[2]

James' grim portrayal tells us about the perilous conditions in adult prisons. These are safer than child penal institutions, which Baroness Linklater described to me in a research interview as having more of a "tinderbox" atmosphere. Comparable statistics for young offender institutions and adult prisons show that, despite comprising just 1% of the prison population,[3] children constitute 16% of those who commit physical attacks, and 18% of those involved in fights. Eleven per cent of prison assault victims are children.[4] The trades union for prison officers says on its website that 'violence and other risks' are part of its members' 'day to day work'.[5] Within juvenile young offender institutions, there were 656 child assault victims in 2013 (meaning each victim was attacked at least once) compared with 306 incidents when staff were assaulted by children.[6] For obvious reasons, literature given to child prisoners and their families omits to mention the high likelihood of physical attack. In a review by the Howard League for Penal Reform of life inside young offender institutions, one interviewee told researchers: 'Everything's about violence.... The violence is unbelievable.'[7] The official body established to help prevent torture and other inhuman and degrading treatment and punishment in UK prisons seems to support this view. Responding to a government consultation on new types of child custody, the National Preventive Mechanism stated:

> Large institutions such as the majority of male YOIs [young offender institutions] are inherently unsafe and rely on high levels of power and control by staff to maintain order.[8]

Government data reveals that there were 587 assaults recorded in Ashfield young offender institution in Bristol in the year to December 2012, making violence at least a daily occurrence.[9] Children were removed from this prison the following year, after which a substantial reduction in assaults was recorded (79 throughout 2013).[10] Feltham young offender institution in London (holding children and young adults) reported 733 assaults during 2013; Wetherby young offender institution in West Yorkshire reported 323; and Hindley young offender institution in Wigan reported 356 assaults in the same 12-month period.[11] Nearly three quarters of children responding to an official survey of gang issues (n=41) said there was fear and intimidation in their prison because of such membership. When children were asked to name the negative effects of gangs operating in prisons, 'the most frequent responses were getting hurt or killed and dealing with the constant feelings of fear, anxiety and lack of safety'.[12] A study by the prisons inspectorate found that child prisoners who have been in care are more than twice as likely as other children to report physical abuse by prison staff (10% compared with 4%). Reports of physical abuse by other prisoners are also higher.[13]

With this backdrop, it came as no surprise to hear the former head of the Youth Justice Board (YJB), John Drew, say in a research interview for this book that "there's a huge culture of violence" in young offender institutions, adding "and that's not to say that anyone deliberately inculcates that. I think those days are probably gone but, nevertheless, it is there."

The days of prison officers inciting and inflicting violence, not as a one-off aberration but as an organised system of control and domination, might well be over, although the absence of independent inquiries has meant no root-and-branch public examination of why serious abuse occurred, how long it went on for, and who failed to stop it. We know a lot about the grave mistreatment of children in residential homes because there have been high-profile inquiries and extensive media coverage, and parliament has passed laws to strengthen child protection in those settings. The senior statutory position of a children's rights director was even created within the social care inspectorate to make sure vulnerable children had a powerful ally in the corridors of power.

Those who have followed developments in children's residential care over the past 20 to 30 years will know the stories behind certain abusive institutions in Islington, Leicestershire, North Wales and Staffordshire, and a great many other areas. These were sites of institutional child abuse over many years. The prison sector has its own skeletons; however, these occupy a much smaller place in our collective consciousness (and, perhaps, conscience).

Chapters Five and Six have considered the unlawful use of restraint in penal settings. There have been other scandals, among the most notorious at Portland young offender institution in Dorset, where the Howard League for Penal Reform exposed allegations of 'systematic abuse' over a decade ago.[14] Medomsley detention centre in Durham, run by the Home Office between 1960 and 1983, is currently the subject of a major police inquiry into institutional child sexual abuse (p 246). Investigations following the murder in 2000 of Zahid Mubarek in Feltham young offender institution, in the London Borough of Hounslow, found instances of horrific emotional and racial abuse. More recently, Her Majesty's Inspectorate of Constabulary has indicated that Duncroft approved school, under the control of the Home Office from 1949 to 1973, had a central place in Jimmy Savile's abuse of vulnerable children (p 234).[15]

A year or so after he became director general of the prison service, Martin Narey told *The Observer* newspaper that he had been 'distressed' by what he found at Portland young offender institution: the prison had 'a culture of violence' and the 'segregation unit was clearly an evil place'.[16] The following year, in February 2001, Narey said at a prison officers' conference that the prison had been a 'hell hole' and conditions were still unacceptable[17] (the YJB stopped placing children there around this time).[18] The Howard League for

Penal Reform first became aware of allegations of physical abuse in the prison in 1998 and interviewed 10 newly released children the following year. Working with the London law firm Hickman and Rose, the charity compiled a dossier of the experiences of 14 former inmates and submitted it to Martin Narey and to Portland's governor. A police investigation followed, called Operation Hourglass, which examined 53 separate complaints of physical abuse, mostly occurring in the prison's segregation unit. Some of the abuse dated back to the 1980s and children gave very similar accounts despite not knowing each other and being incarcerated at different times. The Howard League summarises the nature of children's complaints:

> Slaps to the face/punches to the stomach for insubordinate behaviour such as not addressing an officer as 'Sir' or answering back.[19]

> Repeated banging of heads against a wall or against the floor when an inmate has been restrained.[20]

> Pinning by the throat against a wall, hard slap to back of head causing an inmate to fall to the ground, punches to the kidney area and kicks to the body once an inmate has been restrained on the ground.[21]

The charity reported that a lot of the abuse happened immediately after a child entered the segregation block, or after a strip search, apparently as a strategy to 'humiliate and subjugate inmates seen as "difficult"'.[22] Most of the time children did not suffer injuries from officer assaults, but, when they did, the Howard League reports:

> Not infrequently when inmates did suffer visible injuries false charges of assault or attempted assault were laid against them often resulting in a finding of guilt at adjudications resulting in extra days added to sentences which the inmates then served.[23]

The Crown Prosecution Service brought no criminal charges (in 2001, police were reported to be investigating 35 cases of alleged assault by officers).[24] Internal prison service investigations led to the dismissal of two officers – one after another officer came forward to say she had witnessed an assault. Nine former inmates pursued legal action for the abuse they suffered. The prison service denied liability until the week before the trial, when out-of-court settlement payments totalling £149,000 were made.[25] A few years before, a chaplain at the prison also settled out of court after being subject to a 'huge amount of stress, vulnerability and isolation' after raising concerns about officer abuse.[26] During the children's litigation, the Howard League explains, the new governor of the prison said a system of 'institutionalised intimidation' had operated in the segregation block.[27] This was not simply the work of maverick officers. The Howard League reports one child being slapped on the head for sucking his teeth during an adjudication hearing – an assault that took place in front of a governor.[28] The charity also accused the Independent Monitoring Board of being loyal to the establishment, after it denied there had been any assaults.[29]

Mark Johnson, who set up the criminal justice reform charity UserVoice in 2009, was sent to Portland young offender institution at the age of 17. In a book about his experiences there, he recalls one occasion when a prisoner tried to smuggle a sandwich out of the kitchen. When officers discovered the sandwich in a lift shaft, inmates were told they would go without breakfast as collective punishment. Johnson and others protested by refusing to work. This is what happened next:

> We are pulled out of the recess one by one with agonising force and thrown onto the floor. When it is my turn, my knees are folded under me in one brisk, violent movement and a stick's rammed into the fold. Another stick is run painfully across my back and between my arms and I am carried, a few inches from the floor back to my cell. They tell me I'm going to the Block.
>
> … it's like going to the dungeons because this is the most ancient part of the jail. There's a groove in the step

where it's been rubbed away over many years and the sign outside is blank, because so many busy hands have polished it off ... I see a line-up of screws waiting.

... 'Come on then, you little bastard,' they shout. The door is closed behind me and my feet do not touch the ground. The screws carry me in by my thumbs. I am thrown into a cell and slammed against the wall. I slide down it and they yell at me to get up and when I do I find there are about six of them in my tiny stone cell. They jump on me and pull my shirt over my head and my cuffs over my wrists. They pull my trousers and my underwear down to my ankles and when I'm naked and helpless they beat me. And it is a real beating. They use their fists and knees and elbows.[30]

The padre that later came into Johnson's cell and examined his bruises 'with concern in his eyes'[31] may well have been the same man who suffered abuse himself after reporting officer violence.

Following the brutal murder of Zahid Mubarek in Feltham young offender institution, Hounslow Racial Equality Council facilitated group discussions with 54 young prisoners from black and minority ethnic (BME) communities between January and May 2001, and found that some white officers inflicted frequent racist abuse.[32] The report of the public inquiry into Zahid's death and wider matters records prisoner accounts:

BME prisoners were called 'monkeys' and 'black bastards', and they were told that 'they should be sent back to their own country'. Following Zahid's murder, officers had 'become more discreet in expressing racist attitudes', but that did not mean that they were any less racist than before. They had just become more subtle about it. It was felt that this was being done so that BME prisoners 'would find it difficult to cope and might attempt suicide'.[33]

The inquiry considered the existence of a prison officer game called 'Coliseum', whereby incompatible inmates would be deliberately detained in shared cells to incite violence and staff made bets on the outcome. There was no evidence to support this practice, the inquiry concluded. However, it was equivocal on whether a less extreme system of prisoner abuse existed:

> But the real possibility that unsuitable prisoners have at times been put into the same cell – either to wind them up so that they would misbehave when they were let out or to see whether they would argue with each other – is certainly one which cannot be excluded, even though no hard and fast examples of such a practice have been given otherwise than in the anonymous setting of the Inquiry's focus groups with prisoners and prison staff.[34]

Other racist abuse was described in the inquiry report, including a case where three white prison officers 'handcuffed an ethnic minority prisoner on Raven to the bars of his cell, removed his trousers and smeared his bottom with black shoe polish'. Another case involved 'two white trainee prison officers urinating on a black trainee during a training course'. The trainee officers were dismissed, but the 'Raven Three', as they were called, were given only warnings.[35]

Zahid Mubarek was aged 19 when Robert Stewart, of the same age, clubbed him into a coma with a wooden table leg in the prison cell they shared. Such was the minimal staffing in the institution, and the physical layout, that it was Stewart himself who first drew attention to the ferocious attack by ringing his cell buzzer.[36]

These reflections on Feltham a decade ago are included here for three reasons. The first is to emphasise the inherent dangerousness of prisons, and to show that extreme acts of inhumanity can and do take place. As the inquiry report noted, incidents of 'brutality and serious mistreatment of prisoners on the part of prison officers surface from time to time'.[37] Between 2004/05 and 2009/10, the UK government paid out £1.2 million in compensation for assaults by prison staff and abuse/harassment.[38]

The second reason is to reject any notion that the penal culture enabling grotesque racist abuse in one part of Feltham prison, holding individuals in their late teens and early twenties, would not also have permeated the child unit. Adolescents have been held in this institution since 1859, so the culture cannot be said to have developed around adults only. Moreover, less than six months after Zahid's death, a deputy governor resigned following the suicide attempt of a 17-year-old boy. The child was one of 100 boys housed in adult wings, because the juvenile part of the prison was full. The outgoing governor described the conditions within the prison as Dickensian.[39]

The third reason for considering Feltham's disgraceful past is to highlight the resistance of the then Labour government to launch a public inquiry into Zahid Mubarek's death. Zahid's uncle took his case as far as the House of Lords (since replaced by the Supreme Court) to seek justice for his murdered nephew, and the home secretary was duly ordered, in October 2003, to establish an independent public inquiry. Lord Bingham gave the leading judgment and explained:

> ... while any deliberate killing by state agents is bound
> to arouse very grave disquiet, such an event is likely to
> be rare and the state's main task is to establish the facts
> and prosecute the culprits; a systemic failure to protect
> the lives of persons detained may well call for even more
> anxious consideration and raise even more intractable
> problems.[40]

Lord Slynn of Hadley went further in pointing to the culpability of the state:

> It does not seem to me to be possible to say that there is
> a clear dividing line between those cases where an agent
> of the state kills and those cases where an agent of the
> state or the system is such that a killing may take place.[41]

When *The Guardian* newspaper obtained a leaked copy of an internal investigation into the teenager's death, the head of the prison service, Martin Narey, responded as follows:

There's no element of denial, I've been absolutely up front about the problems we have. It goes beyond institutional racism to blatant malicious pockets of racism.[42]

Narey has been equally candid about the 'norm' of prison officer violence in local prisons in the 1980s. In an online article he recounts an anecdote about Deerbolt borstal in Durham, which held children and young adults between the ages of 16 and 21, showing the close links between different prison service institutions:

> I saw very little violence at Deerbolt [borstal, holding 16-21 year-olds]. I think there genuinely was very little violence there. But I was reminded of the extent to which it was the norm in local prisons. After a minor disturbance at Deerbolt, where I was the only governor on duty, about twenty young men had to be transferred to Durham. I was on duty until after midnight and saw each of those young men, treated professionally, and put on coaches to Durham. When I visited them at Durham the next morning, each of them were black and blue.[43]

Latest inspection data shows that nearly a third of 942 boys held in young offender institutions in 2012/13 had felt unsafe in prison and 11% felt unsafe at the time they filled in their survey.[44] Inspections of the four secure training centres during this same period found that between 8% and 30% of children had felt unsafe at some point, and nearly one in 10 felt unsafe at the time of the inspection.[45] Feltham young offender institution had the worst record, although this was still better than the overall proportion of disabled children who had felt insecure in young offender institutions (42% compared with Feltham's 37%).[46] Seventeen per cent of girls had felt unsafe,[47] considerably fewer than male inmates but still unacceptably high. In an Ofsted survey of children living away from home in foster care, children's homes and educational settings, just 2% of participants reported feeling unsafe in the building in which they lived, and another 4% said their feeling of safety varied.[48]

Children in all settings are bound to minimise their difficulties in surveys, which is why both the prisons inspectorate and Ofsted's children's rights director supplement quantitative data gathering with group discussions (the director's role was subsumed into the Office of Children's Commissioner for England in April 2014). There is also the matter of prison survival depending on boys being invincible rather than needy, and not being a 'grass'. The latest inspection report of a juvenile young offender institution tells of a boy 'who appeared to have fallen out with others [and] meekly 'reported' to a side room off the main association area to meet his assailants. While one boy kept watch, others crowded round to punch and kick him.' The incident only came to light because it was captured on CCTV footage.[49] This reluctance to speak out could also explain why most inmates in Warren Hill young offender institution in Suffolk told inspectors they felt safe in March 2013 despite horrendous levels of violence.[50] The inspection report noted five children and one member of staff 'had required hospital treatment for broken bones, unconsciousness and multiple injuries, including black eyes, stab wounds and grazes as a result of this prison violence'.[51] Private discussions, where the child is shown compassion and concern, may elicit greater openness in the intimidating prison environment. In a study by Professor Barry Goldson on imprisoned children, in-depth interviews with 25 participants revealed that 92% felt unsafe.[52]

As a children's rights officer, I would quickly visit every child admitted to a children's home to check they had basic provisions (toothbrush, somewhere private to lock their possessions and nightclothes, for example), and to tell them they could contact me if they had any concerns. During this initial conversation, I would ask children whether there was anything they were afraid of about living in a children's home. One 12-year-old boy told me his friends had warned him to always keep his back facing a wall and not to bend over in the presence of male staff. This was in the aftermath of the Frank Beck scandal, when there was a spate of media reports about children's homes' residents being raped and sexually assaulted by staff. Little wonder this young child's friends gave him the advice they did. When I returned to County Hall, the director of social services and I composed some wording to be used in a letter to every child entering a children's home from that time onwards. Each letter would contain an assurance that the child would be treated well and the details of whom to contact if they ever felt unsafe.

Young inmates have to come face-to-face with the bogeymen that have petrified children for generations: being sent away to an unknown place full of strangers; being confined in a small, locked space with little natural light and fresh air; hearing shouts and screams and heavy doors slamming and cell buzzers ringing; placed out of sight of parents and other potential rescuers; and suffering random as well as planned attacks on body and mind.

One participant in Goldson's study said he feared he might be killed on his first night in prison:

> You can't sleep. You just think. You wonder, 'Am I going to get beat up? Am I going to get killed?' There was loads of shouting out of the windows. I just didn't know what to do. I didn't even speak with my pad mate. I said nothing. I was too frightened.[53]

As in the world outside, there is usually no neat divide between aggressor and victim in prison. Walking, talking and acting tough is known to be one of the survival techniques adopted by human beings in a nerve-racking situation, be this a war zone or a prison wing. Just as you are not meant to make eye contact with a dangerous dog in case it senses your fear, prison inmates are forced to hide their vulnerabilities. As one interviewee said in a study on safeguarding children remanded in custody, 'I sometimes feel unsafe but I don't show it. I don't want to be a coward.'[54]

It is worth mentioning here the prison officer in Hindley young offender institution found by the Prisons and Probation Ombudsman to have used force unlawfully on a child, resulting in the boy's wrist being broken (p 150). This heavily built man told his line manager 'he could adopt an aggressive attitude with young people to avoid losing face'.[55]

A study of mental healthcare in five prisons, one of them a young offender institution holding boys, found that the need to appear tough was common among male prisoners, although this was no guarantee of safety. A strong exterior would simply defer attacks, with weaker inmates being earlier targets.[56] A five-year study of a men's prison found inmates employed a number of survival strategies, including adopting a 'macho, tough, aggressive façade' (particularly common in the period after admission) and hiding true feelings and personalities:

> Prisoners spoke of the pressure to balance an outward 'public' appearance with their more genuine or private selves.[57]

In a study by the Children's Rights Alliance for England, children with experience of custody talked about feeling compelled to fight within this environment to avoid being seen as the weak one; as a means of releasing pent-up boredom and frustration; and to settle old scores. Their graphic descriptions of violence were counterbalanced by examples of refusals to participate in acts of aggression. The fate of these resisters was to spend long periods alone.[58] That a specialist unit was opened within Wetherby young offender institution in 2008 to provide 'encouragement, support and assistance'[59] to frightened children is official confirmation of such enforced isolation. An evaluation report explains the catalyst for the unit:

> [There were children] being held in healthcare facilities (without healthcare problems), placed on segregation units for their own protection, or refusing to come out of their room.[60]

There are other ways of pre-empting violence. One child, for example, revealed in a study for the Howard League for Penal Reform that he had had all his long hair cut off on admission,[61] while in other research by the Children's Rights Alliance for England two former child prisoners said they had persuaded a fellow inmate to have a wash. The child was avoiding having a shower because he feared sexual assault[62] (in a 2011/12 study of child prisoners, 6% of participants said they had felt unsafe in wing showers; and 9% had felt unsafe in gym showers).[63] Elsewhere, there are stomach-churning tales of children being made by other prisoners to sing nursery rhymes, and perform other 'shout outs', through cell windows at night – ritual degradation that no parent could bear to picture their own child going through – or indeed any child. Despite secure training centres having lower reports of bullying, no doubt associated with higher staffing levels, shouting through windows happens there too. During a prison inspection in Rainsbrook secure training centre in Rugby in December 2012, one third of children said this was a problem.[64] During the latest inspection of Hassockfield secure training centre, in July 2014, 43% of children said they had experienced others shouting or yelling about them through windows.[65]

A team carrying out research for the Prisons and Probation Ombudsman at Lancaster Farms young offender institution in 2008 witnessed 'a sustained and concerted exchange of frightening and disgusting insults' between children locked in their cells at night.[66] The investigators were in the prison following the death of Liam McManus the previous November. This vulnerable child had hanged himself after only one night on a main prison wing. He had been given no opportunity to mix with other children after his transfer from the prison's induction unit because the prison was in 'lockdown' while staff underwent training. A number of reports were received from staff pointing to Liam being subject to repulsive bullying the night before he died, including that he 'had been made to sing and say a nursery rhyme in order to make him feel "stupid"'.[67]

The Ombudsman's report criticised the absence of any up-to-date assessment of Liam's 'ability to cope with the macho environment of a prison establishment',[68] and gave a disturbing account of its evening observations:

> My investigation team visited Windermere 2 Unit by night in order to acquaint themselves with its atmosphere and culture during the dark hours. At about 10.00 pm, they witnessed a prolonged period of concerted banging of doors followed by an exchange of insults of a disgusting nature between a number of young people, most of which seemed to be directed at one particular individual.[69]

'If this is the sort of behaviour the boy experienced, I have no doubt that he would have been frightened,' the Ombudsman concluded.[70] During a research interview with psychotherapist Camila Batmangelidjh, I described the prison practice of forcing fellow captives to recite nursery rhymes, and asked her what a child victim might feel like during this ordeal. Batmangelidjh responded:

> 'Well, that's equivalent to tying someone to a tree and stripping them, because ... it's the group turning on the individual and degrading them and showing them how powerless they are. It's profoundly humiliating. And it's showing the child that there's no line of protection. The savagery of the group dominates.'

In another interview, Professor Barry Goldson agreed that it is no exaggeration to use the term torture to describe what some children are made to suffer in prison:

> 'You've got this continuum between fatality and this profound cruelty which is actually in some senses worse because it's the routine – it's what all young people experience.... We know very little about sexual violence in children's prisons, but we can be certain that it happens. We know more about the kind of emotional and psychological damage that prison imposes, and we know quite a lot about physical violence and bullying and child-on-child bullying and also staff-on-child bullying and also staff-on-staff bullying which children experience as well, and there are all kind of gender politics there.... Let's just imagine ourselves [in that situation] – myself, at 53 years old, I'd be terrified.... It's torture; we're actually subjecting the children to torture.'

Deborah Coles, the co-director of INQUEST, has sat through numerous inquests of children who have died in custody, and said in her interview with me for this book:

'My work in this field has convinced me that we must abolish the use of penal custody for children. An holistic, comprehensive inquiry into the treatment of children in conflict with the law would be a first step in highlighting the failures that have cost the lives of so many children whilst in the "care" of the state.'

Prison must be a place of absolute terror for children who have previously suffered sexual assault. Child sexual abuse victims often report feeling marked out from other children; that the violations they have endured show in their physicality, making them vulnerable to repeat victimisation. Such beliefs are further proof of the nobleness of children who seem forever ready to absorb responsibility. The mother of Joseph Scholes told me her son would have "fought to his death" had officers tried to transfer him from the prison's healthcare unit to a main wing. Joseph had been sexually abused as a young child, and his mother knew what he most feared in prison:

'I know what would've scared him. He wouldn't have been scared physically, because he was very athletic and wiry and strong. He wouldn't have been afraid to have a fight with somebody. He would've been afraid of being sexually abused, 100%, he would've been. That is exactly why, and I know that it was said when they'd been charged and when they were going to get sentenced. Joseph visited me at the cottage and we'd spent time talking about it and he had said that the other children had said about sexual abuse, so I know that Joseph will have thought he would be raped on that wing.... He wasn't afraid of anything physically. It would've been the sexual element.'

The child I first talked about on page xii was terrified about returning to prison because he had previously been in segregation for his own safety. The governor had warned him then that, if he ever returned to the same prison, other inmates would assume he was a sex offender. This child had been sexually and physically abused prior to entering custody, and had profound emotional and social difficulties. Intelligent and self-aware, he had taken the only course available to him within prison to prevent further violations. It is a cruel fact that nearly a third of child prisoners who have been in care spend time in segregation while incarcerated. And boys who have been in care are more likely to report needing protection from other children in their first days of incarceration – 10% compared with 7% of boys generally (and only 26% of children who have been in care say guards have offered them help with such protection).[71]

A 2005 study of child offenders, including 151 who were detained in young offender institutions and secure children's homes, found a quarter of them had learning difficulties. Researchers were told of one boy who was mercilessly bullied:

> We have a young boy in [healthcare] at the moment, as well as an older boy, and they have learning disabilities. We've made him a cleaner, but a member of staff has to be with him to direct him. That can't happen forever, and he's looking at a lengthy sentence; and we'll give him another couple of years, and then he will hit the adult system where he will be absolutely crucified. You couldn't put him anywhere else but here at the moment.[72]

In a study of mental health of children in custody, one child prisoner said that, following segregation, 'the others terrorise you, so you do something to get back in again'.[73] Seventeen-year-old Andrew Batey, who died on the same date as Adam Rickwood hanged himself – albeit 10 years before – asked to be placed in segregation because of bullying. He was told to kill himself by other prisoners and only lasted eight hours in prison.[74] Philip Griffin was found hanging less than an hour after he had been served an evening drink in his cell. His mother reported that her son had run away from home aged 14 because he was bullied at school over his dyslexia.[75] He was bullied again in prison and made an official complaint the day before he died, although this had not been acted on. The 17-year-old had been taking anti-depressants.[76] The inquest considering the death in 2012 of Jake Hardy at Hindley young offender institution heard he had made an official complaint about bullying. He asked on a complaints form for prison staff to 'do their job properly'.[77]

Prisons are unnatural institutions for all sorts of reasons, including the skewed gender balance. While male-dominated environments are customary in the armed forces and boys' boarding schools, continuing with the total captivity of hundreds of teenage boys under the control of mostly men is an extraordinary arrangement. When I interviewed the mother of Jake Hardy, one of the questions she voiced repeatedly was why the prison service did not "send in the mums" to help distressed boys like her son. The vast majority of boys entering prison will have arrived from families headed by mothers. A study of 301 child offenders, half of them incarcerated, found only one third had parents who were still married or living together.[78] In removing boys from their mothers' care, however deficient, and placing them in testosterone-fuelled environments, the authorities are reinforcing the worst elements of 'street culture'. Boys are not sent to prison to learn how to love and to be loved. They are rarely given the skilled care known to heal deep wounds and engender empathy for others. Macho posturing and egocentric survival techniques prevail in prison, and reinforce, rather than reject, what boys have experienced in their own homes and communities. In our research interview, the former head of the YJB, John Drew, cautioned against blaming children for the high level of bullying within young offender institutions:

> 'We very rarely resource a custodial establishment in such a way that the other children present are not a really strong force in how children experience the regime. That links through to bullying and a link between bullying and the behaviour of other children towards children in custody and children who had a really bad time, including children who tried to take their lives or have taken their lives … and that is not to blame the kids themselves

because they didn't ought to be in a position where they can exercise so much influence.'

When I asked Juliet Lyon, an ex-teacher, former foster carer and director of the Prison Reform Trust for over a decade, what she would most fear if one of her own children was sentenced to custody, she replied:

'What wouldn't you fear? The range would be huge, really. I'd fear the treatment they'd get, that they wouldn't be protected, that the staff in charge wouldn't have the time to notice them as an individual. That I might not be able to be in touch with them. Or support them through it because the connection with family is often severed or very weak. I'd worry about the state of other young people in that place. And the whole kind of Lord of the Flies element that happens in institutions that aren't properly staffed. And so the level of bullying and violence, which is very high. I'd worry about self-harm. I'd worry about the things I know I suppose and I'd worry about the outcome because [imprisonment] leaves a lasting mark.'

At the time of my interview with Lyon, there were 890 children held in young offender institutions and 263 children in secure training centres, enough to fill a large secondary school. Each of these children would have had someone, somewhere – be this a parent, grandparent, friend, teacher or social worker – worrying about their safety, with just cause.

ELEVEN

'Listen to the kids'

Institutional child abuse was first officially recognised in the UK nearly five decades ago,[1] though of course there were scandals before. Children who live in institutions are, by definition, profoundly vulnerable. Their parents are physically and emotionally remote, if available at all, and their surroundings are abnormal. When the UK ratified the United Nations Convention on the Rights of the Child nearly a quarter of a century ago, it agreed to provide special protection and assistance to every child deprived of his or her family environment, irrespective of the reasons behind this loss and the length of separation. The notion that institutions can be deeply damaging to children was not a new discovery for Britain. There were child advocates pushing for de-institutionalisation from the late 19th century onwards, culminating in an influential parliamentary report in 1984 pressing for local authorities to increase support to families to prevent children entering care. The Short Committee, so called because it was chaired by Labour MP Renée Short, explained:

> The state can never be a substitute for real parents. But when it is necessary, our communal responsibility to protect children must outweigh everything.[2]

About 40% of the care population – 38,000 children – lived in residential care in 1976. This had decreased to 12% (6,000 children) 20 years later.[3] This transformation arose from an ideological and financial rejection of institutional care in favour of keeping children with their families wherever possible. Although many forms of residential care for children in the past were known to be severe and militaristic, it was not until the 1980s and 1990s that widespread revelations of sexual and physical abuse emerged. Seventeen public inquiries were established into the abuse of children in residential care in the UK between 1985 and 2000.[4] Attention has focused in recent years on the mistreatment of children within institutions run by religious bodies, particularly the Catholic Church and, in December 2013, the Vatican announced the creation of a commission to protect children within its organisation.[5] Our understanding of the vulnerabilities of children separated from their parents increased in 2013 when we were forced to face the fact that one man, Jimmy Savile, had raped and sexually assaulted children in a variety of institutional settings over 40 years.

During the 1990s, inquiries and investigations into allegations of child abuse led to greater understanding among social care agencies of the need for proactive steps to safeguard children in institutions. More recently, revelations of maltreatment at Stafford Hospital and Panorama's exposé of Winterbourne View Hospital – where the ringleader had previously worked in a young offender institution[6] and another of the convicted abusers had formerly been a prison officer for 11 years[7] – reinforced the importance of whistleblowing that creates a response as well as noise. As the shocking scale of Savile's crimes became known, parliamentarians, the media and the public painfully considered the powerlessness of children. The following advice on improving complaints procedures in custody, given by a young participant in a study on safeguarding, could have been the anthem for 2013: 'Listen to the kids and be more supportive to the kids.'[8]

The Metropolitan Police and the National Society for the Prevention of Cruelty to Children (NSPCC) released a joint report at the beginning of that year, called *Giving victims a voice*. This observed a significant rise in the number of individuals reporting past sexual abuse. According to the authors of the study, this was partly a consequence of the media coverage of Savile's abuse and partly because many victims now have more confidence that the authorities will listen to them.[9] That children's evidence is taken more seriously in court was the subject of a lecture given by the then head of the judiciary a few months later. Referring to the more favourable climate for children reporting abuse, Lord Judge explained in his lecture that courts were:

> ... catching up with the consequences of the problems ignored or created by earlier generations. So our [court] lists are filled up not only with contemporary crimes involving our current generation of children, but with the generations of child victims, now mature adults, who for whatever reason did not come within the purview of the criminal justice system contemporaneous with their childhood.[10]

Two months after *Giving victims a voice* was published, the then director of public prosecutions announced on Radio 4's Today programme a 'watershed moment' in child abuse investigations. Keir Starmer QC pledged that police and prosecutors would no longer be overcautious when dealing with child abuse allegations, claiming the pendulum had swung too far from the position in previous decades when the authorities were accused of trawling for child abuse cases.[11] By October 2013, the Crown Prosecution Service had issued guidelines on prosecuting cases of child sexual abuse that warned against inadvertently discriminating against children known to social services who may have had each 'episode of "bad" behaviour, even of the most minor nature' recorded on their files.[12]

Her Majesty's Inspectorate of Constabulary reviewed the police response to Savile's victims, from receipt of the first allegation in Manchester in 1955 to October 2009, when the knighted disc jockey and television presenter was interviewed under caution in Surrey. '[C]ultural mistrust of a child's evidence' was one of the impediments to children finding justice in the past, the inspectorate concluded:

> ... many of Savile's victims were children in vulnerable settings. It appears to us that those victims, who are in the greatest need of the protection of the criminal justice system, are often the ones who have the greatest difficulty in accessing that protection because of the procedures and practices that have been adopted by the

various agencies over the years: a cultural mistrust of a
child's evidence; the need for corroboration; the failure
fully to implement policies that are designed to prevent
or detect offending.[13]

None of these reports considers the unique difficulties one group of
Savile's victims could have faced in accessing justice. These were the
children of Duncroft school, the establishment that police believe
had a pivotal role in the celebrity's abuse:

> It seems as though Duncroft School was at the centre
> of Savile's criminal behaviour: his visits there allowed
> him to identify potential victims and he went on to
> abuse them.[14]

As well as having their integrity dented simply for being children,
it is reasonable to assume that the residents of this school expected
little sympathy because of their perceived status as 'bad', 'rotten',
'damaged' children who had been sent away. Girls often had to endure
the additional character smear of 'immorality', which was associated
with child victims of incest and prostitution in those days. When
interviewed under caution, Savile told police that Duncroft school
was 'a posh borstal for girls who had committed crimes and was an
alternative to custody'.[15] When Alison Levitt, then deputy director
of public prosecutions, asked a former resident who had witnessed
Savile's abuse why she believed girls at the school had not spoken
out at the time, the woman explained that staff 'admired him greatly
because of his wealth, his charity work and the fact that he was on
the television a great deal' and the children were told they were lucky
to be visited by him.[16] The NSPCC held group discussions with 26
of Savile's victims (85% of whom said they were abused by him as
children) and found:

> ... a number remembered how people had laughed at
> them, or had minimised what had happened, and had
> suggested that they should feel 'lucky' that someone like
> Jimmy Savile had paid them attention.[17]

Duncroft staff were not alone in holding Savile in high esteem. Former prime minister Margaret Thatcher tried on four separate occasions to have him knighted, succeeding in 1990 – the same year he was given the highest honour of the Catholic Church which is the Knight Commander of the Pontifical Equestrian Order of Saint Gregory the Great.[18] A parliamentary early day motion, tabled on 31 October 2011, mourned the recent death of the celebrity and warmly remembered his fundraising, the smiles he 'brought to the faces of children' and even his choice of music. Six Members of Parliament sponsored the motion and a further 20 supported it. It is still open for signature at the time of writing.[19] The largesse enjoyed by Savile is in shameful contrast to how his victims at Duncroft school were made to feel. The former resident interviewed by Alison Levitt said:

> Whatever people did to us was ok because we had no self-esteem, we were like second-class citizens. We were always being told we were in care because we were bad.[20]

Another former resident revealed in an interview for *The Mirror* newspaper:

> The girls at Duncroft had been sent there by the courts for prostitution, drugs and because they tried to kill themselves. Who would have believed us against Saint Jimmy?[21]

Duncroft was an approved school from 1949 and then a community home with education between 1972 and 1980. Both incarnations were closed institutions, holding children sent by the courts. Resembling many Category D open prisons, approved schools and community homes with education did not have perimeter security fences, although many had segregation units and locked punishment rooms. Corporal punishment was widespread and sanctioned by law until August 1988.[22] The country's first ever inquiry into institutional child abuse concerned another approved school in Surrey, called Court Lees, holding teenage boys. An internal Home Office inquiry found children had been beaten with the wrong width of cane; teachers had been excessive in their caning and had not adhered to rules restricting corporal punishment to a sanction of last resort; the cane had been administered on children who were wearing pyjamas, rather than ordinary trousers as specified by law; and staff were not properly recording their use of such punishment. The physical abuse of children in Court Lees was not detected and brought to the public's attention by Home Office or local authority officials; a master at the school, Ivor Cook, acted as whistleblower by writing to a London newspaper in March 1967. The *Daily Mail* then took up the story, a judge-led inquiry was established and the school was closed in August 1967. There was no wider inquiry into approved schools. Cook told a Member of Parliament: 'You will not get a report with wider terms of reference, as the [Home Office] children's department has too much to conceal'. [23]

One former resident of Duncroft school, now in her 50s, said in a magazine interview that a fellow resident did tell staff about Savile's sexual abuse and was, as a result, 'put in a padded cell in solitary confinement until she withdrew her wicked allegations'. [24] This was said to have occurred in 1974, a period when children were often subject to regimes in residential care that, at best, robbed them of their individuality. Children held in approved schools had very little parental contact, being restricted to just 24 days' 'home leave' a year. [25]

Children in closed institutions proved to be a blind spot for the National Crime Agency as well. Its thematic review of institutional child sexual abuse, written in the aftermath of the Savile disclosures, considers 18 case studies. Although one of these relates to the sexual, physical and emotional abuse of children in a secure children's unit (pp 96–7), there is no discussion of penal institutions. This is a remarkable omission, especially as the agency's cultural warning signs read like an encyclopedia entry for prisons – closed organisations, male-dominated hierarchies, substantial power differentials between staff and children, poor parental contact and the needs of the institution prevailing over the interests of children. The report's opening words could have been crafted precisely to underline the extreme vulnerability of child prisoners: 'The sexual exploitation and abuse of children is most likely when vulnerability meets power.' [26]

Former BBC director general George Entwhistle, who was told by a colleague that journalists were investigating Savile but did not probe any further, was accused of showing 'an extraordinary lack of curiosity' by the chair of the Commons culture, media and sport select committee in October 2012.[27] What are we to make of the failure of government to investigate why Savile could treat a closed institution supervised by the Home Office, in the words of one of his victims, 'like a paedophile sweetshop'?[28] At the end of November 2013, ministers were asked whether they were conducting any inquiries in relation to Duncroft school. The response shows an absence of inquisitiveness far surpassing Entwhistle's:

> Although the Home Office relinquished control of Duncroft Approved School in 1973, we reviewed the papers that were available and found no references in the material to Savile or concerns about wider abuse allegations that could be passed on to the police to assist in their investigations.[29]

Some may respond that Duncroft school has long been closed, so there is no need to learn the lessons. However, more than 1,000 children continue to be detained in large institutions far from home, with restricted public scrutiny and carrying the scar of 'bad children'. The organisations detaining these children – the prison service, G4S and Serco – are not childcare specialists and one of their legal functions is the punishment of children.[30] Young offender institutions and secure training centres are the descendants of approved schools like Duncroft, just as NHS mental health trusts succeeded county asylums like Saxondale, which closed in 1987/88 but was, nevertheless, investigated following allegations from former patients that Savile abused them. Indeed, nearly a third of the 33 hospitals so far investigated for abuse by Savile[31] have closed.

It was the Home Office that famously refused to accept that child protection legislation applied to child prisoners. This was challenged by the then chief inspector of prisons, David Ramsbotham, who threatened legal action against the home secretary. Ramsbotham's campaign to extend the Children Act 1989 to child prisoners was not a philosophical project. He wanted the law to protect at-risk children he came across during his inspections. For example, in his inspection report on Onley young offender institution in Warwickshire in July 2001, Ramsbotham observed:

> If a child is seen to be at risk of significant harm when judged against a child in another environment, it is possible for a range of public bodies to seek an emergency protection order, enabling that young person to be removed from his or her current environment. We saw a number of individuals for whom this course of action could well apply.[32]

The chief inspector was persuaded not to pursue legal action on the understanding that the Home Office would introduce changes in legislation. The then policy adviser to the home secretary, Norman Warner (later to become inaugural chair of the Youth Justice Board), gave this assurance and, in the interim, the director general of the prison service, Martin Narey, issued an instruction to prison staff referring to the principles and good practice of the Children Act 1989.[33] Ramsbotham continued monitoring the treatment of children and grew increasingly disheartened by the absence of new legislation. In the event, the Howard League for Penal Reform successfully argued in the High Court that the statement in the new prison service instruction issued by Narey – which read: 'The Children Act 1989 does not apply to under 18 year olds in prison establishments'[34] – was wrong in law. (It is fair to note that the court was very complimentary about the remainder of the policy document, describing it as 'eloquent and compassionate – even passionate'.)[35] Ramsbotham provided a witness statement to the court explaining why this legal clarification was vital:

> Applying just the spirit of the Act will never work effectively. The Prison Service does not have a good history of implementing changes that do not carry a legal duty.... In my years as Chief Inspector of Prisons,

I recommended the adoption of 2,800 examples of good practice service wide. Only 70 were taken up.[36]

In a research interview with Frances Crook, the chief executive of the Howard League for Legal Reform and the person responsible for bringing this landmark case, she explained its monumental effect more than a decade later:

> 'Ten years ago if you'd said to a local council leader, "Come and have a look at a prison," they'd say, "What for?".... It's taken a while but that [case] I think was part of the groundwork that children should not be in prison – getting the children out.... It changed mindsets – they are the same children, they do have rights, they need safeguarding, protection, the same say. [That] wasn't there before.'

To test the long-term impact of this child protection breakthrough, I submitted freedom of information (FOI) requests to every local authority in England in March 2013 asking for data on the number of referrals they had received in the last five calendar years and the incidence of section 47 enquiries. These are conducted when a child is known or suspected to be suffering significant harm, and it was this issue that was central to the Howard League case. Since 2005, the law has required that, wherever possible, children's wishes and feelings be ascertained and given due consideration by social workers investigating abuse, so I also asked about the proportion of children seen by a social worker, based within and outside the closed institution.

The vast majority of local authorities without prisons in their locality were unable to say whether there had been any child protection referrals relating to local children imprisoned in a different area. There is no statutory requirement on prisons, and the local authorities in which they are located, to notify children's home authorities of abuse referrals. I was told by some that it would be a matter of 'courtesy' for this information to be passed on. A few local authorities appeared to be very assiduous about collecting data –

critical in establishing trends over time and making assessments of the safety of children presently incarcerated – and gave detailed responses.

At the time of my research, 12 local authorities had a young offender institution and/or a secure training centre in their area. These local authorities were legally required to respond to concerns about a child suffering significant harm in a penal setting. Each local authority was required to have a designated officer to oversee investigations of abuse allegations against individuals working with children. Each had a local safeguarding children board to coordinate action in the local authority area, including relating to child prisons. Table 11.1 shows that nine of the 12 local authorities were able to

Table 11.1: Child protection referrals received by local authorities (LAs) concerning children in young offender institutions and secure training centres, 2008-12 (calendar years unless indicated otherwise): alleged perpetrators

	Referrals	Allegations against staff (%)	Allegations against children (%)	Historic allegations (%)
LA 1	19	19 (100)	0	0
LA 2ª	10	NA	NA	NA
LA 3ᵇ	211	NA	NA	NA
LA 4	15	15 (100)	0	0
LA 5	NA	NA	NA	NA
LA 6	NA	NA	NA	NA
LA 7ᶜ	Approx. 60	NA	NA	NA
LA 8ᵈ	NA	NA	NA	NA
LA 9	182	86 (47)	89 (49)	7 (4)
LA 10ᵉ	93	NA	NA	NA
LA 11ᶠ	53	53 (100)	0	0
LA 12	104	104 (100)	0	0
Total	At least 747 referrals received by nine local authorities (incomplete data) Three local authorities said they could not provide any data without exceeding the FOI time limit (18 working hours)			

Notes:

NA = Data not available/not retrievable within timescale.
ª Data relates to period April 2008 to March 2013.
ᵇ Data relates to period April 2007 to March 2012.
ᶜ Data relates to period April 2009 to March 2013 and is incomplete.
ᵈ Data was provided by this local authority for its secure children's home.
ᵉ Aggregate data was provided by the local authority in relation to two secure establishments in its area, only one of which was a young offender institution or secure training centre.
ᶠ Data relates to last three years only.

indicate how many referrals they had received. Only five of the nine local authorities provided basic data about alleged perpetrators in the different secure settings. Adults working with children were the alleged perpetrators of abuse 100% of the time in four of the five local authorities.

An additional local authority with a young offender institution in its area until 2010 stated that it had received 659 child protection referrals between January 2006 and June 2010. It undertook 45 section 47 inquiries in response to these – accounting for 7% of the total referrals. Table 11.2 gives data on the nature of referrals for the 18-month period to June 2010.

Table 11.2: Child protection referrals from a young offender institution to local authority, 1 January 2009 to 30 June 2010

Nature of allegation	Number	% of total
Physical abuse – by staff	71	41
Physical abuse – by other child	34	20
Physical abuse – historic (not in current prison)	9	5
Sexual abuse – by staff	8	5
Sexual abuse – by other child	15	9
Sexual abuse – historic (not in current prison)	3	2
Emotional abuse – by staff	6	3
Emotional abuse – by other child	7	4
Emotional abuse – historic (not in current prison)	6	3
Neglect	15	9
Total	174	101

Table 11.3 shows that just six of the 12 local authorities provided data on the number of section 47 enquiries they undertook after receiving child protection referrals. Three quarters of abuse allegations in one of the institutions led to a child protection investigation, while between 3% and 9% of allegations in three other local authorities were subject to statutory enquiries. Two local authorities said they had not undertaken any statutory child protection investigations in response to allegations from children in prison in the five years under review. Whenever local authorities decide to take no further action after a child has alleged abuse, they risk deterring the child from seeking

Table 11.3: Child protection referrals received by local authorities (LAs) concerning children in young offender institutions and secure training centres, 2008–12 (calendar years unless indicated otherwise): action taken

	Referrals	Section 47 investigation (%)	Police notified	Child seen by social worker based within institution	Child seen by social worker outside institution	Child protection conference	Child protection plan	Serious case review
LA 1	19	0	19	0	0	0	0	0
LA 2[a]	10	NA	NA	NA	NA	NA	NA	0
LA 3[b]	211	NA	NA	NA	NA	NA	NA	0
LA 4	15[c]	0	NA	NA[d]	NA	0	0	0
LA 5	NA	NA	NA	NA	NA	NA	NA	0
LA 6	NA	NA	NA	NA	NA	NA	NA	NA
LA 7[e]	Approx. 60	NA	Approx. 60	Approx. 80% seen by social worker or other safeguarding staff member	Approx. 5% seen by external social worker or police officer	0	0	0
LA 8[f]	NA	NA	NA	NA	NA	NA	NA	1
LA 9	182	9 (5)	NA	182	NA	0	1	0
LA 10	93	73 (78)	73	0	73	0	0	0
LA 11[g]	53	5 (9)	NA[h]	43	5	0	0	0
LA 12	104	3 (3)	NA	NA	NA	NA	NA	0

Notes:
NA = Data not available/not retrievable within timescale.
[a] Data relates to period April 2008 to March 2013.
[b] Data relates to period April 2007 to March 2012.
[c] All allegations were against staff in current establishment – physical abuse (less than 10); emotional abuse (less than 10); sexual abuse (less than 10); and neglect (less than 10).
[d] This local authority reported that 11 referrals were investigated internally and four had no further action. It also said less than 10 staff members were prosecuted.
[e] Data relates to period April 2009 to March 2013 and is incomplete. Two cases resulted in a prosecution (prosecutions were considered in approximately 6% of cases).
[f] Data was provided for its secure children's home only. However, the local authority stated that no members of staff were prosecuted following any child protection allegations in a secure setting in its area.
[g] Data relates to past three years only.
[h] Police were involved in five strategy meetings.

help in the future. As one advocate working with children in prison told researchers conducting a review of safeguarding:

> I was involved in one allegation where a young person said the restraint had been inappropriate. It was referred to [LA] but they didn't deem it worth investigating. I thought that sent the wrong message to the young person – if you're locked up then you're not worth it.[37]

As Table 11.3 illustrates, only five local authorities provided data about children being seen by a social worker after an allegation of abuse or neglect. The majority of children were seen by social workers based within the institution, although social workers from one local authority (LA 10) visited the child in three out of four referrals. Only one local authority reported that every child was seen by a social worker following a referral (always in-house). Another reported that no child was seen by any social worker. Of the three remaining local authorities, children were not seen by any social worker 9% of the time (LA 11), 15% of the time (LA 7) and 22% of the time (LA 10).

Of the six local authorities that answered my question about what action they took in response to a prison abuse or neglect referral, none indicated a child protection conference had been convened, and only one had agreed a child protection plan for a child at risk. With the benefit of hindsight, Ramsbotham's observation that children in Onley young offender institution could have been candidates for emergency protection orders (p 238) seems hopelessly optimistic. Just one local authority reported having conducted a serious case review in relation to a child in a secure establishment in the past five years. Local safeguarding children boards are required by law to undertake these reviews when abuse or neglect is known or suspected and a child dies or was seriously harmed and there is concern about how local agencies have worked together.[38]

Unless corroborative CCTV evidence exists, or a member of staff backs up the allegation, my impression is that it is virtually impossible a child will be believed when alleging abuse in a penal environment. As Phillip Noyes of the NSPCC reminded me in our research interview, children generally are seen to lack credibility, never mind those in closed institutions: "I think believing children who have been a victim of crime is a minority sport wherever the crime occurs." This could explain the discrepancy between the proportion of children who feel it is easy to make a complaint in young offender institutions (55%) and those who say complaints are resolved fairly (39%).[39] Less than a third (29%) of children from black and minority ethnic communities say complaints are sorted out fairly.[40] Inspection data indicates that it is much easier for children to complain in secure training centres, although there is a yawning gap between perceptions of access and fairness (95% knew how to make a complaint but only 56% felt their complaint had been sorted out fairly). More than one in six (16%) at Rainsbrook secure training centre said they felt too afraid or intimidated to make a complaint.[41] It is notable that the prisons inspectorate asks children about making complaints, and the incidence of staff and peer sexual and physical abuse, but not about their access to child protection social workers.

A separate FOI request to the National Offender Management Service (NOMS) revealed 62 instances of prison officers disciplined for abuse of child prisoners from April 2009 to the end of December 2013. In response to my request, NOMS stated: 'We have removed any cases that have been withdrawn, "auto closed" as no outcome received, or employee resigned.' No further action is recorded as the outcome in two of the cases, and no formal action noted for a third. There were 15 dismissals. Two of the sexual abuse cases did not result in dismissal. Table 11.4 shows the nature and frequency of disciplinary charges. I have added a column indicating the type of child abuse; this is inevitably crude without further information. Most disciplinary action was for physical abuse. Child sexual abuse is classified as 'inappropriate relationship with a prisoner/ex-prisoner' – the same terminology that is used in the adult prison estate. It is possible that these officers were charged with having inappropriate relationships with prisoners in former (prison) workplaces, and not their current juvenile establishments. However, I believe this to be unlikely, as I was clear with NOMS throughout that I was seeking data relating to children (the request went to an internal review because it was initially refused).

Table 11.4: Prison officers disciplined in nine juvenile prisons/units, 1 April 2009 to 28 December 2013

Disciplinary charge (NOMS)	Type of child abuse	Number of staff	% of cases
Assault/unnecessary use of force on a prisoner	Physical abuse	26	42
Abusive language/behaviour towards a prisoner	Emotional abuse	12	19
Inappropriate relationship with a prisoner/ex-prisoner	Sexual abuse	6	10
Bullying/harassment	Emotional abuse	4	6
Police caution	Insufficient information	13	21
Criminal conviction	Insufficient information	1	2
Total		62	100

An additional FOI request to police forces in England extracted data from 32 forces (82% of the total). Interested in whether the 'Savile effect' had extended to current or former child prisoners, in September 2013 I asked each force whether it had received any reports of sexual or physical abuse by staff within a young offender institution, secure training centre or other type of penal institution within the past 12 months. Half of the responding police forces said that retrieving the information would exceed the time limit set for such requests; two said they could neither confirm nor deny that they held the information; and one claimed other exemptions. Of the police forces that answered my questions, eight said they had received no such reports in the past year and five indicated they had. The five forces that told me they had received reports of child abuse were Derbyshire, Durham, Greater Manchester, Kent and West Yorkshire.

There were three reports of staff sexual abuse and nine reports of staff physical abuse allegedly occurring in the past 12 months. In addition, there were 43 reports of staff sexual abuse of child prisoners said to have occurred more than 10 years ago (42 of these in one county, Durham) and one further allegation of staff sexual abuse relating to the period between one and five years ago. As well as 42 reports of sexual abuse in Medomsley detention centre, Durham police force had received 27 reports of physical abuse in the year to end September 2013. Detention centre staff were the alleged perpetrators of all of these crimes.

By the end of October 2013, *The Mirror* newspaper, which is collaborating with Durham constabulary in appealing for victims to come forward, reported that 94 people had contacted the police to date. The article observed that Medomsley 'is fast becoming one of the worst cases of mass scale sexual abuse at a government-run institution seen in this country'.[42] More than 750 former inmates had reported abuse to the police by May 2014.[43] Despite this, ministers confirmed in December 2013 that, besides the police investigation, no government or independent inquiries have been launched to examine the abuse of children in this institution.[44] That said, one line of investigation could surely be the extent to which the law empowered child abusers. Until 1989,[45] it was a disciplinary offence in detention centres (and subsequently in young offender institutions) to make a false and malicious allegation against an officer and to repeatedly make groundless complaints – a sure-fire means of silencing children.

I propose four explanations for the parsimonious attention given to penal child abuse: first, the naïve view that such abuse, particularly sexual assault, could not happen in the panoptic prison environment; second, that child protection and child welfare are not core functions of prisons; third, that at some deep level we believe child offenders can take care of themselves; and finally – the most unsettling reason of all – that perhaps we want child prisoners to suffer.

Returning to the first explanation, it is a giant leap from recognising the ordinary pains of confinement – the hunger and other forms of material deprivation, loneliness, strip searching, peer violence, self-harming and suicide attempts, the near-frenetic use of physical restraint in some prisons and the isolation and despair of segregation – to accepting that children could be sexually assaulted and beaten up by staff.

Some might argue that sexual abuse is unlikely because of the limited opportunities for officers to be alone with children. In many of the children's homes scandals, for example, residents had been taken off the premises to be abused, or staff had been able to manipulate situations to spend long periods alone with individual children. Then there are visits from inspectors, YJB officials, members of independent monitoring boards and the Office of the Children's Commissioner, and advocates and social workers are also close to hand. This is in addition to those employed within the institutions who would feel morally and professionally compelled to report any abuse. Moreover, children can take complaints to their local authority, the Prisons and Probation Ombudsman or their MP.

In my view, however, the availability of authority figures is not a fail-safe way of preventing abuse – principally because children have no way of leaving the institution. What's more, there are limitations on all of the safeguarding roles as currently organised. Even the independent advocates employed by Barnardo's have to sign the Official Secrets Act[46] and, according to the contract documents, record their contacts with child prisoners on the YJB's electronic management system[47] – in breach of the government's confidentiality standard for such services.[48]

In our research interview, Phillip Noyes, the NSPCC's chief advisor on child protection, and I discussed the challenges facing children abused in custody. Noyes stressed that retribution is "the number one fear" preventing abuse disclosures of any kind in any setting; children are fearful of being blamed and punished. He reminded me of the research his organisation conducted with young adults who were sexually abused as children. Running away, finding sympathetic adults and the perpetrator losing the opportunity to abuse were the main reasons behind the abuse stopping (although for some the abuse continued long into adulthood). Only a small minority of children reported sexual abuse to the police and social services.[49] Noyes reflected:

> 'Then of the rest: they either stopped it themselves – well, would that be more difficult in a custodial institution? Yes, it would. Or it was stopped by someone they loved or trusted and told. Would that be more difficult in a custodial institution? Yes, it would. Or the perpetrator got fed up and went away. Well, is that more difficult in a custodial institution? Yes, it is. Or it didn't stop. And you just think which of those four [outcomes] are you putting money on in a locked-in space?'

A particularly distressing allegation to come out of Medomsley detention centre was that boys would lie at the bottom of the stairs and ask other children to jump on them in the hope their legs would be broken and they would be taken off the premises and therefore escape more abuse.[50] It is hard to imagine children in locked institutions today being so utterly desperate, but testimonies like this serve as markers of how bad things can get.

One UK study found that, when male offenders 'talked about abuse it was hesitantly, with reticence and often under-reported'.[51] Other NSPCC research shows that it takes on average seven years for children to disclose sexual abuse.[52] The resourcefulness of abusers should not be underestimated. Sexual offenders have great skill in creating occasions to violate children – within family homes, when other family members are in the same or next room (even in the same bed); in schools, when a child can be legitimately asked to stay behind or given a role that involves entering a storeroom or remote area of the building; and in children's homes, when a child is supposedly being checked on, talked to or given some special time. A former social work manager reminded me of a case in our local authority where several children – in care because of multiple family abuse – were sexually assaulted by family members during supervised contact visits.

We considered earlier (p 40) the difficulties children with literacy and other learning difficulties have in understanding and using formal complaints processes. The fundamental impediment is that these systems have been designed for adults. Within the social care context, there have been numerous reviews and reforms to complaints procedures to make them work easily and fairly for children. There are separate laws, policies and personnel for dealing with children's complaints in social care. But still there are problems. The position in penal institutions is far worse. Over a decade ago, a review was undertaken to try to establish why young prisoners make little use of prison complaints procedures. Stephen Shaw, then Prisons and Probation Ombudsman (PPO), asked at the start of the report: 'Is it a paradox or actually part of the explanation that the worst institutions seem to generate the fewest formal complaints?'[53] His conclusion mirrored the findings of earlier major inquiries into abuse in children's homes:

> Young people in custody are peculiarly vulnerable. Safeguards of prisoners' rights designed for adults may simply be unsuitable to the needs of children and young people.[54]

During my research for this book, I asked the PPO to supply information on the number and types of complaints it has received from child prisoners in the past five years, and discovered that only 29 cases were lodged and 19 considered eligible for investigation. This amounts to just 0.1% of the total complaints submitted by prisoners. What is particularly eye-catching about the PPO data is that 17 (59%) of the children who made a complaint did so after leaving the establishment. The reasons are not hard to comprehend, and were no doubt behind the Howard League for Penal Reform's decision some years ago to interview children who had recently left Portland young offender institution about the abusive regime, instead of those still in the prison (p 215). Furthermore, only two of the complaints investigated by the PPO surrounded allegations of officer abuse; most were about loss of possessions and adjudications.

The lawyers I interviewed for this book were clear about both the necessity and limitations of complaints procedures. Chris Callender told me about the worker who ended up being "hounded out" of a prison because she contacted him about a client while he was legal director at the Howard League for Penal Reform. He said that "outstanding individuals who were prepared to put their livelihoods and reputations at risk" had referred nearly all of the child prisoner cases he dealt with. Children very rarely came directly to the charity's legal service. Richard Hermer QC summed up:

> 'With children you just can't leave it by saying, in a leaflet or during induction, that if you've got any issues you can go to the Ombudsman. One needs to create an environment in which children feel and understand

that they have those remedies available to them, and feel comfortable about using them.'

The law entitles children who are dissatisfied with the outcome of a complaint in a secure training centre to appeal to the YJB monitor.[55] I asked the YJB for data on children's use of this procedure and discovered that only 15 such appeals were made between 2009 and February 2014. I was told that children have to go through an internal appeals process before approaching the monitor, although this is not something that appears in the statutory rules. One of the 15 appeals related to staff physical assault and another to other staff mistreatment. The YJB upheld four appeals (27%). Children directly communicated their appeals to the YJB monitor on 11 occasions and lawyers did so on their behalf four times. Social workers or independent advocates lodged no appeals. In December 2013, legal aid entitlement for advice and assistance on matters relating to their treatment in prison was withdrawn from children in young offender institutions and secure training centres, and limitations were introduced on legal representation in prison disciplinary proceedings.[56] The following month, Lord Pannick led a debate in the House of Lords on opposition to the changes:

> The Minister's main argument, that the internal complaints system and the ombudsman system are an effective substitute for legal assistance and advice, is simply contrary to the advice of the Parole Board, the inspector of prisons and the ombudsman. It is contrary to court judgments over the years. It is contrary to the experience of all those who have spoken tonight, apart from the Minister. Indeed, it is irrational, given the lack of literacy, the youth, the immaturity and the mental health difficulties of so many prisoners, let alone their obvious inability to identify and present the issues that arise in their cases.[57]

The Howard League for Penal Reform and the Prisoners' Advice Service unsuccessfully challenged the changes in the High Court and, at the time of writing, have been given leave to appeal their case. Any reduction in children's access to individuals truly independent of prisons is clearly very dangerous.

It is not that the state refuses to countenance the notion that children might be gravely harmed in prison. Children are routinely asked about sexual and physical abuse during official prison inspections. Moreover, following the publication of a major review into safeguarding children living away from home (p 18), the Home Office conducted a unique study into abuse in young offender institutions. Face-to-face interviews were undertaken with 979 children, aged 15 to 17, in 28 young offender institutions between October 1999 and February 2000. The interviewers were experienced police officers and psychologists. In addition to questions about safety, physical abuse and coercion, children were asked about 'sexual behaviour'. Eight per cent of the children (77 in all) had heard of prisoners having to do something sexual against their will. Three children said they had witnessed this happening, and another three reported that it had happened to them. Staff were said to be aware of just two of these six incidents.

None of the children alleged sexual abuse by staff, leading the authors to comment: 'The lack of evidence for any wrongdoing on the part of prison staff must be gratifying to the prison authorities when so many examples of abuse by staff have emerged from children's homes.'[58] A number of explanations were proposed for the total absence of reports of staff sexual violence, including this remarkable theory:

> Many of the abuses reported from children's homes involve children under ten years old. In most cases, the abuses committed against them tend to reduce in their teens and disappear altogether as they approach adulthood and are better able either to defend themselves, or to articulate complaints. It is also the case that many paedophiles are attracted to younger children. Our youngest participants were 15 years old, generally 'streetwise', and not, on the face of it, the likeliest victims.[59]

Had Home Office officials consulted colleagues in the Department of Health (then responsible for government policy on children's homes) about the characteristics of abuse victims in residential care, they would have been told of the similarities with their own cohort of vulnerable children. A report published two years earlier had summarised 36 separate NSPCC investigations into child abuse in residential and day care settings. Of 67 children alleging abuse in these settings, 55% were aged between 15 and 17 years. Only 4% were aged 10 and under.[60] It is very unlikely that sexual abuse disclosures would arise in a 15-minute prison research interview, particularly as children were never asked directly about any mistreatment by staff. Indeed, the introduction to the interview – read aloud to children – included this instruction: 'We don't want your name, or the name of anyone else, and your answers will not be shown to anyone else.'[61] This was hardly an invitation to report abuse. Some years later, Martin Narey, who was the prison service's director general at the time of the flawed research, was reported as saying:

> As director-general, I was intolerant of physical abuse and racism and sacked a lot of staff ... but at that time there was very little awareness of male-on-male sexual abuse, either in prisons or in wider society.[62]

Nobody would bat an eyelid if a person working in road maintenance or car sales regretted being oblivious to child rape and sexual assault a decade or two ago, but what is perplexing is that Narey was in charge of institutions detaining people convicted of these very crimes. The most notorious abuser of children in care, Frank Beck, was in November 1991 handed 'one of the most severe sentences seen in this country since the abolition of the death penalty' – five life sentences plus 24 years.[63] Prisons officers surely sit alongside child protection social workers, police officers, lawyers and specialist paediatricians in terms of exposure to levels of suffering and depravity unknown to most.

A study conducted by the US government in 2012, where almost 9,000 child prisoners were asked to complete a detailed online survey with explicit questions about sexual victimisation by staff (and fellow inmates), found that 8.2% of boys and 2.8% of girls reported sexual activity with staff.[64]

The results of the flawed Home Office research have cast a long shadow. Even today, there is no central data on the numbers of staff working in penal establishments that have been suspended, disciplined, dismissed or convicted for matters relating to child protection (although I was able to obtain some information after persisting for months with an FOI request – p 245). In July 2013, Lord McNally in the Ministry of Justice, in an answer to a parliamentary question, said the 'information is not held centrally' and explained:

> [G4S and Serco, which run secure training centres,] do hold internal records of reasoning behind staff dismissals however the YJB do not have access to this.

> [The National Offender Management Service, which runs young offender institutions,] provides improved centralised information in a number of areas, including the number of staff subject to disciplinary procedures. However it is not possible to filter the results to show the numbers of staff working in the young people's estate at the time of their disciplinary award, nor the number of disciplinary investigations specifically triggered by complaints from young people.[65]

If the head of a local authority children's services department was unable to tell Ofsted, government ministers, or a local newspaper how many childcare staff had been subject to disciplinary action following allegations of abuse, they would invite scorn and disbelief.

This leads to my second theory for why penal institutions evade proper child protection scrutiny: because looking after vulnerable children is not their core function. Children are not sent to prison for a better life, to be protected, saved or rescued. The twin obsessions of penal administrators are discipline and security, not child welfare, and this is what they are judged on. Prison service performance data, for example, tracks drug testing, overcrowding, escape attempts and absconding; there is no differentiation between child and adult institutions. At the same time, there is little indication that young offenders are current priorities for children's charities. Even the NSPCC's 'first national child abuse tracker', launched in 2013, stresses the risks for children in care but says nothing about penal institutions:

> The types of abuse [looked after] children may suffer include targeted abuse by carers or other adults, poor standards of care, abuse disguised as treatment or behaviour modification techniques, systematic abuse by staff against children, and further emotional damage caused by placement instability.... The full extent of abuse while in care is unknown, but for this extremely vulnerable group, it is important to remain vigilant.[66]

This relates to my third explanation for the lack of sustained interest in child prisoners, which is that we choose to swallow whole the representations of young offenders as strong and powerful. Like the Home Office officials who found no sexual abuse, at some deep level we believe child prisoners can take care of themselves. We considered in Chapter One the extraordinary denials from past government ministers that child prisoners are actually children. This practice of emboldening child offenders to the point where they are no longer perceived to be children even led the former justice secretary, Kenneth Clarke, a man not lacking in physical stature, to warn that some child prisoners 'are much bigger than I am'.[67] The day after Clarke's disclosure, Lord McNally cautioned peers against using 'the word "children" very casually'.[68] Both ministers were at the time defending the deliberate infliction of pain on children in penal institutions, a practice prohibited in secure children's homes regardless of the height, weight or strength of residents. Even in moments of mercy, such as when the children's charity Barnardo's called for children to be removed from custody, there is a cut-off point. Barnardo's argued for custody to be reserved for children aged 15 and over, unless they have committed serious and violent crimes, in which case younger children should also continue to be detained. What was it is about 15-, 16- and 17-year-olds that made Barnardo's believe custody was justified? It could not have been the success rate: it rightly described the practice of incarceration as 'costly and ineffective'.[69]

In a research interview, the Labour peer Lord Judd told me he finds it "absolutely intolerable that we treat children who are disadvantaged in a way we would never, ever dream of treating our own children". Incarcerated children are most definitely seen as 'other' children,[70] banished from normal conceptions of what makes a child, and how we should treat a child. In disturbing the received wisdom, child offenders hurt not only their victims. They have taken risks and been daring; some have behaved appallingly. Virtually all have acted outside what we understand children to be like, and this seems to hit a raw nerve in many. Unlike smaller and younger victims of childhood trauma and deprivation, adolescent law-breakers tend not to present as pitiful or fragile – at least not in photographs taken in police stations and used by the media. Within penal establishments, Baroness Veronica Linklater explained in our interview, many officers:

> '... just don't have the background or the training to appreciate the lengths and the depths and the breadths of the vulnerability and the insecurity of children who very often look very big and beefy, and confident and loud, all of which is very counterintuitive if you then start talking about vulnerabilities.'

It is as if we would rather get them out of our sight altogether than deal with difficult and demanding children – especially teenagers. It is Oliver Twist we are rooting for, not the Artful Dodger. All too late, thoughtful examinations of young offenders' lives, as occasionally happen after a child dies with a ligature around their neck, or when they have committed a particularly odious offence, bring forth biographies heaving with tragedy and hardship. The serious case review into the death of 15-year-old Alex Kelly at Cookham Wood young offender institution (p 12) observed:

> The severity of Child F's abuse in early childhood and the fact that it occurred in parallel with neglect and emotional abuse is likely to have had a lasting negative

impact on all aspects of his emotional and behavioural development.[71]

A later statement points to the devastating consequences of adults 'forgetting' what children have been through:

> Increasingly Child F's behaviour began to reflect the very severe impact on him of the abuse that he had suffered, leading to more and more difficulties in controlling his emotions and his behaviour... gradually over the years detailed knowledge of the gravity of what had happened to Child F was lost.[72]

It is as if children who started out as abused, neglected or struggling but have then acted in unpalatable ways – lashing out, bunking off school, setting fires, inflicting harm, running away and not responding to help – have switched sides. Defected. They are victims no longer. The more challenging the behaviour, the less we want to understand and truly know them. A core textbook on child abuse and neglect refers to a 1970s study of the characteristics of the behaviour of abused children, beginning with 'impaired capacity to enjoy life – abused children often appear sad, preoccupied and listless'.[73] It may be in our quest to rescue those who show obvious signs of childhood sadness that we walk right past children who show their hurt in more puzzling and defiant ways.

The final possible explanation for not listening – really listening – to incarcerated children is the most troubling. Could it be that this group of children acts as a lightning rod for the worst of our attitudes towards the young? Just as the undeserving poor and migrants act as a steady supply of adult hate figures, could it be that young prisoners function as the only children for whom it is legitimate for state bodies to frighten, demean and hurt? That this group has been (subconsciously) selected as a receptacle of levels of anger, frustration and intolerance deemed far too dangerous and damaging for our own children? Criminologists have long shown the forces and prejudices at play in the rounding up, branding and punishment of criminals – control of the underclass, racial superiority and rigid gender rules among them. Children are part of this too. Could there be an additional dynamic in child imprisonment conserving, albeit in tucked-away places and hidden from view, archaic beliefs about children and punishment? Fear and suffering were once the golden strategies of schools, residential institutions and families determined to 'make' good children. We now appreciate the importance of listening to children, understanding them and treating them gently, and we have passed laws and signed up to international treaties to prove we know better. However, like the ex-smoker who hides a pack of 10 at the back of a kitchen cupboard, or the jilted lover who has sadly held on to birthday cards and text messages sent by their ex-partner, might the preservation of juvenile prisons be a flashing neon sign broadcasting the fact that we haven't altogether moved on from making children suffer? Child prisoners are not literally whipping boys – state corporal punishment was banned nearly half a century ago – but they are victim to ideas and practices long since abandoned for their peers.

TWELVE

They shouldn't be there

The sociologist Stanley Cohen describes three types of information denial – literal, interpretative and implicatory. These encompass flat denials that events occurred; giving different meaning to events but not denying them; and not feeling compelled to act.[1] The state exhibited all three forms of denial in the years of intense scrutiny and censure after child prisoners Gareth Myatt and Adam Rickwood died in scandalous conditions. The light shone on child prisons as a consequence of these boys' deaths exposed more than brutal, unlawful restraint. Two years after Gareth and Adam died, for example, the Carlile Inquiry reported disturbing incidents of child prisoners being routinely forced to remove their clothes and had this to say about prison solitary confinement:

> ... the inquiry found that most segregation units in [juvenile] prisons were little more than bare, dark and dank cells which in effect were inducements to suicide.[2]

The Youth Justice Board (YJB) subsequently reviewed a number of contentious prison practices and the former Labour government commissioned an independent review of restraint. The past few years have seen some movement in some entrenched behaviours, including the belated surrendering of habitual strip searching – although, notably, not the procedure itself. That the number of children sent to custody continues to fall, which itself is partly attributable to the actions of the YJB, inevitably means fewer are exposed to the dangers of incarceration. It is nonetheless a cause for head shaking that the exile of children to prison has survived these revelations as well as the scandals of former decades (pp 214–20) and has been impervious to transformations in the treatment of children elsewhere. What more would have needed to be uncovered about Gareth and Adam, and other imprisoned children who have suffered, to have led our politicians to declare 'enough is enough'?

Deborah Coles, co-director of INQUEST, has had more than 20 years' worth of exposure to the hidden realities of child prisons. In our research interview, she told me:

> 'Nobody's willing to engage with the fact that what we need for the first time ever is a far-reaching inquiry that can properly look at all the interrelating issues that your book is essentially dealing with.... I think the cases of Joseph and Gareth and Adam will haunt me forever, because when you sit through an inquest where you actually hear the reality of what we're doing to those children alongside the family, it's shameful.... I must admit I was struck when we came out of the second inquest into Adam's death. The jury waited behind and, as we walked out, a woman came up to me and she said … "Why don't we know about what takes place in these places?" and I said, "That is the question." The truth about what we do behind the closed doors of prisons tends only to come out when: one, there's a death; two, when you've got a family who are prepared to stand up and demand questions be asked; and, importantly, [they] have the legal aid and specialist lawyers to actually ensure that those questions are answered.'

Jake Hardy's mother recounted a similar story. At the conclusion of the inquest into her son's death, individual jurors approached her and said they could not believe how he was treated in prison. Pam Wilton, the mother of Gareth Myatt, was still grateful a decade later for the solidarity she received from those working in the conference centre in which her son's inquest was held.

Less than three weeks after the convictions of three adults for causing or allowing the horrific death of 17-month-old Peter

Connolly (known in the media as Baby Peter), Ed Balls, then secretary of state for children, schools and family, announced on television that he had replaced Haringey council's director of children's services, Sharon Shoesmith, and wanted her to be sacked without any 'pay-off'. This intervention was later found by the Court of Appeal to be unlawful.[3] Nevertheless, it is to be assumed the minister's actions were influenced by public concern about a baby dying in horrific circumstances. There were no such ramifications for those in charge of penal institutions.

Baby Peter was living at home with his mother, one of those convicted of his death, even though he met the threshold for care proceedings – a process that would have made him a child in public care. Children who die in prison are not in any sense concealed from the authorities. The state has complete control and oversight of them. During our research interview, I asked Phillip Noyes, chief advisor for child protection at the National Society for the Prevention of Cruelty to Children (NSPCC), whether he believes the risks facing children in prison are heightened because they are frequently detained many miles away from home, or due to the hidden nature of penal institutions. He replied:

> 'I think fear and secrecy are even more important because you can imagine a child's family living next door to a penal institution but fear and secrecy will still be the institutional norm.'

Lack of public scrutiny is one of the reasons independent inspection is so important, says Nick Hardwick, the current chief inspector of prisons, in a report for the National Preventive Mechanism. He continues:

> The nature of those held, the imbalance of power between detainee and gaoler and the fact that the work of the institution takes place behind high walls, out of sight, creates the conditions in which it is all too easy for abuse to take place. However, in my view, the greatest risk is the normative effect those conditions create. Away from

public scrutiny, it is all too easy for even well intentioned staff to become accepting of standards that in any other setting would be unacceptable.[4]

Eight-year-old Victoria Climbié was tortured and murdered by her aunt and aunt's partner in 2000, the same year as three teenage boys – David Dennis, Philip Griffin and Kevin Henson – died in young offender institutions in Wolverhampton, Wetherby and London respectively. Only Victoria's death led to sustained media coverage, a public inquiry and changes in children's services. The terrifying treatment of Victoria by her guardians, her young age and the fact that she was sent to this country for a better life were elements of her 'story' that appalled the nation. But was the suffering of three teenage boys who perished in our prisons that year any less shocking than that of this vulnerable little girl? Was their distress so insignificant as to warrant a virtual media and political blackout?

In March 2014, the YJB published a report summarising its actions in response to the 16 child deaths occurring since it took on responsibility for allocating children to institutions. It confessed to having only minimal paperwork for five of the children, including the three who died the same year as Victoria Climbié.[5]

Stories of infants being starved, beaten and abandoned rightly evoke public anger and political action. These tiny human beings are completely powerless. But empathy, like love and compassion, is not a scarce resource and I refuse to accept we are incapable of defending the rights of older, bigger and more challenging children. Lord Laming, former chief of the social services inspectorate, led the Victoria Climbié Inquiry and one area he considered was the assumptions made by health and social care staff about Victoria and the adults who killed her. The relationship between Victoria and her aunt was said, for example, to reflect 'master and servant'; she was seen in hospital 'standing to attention' and had wet herself while being told off by her aunt. This cruel formality was believed by some professionals to be normal for African-Caribbean families.[6] Lord Laming penned a reminder of the universal norms of child protection:

The basic requirement that children are kept safe is universal and cuts across cultural boundaries. Every child living in this country is entitled to be given the protection of the law, regardless of his or her background.[7]

Gareth Myatt and Adam Rickwood must have felt absolutely defeated in the moments before their death. These two boys were victims of serious child abuse in penal institutions that had been open for less than five years. There have been no criminal prosecutions, no sackings, no independent inquiries and no public apologies arising from this severe mistreatment. In October 2014, the YJB announced it would no longer be sending children to Hassockfield secure training centre from March 2015. This might have been the moment for officials to publicly express regret and remorse for their abject failure to protect children in Hassockfield from unlawful restraint in the past, and to remember the ultimate price paid by Adam Rickwood. Instead, the YJB indicated a number of factors lay behind its decision, but concerns about Hassockfield's performance was not one of them. It is now known that several hundred former inmates of Medomsley detention centre, which previously occupied the land on which Hassockfield stands, have reported to the police that Medomsley officers sexually abused them (p 246). This therefore could have also been the moment for government ministers to pledge the place would never again be used to imprison children. There were no such reassurances. The site would be handed back to the Ministry of Justice, 'who will decide on [its] future use', the YJB added.[8]

Rainsbrook secure training centre, the institution in which Gareth died, was in the constituency of the then Labour MP, Sally Keeble. Three years after his death she was still outraged:

> When I first set out to look into the matter, I thought that it might have been individual wrongdoing by a member of staff that led to Gareth's death, but it was much worse than that. It was a complete systematic collective failure, which so far has not been put right. On a personal note, what particularly appals me is the complete lack of any sense of horror on the part of officialdom at what

happened. As the jury found, the gruesome death of a boy was caused by profound failures in a system for which, ultimately, Ministers are responsible to the House.[9]

Unlike Winterbourne View, the hospital for adults with learning disabilities that was shut down after several care staff were caught on film unlawfully restraining their patients and subjecting them to sickening cruelty (p 107), Rainsbrook and Hassockfield secure training centres thrived in the years following Gareth and Adam's deaths. G4S was contracted by the government to train immigration officials in child protection a few years after three of its employees fatally restrained Gareth.[10] Serco, the multinational running the prison in which Adam died, was praised by the deputy prime minister, Nick Clegg, for its work with young people[11] within days of the High Court concluding that widespread unlawful restraint had occurred in all four secure training centres.

The invitation issued to Adam's mother to join in with a prayer service for her son could have represented genuine concern. However, the offer was hollow because it came from a prison in which a powerless 14-year-old boy hanged himself after a catalogue of punishing events – sanctions for accepting two cigarettes and some matches during a family visit; restraint for non-compliance that included a swipe to the nose; and no immediate prospect of bail. The Prisons and Probation Ombudsman summed up:

> Tragedy is not a word to be used lightly…. However, I have found this a uniquely troubling story. At its centre is an intelligent but damaged and vulnerable 14 year old boy who took his life while in the care of the state, having planned the details of his own funeral. If this does not constitute a tragedy, the word has lost all meaning.[12]

In our interview, Carol spoke to me about her feelings when she went to collect her son's belongings from the prison after she had been to the hospital morgue:

'Their words to me were, "Mrs Pounder, once this has all blown over would you like to come for prayers?" I said, "Once this is all blown over?": I lost it.'

In another example of a deeply insensitive institutional response, Pam Wilton told me that when she went to visit Rainsbrook secure training centre after her son's death, she was given a tour of the building and told about the centre's educational achievements.

Other shocking 'non-accidental' deaths of children living with their parents have resulted in high-level reviews and policy announcements. Some local authorities have had external agencies and individuals parachuted in by central government, because they are no longer deemed capable of protecting children in neighbourhoods where professionals and the public can readily see and hear when things are not right. The lack of comparable action for penal child deaths is stark. Mark Scott, the solicitor representing the mothers of Gareth and Adam, told me in his interview:

'I suppose when I was young and naïve, a long time ago, you'd always hope that someone at an inquest would actually really engage with the family and say, "Look, we really messed up here, and I'm so terribly sorry for this." But I can't remember any apology like that, that's ever been made in a really meaningful way. If these deaths happened in any other sort of institution, you'd be pushing at an open door to get some sort of systemic inquiry.'

I asked Scott what he hoped as an inquest lawyer to achieve for the parents of children who have died in custody, and received this reply:

'Nothing can bring the child back for the parent, and so what they want is for meaningful lessons to be learnt. The parent doesn't want someone else – other parents – to go through what they've been through. But that's a difficult thing to achieve ... a lawyer can't say you're going to change the system, that this isn't going to happen again, particularly when experience is you've seen the cases again and again and again, effectively. So it's to try and expose the truth as to what happened, to try and get some level of accountability for what's happened. And to try and ensure that some lessons are learnt.'

The government's March 2011 announcement that 'any technique for restraining a child should never be intended to inflict pain'[13] would have been a major lesson learnt had it applied to prisons. Besides representing a move towards compliance with human rights treaties, it would have shown that state officials now understand the risks inherent in allowing the deliberate infliction of severe pain as a form of child restraint. For those still wondering how officers can protect themselves and others in situations of dire emergency, remember that they are also trained in personal safety techniques (p 141). Adam can be credited with the withdrawal of the nose distraction, but what if his brave note had asked, 'What gives them the right to hit a child?'? What if it had not mentioned the nose? It is a sad irony that the prohibition of pain was ordered only for children's homes, the type of establishment Adam was meant to have been in. In our research interview, barrister Richard Hermer QC summed up the impact on the state of years of concerted pressure around unlawful restraint:

> 'It had some uncomfortable moments in court, but that's about as far as it goes. They're facing damages on some cases, but not very much.'

Professor Mike Stein has written a book about the formidable efforts of children and young people to humanise the 'care system' over the past 40 years.[14] Some of the accounts of life in care in the past would be unrecognisable to children in residential care today, including children having to bathe and shower in front of staff; calling carers 'auntie' and 'uncle'; sleeping on the floor as punishment for wetting the bed; having dinner money paid directly from the council to schools (and therefore being singled out as a child in care); not having any influence over children's homes rules; and being denied family visits as a penalty for poor behaviour.

Many of these discarded practices are alive and kicking in child prisons. Routine strip searching, only recently abolished and still available for those deemed to be a security risk, is not dissimilar to the institutional bathing once imposed on care entrants. Inmates addressing officers as 'Boss', 'Gov' or 'Miss', and being identified by numbers and surnames in official procedures, harks back to a bygone era when pretend titles were common within care settings – though at least in that context the motive was to emulate loving relationships. What is clear about these formalities is that they firmly cast prison as institution, not home. Child prisoners may not have to sleep on the floor as punishment for wetting the bed, but showing extreme distress or agitation may result in time in segregation and adjudication 'awards' (p 68). The practice of delivering meals to cell doors is plainly not aimed at boosting children's self-esteem.

Listening to children is one of the principal policy requirements of social care. In addition to social workers' legal duty to consult looked after children before making decisions about them (a requirement since 1975), care workers have wide-ranging obligations to take account of the views of children's homes residents. The same cannot be said about prison. Why should it? People are incarcerated as the ultimate act of disempowerment; expecting children's free expression and human agency to grow in this environment is as absurd as looking for clean fingernails in a gardener. As for the withdrawal of parental contact as a punishment, this was outlawed in children's homes in 1990. Conversely, young offender institutions and secure training centres are permitted to vary the quantity and quality of family visits as a means of regulating the child's behaviour (p 163). The former head of the YJB, John Drew, put this into context by reminding me that rewards and sanctions are the lifeblood of prisons. It follows that family contact acts as both carrot and stick.

Anyone visiting our country for the first time in 2013 would have deduced that we are a nation that loathes child abuse. Some of our most iconic institutions – the BBC, NHS, Crown Prosecution Service and the police – offered *mea culpas* following the Savile exposures. The NSPCC's child abuse helpline was contacted 9,000 times in a single month also in the aftermath of the Savile case.[15] Working on the assumption that it is not only sexual assaults on vulnerable children but any form of suffering and extreme powerlessness that we cannot tolerate, the continuation of child prisons is anomalous. Any parent found to be keeping their child detained in a tiny room more than 20 hours a day would, at the very least, be sent on a compulsory course to correct their abusive behaviour and yet prison inspectors routinely report this kind of practice in institutions run by the state. The UN Special Rapporteur on Torture has advised states that 'some of the harmful psychological effects of isolation can become irreversible' once a person of any age has been kept in solitary confinement for 15 days or more.[16] For children, the anti-torture expert concludes, any period in physical or social isolation in prison 'is cruel, inhuman or degrading treatment'.[17] The UN Committee on the Rights of the Child is clear that solitary confinement as punishment 'must be strictly forbidden'.[18] What makes us continue to treat children like this?

In our interview, Deborah Coles reflected on the use of restraint in prisons and how this would never be tolerated within a family setting. Using the example of her teenage son, she explained:

> 'It will be like me ringing up a couple of mates and going, "Oh come on give us a hand we're going to restrain him and take him up to his room and sit on his bed and force him down until he submits."… It's horrible actually to even think it.'

Chris Callender, former legal director of the Howard League for Penal Reform, told me about the impersonal and sometimes abusive language used in prisons:

> 'People live in blocks [in prisons]. I don't live in a block I live in a home, do you know what I mean? I've been on the phone to kids who are self-harmers being called all sorts of names, all totally contrary to the so-called guidance. I mean one lad who's now ended up in a high secure hospital, who I represented in HMYOI Ashfield and I'm still in contact with, I was on the phone and you could hear the way officers were talking to him and calling him "slasher" and he's stuck with that. This all

relates to self-harm. It's just completely depressing to see these really needy, vulnerable children who are extremely bright, extremely insightful, sometimes really articulate, sometimes much more articulate than the prison officers, which is often a problem for them, crushed. And where you can see there's a whole level of need and it's just unmet. It will continue to be unmet.'

An evaluation of one of the prison service's few dedicated units for especially vulnerable children, operating to a specification provided by the YJB, underlines what is missing for most incarcerated children:

It was designed to be a 'less institutional environment' with smaller wings and no bars on the windows.... A central hub on each floor contains multi-function rooms for education, group work, one-to-one interviews and other activities, as well as space for health services, cooking facilities and staff areas. The unit has been designed to ensure that there are open spaces and natural light.[19]

Baroness Vivien Stern has spoken about how we adjust our perceptions by wearing 'crime spectacles'.[20] Everything is viewed through the prism of the child (or adult) being an offender. Popular narratives tell us these children are not the same as our own children. Looking to the backgrounds and earlier traumas of child prisoners to understand and change their behaviour is seen as making excuses. This dangerous practice of viewing children who have committed crimes as essentially different from other children is, I believe, not a stone's throw away from a belief in witchcraft.

Mark Scott, a solicitor who has represented many of the families of children who have died in prison, told me that the problem with inquests is that they deal with only the very final part of a child's life:

'If there are 10 stages of the child's life, the inquest is looking at stage 9.9 of 10 when some of the really fundamental failings happened at a much earlier stage.'

The same applies to criminal acts. From everything that could be known about a child, we select a fraction of his or her behaviour – that which has breached the law – and construe their 'master-status' as young offender.[21] We saw in Chapter Two the many other descriptors that could be used (if label we must) to more accurately reflect children's lives and circumstances, including victims of poverty, maltreatment, bereavement, educational exclusion and institutional racism. There is no question that the vast majority of child prisoners will have suffered serious human rights violations. This is why the UN urges its member states to locate measures to prevent and respond to juvenile offending within their wider 'comprehensive framework of social justice for all juveniles'.[22] England's first children's commissioner articulated this in straightforward terms when he said, 'Shutting children away in prison sends a message that we are giving up on them. If progress is to be made, we need to tackle the root causes of crime.'[23]

Grave crimes committed by children remain very rare. The number of children presently serving custodial sentences for murder is the size of a football team with two reserves. Youth justice academic Tim Bateman made the obvious point in our research interview that "one of the most powerful ways of reducing the custodial population" would be to increase the age of criminal responsibility:

'By and large most kids in custody are still there for persistence rather than seriousness. If you can start offending at 10 you can build up quite a record by the time you're 17.'

Bateman is confident that removing younger children from the purview of criminal justice agencies would force mainstream welfare services to provide for those who offend and they would then develop "an ethos and a culture and a practice that suggests there are ways of dealing with these children without criminalising them". The other practical step he advocates is the decoupling of sentencing rules for adults and children, to bring an end to children being deprived of their liberty for the same crimes as adults.

The dangers of criminalisation are long proven, including through respected research in the UK. A longitudinal study of 4,300 children in Edinburgh started in 1998, when the subjects were aged around 12.[24] Information about the children was collected on six separate occasions during a five-year period. Researchers found that previous contact with criminal justice agencies was the most significant predictor of future intervention – greater than the nature of the child's offending or level of need. Children who became entrenched in the system ('the usual suspects') were significantly less likely to report that they had stopped serious offending than those who had no or minimal contact but had initially exhibited similar offending behaviour. Since the late 1960s, Scotland's overall approach to child offending has been welfare-focused and deliberately non-punitive. Yet even within this framework the results of the Edinburgh study 'add further weight to the international research evidence that youth justice systems may be congenitally unable to deliver the reductions in offending'[25] governments expect them to.

That we retain an age of criminal responsibility of 10 is entirely defeatist, showing an embarrassing lack of confidence in intervening in the lives of even very young children without organised punishment. It is also dangerous. Like the disciplinarian who keeps a belt hung on the wall, the extreme options of arrest and custody will be brought down and used so long as they are available.

Imprisoned children inhabit a peculiar world of last resorts. Separation from parents is meant to be a last resort; criminal proceedings are meant to be a last resort; deprivation of liberty is meant to be a last resort; use of force is meant to be a last resort; the removal of clothes is meant to be a last resort; the deliberate infliction of severe pain as a form of restraint is meant to be a last resort; and personal safety techniques even more of a last resort. In a rich country like ours, with decades of learning about the needs of children – and health, education and child welfare services among the best in the world – it is incongruous that prisons remain part of the landscape. Are we really to believe that children who end up in prison are there because we have nothing else to offer them? A roll call of the children who have died in prison since the UK accepted the last resort obligations of the United Nations Convention on the Rights of the Child stands as a towering memorial of our collective failure.

Philip Knight, who died in 1990, was adopted as an infant and started showing behaviour problems from around the age of seven. He was 'returned' to social services when he was 14. He killed himself in the hospital wing of an adult prison, having cut his wrists the week before.[26] Craig Walsh (died 1990) had been in a youth treatment centre for 18 months and was expected to return there on sentencing. There was no room so he was sent to Glen Parva young offender institution, where he hanged himself aged 15.[27] Jeffrey Horler (died 1991) was sent to prison for setting fire to a shed and was devastated by the death of his grandmother during his incarceration.[28] Patrick Murphy (died 1992) was given a custodial sentence for burglary and theft, and was said to have a serious alcohol problem. He had tried to kill himself in a court cell and was beaten up the day he hanged himself.[29] Andrew Batey (died 1994) had asked to go into segregation for his own protection but the bullying and threats he had been subjected to continued.[30] Chris Greenaway (died 1995) was found hanging in his cell, aged 16; his cellmate was later convicted of his murder.[31] Nicholas Whelan (died 1998) had attention deficit hyperactivity disorder (ADHD) and prison staff had apparently stopped giving him his drug Ritalin before he killed himself.[32] John Keyworth (died 1998) had tried to cut his wrists when he was imprisoned previously and there were claims at his inquest that he had been bullied.[33] Kirk Edwards (died 1999), a boy with severe learning difficulties, was found hanging two days into his sentence; on admission, he had told a prison nurse he felt very guilty because both his parents had cancer and he could not help them.[34] Philip Griffin (died 2000), a child with dyslexia who, until a few years before, had been 'a lovely lad who would have helped anyone', was given his first prison sentence for stealing from a shop, a house burglary and robbing a person in the street.[35] He was homeless at the time of sentencing.[36] Kevin Henson (died 2000) had turned to drink after his mother died on his 14th birthday; he told his father Feltham young offender institution was the worst place in the world.[37] Anthony Redding (died 2001) had been taken out of school because of bullying[38] and had made three other suicide attempts during the previous three weeks (one in the escort vehicle taking him to prison).[39] Mark Dade (died 2001) was addicted to drugs on admission to custody and apparently had no help with withdrawal. He was dead within a fortnight.[40] Kevin Jacobs (died 2001) had been in care since a toddler, suffered sexual abuse in a children's home and was severely psychiatrically disturbed; some of his offending involved stealing knives and insulin to self-harm.[41] Joseph Scholes (died 2002) was praised as a polite and well-behaved boy days before he hanged himself; he had been sexually abused as a young child and was known to be a suicide risk. Ian Powell (died 2002) had lived in a number of children's homes and was on remand for motoring offences; his probation officer had found alternative accommodation but had not had time to tell the prison.[42] Gareth Myatt (died 2004) was an academically very able child; two months before his death, his youth offending team worker told a court he was vulnerable because of his 'size, low self-esteem and also his confusion over his ethnic identity'.[43] Adam Rickwood (died 2004) was a very intelligent boy who settled in well at a local children's home the month before he died.[44] Gareth Price (died 2005) had found his brother hanging when he was aged 12; he was subsequently bullied at school and later crashed a car in which his best friend died. He was remanded to prison for a serious sexual offence and, because of this, his red hair and Romany background, was seen to be at risk of bullying.[45] Sam Elphick (died 2005) had lived in residential care and with foster carers: the local authority was said by Barnardo's to be pushing him into independent living too early.[46] Liam McManus (died 2007) had been moved from prison to a children's home previously because of his vulnerability and suicide attempts. He had had multiple carers and had suffered neglect and bereavement before the age of three.[47] Ryan Clark (died 2011) had been in care since he was 16 months old and was remanded into custody while living in 'dire' housing and receiving hardly any support from social services.[48] Jake Hardy (died 2012) was a child with ADHD who had attended special school and had a long history of being bullied; he begged the prison to send him home to his mother. Alex Kelly (died 2012) had been on the child protection register from the age of four and entered care when he was six, after he was raped in his family. Over the years, professionals working with Alex failed to recognise the devastation caused by earlier abuse.[49]

Other children to have died in prison were: Simon Willerton (died 1990); David Stewart (died 1993); Joseph Stanley (died 1994); Mark Weldrand (died (1995); Ryan Winter (died 1996); Lee Wagstaff (died 1997); Colin Scarborough (died 1998); Anthony Howarth (died 1999); and David Dennis (died 2000 after eight days in custody).[50] I have been unable to track down any information about them other than the date and place of their death.

Was prison a genuine last resort for all of these boys?

Courts in England and Wales sentenced children to immediate custody 49,709 times in the last 11 years.[51] The names of all of these children could be listed in the remaining pages of this book, with the same headline question: was this child locked up after we had applied the best of our knowledge, skill and resources and found that nothing worked? To borrow a feminist rejoinder, which part of last resort do we not understand?

Some might point to the positive changes occurring in the 'secure estate' and brightly cite this as evidence of child prisons being 'transformed'.[52] There is a social work term for wishing so hard for children's lives to be different that the grim realities pass us by. This is the 'rule of optimism' and the child penal industry has it in abundance, with institutions being renamed and redesigned every few decades. Over the past 160 years, we have had reformatories, borstals, approved schools, remand centres, detention centres, youth custody centres, young offender institutions and secure training centres,[53] and next we are to have secure colleges. Each rebranding has retained the core aim of locking child offenders in institutions markedly inferior in design, safety and status to those provided for more deserving children. We cannot rely on the judgements of those who are deeply invested in the incarceration of children, for this attachment – whether motivated by their own psychological needs or professional, financial or political interests – makes them incapable of recognising the pathology. The May 2014 contract notice for three of the four secure training centres in the UK, promising an income of around £236 million over a seven-year period, embodies the inability of those in the system to see the harm:

> The Authority believes that the success of youth custody in the long-term will require a competitive, diverse and open market with a number of credible providers.[54]

Like the social worker who believes resources and time will bring happiness to every child, administrators who believe they can make prisons fit for children are deluded. Terrible things happen to children in prison because they are in prison, just as unloved children feel that way because they are unloved.

Barrister Shauneen Lambe, who represents children in trouble with the law, told me in our interview:

> 'I think, to some degree, I've become normalised to Feltham [young offender institution], because I go there so often, maybe. It doesn't shock me in the same way. I really like going with people for the first time, because it reminds me to be shocked by it.'

In a newspaper interview in 2013, Nick Hardwick, the chief inspector of prisons, described his experience of visiting inmates in the juvenile section of Feltham young offender institution: 'When you see them all together, the striking thing is how young they look ... it's important that you never forget it. They are children.'[55]

There are many things about child prisons we must never forget, including: the ritual undressing of children; the nose distraction inflicted to make children follow orders; the placing of mentally ill and profoundly unhappy children in 'safe clothing' without their underwear in 'safe cells' with blocks of concrete for beds; the ministers and officials who went to court to prevent child protection legislation from applying to child prisoners; the restraint trainers calling themselves Clubber and Breaker; the ministers and officials who went to court to defend new restraint powers in secure training centres that breached children's right to protection from inhuman and degrading treatment or punishment; the children mentally tortured by 'shout outs' and those who beg to be allowed to go home to their mothers; the prison managers and social workers who watched the CCTV footage of a child whose wrist snapped like a pencil[56] and concluded officers had acted reasonably; and now the ministers and officials preparing to build a 320-place prison and shamefully closing their ears to warnings that permitting staff in the new 'colleges' to use restraint for disobedience risks serious breaches of children's human rights. The 33 boys who died as prisoners must be remembered especially, not least because a large proportion of them had been subject to care orders[57] – the highest level of state protection given to abused and abandoned children. Let us also not forget the sordid history of gangs of booted prison officers ripping off children's clothes, as a form of sadistic humiliation (p 217). This was one of the practices causing Martin Narey, as director general of the prison service from 1998 to 2003, to introduce his 'decency agenda'. With terminology like this, the public might have assumed Narey was seeking to enhance the dignity of prisoners, not stamp out officer violence. Then again, Narey told a national newspaper of his lack of success in improving conditions in Feltham young offender institution and reducing prison suicides:

> Do you know, 594 people killed themselves on my watch; 19 of them were children. And nobody gave a toss.[58]

Even with the most dedicated and skilful staff, prison can never be a suitable place for children. No matter how many cosmetic improvements are made, the institutions are fundamentally flawed. As Richard Hermer QC reflected in our research interview:

> 'Seen through my experience, which is through the prism really of Adam Rickwood, you have people who see their role of looking after children in terms of control. So not in terms of welfare, they don't see it from the child's eye. They don't see it. And you get these institutions in which it must be deeply alienating for children, reinforcing trauma and dehumanising. I mean, the treatment of children through these restraint techniques is dehumanising. It reinforces no doubt all sorts of views the children already have [about themselves].'

Former senior civil servant Malcolm Stevens told me of his exasperation at the Home Office being in charge of child incarceration in the 1990s. He asked a question that remains extremely relevant:

'Why are you shutting your eyes and ears like the monkeys? Would you really want your children to be looked after by "libertarians" like Ann Widdecombe?'

During her stint as prisons minister, Widdecombe defended the practice of shackling pregnant women in hospital until the point of labour, telling fellow parliamentarians about a remarkable case where 'a male prisoner who was diagnosed as completely paralysed jumped up and ran away as soon as his bed watch was withdrawn'.[59] Civil servants would have familiarised the minister with current issues ahead of her parliamentary grilling. As someone who has briefed many MPs and peers, and watched a lot of parliamentary debates, I have sometimes wondered whether officials plant outlandish statements into their ministers' scripts and devilishly wait to see if they read them aloud. If so, the incident of the paralysed man must surely have been a hoax.

The question of who should be responsible for child offenders, at government and operational level, is not about individual personalities; there are decent people in all organisations and areas of public life. Reading hundreds of documents in the course of researching this book, I came across some truly moving accounts of prison officer kindness. Two examples that stick in my mind are the officer at Lancaster Farms young offender institution who gave Liam McManus several extra biscuits at supper, hours before he hanged himself,[60] and, five years later, the officer who managed to bring a horse into Hindley young offender institution for a Traveller boy with very difficult behaviour.[61]

In our interview, Labour peer Frank Judd reminisced about attending a Geneva conference, aged 13, organised by his father:

'While I was there I had the great privilege of meeting Eleanor Roosevelt, who was central to the cause. Now, when human rights were first being highlighted in mainstream politics, the UN Declaration of Human Rights, they weren't seen as a nice option … they were seen as absolutely indispensable for stability and security. Well I think what you and I are talking about in terms of keeping kids safe, and the rest of it, is exactly the same. It's whether we want to have a decent society, a stable society, a society which is able with more optimism to live comfortably with itself. We must see these things as fundamental: how are we treating our kids?'

There will always be a small number of children whose behaviour is so chaotic, risky and disturbed that time in a protective environment is necessary. However, just as we would not expect a phlebotomist to carry out open-heart surgery, we cannot pretend prisons are capable of dealing with the childhood traumas and difficulties that catapult a very small number of children into very dangerous and self-destructive behaviour. And we must recognise the limitations of any kind of institution in changing a child's life – for this, skilled support has to be given to their families (or carers if they are looked after), schools and colleges, and a vast number of community resources – material, social and psychological – have to be gathered around the child. When I interviewed Juliet Lyon, the director of the Prison Reform Trust, she reflected on what she had learnt about the needs of abused and neglected children as a foster carer in the 1970s:

'The unmet need that is just so obvious … at heart it's a need for love. It's a need for somebody to really care about you and care what happens to you.'

The director of Kids Company, Camila Batmangelidjh, advocates tenderness as a means of recovering from childhood trauma, to which I would add respect. Chris Callender says we need to learn to give "second, third, fourth [and] fifth chances to our children and more". That penal policy is so far removed from childcare norms – even access to fresh air remains elusive – makes the advocacy of love, tenderness, respect and fortitude sound positively revolutionary. Which it would be if all we had ever known were child prisons. This is not the situation we are in. Secure children's homes are small, locked childcare establishments run by local authority children's services. This is the model we must develop; and it is what the inquest jury considering the death of Joseph Scholes asked for a decade ago. 'Perhaps more money could be put into building more secure units',[62] its members implored months before Adam Rickwood died. In a similar vein, the latest parliamentary investigation concluded:

> It is safer and more humane to detain young offenders in small, local units with a high staff ratio and where they can maintain links with their families and children's services.[63]

Substantial investment, and learning from international best practice, are necessary if we are to reach a position of national pride in our humane and specialist care for troubled and troublesome children. The goal must be interventions that genuinely and fully rehabilitate children – not by narrowly stopping them committing crimes but restoring them to a state of happiness and positive mental and physical health that most will not have experienced for many years. Children must never leave an establishment to return to the same hopeless social and economic conditions from which they came (in conspicuous contrast to the welcome home Vicky Pryce enjoyed – p 37). The standards and norms in locked settings must be the same as for children in other childcare placements, operating to the highest level of transparency, with children able to raise concerns and express their views with ease. Respect and humanity must be the touchstone of behaviour management, with the deliberate and organised infliction of pain and humiliation left to the history books. Inspections must be transformed so they focus on children's experiences, as told by them, and the success (or otherwise) of establishments in transforming children's lives. Working in secure children's homes should be prized roles in the service of children, attracting the most capable from a variety of professions and occupations, including social work, psychology, education, health, youth work, law and welfare rights. Given the threat of rights violations in closed institutions, however child-centred, detained children must be a permanent priority group for child protection agencies locally and nationally. As Allan Levy QC, one of the chairs of the pindown inquiry and a commissioner for the Howard League for Penal Reform's inquiry into violence in child prisons, rightly cautioned: '[Child prisoners] must not also suffer the added burden of being forgotten and unforgiven.'[64]

At the time of writing, there are 16 secure children's homes in England, eight of which look after children sent through a criminal justice route (the remainder care for children officially detained on welfare grounds). The homes have high staff-to-child ratios and the registered manager must be a qualified social worker or have another professional qualification for work with children. A recent evaluation found them to be particularly successful in improving children's educational achievements.[65] After eight weeks in a secure children's home, the reading age of children increases, on average, by a year (meaning a 15-year-old improves to the reading level of a 12-year-old).[66] The childcare standards are exactly the same as for ordinary children's homes, and require staff to put the child's welfare, safety and needs at the centre; promote a loving environment; and organise care around the development of the child's identity and self-worth.[67]

Secure children's homes are more expensive to run than prisons, which is to be expected; hospital intensive care units cost more to run than general medical wards. Current prices are equivalent to therapeutic hospital placements or therapeutic residential care with education.[68]

Research for the Prison Reform Trust shows many other countries have a welfare approach to child offending and social services in countries like Norway and Sweden are running open residential centres for children who have serious behaviour problems, including those who have committed violent offences.[69] In our interview, the former chief inspector of prisons, David Ramsbotham, told me about visiting children in prison:

> 'There's a wonderful phrase of Winston Churchill's that there is a treasure in the heart of every man, if only you can find it. If you took the trouble to identify some talent in any of these young people they invariably responded. I met very few who did not respond. They

were responding as much to the fact that somebody had
taken notice of them as the fact that there was someone
to whom they could go to discuss something which they
could not excel in but at least make progress in. [This]
convinced me that they are all looking for long-term
contact with a responsible adult to act as their guide.'

I asked Ramsbotham if prison is the best route for delivering this to
children, and he replied:

'No, it's not. It's not. Prison is not the best route; prison
is the worst route as conducted by the prison service.'

He went on to describe the dogged efforts staff have to make to
identify "where [the children] might have an ability" and to offer as
many opportunities as possible so they can achieve and grow their
self-esteem. "That's the first thing," he told me.

The mother of Jake Hardy, who hanged himself in prison in January
2012, recalled the happiest day of her life being when, at the age of
12, her son was diagnosed with ADHD, conduct disorder and dyslexia,
and he was given tablets to manage his behaviour. Jake then attended
a special unit and subsequently a school with only 78 students where
he could learn in small groups, and "he came on leaps and bounds".
In this new, safe environment, he was one of the cleverest in his class,
and he grew in self-confidence and happiness. Once in prison, he
was back to being bullied because of his difficulties. Even staying in
his cell was no protection, as other boys hurled insults (calling him
a 'pad-rat'),[70] and urinated and smeared faeces on his cell hatch. Six
months after an inquest jury found 12 separate failures by Hindley
young offender institution had caused or contributed to Jake's death,[71]
the YJB said it would no longer be sending children to that prison
from March 2015. The news was delivered in the same press release
announcing the decommissioning of Hassockfield secure training
centre, with the YJB stating: 'The decisions were not taken because
of any concerns with the establishments' performance…'.[72] Before
he hanged himself, Jake had written a note which said: 'so mum if

you are reading this I not alive cos I can not cope in prison people giveing [sic] me shit even staff'.[73]

Psychotherapist Camila Batmangelidjh is convinced that only stupidity will keep us invested in penal incarceration. I asked her why we keep imprisoning children, when it is known to be so harmful. I expected her to give me a rundown of the deepest psychological processes at work, but her response was much more down to earth:

'Well, I'll tell you – it's because we're blooming idiots. That's all there is to it. We are idiots.... In every aspect, if you were absolutely objective and you wanted to measure the efficacy of custody of vulnerable children, there is no logical argument for sustaining it. So the conclusion is – stupidity. It suits us to be stupid so we remain stupid. No other word.'

Seeking to remove children from penal institutions is not an attack on officers who begin each shift determined to do their best for vulnerable boys and girls. It is not a refusal to believe or value the individual stories of hope and change. The human price in fear, misery and violence is an unbearable cost for, at best, the occasional breakthrough. Sanatoriums, asylums and large children's homes were closed after scandals broke and the welfare of inhabitants was seen to be subservient to the interests of the institution. This breaking with the past must happen again. High-calibre staff from those sectors found new roles and organisations keen to use their skills, and the same would happen if prisons were to be abolished. One of the hazards of the prison officer role, according to the prison officers' trades union, is 'being stigmatised and institutionalised',[74] so able and motivated officers would have much to gain from being transferred to highly regarded childcare settings.

The number of children in our prisons today is the lowest for more than 20 years (although this is no guarantee numbers will not soar again – Bateman reports a fall from 7,000 to 1,400 of children in custody between 1979 and 1990;[75] by 2002, this had increased to more than 3,000).[76] We must seize this moment to completely sever our links with the Victorian prison project, when children were deemed no different from adults and fear and isolation ruled. We know much better now.

If the real block to progress is our desire to punish, let us come clean. We want to go on inflicting harm because children have made others suffer. Notwithstanding the fact that most children are not imprisoned because of violence against others, such an open declaration of combat with child offenders would imply that the abuses depicted in this book were meant to happen, and have our consent.

Yvonne Bailey knew nothing about prisons before her son, Joseph Scholes, was incarcerated. She knew about children, though, as a mother of four. Having spent the past decade immersed in the minutiae of children's experiences of prison, Yvonne told me in our interview that she is no longer naïve about what goes on behind high perimeter fences in these sad buildings:

> 'If I thought a child I knew was sent to prison, I'd be chained to the prison, and they would have to kill me to get me off the door.'

Notes

Preface

[1] Morgan, R. (2009) 'Children in custody', in M. Blyth, R. Newman and C. Wright (eds) *Children and young people in custody. Managing the risk*, Bristol: The Policy Press, p 14.

[2] Mathiesen, T. (2002) 'The future of imprisonment', in J. Muncie, G. Hughes and E. McLaughlin (eds) *Youth justice. Critical readings*, London: Sage Publications, p 381.

[3] Butler, I. and Williamson, H. (1994) *Children speak. Children, trauma and social work*, Essex: Longman, p 95.

Chapter One

[1] House of Commons *Hansard*, 15 October 2012: Column 27.

[2] ITN News, 22 October 2012, 'David Cameron: nation "appalled" by Jimmy Savile scandal', www.itn.co.uk/UK/59328/david-cameron--nation-appalled-by-jimmy-savile-scandal

[3] House of Commons *Hansard*, 6 November 2012: Column 733.

[4] Gray, D. and Watt, P. (2013) *Giving victims a voice. Joint report into sexual allegations made against Jimmy Savile*, London: Metropolitan Police and NSPCC, p 22.

[5] League of Nations (1924) Geneva Declaration of the Rights of the Child, Geneva: League of Nations.

[6] Her Majesty's Inspectorate of Prisons (2014) *Report on an unannounced inspection of HMYOI Werrington 23 September-4 October 2013 by HM Chief Inspector of Prisons*, London: HMIP, p 33.

[7] Her Majesty's Inspectorate of Prisons (2014) *Report on an unannounced inspection of HMYOI Werrington 23 September-4 October 2013 by HM Chief Inspector of Prisons*, London: HMIP, p 33. At the time of the inspection, 119 children were detained and 44 single cells were said to be in double occupancy (88 children).

[8] Her Majesty's Inspectorate of Prisons (2014) *Report on an unannounced inspection of HMP &YOI Wetherby 7-18 October 2013 by HM Chief Inspector of Prisons*, London: HMIP, p 33.

[9] Her Majesty's Inspectorate of Prisons (2014) *Report on an unannounced inspection of HMYOI Hindley 3 – 14 March 2014 by HM Chief Inspector of Prisons*, London: HMIP, pp 17 and 5.

[10] In March 2012, Her Majesty's Inspectorate of Prisons reported to parliament that few young offender institutions, which hold the majority of imprisoned children, meet the target of 10 hours a day time out of cell. House of Commons Justice Committee (2013) *Youth justice. Seventh report of session 2012-13. Volume I*, London: The Stationery Office, ev 125.

[11] In March 2011, 30% of child prisoners were held more than 50 miles from home and 10% more than 100 miles from home. Murray, R. (2012) *Children and young people in custody 2011-12. An analysis of the experiences of 15–18-year-olds in prison*, London: Her Majesty's Inspectorate of Prisons, p 17.

[12] *Children's Rights Alliance for England v Secretary of State for Justice and G4S Care and Justice Services (UK) Limited and Serco PLC* [2012] EWHC 8 (Admin) at 91. The case went to the Court of Appeal where this conclusion was not disputed.

[13] Coyle, A. (1994) *The prisons we deserve*, London: HarperCollins Publishers, p 5.

[14] Coyle, A. (2011) 'Foreword', in A. Liebling and S. Maruna (eds) *The effects of imprisonment* (2nd edn), Abingdon: Routledge, p xix.

[15] Bradley, K. (2009) *The Bradley report. Lord Bradley's review of people with mental health problems or learning disabilities in the criminal justice system*, London: Department of Health, p 99.

[16] Berelowitz, S. (2011) *'I think I must have been born bad.' Emotional well-being and mental health of children and young people in the youth justice system*, London: Office of the Children's Commissioner for England, p 22.

[17] Howard League for Penal Reform (2010) *Life inside 2010. A unique insight into the day to day experiences of 15-17 year old males in prison*, London: Howard League for Penal Reform, p 10.

[18] NSPCC (2013) *Annual report 2012/13*, London: NSPCC, p 32.

[19] Her Majesty's Inspectorate of Prisons (2012) *Report on an unannounced short follow-up inspection of HMYOI Wetherby The Keppel Unit 13-16 February 2012 by HM Chief Inspector of Prisons*, London: HMIP, p 10.

[20] National Offender Management Service (2012) *Minimising and managing physical restraint 2012. Volume 5. Physical restraint*, London: MoJ, p 10.

[21] Ofsted, Care Quality Commission and Her Majesty's Inspectorate of Prisons (2014) *Inspection of Oakhill secure training centre: February 2014*, Manchester: Ofsted, p 5 and p 19.

[22] House of Commons Justice Committee (2009) *Draft sentencing guideline: overarching principles – sentencing youths. Tenth report of session 2008-09*, London: The Stationery Office, ev 21.

[23] Children Act 1989, s 31(9).

[24] HM Government (2013) *Working together to safeguard children. A guide to inter-agency working to safeguard and promote the welfare of children*, London: The Stationery Office, pp 85-6.

[25] Howard League for Penal Reform (1993) *Banged up. Beaten up. Cutting up. Report of the Howard League Commission of Inquiry into violence in penal institutions for teenagers under 18*, London: Howard League for Penal Reform, p 41.

[26] Her Majesty's Inspectorate of Prisons (2013) *Report on an unannounced inspection of HMP/YOI Feltham (Feltham A – children and young people 21–25 January 2013 by HM Chief Inspector of Prisons)*, London: HMIP, pp 31, 36 and 30.

[27] Murray, R. (2012) *Children and young people in custody 2011-12. An analysis of the experiences of 15–18-year-olds in prison*, London: HMIP, pp 10 and 16.

[28] Murray, R. (2012) *Children and young people in custody 2011-12. An analysis of the experiences of 15–18-year-olds in prison*, London: HMIP, pp 153, 115 and 116.

[29] Gyateng, T., Moretti, A., May, T. and Turnbull, P. (2013) *Young people and the secure estate: needs and interventions*, London: Youth Justice Board for England and Wales, p 3.

[30] The prison inspectorate spreadsheet I was sent records 126 allegations in total from English young offender institutions and secure training centres but the individual allegations amount to 130, so this is what I have included in the table.

[31] Response to freedom of information request dated 25 April 2014.

[32] Response to freedom of information request dated 3 February 2014.

[33] Children and Young Persons Act 1933, s 53(1). The Children Act 1908 introduced a minimum age of 16 for capital punishment.

[34] Criminal Justice Act 1948, s 2.

[35] Latest available data: for the six months between February and July 2014, the monthly number of children in young offender institutions and secure training centres never exceeded 1,059. Youth Justice Board for England and Wales (2014) *Youth custody report. July 2014*, Table 2.4: Accommodation type, London: YJB.

[36] Youth Justice Board for England and Wales, Home Office and Ministry of Justice (2013) *Youth justice statistics 2011/12. England and Wales*, Table 7.4: Custody population, year on year monthly trends (under 18s only), 2002/03 and 2008/09 to 2012/13, London: MoJ.

[37] Aebi, M.F. and Delgrande, N. (2013) *Council of Europe annual penal statistics. Space I survey 2011*, Strasbourg: Council of Europe, pp 68-9.

[38] Schofield, G. and others (2012) *Looked after children and offending: reducing risk and promoting resilience*, Norwich: University of East Anglia, p 157.

[39] Goldson, B. (2009) 'Child incarceration: institutional abuse, the violent state and the politics of impunity', in P. Scraton and J. McCulloch (eds) *The violence of incarceration*, London: Routledge, p 96.

[40] Goldson, B. (2009) 'Child incarceration: institutional abuse, the violent state and the politics of impunity', in P. Scraton and J. McCulloch (eds) *The violence of incarceration*, London: Routledge, pp 86-106.

[41] Sykes, G.M. (2007) *The society of captives. A study of maximum security prison* (2nd edn), Woodstock, Oxfordshire: Princeton University Press, p 65.

[42] House of Lords *Hansard*, 7 November 2011: Column 95.

[43] Youth Justice Board for England and Wales (2009) *Girls and offending – patterns, perceptions and interventions*, London: YJB, pp 61-62.

[44] Goldson, B. (2002) *Vulnerable inside. Children in secure and penal settings*, London: The Children's Society, p 128.

[45] James, E. (2003) *A life inside. A prisoner's notebook*, London: Atlantic Books, p 77.

[46] House of Commons *Hansard*, 29 January 2014: Column 605W.

[47] House of Commons *Hansard* 18 June 2013: Column 660W.

[48] Ofsted, Her Majesty's Inspectorate of Prisons and Care Quality Commission (2013) *The inspection of Hassockfield secure training centre: February/March 2013*, Manchester: Ofsted, p 22.

[49] The Youth Justice Board's annual accounts indicate average annual expenditure of £43.4 million on the four secure training centres between 2003/04 and 2012/13. Expenditure in 2012/13 was the lowest across this whole period – £14.4 million compared with £58.5 million the year before.

[50] Children's Food Trust (2013) *Food provision in juvenile young offender institutions in England and Wales. Prepared for the Youth Justice Board*, Sheffield: Children's Food Trust, p 32.

[51] Children's Food Trust (2013) *Food provision in juvenile young offender institutions in England and Wales. Prepared for the Youth Justice Board*, Sheffield: Children's Food Trust, p 21.

[52] Her Majesty's Inspectorate of Prisons (2014) *Report on an unannounced inspection of HMYOI Cookham Wood 9-20 June 2014 by HM Chief Inspector of Prisons*, London: HMIP, p 46.

[53] Coles, D. (2007) *INQUEST's submission to the Ministry of Justice & Department for Children, Schools and Families on the 'Review of restraint'*, London: INQUEST, p 8.

[4] House of Lords *Hansard*, 9 November 2011: Column WA72.

House of Commons *Hansard*, 5 December 2007: Column 1266W.

House of Commons *Hansard*, 9 September 2009: Column 15MC.

House of Commons *Hansard*, 22 July 2013: Column WA177.

Tower Hamlets Safeguarding Children Board (2013) *Serious case review executive summary. Services provided for child F June 2004–January 2012*, London: Tower Hamlets Safeguarding Children Board, p 6.

Tower Hamlets Safeguarding Children Board (2013) *Serious case review executive summary. Services provided for child F June 2004–January 2012*, London: Tower Hamlets Safeguarding Children Board, p 10.

[60] Prisons and Probation Ombudsman for England and Wales (2013) *Child deaths. Learning from PPO investigations into three recent deaths of children in custody*, London: PPO, p 5. This report does not link particular incidents to named children: in light of the serious case review observations, I have made the supposition that the PPO's comment related to Alex.

[61] Tower Hamlets Safeguarding Children Board (2013) *Serious case review executive summary. Services provided for child F June 2004-January 2012.* London: Tower Hamlets Safeguarding Children Board, p 10.

[62] Carlile, A. (2006) *An independent inquiry into the use of physical restraint, solitary confinement and forcible strip searching of children in prisons, secure training centres and local authority secure children's homes*, London: Howard League for Penal Reform, p 53.

[63] Morgan, R. (2006), 'Difficult youngsters in difficult circumstances', *The Guardian*, 23 March.

[64] Miller, J.G. (1998) *Last one over the wall. The Massachusetts experiment in closing reform schools*, Columbus: Ohio State University Press, p 146.

[65] Miller, J.G. (1998) *Last one over the wall. The Massachusetts experiment in closing reform schools*, Columbus: Ohio State University Press, p 18.

[66] Levy, A. and Kahan, B. (1991) *The pindown experience and the protection of children. The report of the Staffordshire child care inquiry*, Stafford: Staffordshire County Council, pp 167-8.

[67] Her Majesty's Inspectorate of Prisons (2011) *Report on an unannounced full follow-up inspection of HMYOI Lancaster Farms 1-10 June 2011 by HM Chief Inspector of Prisons*, London: HMIP, p 30.

[68] Her Majesty's Inspectorate of Prisons (2000) *A full announced inspection of HM young offender institution Lancaster Farms 8-12 May 2000 by HM Chief Inspector of Prisons*, London: HMIP, p 47.

[69] Safe and Sound in partnership with NSPCC (1995) *So who are we meant to trust now? Responding to abuse in care: the experiences of young people*, London: NSPCC, p 7.

[70] Her Majesty's Inspectorate of Prisons (2013) *Report on an announced inspection of HMYOI Warren Hill 4-8 March 2013 by HM Chief Inspector of Prisons*, London: HMIP, p 32.

[71] National Children's Bureau (2008) *A review of safeguarding in the secure estate*, London: NCB, p v.

[72] House of Commons *Hansard*, 1 July 2009: Column 269W.

[73] House of Commons *Hansard*, 20 May 2013: Column 582W.

[74] Care Inspectorate (2013) *A report into the deaths of looked after children in Scotland 2009-2011*, Dundee: Care Inspectorate, p 6.

[75] A narrative verdict was also given in addition to the accidental verdict in respect of Gareth Myatt.

[76] For more information, see INQUEST (2011) *The inquest handbook. A guide for bereaved families, friends and their advisers*, London: INQUEST.

[77] Gyateng, T., Moretti, A., May, T. and Turnbull, P. (2013) *Young people and the secure estate: needs and interventions*, London: Youth Justice Board for England and Wales, p 9.

[78] *Children and Young People Now*, 'YOI child-to-staff ratio to rise', 10 May 2013.

[79] Gyateng, T., Moretti, A., May, T. and Turnbull, P. (2013) *Young people and the secure estate: needs and interventions*, London: Youth Justice Board for England and Wales, p 10.

[80] Gyateng, T., Moretti, A., May, T. and Turnbull, P. (2013) *Young people and the secure estate: needs and interventions*, London: Youth Justice Board for England and Wales, p 10.

[81] Department for Education (2012) *School workforce in England: November 2011*, Table 17, London: DfE.

[82] Cunningham, H. (2005) *Children and childhood in western society since 1500* (2nd edn), Harlow: Pearson Education, p 148.

[83] Cited in Goldson, B. (2009) 'Counterblast: 'Difficult to understand or defend': A reasoned case for raising the age of criminal responsibility', *The Howard Journal of Criminal Justice*, vol 48, no 5, p 514.

[84] House of Commons *Hansard*, 10 June 2008: Column 156.

[85] House of Commons *Hansard*, 10 June 2008: Column 235W.

[86] Utting, W. (1997) *People like us. The report of the review of the safeguards for children living away from home*, London: The Stationery Office, p 64.

[87] Her Majesty's Inspectorate of Prisons (1997) *Young prisoners. A thematic review by HM Chief Inspector of Prisons for England and Wales*, London: HMIP, para 8.07.

[88] Cited in 'Developing the secure estate for children and young people in England and Wales – responses to the consultation', Public and Commercial Services Union, https://consult.justice.gov.uk/digital-communications/secure_estate_youth

[89] House of Lords *Hansard*, 19 July 2013: Column 154W.

[90] House of Commons Justice Committee (2013) *Youth justice. Seventh report of session 2012-13. Volume I*, London: The Stationery Office, ev 54.

[91] Prisons and Probation Ombudsman for England and Wales (2006) *Circumstances surrounding the death of a boy at Hassockfield secure training centre on 8 August 2004*, London: PPO, p 102.

[92] BBC Face the Facts, 26 August 2005.

[93] Ministry of Justice (2014) *Proven re-offending statistics. Quarterly bulletin. October 2011 to September 2012, England and Wales*, Table 23: Juvenile proven re-offending data, by individual prison or secure accommodation, based on first release from each prison or secure accommodation 2007 to June 2012, London: MoJ.

[94] Information obtained from theYouth Justice Board's annual accounts.The 2013 report showed expenditure on 'secure accommodation' below £200 million for the first time since 2003/04.Youth Justice Board for England and Wales (2013) *Annual report and accounts 2012/13*, London:The Stationery Office, p 63.

[95] Ministry of Justice (2014) *Proven re-offending statistics. Quarterly bulletin. October 2011 to September 2012, England and Wales*,Table 19b:Juvenile proven re-offending data, by custodial sentence length, 2000, 2002 to September 2012, London: MoJ.

[96] BBC press release, 26 January 2007, 'Chairman of Youth Justice Board resigns condemning government policy'.

[97] Batmanghelidjh, C. (2006) *Shattered lives. Children who live with courage and dignity*, London: Jessica Kingsley, p 83.

[98] Hennesy,P. (2013) 'Crackdown on perks for young offenders', *The Telegraph*, 7 July.

[99] Robins, L. (2012) *Mother and baby prison units. An investigative study*, Wellington: New Zealand Winston Churchill Memorial Trust, p 90.

[100] Ministry of Justice press release, 30 June 2014, 'Early lights out for young offenders'.

Chapter Two

[1] www.chelsea-pensioners.co.uk/origins-and-history-0

[2] Berelowitz, S. (2011) '*I think I must have been born bad.' Emotional well-being and mental health of children and young people in the youth justice system*, London: Office of the Children's Commissioner for England, p 24.

[3] Wilkinson, R. and Pickett, K. (2010) *The spirit level.Why equality is better for everyone*, London: Penguin, pp 150 and 155.

[4] Duffell, N. (2010) *The making of them.The British attitude to children and the boarding school system* (3rd edn), London: Lone Arrow Press, pp 135-57.

[5] Jacobson, J. (2010) *Punishing disadvantage. A profile of children in custody*, London: Prison Reform Trust, p 52.

[6] Liddle, M. and Solanki, A.-R. (2002) *Persistent young offenders. Research on individual backgrounds and life experiences. Research briefing 1*, London: Nacro, p 4.

[7] Renshaw, J. (2010) *Young people held in the juvenile secure estate for serious offences on Section 228, Section 226 and Section 90 sentences*, London:Youth Justice Board for England and Wales, p 28.

[8] *R (L) v West London MH NHS Trust* (2012) EWHC 3200 (Admin).

[9] *R v Nottingham Magistrates' Court, ex parte SR* (2001) EWHC (Admin) 802.

[10] Barnardo's and Nacro with NSPCC (2006) *Past abuse suffered by children in custody. A way forward*, London: Howard League for Penal Reform, p 8.

[11] Jacobson, J. (2010) *Punishing disadvantage. A profile of children in custody*, London: Prison Reform Trust, p 52.

[12] Glover, J. and Hibbert, P. (2009) *Locking up or giving up? Why custody thresholds for teenagers aged 12, 13 and 14 need to be raised*, London: Barnardo's, p 18.

[13] Lader, D., Singleton, N. and Meltzer, H. (2000) *Psychiatric morbidity among young offenders in England and Wales. Further analysis of data from the ONS survey of psychiatric morbidity among prisoners in England and Wales carried out in 1997 on behalf of the Department of Health*, London: Office for National Statistics, p 89.

[14] Williams, K., Papadopoulou, V. and Booth, N. (2012) *Prisoners' childhood and family backgrounds. Results from the Surveying Prisoner Crime Reduction (SPCR) longitudinal cohort study of prisoners*, London: Ministry of Justice, p 9.

[15] Williams, K., Papadopoulou, V. and Booth, N. (2012) *Prisoners' childhood and family backgrounds. Results from the Surveying Prisoner Crime Reduction (SPCR) longitudinal cohort study of prisoners*, London: Ministry of Justice, p 9.

[16] Williams, K., Papadopoulou, V. and Booth, N. (2012) *Prisoners' childhood and family backgrounds. Results from the Surveying Prisoner Crime Reduction (SPCR) longitudinal cohort study of prisoners*, London: Ministry of Justice, p 8.

[17] Department for Education (2014) *Outcomes for children looked after by local authorities*, Table 4: Offending by children who have been looked after continuously for at least 12 months, by age and gender, London: Department for Education.

[18] House of Lords *Hansard*, 12 June 2007: Column 1583.

[19] Barnardo's and Nacro with NSPCC (2006) *Past abuse suffered by children in custody. A way forward*, London: Howard League for Penal Reform, p 18.

[20] Day, C., Hibbert, P. and Cadman, S. (2008) *A literature review into children abused and/or neglected prior custody*, London: Youth Justice Board for England and Wales, p 30.

[21] *Children and Young People Now*, 'Youth justice: Anger over "stifled" report into abuse', 11 September 2007.

[22] Coroners and Justice Act 2009, ss 54 and 55.

[23] Emma Humphreys sought help from Justice for Women, which campaigned for her release; www.justiceforwomen.org.uk/emma-humphreys/

[24] User Voice (2011) *What's your story? Young offenders' insights into tackling youth crime and its causes*, London: User Voice, p 30.

[25] Schofield, G. and others (2012) *Looked after children and offending: reducing risk and promoting resilience*, Norwich: University of East Anglia.

[26] Afifi, T.O. (2012) 'The relationship between child maltreatment and Axis I mental disorders: a summary of the published literature from 2006 to 2010', *Open Journal of Psychiatry*, 2, pp 21-32.

[27] Jacobson, J. (2010) *Punishing disadvantage. A profile of children in custody*, London: Prison Reform Trust, p 61.

[28] Glover, J. and Hibbert, P. (2009) *Locking up or giving up? Why custody thresholds for teenagers aged 12, 13 and 14 need to be raised*, London: Barnardo's, p 4.

[29] Miller, J.G. (1998) *Last one over the wall. The Massachusetts experiment in closing reform schools*, Columbus: Ohio State University Press, pp 108-9.

[30] Barnardo's and Nacro with NSPCC (2006) *Past abuse suffered by children in custody. A way forward*, London: Howard League for Penal Reform, p 22.

[31] Ministry of Justice (2013) *Transforming youth custody. Putting education at the heart of detention*, London: The Stationery Office, p 20.

[32] Ministry of Justice (2013) *Transforming youth custody. Putting education at the heart of detention*. London: The Stationery Office, p 20.

[33] Youth Justice Board for England and Wales and Ministry of Justice (2013) *Developing the secure estate for children and young people in England and Wales. Plans until 2015*, London: Youth Justice Board for England and Wales, p 12.

[34] Youth Justice Board for England and Wales (2014) *YJB corporate plan 2014-17 and business plan 2014/15*, London: YJB, pp 27 and 30.

[35] Goldson, B. (2009) 'Child incarceration: institutional abuse, the violent state and the politics of impunity', in P. Scraton and J. McCulloch (eds) *The violence of incarceration*, London: Routledge, pp 96-7.

[36] Jacobson, J. (2010) *Punishing disadvantage. A profile of children in custody.* London: Prison Reform Trust, p 52.

[37] Kennedy, E. (2013) *Children and young people in custody 2012-13. An analysis of 15–18-year-olds' perceptions of their experiences in young offender institutions*, London: The Stationery Office, pp 27 and 30.

[38] Ministry of Justice (2013) *Youth justice statistics 2011/12. England and Wales*, London: MoJ, p 39.

[39] Ministry of Justice and Youth Justice Board for England and Wales (2014) *Youth justice statistics. Use of custody YOT and region 2012-13*, London: The Stationery Office.

[40] Houchin, R. (2005) *Social exclusion and imprisonment in Scotland. A report*, Glasgow: Glasgow Caledonian University, pp 11 and 20.

[41] Ministry of Justice and Youth Justice Board for England and Wales (2014) *Youth justice statistics. Use of custody YOT and region 2012-13*, London: The Stationery Office.

[42] Prison Reform Trust (2008) *Criminal damage: why we should lock up fewer children. A Prison Reform Trust briefing*, London: Prison Reform Trust, p 3.

[43] HMI Probation, HMI Courts Administration, HM Crown Prosecution Service Inspectorate (2011) *Not making enough difference: a joint inspection of youth offending court work and peports*, Manchester: HM Inspectorate of Probation, pp 46.

[44] HMI Probation, HMI Courts Administration, HM Crown Prosecution Service Inspectorate (2011) *Not making enough difference: a joint inspection of youth offending court work and peports*, Manchester: HM Inspectorate of Probation, p 47.

[45] HMI Probation, HMI Courts Administration, HM Crown Prosecution Service Inspectorate (2011) *Not making enough difference: a joint inspection of youth offending court work and peports*, Manchester: HM Inspectorate of Probation, pp 47-50.

[46] Townsend, P. (1979) *Poverty in the United Kingdom*, London: Allen Lane, p 915.

[47] Willow, C. (2001) *Bread is free. Children and young people talk about poverty*, London: Children's Rights Alliance for England, p 61.

[48] Social Mobility and Child Poverty Commission (2013) *State of the nation 2013: social mobility and child poverty in Great Britain*. London: The Stationery Office, p 41.

[49] Pryce, V. (2013) *Prisonomics. Behind bars in Britain's failing prisons*, London: Biteback Publishing, pp 217-19.

[50] Kennedy, E. (2013) *Children and young people in custody 2012-13. An analysis of 15–18-year-olds' perceptions of their experiences in young offender institutions*, London: The Stationery Office, pp 72-3.

[51] Kennedy, E. (2013) *Children and young people in custody 2012-13. An analysis of 15–18-year-olds' perceptions of their experiences in young offender institutions*, London: The Stationery Office, p 74.

[52] Kennedy, E. (2013) *Children and young people in custody 2012-13. An analysis of 15–18-year-olds' perceptions of their experiences in young offender institutions*, London: The Stationery Office, p 94.

[53] Her Majesty's Inspectorate of Prisons (2011) *Resettlement provision for children and young people. Accommodation and education, training and employment*, London: HMIP, p 15.

[54] Curtis, P. (2003) 'Twice as many black people in prison as on campus', *The Guardian*, 15 December.

[55] Ministry of Justice (2014) *Youth custody report – July 2014*, Table 2.6, www.gov.uk/government/publications/youth-custody-data

[56] www.nomisweb.co.uk/census/2011/DC2101EW/view/2092957699?rows=c_age&cols=c_ethpuk11

[57] May, T., Gyateng, T., Hough, M. and others (2010) *Differential treatment in the youth justice system*, London: Equality and Human Rights Commission, pp 86-7.

[58] House of Commons Home Affairs Committee (2007) *Young black people and the criminal justice system. Second report of session 2006-07. Volume I*, London: The Stationery Office, p 13.

[59] House of Commons Home Affairs Committee (2007) *Young black people and the criminal justice system. Second report of session 2006-07. Volume I*, London: The Stationery Office, p 53.

[60] House of Commons Home Affairs Committee (2007) *Young black people and the criminal justice system. Second report of session 2006-07. Volume I*, London: The Stationery Office, pp 30-1.

[61] Letter to the Home Secretary Jack Straw MP from His Honour Richard Pollard, Assistant Deputy Coroner for the County of Northampton, 18 July 2007, p 7.

[62] UK Government (2008) *The Government's response to coroners' recommendations following the inquests of Gareth Myatt and Adam Rickwood*, London: Ministry of Justice, Youth Justice Board for England and Wales and the Department for Children, Schools and Families, p 16.

[63] ECOTEC Research and Consulting (2001) *An audit of education provision within the juvenile secure estate. A report to the Youth Justice Board*, London: Youth Justice Board for England and Wales, pp 30-31.

[64] Gyateng, T., Moretti, A., May, T. and Turnbull, P.J. (2013) *Young people and the secure estate: needs and interventions*, London: Youth Justice Board for England and Wales, p 4.

[65] Harrington, R. and Bailey, S. with others (2005) *Mental health needs and effectiveness of provision for young offenders in custody and in the community*, London: Youth Justice Board for England and Wales, p 27.

[66] Talbot, J. (2008) *No one knows. Prisoners' voices. Experiences of the criminal justice system by prisoners with learning disabilities and difficulties*, London: Prison Reform Trust, p 33.

[67] Her Majesty's Inspectorate of Prisons (2014) *Report on an unannounced inspection of HMYOI Cookham Wood 9-20 June 2014 by HM Chief Inspector of Prisons*, London: HMIP, p 39.

[68] Her Majesty's Inspectorate of Prisons (2013) *Report on an unannounced inspection of HMP/YOI Feltham (Feltham A – children and young people) 21-25 January 2013 by HM Chief Inspector of Prisons*, London: HMIP, p 46.

[69] Ministry of Justice (2014) *Youth justice annual statistics 2012-2013*, Table 7.5a: Custody population by primary offence group (under 18s only), 2012/13, London: The Stationery Office.

[70] Ministry of Justice (2014) *Youth justice annual statistics 2012-2013*, Table 7.5b: Average custody population by primary offence group (under 18s only), 2008/09 to 2012/13, London: The Stationery Office.

[71] See Prison Reform Trust's analysis of the positive impact of the Youth Justice Board in House of Commons Justice Committee (2011) *The proposed abolition of the Youth Justice Board*, London: The Stationery Office, ev 34.

[72] Hart, D. (2011) *Into the breach. The enforcement of statutory orders in the youth justice system*, London: Prison Reform Trust, pp 16-17.

[73] House of Commons Justice Committee (2013) *Youth justice*, London: The Stationery Office, p 30.

[74] Ministry of Justice (2014) *Youth justice annual statistics 2012-2013. Table 7.5a: Custody population by primary offence group (under 18s only), 2012/13 and Table 7.2: Custody population by legal basis for detention (under 18s only), 2012/13*, London: The Stationery Office.

[75] Miller, J.G. (1998) *Last one over the wall. The Massachusetts experiment in closing reform schools*, Columbus: Ohio State University Press, p 128.

[76] Youth Justice Board (2014) *Youth custody report – July 2014*, London: Ministry of Justice.

[77] Ministry of Justice (2014) *Transforming youth custody. Government response to the consultation*, London: The Stationery Office, p 9.

[78] Ministry of Justice (2013) *Transforming youth custody. Putting education at the heart of detention*, London: The Stationery Office, p 14.

[79] Ministry of Justice (2013) *Transforming youth custody. Putting education at the heart of detention*, London: The Stationery Office, p 5.

[80] The Young Offender Institution Rules 2000, rule 3.

Chapter Three

[1] Her Majesty's Inspectorate of Prisons (2001) *Report of an unannounced inspection HMYOI Stoke Heath 29-31 May 2001 by HM Chief Inspector of Prisons*, London: HMIP, p 13.

[2] Lambert, D. (2005) *Review of the effectiveness of operational procedures for the identification, placement and safeguarding of vulnerable young people in custody*, London: Home Office, p 14.

[3] Crown Prosecution Service (2006) *Guidance on the prosecution of offending behaviour in children's homes*, London: CPS.

[4] Lambert, D. (2005) *Review of the effectiveness of operational procedures for the identification, placement and safeguarding of vulnerable young people in custody*, London: Home Office, p 15.

[5] Lambert, D. (2005) *Review of the effectiveness of operational procedures for the identification, placement and safeguarding of vulnerable young people in custody*, London: Home Office, p 15.

[6] INQUEST (2003) *A child's death in custody. Call for a public inquiry. Campaign briefing*, London: INQUEST, p 2.

[7] *Yvonne Scholes v Secretary of State for the Home Department* [2006] EWCA Civ 1343 [7].

[8] Her Majesty's Inspectorate of Prisons (2001) *Report of an unannounced inspection HMYOI Stoke Heath 29-31 May 2001 by HM Chief Inspector of Prisons*, London: HMIP, pp 51-2.

[9] Her Majesty's Inspectorate of Prisons (2001) *HMYOI Stoke Heath. Report of an announced inspection 2-6 October 2000 by HM Chief Inspector of Prisons*, London: HMIP, pp 3 and 22.

[10] Her Majesty's Inspectorate of Prisons (2001) *HMYOI Stoke Heath. Report of an announced inspection 2-6 October 2000 by HM Chief Inspector of Prisons*, London: HMIP, pp 66-7.

[11] *North Wales Daily Post*, 21 April 2004, 'Social worker feared for tragic teenage prisoner'.

[12] Fazel, S., Benning, R. and Danesh, J. (2005) 'Suicides in male prisoners in England and Wales, 1978–2003', *Lancet*, 366, pp 1301-2.

[13] *Bailey v The United Kingdom*, application no. 39953/07, p 3.

[14] Edmundson, A. and Coles, D. (2012) *Fatally flawed. Has the state learned lessons from the deaths of children and young people in prison?*, London: Prison Reform Trust, pp 3 and 51.

[15] INQUEST press release, 30 April 2004, 'Coroner calls for public inquiry following verdict returned at inquest into the death in prison of 16 year-old Joseph Scholes', p 2.

[16] INQUEST press release, 30 April 2004, 'Coroner calls for public inquiry following verdict returned at inquest into the death in prison of 16 year-old Joseph Scholes', p 2.

[17] INQUEST press release, 30 April 2004, 'Coroner calls for public inquiry following verdict returned at inquest into the death in prison of 16 year-old Joseph Scholes', p 2.

[18] House of Commons *Hansard*, 16 September 2004: Column 160WS.

[19] Lambert, D. (2005) *Review of the effectiveness of operational procedures for the identification, placement and safeguarding of vulnerable young people in custody*, London: Home Office, p 105.

[20] Davies, N. (2004) 'Wasted lives of the young let down by jail system', *The Guardian*, 8 December.

[21] Hall, S. (2002) 'Inquest blames Feltham for teenager's suicide', *The Guardian*, 27 September.

[22] INQUEST press release, 26 September 2002, 'Jury to consider verdict at inquest into death of 16 year old in Feltham young offender institution'.

[23] Shaw, J., Senior, J., Hayes, A., Roberts, A., Evans, G., Rennie, C., James, C., Mnyamana, M., Senti, J., Trwoga, S., Taylor, P., Maslin, L., De Viggiani, N. and Jones, G. (2008) *An evaluation of the Department of Health's 'Procedure for the transfer of prisoners to and from hospital under sections 47 and 48 of the Mental Health Act 1983' initiative*, Manchester: Offender Health Research Network, p 38.

[24] Her Majesty's Inspectorate of Prisons (2012) *Report on an announced inspection of HMYOI Wetherby. 30 January-3 February 2012 by HM Chief Inspector of Prisons*, London: HMIP, p 6.

[25] Her Majesty's Inspectorate of Prisons (2010) *Report on an announced inspection of HMP/YOI Downview Josephine Butler Unit. 1- 4 February 2010 by HM Chief Inspector of Prisons*, London: HMIP, pp 53 and 56.

[26] 'The history of the SP inquiry is summarised by the Howard League for Penal Reform', www.howardleague.org/history/

[27] House of Lords *Hansard*, 9 January 2014: Column WA318.

[28] Glover, J., Webster, L., White, J. and Jones, N. (2012) *Developing the secure estate for children and young people in England and Wales – young people's consultation report. A report produced for the Youth Justice Board by Voice and Barnardo's*, London: Youth Justice Board for England and Wales, p 30.

[29] Prisons and Probation Ombudsman for England and Wales (2009) *Investigation into the circumstances surrounding the death of a boy at HMYOI Lancaster Farms in November 2007*, London: PPO, p 41 and p 55.

[30] INQUEST press release, 13 November 2009, 'Systemic failings in the care and support of vulnerable boy contributed to death in prison'.

[31] Prisons and Probation Ombudsman for England and Wales (2009) *Investigation into the circumstances surrounding the death of a boy at HMYOI Lancaster Farms in November 2007*, London: PPO, pp 2 and 6.

[32] House of Commons *Hansard*, 9 February 2005: Column 454WH.

[33] House of Commons *Hansard*, 9 February 2005: Column 456WH.

[34] Coroner's note 'Summing up in the inquest touching upon the death of Gareth Price', p 15.

[35] Kennedy, E. (2013) *Children and young people in custody 2012-13. An analysis of 15–18-year-olds' perceptions of their experiences in young offender institutions*, London: The Stationery Office, pp 11 and 51.

[36] Shaw, S. (2008) *Circumstances surrounding the death of a trainee at HMP and YOI Hindley, in September 2005*, London: Prisons and Probation Ombudsman for England and Wales, p 7.

[37] *Yorkshire Evening Post*, 17 October 2013, 'Hanged Leeds teenager was taunted in jail'.

[38] Toch, H. (1992) *Living in prison. The ecology of survival* (2nd edn), Washington DC: American Psychological Association, p 196.

[39] House of Lords *Hansard*, 1 April 2004: Column 1573.

[40] Selwyn, J., Wijedasa, D. and Meakings, S. (2014) *Beyond the adoption order: challenges, interventions and adoption disruption. Research report*, London: Department for Education, p 44.

[41] Jaffe, M. (2012) *The Listener scheme in prisons: final report on the research findings*, Surrey: Samaritans, p 30.

[42] Morris, S. and Wheatley, H. (1994) *Time to listen. The experiences of children in residential and foster care*, London: ChildLine, pp 111-12.

[43] Zimbardo, P. (2009) *The Lucifer effect. How good people turn evil*, London: Rider, p 237.

[44] Bartollas, C. (1982) 'Survival problems of adolescent prisoners', in R. Johnson and H. Toch (eds) *The pains of imprisonment*, London: Sage Publications, p 174.

[45] Berelowitz, S. (2011) '*I think I must have been born bad.' Emotional well-being and mental health of children and young people in the youth justice system*, London: Office of the Children's Commissioner, p 10.

[46] Goldson, B. (2005) 'Child imprisonment: a case for abolition', *Youth Justice*, 5, p 80.

[47] Dimond, C., Misch, P. and Goldberg, D. (2001) 'On being in a young offender institution. What boys on remand told a child psychiatrist', *The Psychiatrist*, 25, pp 342-5.

[48] Goldson, B. (2002) *Vulnerable inside. Children in secure and penal settings*, London: The Children's Society, p 138.

[49] Lyon, J., Dennison, C. and Wilson, A. (2000) '*Tell them so they listen': messages from young people in custody*, London: Home Office, p 30.

[50] Derbyshire, P. (2007) *Report of the serious case review panel upon the circumstances surrounding the death of AR at Hassockfield secure training centre on 9th August 2004. Part II*, Preston: Lancashire Safeguarding Children Board, p 56.

[51] Coles, D. with Scott, M. and Dias, D. (2007) *INQUEST's submission to the Ministry of Justice & Department for Children, Schools and Families on the 'Review of restraint'*, London: INQUEST, p 25.

[52] Shaw, S. (2006) *Circumstances surrounding the death of a boy at Hassockfield Secure Training Centre on 8 August 2004*, London: Prisons and Probation Ombudsman, p 78.

[53] Shaw, S. (2006) *Circumstances surrounding the death of a boy at Hassockfield Secure Training Centre on 8 August 2004*, London: Prisons and Probation Ombudsman, p 78.

[54] Shaw, S. (2006) *Circumstances surrounding the death of a boy at Hassockfield Secure Training Centre on 8 August 2004*, London: Prisons and Probation Ombudsman, p 15.

[55] Shaw, S. (2006) *Circumstances surrounding the death of a boy at Hassockfield Secure Training Centre on 8 August 2004*, London: Prisons and Probation Ombudsman, p 23.

[56] Shaw, S. (2006) *Circumstances surrounding the death of a boy at Hassockfield Secure Training Centre on 8 August 2004*, London: Prisons and Probation Ombudsman, pp 27-8.

[57] Shaw, S. (2006) *Circumstances surrounding the death of a boy at Hassockfield Secure Training Centre on 8 August 2004*, London: Prisons and Probation Ombudsman, p 80.

[58] Howard League for Penal Reform (2010) *Life inside. A unique insight into the day to day experiences of 15-17 year old males in prison*, London: Howard League for Penal Reform, p 20

[59] Data was provided by the Youth Justice Board in April 2014. I was told data relating to 2013 was still provisional.

[60] House of Lords *Hansard*, 22 July 2013: Column WA176.

[61] Harrington, R. and Bailey, S. with others (2005) *Mental health needs and effectiveness of provision for young offenders in custody and in the community*, London: Youth Justice Board for England and Wales, p 19.

[62] *The Press*, 19 July 2000, 'Kirk's cellmate on jail suicide watch'.

[63] NSPCC press release, 27 February 2014, 'Young people self-harm because of bullying and loneliness'.

[64] Durcan, G. (2008) *From the inside. Experiences of prison mental health care*, London: Sainsbury Centre for Mental Health, p 30.

[65] Shaw, S. (2008) *Circumstances surrounding the death of a trainee at HMP and YOI Hindley, in September 2005*, London: Prisons and Probation Ombudsman for England and Wales, pp 6, 32 and 46.

[66] Shaw, S. (2008) *Circumstances surrounding the death of a trainee at HMP and YOI Hindley, in September 2005*, London: Prisons and Probation Ombudsman for England and Wales, p 6.

[67] House of Commons Justice Committee (2009) *Role of the prison officer*, London: The Stationery Office, ev 76.

[68] The focus was on 11- to 25-year-olds.

[69] Brophy, M. (2006) *Truth hurts. Report of the national inquiry into self-harm among young people*, London: Mental Health Foundation, p 18.

[70] Brophy, M. (2006) *Truth hurts. Report of the national inquiry into self-harm among young people*, London: Mental Health Foundation, p 12.

[71] Tower Hamlets Safeguarding Children Board (2013) *Tower Hamlets Safeguarding Children Board serious case review. Executive summary. Services provided for Child F June 2004-January 2012*, London: Tower Hamlets SCB, p 10.

[72] Prisons and Probation Ombudsman for England and Wales (March 2013) *Learning lessons bulletin. Fatal incidents investigations issue 3*, London: PPO, p 1.

[73] Prisons and Probation Ombudsman for England and Wales (March 2013) *Learning lessons bulletin. Fatal incidents investigations issue 3*, London: PPO, p 2.

[74] This system was designed for adults. It is called Assessment, Care in Custody and Teamwork (ACCT).

[75] Prisons and Probation Ombudsman for England and Wales (March 2013) *Learning lessons bulletin. Fatal incidents investigations issue 3*, London: PPO, p 7.

[76] INQUEST press release, 'Serious failures identified by jury at inquest into death of 17 year old Ryan Clark at HMYOI Wetherby', 28 January 2014.

[77] House of Lords *Hansard*, 24 June 1992: Columns 504-38.

[78] Goldson, B. and Coles, D. (2005) *In the care of the state. Child deaths in penal custody in England and Wales*, London: INQUEST, pp 39-40.

[79] http://news.bbc.co.uk/1/hi/programmes/panorama/archive/1211953.stm

[80] Transcript from BBC Panorama programme, 11 March 2001, http://news.bbc.co.uk/hi/english/static/audio_video/programmes/panorama/transcripts/transcript_11_03_01.txt

[81] *The Press*, 24 August 2000, 'Last hours of cell hanging teenager'.

[82] Prisons and Probation Ombudsman for England and Wales (2006) *Investigation into the circumstances surrounding the death in custody of a male trainee at a hospital in January 2005*, London: PPO, p 53.

[83] Information contained in coroner's summing-up statement.

[84] BBC News, 11 December 2001, 'Teenager "attempted suicide four times"'.

[85] House of Lords *Hansard*, 22 July 2013: Column WA175.

[86] House of Lords *Hansard*, 22 July 2013: Column WA175.

[87] Spurr, M. (2008) 'Background on the English and Welsh prison system', in *Prison policy and prisoners' rights, proceedings of the colloquium of the International Penal and Penitentiary Foundation, Stavern, Norway, 25-28 June 2008, Nijmegen: Wolf Legal Publishers, p 313*.

[88] Rose, J. (2014) *Working with young people in secure accommodation. From chaos to culture* (2nd edn), London: Routledge, p 184.

[89] TheYouth Justice Board's annual report for 2012/13 states that the 'Working with young people in custody programme' has replaced the seven-day 'Juvenile awareness staff programme' but gives no further details: Youth Justice Board for England and Wales (2013) *Annual report and accounts 2012/13*, London: The Stationery Office, p 17.

[90] House of Lords *Hansard*, 16 July 2013: Column WA117.

Chapter Four

[1] NSPCC press release, 8 July 2013, 'Campaign launched to teach children the Underwear Rule'.

[2] Goffman, E. (1974) *Asylums. Essays on the social situation of mental patients and other inmates* (6th edn), Harmondsworth: Penguin Books, p 85.

[3] National Offender Management Service (2011) *National security framework. Ref: NSF 3.1. Searching of the person. PSI 67/2011*, London: Ministry of Justice, p 26.

[4] House of Lords *Hansard*, 6 May 2014; Column 338W.

[5] Education Act 1996, s 550AA (inserted by Violent Crime Reduction Act 2006, s 45).

[6] National Offender Management Service (2011) *National security framework. Ref: NSF 3.1. Searching of the person. PSI 67/2011*, London: Ministry of Justice, p 17.

[7] National Offender Management Service (2014) *National security framework. Ref: NSF 2.1. Control and order function. Use of force – implementation of minimising and managing physical restraint*, London: Ministry of Justice, p 8.

[8] Anne Owers CBE, HM Chief Inspector of Prisons, 'Prison inspection and the protection of human rights', BIHR Human rights lecture, 22 October 2003, p 6.

[9] Personal communication from Liz Hardy.

[10] Her Majesty's Inspectorate of Prisons (2009) *Report on a full announced inspection of HMYOI Castington 19-23 January 2009 by HM Chief Inspector of Prisons*, London: HMIP, p 21.

[11] Her Majesty's Inspectorate of Prisons (2011) *Report on an unannounced full follow-up inspection of HMYOI Feltham (young people under 18) 18-22 July 2011 by HM Chief Inspector of Prisons*, London: HMIP, p 80.

[12] Carlile, A. (2006) *An independent inquiry into the use of physical restraint, solitary confinement and forcible strip searching of children in prisons, secure training centres and local authority secure children's homes*, London: Howard League for Penal Reform, p 55.

[13] Her Majesty's Inspectorate of Prisons (2006) *Report on an announced inspection of HMYOI Huntercombe 8-12 May 2006 by HM Chief Inspector of Prisons*, London: HMIP, p 38.

[14] Her Majesty's Inspectorate of Prisons (2007) *Report on an unannounced full follow-up inspection of HMYOI Brinsford 5-9 February 2007 by HM Chief Inspector of Prisons*, London: HMIP, p 91.

[15] Her Majesty's Inspectorate of Prisons (2007) *Report on an unannounced short follow-up inspection of HMYOI Werrington 16-20 April 2007 by HM Chief Inspector of Prisons*, London: HMIP, p 5.

[16] Her Majesty's Inspectorate of Prisons (2007) *Report on an unannounced short follow-up inspection of HMYOI Wetherby 6-9 March 2007 by HM Chief Inspector of Prisons*, London: HMIP, p 17.

[17] Her Majesty's Inspectorate of Prisons (2007) *Report on an unannounced short follow-up inspection of HMYOI Warren Hill 16-18 July 2007 by HM Chief Inspector of Prisons*, London: HMIP, p 44.

[18] Her Majesty's Inspectorate of Prisons (2009) *Report on an unannounced short follow-up inspection of HMYOI Huntercombe 9-12 December 2008 by HM Chief Inspector of Prisons*. London: HMIP, p 17.

[19] Her Majesty's Inspectorate of Prisons (2009) *Report on an announced inspection of HMYOI Cookham Wood 2-9 February 2009 by HM Chief Inspector of Prisons*, London: HMIP, p 10.

[20] Her Majesty's Inspectorate of Prisons (2009) *Report on an announced inspection of HMYOI Cookham Wood 2-9 February 2009 by HM Chief Inspector of Prisons*, London: HMIP, p 21.

[21] Her Majesty's Inspectorate of Prisons (2009) *Report on an announced inspection of HMYOI Cookham Wood 2-9 February 2009 by HM Chief Inspector of Prisons*, London: HMIP, p 21.

[22] Her Majesty's Inspectorate of Prisons (2009) *Report on an announced inspection of HMYOI Werrington 29 June-3 July 2009 by HM Chief Inspector of Prisons*, London: HMIP, p 68.

[23] Her Majesty's Inspectorate of Prisons (2007) *Report on an unannounced short follow-up inspection of HMP/YOI Downview Josephine Butler Unit 1-4 February 2010 by HM Chief Inspector of Prisons*, London: HMIP, pp 11 and 54.

[24] Her Majesty's Inspectorate of Prisons (2014) *Report on an unannounced inspection of HMYOI Wetherby Keppel Unit 12-23 August 2013 by HM Chief Inspector of Prisons*, London: HMIP, p 5.

[25] Her Majesty's Inspectorate of Prisons (2014) *Report on an unannounced inspection of HMYOI Wetherby Keppel Unit 12-23 August 2013 by HM Chief Inspector of Prisons*, London: HMIP, p 70.

[26] Her Majesty's Inspectorate of Prisons (2014) *Report on an unannounced inspection of HMYOI Werrington 23 September-4 October 2013 by HM Chief Inspector of Prisons*, London: HMIP, p 26.

[27] Her Majesty's Inspectorate of Prisons (2014) *Report on an unannounced inspection of HMYOI Hindley 3-14 March 2014 by HM Chief Inspector of Prisons*, London: HMIP, p 25.

[28] Her Majesty's Inspectorate of Prisons (2014) *Report on an unannounced inspection of Cookham Wood 9-20 June 2014 by HM Chief Inspector of Prisons*, London: HMIP, p 27.

[29] Ofsted, Her Majesty's Inspectorate of Prisons and Care Quality Commission (2014) *Inspection of Hassockfield Secure Training Centre: July 2014*, Manchester: Ofsted, p 11.

[30] House of Commons *Hansard*, 28 March 2006: Column 62WS.

[31] Lader, D., Singleton, N. and Meltzer, H. (2000) *Psychiatric morbidity among young offenders in England and Wales. Further analysis of data from the ONS survey of psychiatric morbidity among prisoners in England and Wales carried out in 1997 on behalf of the Department of Health*, London: Office for National Statistics, p 89.

[32] Her Majesty's Inspectorate of Prisons (2008) *Report on an announced inspection of HMYOI Wetherby 30 June-4 July 2008 by HM Chief Inspector of Prisons*, London: HMIP, p 69.

[33] Ofsted (2012) *The inspection of Rainsbrook secure training centre: December 2012*, Manchester: Ofsted, p 10.

[34] Corston, J. (2007) *The Corston report. A review of women with particular vulnerabilities in the criminal justice system*, London: Home Office, p 31.

[35] Pryce, V. (2013) *Prisonomics. Behind bars in Britain's failing prisons*, London: Biteback Publishing, p 20.

[36] User Voice (2011) *Young people's views on safeguarding in the secure estate. A User Voice report for the Youth Justice Board and the Office of the Children's Commissioner*, London: Youth Justice Board for England and Wales, p 21.

[37] Her Majesty's Inspectorate of Prisons (2005) *Report on a full announced inspection of HM young offender institution Feltham 15-20 May 2005 by HM Chief Inspector of Prisons*, London: HMIP, p 23.

[38] Her Majesty's Inspectorate of Prisons (2005) *Report on an announced inspection of HMYOI Wetherby 19-23 July 2004 by HM Chief Inspector of Prisons*, London: HMIP, p 12.

[39] Council of Europe (2009) *Report to the government of the United Kingdom on the visit to the United Kingdom carried out by the European Committee for the Prevention of Torture and Inhuman or Degrading Treatment or Punishment (CPT) from 18 November to 1 December 2008*, Strasbourg: Council of Europe, para 106.

[40] Council of Europe (2009) *Response of the United Kingdom government to the report of the European Committee for the Prevention of Torture and Inhuman or Degrading Treatment or Punishment (CPT) following its visit to the United Kingdom from 18 November to 1 December 2008*, London: Ministry of Justice, paras 364-8.

[41] Youth Justice Board for England and Wales (2006) *A response to Lord Carlile's Inquiry into children in custody*, London: YJB, pp 9-10.

[42] Youth Justice Board for England and Wales (2011) *Review of full searches in the secure estate for children and young people. Summary of findings and action plan*, London: YJB, p 11.

[43] Youth Justice Board for England and Wales (2011) *Review of full searches in the secure estate for children and young people*, London: YJB, p 43.

[44] Youth Justice Board for England and Wales (2011) *Review of full searches in the secure estate for children and young people*, London: YJB, pp 11–12.

[45] Youth Justice Board for England and Wales (2011) *Review of full searches in the secure estate for children and young people*, London: YJB, p 12.

[46] Youth Justice Board for England and Wales press release, 2 July 2013, 'YJB reduces number of commissioned places in youth custody'.

[47] Youth Justice Board for England and Wales (2011) *Review of full searches in the secure estate for children and young people*, London: YJB, p 24.

[48] Youth Justice Board for England and Wales (2011) *Review of full searches in the secure estate for children and young people*, London: YJB, p 26.

[49] Goffman, E. (1974) (6th edn) *Asylums. Essays on the social situation of mental patients and other inmates*, Harmondsworth: Penguin Books, p 27.

[50] *Wainwright v UK* 2006 (Application no. 12350/04).

[51] *Wainwright v UK* 2006 [7].

[52] *Frérot v France* 2007 (Application no. 70204/01).

[53] Youth Justice Board press release, 1 March 2011, 'Youth Justice Board commits to improve practice in response to children and young people's views'.

[54] Youth Justice Board for England and Wales (2011) *Review of full searches in the secure estate for children and young people. Summary of findings and action plan*, London: YJB, pp 7 and 28.

[55] Youth Justice Board for England and Wales Order 2000.

[56] Her Majesty's Inspectorate of Prisons (2013) *Report on an unannounced inspection of HMYOI Ashfield 11-14 February 2013 by HM Chief Inspector of Prisons*, London: HMIP, p 9.

[57] User Voice (2011) *Young people's views on safeguarding in the secure estate. A User Voice report for the Youth Justice Board and the Office of the Children's Commissioner*, London: Youth Justice Board for England and Wales, p 28.

[58] User Voice (2011) *Young people's views on safeguarding in the secure estate. A User Voice report for the Youth Justice Board and the Office of the Children's Commissioner*, London: Youth Justice Board for England and Wales, p 31.

[59] User Voice (2011) *Young people's views on safeguarding in the secure estate. A User Voice report for the Youth Justice Board and the Office of the Children's Commissioner*, London: Youth Justice Board for England and Wales, p 29.

[60] Coles, D. and Shaw, H. (2012) 'Physical control, strip searching and segregation: observations on the deaths of children in custody', in A. Briggs (ed) (2012) *Waiting to be found. Papers on children in care*, London: Karnac Books, p 264.

[61] Prisons and Probation Ombudsman (2013) *Sexual abuse in prisons*, London: PPO, p 2.

[62] User Voice (2011) *Young people's views on safeguarding in the secure estate. A User Voice report for the Youth Justice Board and the Office of the Children's Commissioner*, London: Youth Justice Board for England and Wales, pp 28-42.

[63] Youth Justice Board for England and Wales (2011) *Review of full searches in the secure estate for children and young people*, London: YJB, p 29.

[64] Lambert, D. (2005) *Review of the effectiveness of operational procedures for the identification, placement and safeguarding of vulnerable young people in custody*, London: Home Office, p 76.

[65] Youth Justice Board for England and Wales (2011) *Review of full searches in the secure estate for children and young people*, London: YJB, p 18.

[66] Carlile, A. (2006) *An independent inquiry into the use of physical restraint, solitary confinement and forcible strip searching of children in prisons, secure training centres and local authority secure children's homes*, London: Howard League for Penal Reform, p 56.

[67] Levy, A. and Kahan, B. (1991) *The pindown experience and the protection of children. The report of the Staffordshire child care inquiry 1990*, Stafford: Staffordshire County Council, p 111.

[68] Levy, A. and Kahan, B. (1991) *The pindown experience and the protection of children. The report of the Staffordshire child care inquiry 1990*, Stafford: Staffordshire County Council, pp 115-16.

[69] Levy, A. and Kahan, B. (1991) *The pindown experience and the protection of children. The report of the Staffordshire child care inquiry 1990*, Stafford: Staffordshire County Council, p 167.

[70] Children's Homes Regulations 1991, reg 8(2)(h).

[71] Department of Health (1991) *The Children Act 1989. Guidance and regulations. Volume 4 residential care*, London: HMSO, p 19.

[72] Children's Homes Regulations 2001, reg 17(5)(h).

[73] Office for Standards in Education, Children's Services and Skills (2008) *Safeguarding children: the third joint chief inspectors' report on arrangements to safeguard children, Manchester: Ofsted, p 18.

[74] Hunter, N. (2013) 'Darlington prison worker found guilty of sex crimes', *The Northern Echo*, 20 May; Hunter, N. (2013) 'Former prison worker is behind bars himself after child sex conviction', *The Northern Echo*, 15 June.

[75] Bhatt Murphy press release, 23 August 2012, 'MOJ agrees to pay compensation to a young man for sexual assaults at HMYOI Huntercombe'.

[76] Woodfield, A. (2012) 'Prolific sex offender jailed', www.heart.co.uk/watfordhemel/news/local/prolific-sex-offender-gets-life-jail/

[77] CPS Thames and Chiltern News, 4 July 2012, 'Paedophile John Maber sentenced – Hertfordshire'.

[78] www.thelawpages.com/court-cases/John-Dominic-Maber-8438-1.law

[79] BBC News, 4 July 2012, 'John Maber: paedophile prison officer jailed for life'.

[80] BBC News, 18 July 2011, 'Downview sex case prison governor jailed'.

[81] Watts, M. (2011) 'Sutton prison officer fell to death day he faced sex with inmates trial', *Epsom Guardian*, 12 December.

[82] *Surrey Mirror*, 13 January 2012, 'Review launched at HMP Downview after prison sex scandal'.

[83] Information Commissioner's Office decision notice FS50525192, 24 April 2014, para 57.

[84] BBC News, 10 June 2011, 'Prison governor Barry Cummings jailed for child sex crimes'.

[85] *Daily Mail*, 16 May 2011, '"I raped a child hundreds of times": ex-prison officer, 68, walks up to policeman to confess 20 years after attacks'.

[86] *The Journal*, 11 November 2010, 'Prison officer Leslie Winnard jailed over child porn'; Unwin, B. (2010) 'Officer jailed over child porn', *The Northern Echo*, 11 November.

[87] *The York Press*, 31 August 2010, 'Child porn shame of ex-prison guard Andrew Burns'.

[88] Hunt, J. (2010) 'Prison officer jailed over inmate abuse', *East Anglian Daily Times*, 11 May.

[89] Hendy, A. (2010) 'Portland prison officer jailed for child porn offences', *Dorset Echo*, 13 February.

[90] Hunter, N. (2009) 'David George Lamb found guilty of making and distributing the obscene photographs', *The Northern Echo*, 6 October.

[91] Allison, E. and Hattenstone, S. (2012) 'A true horror story: the abuse of teenage boys in a detention centre', *The Guardian*, 13 April.

[92] Wearmouth, R. (2014) 'Government could pay out £12m to victims of abuse at Medomsley Detention Centre', *The Journal*, 30 January.

[93] Pyatt, J. (2007) 'Perv prison officer jailed', *The Sun*, 31 July.

[94] BBC News, 19 May 2006, 'Life term for rapist prison guard'.

[95] *The Telegraph*, 20 May 2006, 'Life for sadistic prison officer who posed as PC to rape and kidnap girls'.

[96] *Lancaster Guardian*, 15 November 2002, 'Internet child porn – prison officer and ambulanceman cautioned'.

[97] Her Majesty's Inspectorate of Prisons (2004) *Report on an announced inspection of HMP/YOI Lancaster Farms 12-16 January 2004 by HM Chief Inspector of Prisons*, London: HMIP, p 11.

[98] National Offender Management Service (2014) *Revised searching policy for young people. Ref: National security framework function 3. PSI 16/2014*, London: Ministry of Justice.

[99] National Offender Management Service (2014) *National security framework NSF 2.1. Control and order function. Use of force – implementation of minimizing and managing physical restraint*, London: Ministry of Justice, p 8.

[100] Child Exploitation and Online Protection (2013) *The foundations of abuse: a thematic assessment of the risk of child sexual abuse by adults in institutions*, London: National Crime Agency, p 11.

Chapter Five

[1] BBC News Wales, 8 July 2013, 'Jillings report: "extensive" abuse at children's homes'.

[2] Jillings, J. (2012) *Child abuse. An independent investigation commissioned by Clwyd County Council. Period 1974-1995*, Wrexham: Wrexham Borough Council, p 12.

[3] Jillings, J. (2012) *Child abuse. An independent investigation commissioned by Clwyd County Council. Period 1974-1995*. Wrexham: Wrexham Borough Council, p 12.

[4] Ministry of Justice (2013) *Transforming youth custody. Putting education at the heart of detention*, London: MoJ, p 8.

[5] Her Majesty's Inspectorate of Prisons (2013) *Report on an unannounced inspection of HMYOI Hindley 19-23 November 2012 by HM Chief Inspector of Prisons*, London: HMIP, p 7.

[6] Her Majesty's Inspectorate of Prisons (2014) *Report on an unannounced inspection of HMYOI Hindley 3–14 March 2014 by HM Chief Inspector of Prisons*, London: HMIP, p 6.

[7] Ministry of Justice (2014) *Transforming youth custody. Government response to the consultation*, London: MoJ, p 7.

[8] Kennedy, E. (2013) *Children and young people in custody 2012-13. An analysis of 15–18-year-olds' perceptions of their experiences in young offender institutions*, London: The Stationery Office, pp 27 and 30.

[9] Her Majesty's Inspectorate of Prisons (2009) *The prison characteristics that predict prisons being assessed as performing 'well': a thematic review by HM Chief Inspector of Prisons*, London: HMIP, p 18.

[10] Letter to Dr Hywel Francis MP, Chair of Joint Committee on Human Rights, from Chris Grayling MP, Secretary of State for Justice, 31 March 2014, p 4.

[11] National Children's Bureau (2008) *A review of safeguarding in the secure estate*, London: Youth Justice Board for England and Wales, p 24.

[12] Her Majesty's Inspectorate of Prisons (2013) *Report on an unannounced inspection of HMYOI Cookham Wood 7-17 May 2013 by HM Chief Inspector of Prisons*, London: HMIP, p 7.

[13] Ofsted, Her Majesty's Inspectorate of Prisons and Care Quality Commission (2013) *Inspection of Hassockfield Secure Training Centre: September 2013*, Manchester: Ofsted, p 8.

[14] Ofsted, Her Majesty's Inspectorate of Prisons and Care Quality Commission (2014) *Inspection of Hassockfield Secure Training Centre: July 2014*, Manchester: Ofsted, pp 7 and 14.

[15] Ofsted, Her Majesty's Inspectorate of Prisons and Care Quality Commission (2012) *Inspection of Medway Secure Training Centre: November 2012*, Manchester: Ofsted, p 9.

[16] Ofsted, Her Majesty's Inspectorate of Prisons and Care Quality Commission (2013) *Inspection of Medway Secure Training Centre: June 2013*, Manchester: Ofsted, pp 13 and 8.

[17] Ofsted, Her Majesty's Inspectorate of Prisons and Care Quality Commission (2014) *Inspection of Oakhill Secure Training Centre: February 2014*, Manchester: Ofsted, pp 13 and 24.

[18] Her Majesty's Inspectorate of Prisons (2009) *Expectations. Her Majesty's Inspectorate of Prisons criteria for assessing the treatment and conditions for children and young people held in prison custody*, London: HMIP.

[19] Her Majesty's Inspectorate of Prisons (1993) *Doing time or using time. Report of a review by Her Majesty's Inspectorate of Prisons for England and Wales*, London: HMSO, p 35.

[20] In March 2012, the prisons inspectorate reported to parliament that few young offender institutions, which hold the vast majority of imprisoned children, meet its target of 10 hours a day time out of cell: House of Commons Justice Committee (2013) *Youth justice. Seventh report of session 2012-13. Volume I*, London: The Stationery Office, ev 125.

[21] Her Majesty's Inspectorate of Prisons (2014) *Report on an unannounced inspection of HMYOI Werrington 23 September-4 October 2013 by HM Chief Inspector of Prisons*, London: HMIP, p 47; and Her Majesty's Inspectorate of Prisons (2014) *Report on an unannounced inspection of HMP & YOI Wetherby 7-18 October 2013 by HM Chief Inspector of Prisons*, London: HMIP, p 47.

[22] Her Majesty's Inspectorate of Prisons (2014) *Report on an unannounced inspection of HMP & YOI Wetherby 7-18 October 2013*, London: HMIP, p 47.

[23] Her Majesty's Inspectorate of Prisons (2014) *Report on an unannounced inspection of HMYOI Werrington 23 September-4 October 2013*, London: HMIP, p 47.

[24] Her Majesty's Inspectorate of Prisons (2014) *Report on an announced inspection of HMYOI Hindley 3-14 March 2014 by HM Chief Inspector of Prisons*, London: HMIP, pp 14 and 33.

[25] Her Majesty's Inspectorate of Prisons (2014) *Report on an unannounced inspection of HMYOI Cookham Wood 9-20 June 2014 by HM Chief Inspector of Prisons*, London: HMIP, pp 49 and 7.

[26] Her Majesty's Inspectorate of Prisons (2013) *Report on an announced inspection of HMYOI Warren Hill 4-8 March 2013 by HM Chief Inspector of Prisons*, London: HMIP, p 43.

[27] Her Majesty's Inspectorate of Prisons (2013) *Report on an unannounced inspection of HMP/YOI Feltham (Feltham A – children and young people) 21–25 January 2013 by HM Chief Inspector of Prisons*, London: HMIP, p 47.

[28] Independent Monitoring Board (2014) *Annual Report HMP YOI Feltham 2012-13*, London: Ministry of Justice, p 17.

[29] Independent Monitoring Board HMP/YOI Downview (2013) *Annual report January-December 2012*, London: Ministry of Justice, p 12.

[30] Independent Monitoring Board HMP/YOI Downview (2013) *Annual report January-December 2012*, London: Ministry of Justice, p 12.

[31] Youth Justice Board press release, 2 July 2013, 'YJB reduces number of commissioned places in youth custody'.

[32] Aynsley-Green, A. (2013) 'Does the Westminster government want to improve youth custody, or not?', OurKingdom website: www.opendemocracy.net/ourkingdom/al-aynsley-green/does-westminster-government-want-to-improve-youth-custody-or-not, 14 February.

[33] Ipsos MORI (2002) 'Bungalows are "people's choice" in England', London: Ipsos MORI.

[34] Her Majesty's Inspectorate of Prisons (2011) *The Carlile Inquiry: five years on. The use of force on children in custody. Memorandum*, London: HMIP, paras 30 and 31.

[35] Her Majesty's Inspectorate of Prisons (2011) *The Carlile Inquiry: five years on. The use of force on children in custody. Memorandum*, London: HMIP, paras 30 and 31.

[36] Murray, R. (2012) *Children and young people in custody 2011-12. An analysis of the experiences of 15–18-year-olds in prison*, London: Her Majesty's Inspectorate of Prisons, p 106; Kennedy, E. (2013) *Children and young people in custody 2012-13. An analysis of 15–18-year-olds' perceptions of their experiences in young offender institutions*, London: The Stationery Office, p 66.

[37] Youth Justice Board and Ministry of Justice (2013) *Service level agreement for young people's public sector YOIs*, London: YJB, p 8.

[38] Department of Health (2011) *Start active, stay active. A report on physical activity for health from the four home countries' Chief Medical Officers*, London: DH, p 26.

[39] Ministry of Justice press release, 14 February 2013, 'Greater focus on education in youth estate'.

[40] www.etoncollege.com/MinorSports.aspx

[41] Kennedy, H. (1995) *Banged up. Beaten up. Cutting up. Report of the Howard League Commission of Inquiry into violence in penal institutions for teenagers under 18*, London: Howard League for Penal Reform, p 43.

[42] House of Commons Justice Committee (2009) *Role of the prison officer. Twelfth report of session 2008-09*, London: The Stationery Office, p 30.

[43] Her Majesty's Inspectorate of Prisons (1997) *Young prisoners. A thematic review by HM Chief Inspector of Prisons for England and Wales*, London: HMIP, para 4.28.

[44] Her Majesty's Inspectorate of Prisons (1997) *Young prisoners. A thematic review by HM Chief Inspector of Prisons for England and Wales*, London: HMIP, para 4.35.

[45] Smallridge, P. and Williamson, A. (2008) *Independent review of restraint in juvenile secure settings*, London: Ministry of Justice, p 50.

46 Plomin, J. (2013) 'The abuse of vulnerable adults at Winterbourne View Hospital: the lessons to be learned' *Journal of Adult Protection*, vol 15, no 4, p 187.

47 Plomin, J. (2013) 'The abuse of vulnerable adults at Winterbourne View Hospital: the lessons to be learned' *Journal of Adult Protection*, vol 15, no 4, p 187.

48 Gilroy, D. (2004) *Youth Justice Board serious incident review. Gareth Paul Myatt*, London: Youth Justice Board, p 10.

49 Smith, L. (2007) 'Nobody can hurt him now', *The Guardian*, 4 July.

50 Gilroy, D. (2004) *Youth Justice Board serious incident review. Gareth Paul Myatt*, London: Youth Justice Board, p 11.

51 *Smith v Youth Justice Board for England and Wales & Another* [2010] EWCA Civ 99 [15].

52 *Community Care*, 16 February 2007, 'Rainsbrook chief admits restraint used on Gareth Myatt was "default" method for offenders'.

53 *(W) v HM Deputy Coroner for Northamptonshire* [2007] EWHC 1649 (Admin) [1].

54 *Smith v Youth Justice Board for England and Wales & Another* [2010] EWCA Civ 99. [18].

55 *R (C) v Secretary of State for Justice* [2008] EWCA Civ 882 [12].

56 'Physical Control in Care introduction', produced by Leanne Clay (undated).

57 Rainsbrook secure training centre, PCC statistics, October 2003, commentary.

58 *Community Care*, 14 March 2007, 'Myatt officer investigated for previous restraint, inquest hears'.

59 Coles, D. with Scott, M. and Dias, D. (2007) *INQUEST's submission to the Ministry of Justice & Department for Children, Schools and Families on the 'Review of restraint'*, London: INQUEST, pp 33-5.

60 BBC News, 17 June 2004, 'Restraint hold banned after death'.

61 *(W) v HM Deputy Coroner for Northamptonshire* [2007] EWHC 1649 (Admin) [29].

62 INQUEST press release, 28 June 2007, 'Gareth Myatt inquest verdict – failings of the Youth Justice Board cause death of a child'.

63 Letter to Jack Straw MP from His Honour Richard Pollard, Assistant Deputy Coroner for the County of Northampton, 18 July 2007, p 5.

64 Hart, D. and Howell, S. (2003) *Report to the Youth Justice Board on the use of physical intervention within the juvenile secure estate*, London: Youth Justice Board, p 58.

65 INQUEST press release, 28 June 2007, 'Gareth Myatt inquest verdict – failings of the Youth Justice Board cause death of a child'.

66 *Children and Young People Now*, 21 February 2007, 'Youth custody: Myatt inquiry hears of restraint failures'.

67 *Daily Mail*, 14 February 2007, 'Jail teenager died "being restrained by guards"'.

[68] House of Commons *Hansard*, 12 July 2007: Column 1716.

[69] Crown Prosecution Service press release, 19 December 2005, 'CPS advises no prosecution following death of teenager in custody'.

[70] House of Commons *Hansard*, 12 July 2007: Column 1715.

[71] *Smith v Youth Justice Board for England and Wales & Another* [2010] EWCA Civ 99 [35].

[72] *Community Care*, 16 February 2006, '"No wrongdoing" in Rainsbrook death'.

[73] Sambrook, C. (2013) 'G4S teaches UK Border Agency how to care for children', OurKingdom website: www.opendemocracy.net/ourkingdom/clare-sambrook/g4s-teaches-uk-border-agency-how-to-care-for-children, 10 July

[74] Sambrook, C. (2013) 'G4S guard fatally restrains 15 year old – gets promoted', OurKingdom website: www.opendemocracy.net/ourkingdom/clare-sambrook/g4s-guard-fatally-restrains-15-year-old-gets-promoted, 22 July.

[75] *Smith v Youth Justice Board for England and Wales & Another* [2010] EWCA Civ 99 [9].

[76] *(W) v HM Deputy Coroner for Northamptonshire* [2007] EWHC 1649 (Admin) [25].

[77] BBC News, 28 June 2007, 'Criticism over youth jail death'.

[78] *Smith v Youth Justice Board for England and Wales & Another* [2010] EWCA Civ 99 [35].

[79] Baroness Ashton at Second Reading of the Children Bill: House of Lords *Hansard*, 30 March 2004: Column1208.

[80] HM Prison Service Training and Development Group (2005) *Physical control in care manual*, London: HM Prison Service, p 49.

[81] Carlile, A. (2006) *An independent inquiry into the use of physical restraint, solitary confinement and forcible strip searching of children in prisons, secure training centres and local authority secure children's homes*, London: Howard League for Penal Reform, p 12.

[82] Youth Justice Board for England and Wales (2006) *A response to Lord Carlile's inquiry into children in custody*, London: YJB, p 9.

[83] Ministry of Justice (2008) *The Government's response to the report by Peter Smallridge and Andrew Williamson of a review of the use of restraint in juvenile secure settings*, London: MoJ, p 4.

[84] Information made available during legal proceedings.

[85] Information made available during legal proceedings.

[86] Commission for Social Care Inspection, HM Inspectorate of Court Administration, Healthcare Commission, HM Inspectorate of Constabulary, HM Inspectorate of Probation, HM Inspectorate of Prisons, HM Crown Prosecution Service Inspectorate and Office for Standards in Education (2005) *Safeguarding children: the second joint chief inspectors' report on arrangements to safeguard children*, London: Commission for Social Care Inspection, pp 11-12.

[87] Youth Justice Board for England and Wales (2006) *Managing the behaviour of children and young people in the secure estate*, London: YJB, p 11.

[88] *The Guardian*, 21 June 2007, Letter from Graham Robb.

[89] Smallridge, P. and Williamson, A. (2008) *Independent review of restraint in juvenile secure settings*, London: Ministry of Justice, pp 15-16.

[90] House of Lords *Hansard*, 9 November 2011: Column WA72.

[91] National Offender Management Service (2012) *Minimising and managing physical restraint. Volume 2. Behaviour recognition and decision making*, London: MoJ.

[92] www.justice.gov.uk/youth-justice/custody/behaviour-management/behaviour-management-and-restraint-update

[93] National Offender Management Service (2014) *National security framework NSF 2.1. Control and order function. Use of force – implementation of minimising and managing physical restraint*, London: Ministry of Justice, p 15.

[94] Social Services Inspectorate (1993) *A place apart: an investigation into the handling and outcomes of serious injuries to children and other matters at Aycliffe Centre for Children*, County Durham, London: SSI, p 20.

[95] Social Services Inspectorate (1993) *A place apart: an investigation into the handling and outcomes of serious injuries to children and other matters at Aycliffe Centre for Children*, County Durham, London: SSI, p 7.

Chapter Six

[1] Secure Training Centre (Amendment) Rules 2007 (2007 No 1709).

[2] House of Commons *Hansard*, 21 June 2007: Column 113WS.

[3] Joint Committee on Human Rights (2008) *The use of restraint in secure training centres. Eleventh report of session 2007-08*, London: The Stationery Office, ev 28.

[4] The first inquest concluded on 1 June 2007, the coroner wrote to the secretary of state for justice the following week and the amendment rules were signed 13 June 2007.

[5] Extract of letter to directors from Ellie Roy, Youth Justice Board chief executive, 27 May 2007, cited in *R (C) v Secretary of State for Justice* [2008] EWCA Civ 882 [16].

[6] BBC News, 1 June 2011, 'Moat Taser man Peter Boatman's inquest records open verdict'.

[7] *Children's Rights Alliance For England v Secretary of State for Justice and G4S Care and Justice Services (UK) Limited and Serco PLC* [2012] EWHC 8 (Admin) [45].

[8] *Children's Rights Alliance For England v Secretary of State for Justice and G4S Care and Justice Services (UK) Limited and Serco PLC* [2012] EWHC 8 (Admin) [61].

[9] House of Commons *Hansard*, 12 July 2007: Column 70WS.

[10] Reilly, G. and Larkins, S. (2007) *Restraint in secure training centres. A stakeholder briefing*, London: Youth Justice Board for England and Wales, pp 2 and 5.

[11] Reilly, G. and Larkins, S. (2007) *Restraint in secure training centres. A stakeholder briefing*, London: Youth Justice Board for England and Wales, p 5.

[12] *R (C) v Secretary of State for Justice* [2008] EWCA Civ 882 [21] and [26].

[13] *R (C) v Secretary of State for Justice* [2008] EWCA Civ 882 [12].

[14] *R (C) v Secretary of State for Justice* [2008] EWCA Civ 882.

[15] *R (C) v Secretary of State for Justice* [2008] EWCA Civ 882 [74].

[16] House of Commons *Hansard*, 6 October 2008: Column 188W.

[17] Between 1 August 2009 and 31 March 2010, there were nine incidents of restraint for concerted indiscipline leading to injury; between December 2010 and April 2011, there were five incidents of restraint for concerted indiscipline leading to injury; and between August 2010 and March 2012, there were 26 incidents of restraint for concerted indiscipline leading to injury.

[18] Durham Safeguarding Children Board (2011) *Restraints leading to injuries to children within Newton Aycliffe secure children's home and Hassockfield secure training centre*, Durham: Durham Safeguarding Children Board, p 6.

[19] Durham Safeguarding Children Board (2012) *Annual report to the Youth Justice Board. Use of restraint in the secure estate for children and young people – April 2012*, Durham: Durham Safeguarding Children Board, p 8.

[20] Letter from Youth Justice Board, 7 November 2013.

[21] Letter from Youth Justice Board, 7 November 2013.

[22] Joint Committee on Human Rights (2008) *The use of restraint in secure training centres. Eleventh report of session 2007-08,* London: The Stationery Office, ev 53.

[23] Joint Committee on Human Rights (2008) *The use of restraint in secure training centres. Eleventh report of session 2007-08*, London: The Stationery Office, ev 29.

[24] Joint Committee on Human Rights (2008) *The use of restraint in secure training centres. Eleventh report of session 2007-08*, London: The Stationery Office, ev 29.

[25] Early Day Motion 1727, tabled 18 June 2007, 'Restraint in secure training centres'.

[26] House of Lords *Hansard*, 18 July 2007: Column 283.

[27] House of Lords *Hansard*, 18 July 2007: Column 301.

[28] House of Lords *Hansard*, 18 July 2007: Column 297.

[29] House of Lords *Hansard*, 18 July 2007: Column 287.

[30] Joint Committee on Human Rights (2008) *The use of restraint in secure training centres. Eleventh report of session 2007-08*, London: The Stationery Office, p 21.

[31] Allison, E. and Hattestone, S. (2007) 'What gives them the right to hit a child in the nose?', *The Guardian*, 2 June.

[32] *R (Carol Pounder) v HM Coroner for the North and South Districts of Durham and Darlington & Ors* [2009] EWHC 76 (Admin) [71].

[33] INQUEST press release (2011) 'Youth justice agencies condemned for unlawful treatment of vulnerable boy in custody', pp 1 and 2, 27 January.

[34] INQUEST press release (2011) 'Youth justice agencies condemned for unlawful treatment of vulnerable boy in custody', pp 2 and 3, 27 January.

[35] Crown Prosecution Service press release, 20 March 2014, 'Death of Jimmy Mubenga – charging decisions following inquest'.

[36] House of Commons Home Affairs Committee (2012) *Rules governing enforced removals from the UK*, London: The Stationery Office, ev 4.

[37] Reilly, G. and Larkins, S. (2007) *Restraint in secure training centres. A stakeholder briefing*, London: Youth Justice Board for England and Wales, p 3.

[38] Carlile, A. (2006) *An independent inquiry into the use of physical restraint, solitary confinement and forcible strip searching of children in prisons, secure training centres and local authority secure children's homes*, London: Howard League for Penal Reform, p 43.

[39] Lord Carlile of Berriew QC (2006) *An independent inquiry into the use of physical restraint, solitary confinement and forcible strip searching of children in prisons, secure training centres and local authority secure children's homes*, London: Howard League for Penal Reform, p 48.

[40] Lord Carlile of Berriew QC (2006) *An independent inquiry into the use of physical restraint, solitary confinement and forcible strip searching of children in prisons, secure training centres and local authority secure children's homes*, London: Howard League for Penal Reform, p 49.

[41] Lord Carlile of Berriew QC (2006) *An independent inquiry into the use of physical restraint, solitary confinement and forcible strip searching of children in prisons, secure training centres and local authority secure children's homes, London: Howard League for Penal Reform*, p 45.

[42] Voice (2008) *A submission from Voice to the joint review on the use of restraint in juvenile secure settings*, London: Voice, p 4.

[43] NSPCC (2008) *A consultation with young people on the use of restraint in custody*, London: NSPCC, p 7.

[44] NSPCC (2008) *A consultation with young people on the use of restraint in custody*, London: NSPCC, p 9.

[45] Owen, J. and Brady, B. (2008) 'NSPCC calls for end to abuse in custody', *The Independent*, 16 March 2008.

[46] Hale, B. (2013) 'Who's afraid of children's rights', Lecture, Swansea University, 14 June.

[47] Criminal Justice Act 1967, s 65.

[48] Criminal Justice Act 1988, s 134.

[49] HM Prison Service Training and Development Group (2005) *Physical control in care training manual*, London: HM Prison Service, p 75.

[50] HM Prison Service Training and Development Group (2005) *Physical control in care training manual*, London: HM Prison Service, p 97.

[51] HM Prison Service Training and Development Group (2005) *Physical control in care training manual*, London: HM Prison Service, p 93.

52 Kirkwood, A. (1992) *The Leicestershire inquiry. The report of an inquiry into aspects of the management of children's homes in Leicestershire between 1973 and 1986*, Leicester: Leicestershire County Council, p 1.

53 *R (Carol Pounder) v HM Coroner for the North and South Districts of Durham and Darlington & Ors* [2009] EWHC 76 (Admin) [67].

54 *R (Carol Pounder) v HM Coroner for the North and South Districts of Durham and Darlington & Ors* [2009] EWHC 76 (Admin) [67].

55 House of Commons *Hansard*, 16 June 2009: Column 272W.

56 *R (C) v Secretary of State for Justice* [2008] EWCA Civ 882 [73].

57 Ministry of Justice and Department for Children, Schools and Families (2008) *The government's response to the report by Peter Smallridge and Andrew Williamson of a review of the use of restraint in juvenile secure settings*, London: The Stationery Office, p 9.

58 House of Lords *Hansard*, 22 January 2008: Column 166.

59 Prisons and Probation Ombudsman for England and Wales (2010) *Annual report 2009-2010*, London: PPO, p 37.

60 Prisons and Probation Ombudsman for England and Wales (2010) *Annual report 2009-2010*, London: PPO, p 37.

61 Ministry of Justice officials told the Equality and Human Rights Commission that the nose control was removed in January 2011, although contradictory information appears in the report of a group of experts appointed by the government to review restraint. The Restraint Advisory Board's report states that the mandibular angle technique was introduced in August 2010 after the nose distraction was removed: Restraint Advisory Board (2011) *Assessment of behaviour recognition & physical restraint (BRPR) for children in the secure estate. Submitted by the National Offender Management Service*, London: Ministry of Justice, p 66.

62 Ryan, J. (undated) *Report of the panel of specialists, chaired by Professor Jim Ryan, to assess the mandibular angle technique for use on young people under 18 in secure establishments*, London: Ministry of Justice, p 17.

63 Ministry of Justice (2012) *Minimising and managing physical restraint 2012. Volume 5 physical restraint*, London: Ministry of Justice, pp 45-8.

64 Ministry of Justice (2012) *Minimising and managing physical restraint 2012. Volume 5 physical restraint*, London: Ministry of Justice, p 45.

65 Dunhill, L. (2010) 'Police officer tells inquest why he was seen gripping Habib Ullah's throat', Buck Free Press, www.bucksfreepress.co.uk/news/8732181.Police_officer_tells_inquest_why_he_was_seen_gripping_Habib_Ullah_s_throat/, 11 December.

66 IPCC press release, 3 February 2014, 'IPCC refers Habib Ullah case to the Crown Prosecution Service'.

67 IPCC response to my freedom of information request, 30 May 2014.

68 IPCC news release, 8 August 2014, 'No further action to be taken following the death of Habib Ullah'.

[69] Restraint Advisory Board (2012) *The final report from the Restraint Advisory Board (RAB) on the reporting and analysis on the mandibular angle technique (MAT)*, London: Ministry of Justice.

[70] Restraint Advisory Board (2012) *The final report from the Restraint Advisory Board (RAB) on the reporting and analysis on the mandibular angle technique (MAT)*, London: Ministry of Justice, p 14.

[71] Restraint Advisory Board (2012) *The final report from the Restraint Advisory Board (RAB) on the reporting and analysis on the mandibular angle technique (MAT)*, London: Ministry of Justice, p 8.

[72] Restraint Advisory Board (2012) *The final report from the Restraint Advisory Board (RAB) on the reporting and analysis on the mandibular angle technique (MAT)*, London: Ministry of Justice, p 12.

[73] Restraint Advisory Board (2012) *The final report from the Restraint Advisory Board (RAB) on the reporting and analysis on the mandibular angle technique (MAT)*, London: Ministry of Justice, p 4.

[74] Restraint Advisory Board (2012) *The final report from the Restraint Advisory Board (RAB) on the reporting and analysis on the mandibular angle technique (MAT)*, London: Ministry of Justice, p 6.

[75] Restraint Advisory Board (2012) *The final report from the Restraint Advisory Board (RAB) on the reporting and analysis on the mandibular angle technique (MAT)*, London: Ministry of Justice, p 12.

[76] Her Majesty's Inspectorate of Prisons (2013) *Report on an announced inspection of HMYOI Warren Hill 4-8 March 2013 by HM Chief Inspector of Prisons*, London: HMIP, p 27.

[77] Her Majesty's Inspectorate of Prisons (2014) *Report on an unannounced inspection of HMP &YOI Wetherby 7-18 October 2013 by HM Chief Inspector of Prisons*, London: HMIP, p 29.

[78] Her Majesty's Inspectorate of Prisons (2014) *Report on an unannounced inspection of HMYOI Werrington 23 September-4 October 2013 by HM Chief Inspector of Prisons*, London: HMIP, p 29.

[79] Prisons and Probation Ombudsman (2014) *Use of force. Learning from PPO complaints relating to the use of force on prisoners*, London: PPO, p 3.

[80] The Youth Justice Board released data for Rainsbrook secure training centre on 17 January 2014, relating to the period March to August 2013: www.justice.gov.uk/youth-justice/custody/behaviour-management/behaviour-management-and-restraint-update#Rainsbrook

[81] Written ministerial statement, 10 July 2012, 'Approval of a new system of restraint for use in secure training centres and young offender institutions', Ministry of Justice.

[82] Youth Justice Board for England and Wales (2012) *Minimising and managing physical restraint. Safeguarding processes, governance arrangements, and roles and responsibilities*, London: YJB.

83 D'Arcy, M. and Gosling, P. (1998) *Abuse of trust. Frank Beck and the Leicestershire children's homes scandal*, London: Bowerdean Publishing Company Ltd, pp 123-25.

84 House of Commons Home Affairs Committee (2002) *The conduct of investigations into past cases of abuse in children's homes*, London: The Stationery Office, para 1.

85 BBC News, 24 November 2011, 'British Gas to make changes after "loss of trust"'.

86 Jameson, N. and Allison, E. (1995) *Strangeways 1990. A serious disturbance*, London: Larkin Publications, p 138.

87 BBC News, 13 March 2012, 'G4S annual profits fall after failed takeover bid'.

88 Wallop, H. (2012) 'Serco profits rise despite flat performance in Britain', *The Telegraph*, 28 February.

89 *Children's Rights Alliance for England v Secretary of State for Justice and G4S Care and Justice Services (UK) Limited and Serco PLC* [2012] EWHC 8 (Admin) [78].

90 *Children's Rights Alliance for England v Secretary of State for Justice and G4S Care and Justice Services (UK) Limited and Serco PLC* [2012] EWHC 8 (Admin) [50-52].

91 *Children's Rights Alliance for England v Secretary of State for Justice and G4S Care and Justice Services (UK) Limited and Serco PLC* [2012] EWHC 8 (Admin) [199].

92 Francis, R. (2013) *Report of the Mid Staffordshire NHS Foundation Trust public inquiry volume 1: Analysis of evidence and lessons learned (part 1)*, London: The Stationery Office, p 9.

93 Department of Health (2014) *Introducing the statutory duty of candour. A consultation on proposals to introduce a new CQC registration regulation*, London: DH, pp 17-20.

94 House of Commons *Hansard*, 27 July 2010: Column 929W.

95 House of Lords *Hansard*, 30 October 2013: Column WA275.

96 House of Lords *Hansard*, 22 July 2013: Column WA178.

97 Ministry of Justice and Youth Justice Board for England and Wales (2014) *Youth justice annual statistics 2012-2013*, Table 8.7 RPIs involving injury by sector, 2008/09 to 2012/13, London: MoJ.

98 Her Majesty's Inspectorate of Prisons (2009) *Report on a full announced inspection of HMYOI Castington 19-23 January 2009 by HM Chief Inspector of Prisons*, London: HMIP, p 10

99 Casciani, D. (2009) 'Injuries prompt youth jail review', BBC News, 23 June.

100 National Offender Management Service (2010) *Review of the management and use of control and restraint at HMYOI Castington*, London: Ministry of Justice, p 16.

101 National Offender Management Service (2010) *Review of the management and use of control and restraint at HMYOI Castington*, London: Ministry of Justice.

[102] Sam Riley Law Associates, 15 June 2012, 'Prison guard loses unfair dismissal claim at employment tribunal'.

[103] Chronicle Live, 10 June 2012, 'Former guard loses appeal over '"unfair dismissal"'.

[104] BBC News, 22 February 2010, 'Castington Young Offenders to phase out under-18 places'.

[105] UKEAT/0638/11/SM [14].

[106] Her Majesty's Inspectorate of Prisons (2013) *Report on an unannounced inspection of the decommissioning of HMYOI Ashfield 11-14 February 2013 by HM Chief Inspector of Prisons*, London: HMIP, p 10.

[107] Puffett, N. (2013) 'Ashfield YOI to close in response to falling custody levels', *Children and Young People Now*, 10 January.

[108] Prisons and Probation Ombudsman for England and Wales (2013) *A report by the Prisons and Probation Ombudsman Nigel Newcomen CBE*, London: PPO, para 57.

[109] Prisons and Probation Ombudsman for England and Wales (2013) *A report by the Prisons and Probation Ombudsman Nigel Newcomen CBE*, London: PPO, paras 133 and 135.

[110] National Offender Management Service (2006) *Use of force training manual*, London: Ministry of Justice, p 90.

[111] House of Lords *Hansard*, 21 October 2013: Column WA134.

[112] Prisons and Probation Ombudsman for England and Wales (2013) *A report by the Prisons and Probation Ombudsman Nigel Newcomen CBE*, London: PPO, para 37.

[113] Prisons and Probation Ombudsman for England and Wales (2013) *A report by the Prisons and Probation Ombudsman Nigel Newcomen CBE*, London: PPO, para 94.

[114] Prisons and Probation Ombudsman for England and Wales (2013) *A report by the Prisons and Probation Ombudsman Nigel Newcomen CBE*, London: PPO, para 139.

[115] Prisons and Probation Ombudsman for England and Wales (2013) *A report by the Prisons and Probation Ombudsman Nigel Newcomen CBE*, London: PPO, paras 86 and 87.

[116] Prisons and Probation Ombudsman for England and Wales (2013) *A report by the Prisons and Probation Ombudsman Nigel Newcomen CBE*, London: PPO, para 71.

[117] Prisons and Probation Ombudsman for England and Wales (2013) *A report by the Prisons and Probation Ombudsman Nigel Newcomen CBE*, London: PPO, para 5.

[118] Prisons and Probation Ombudsman for England and Wales (2013) *A report by the Prisons and Probation Ombudsman Nigel Newcomen CBE*, London: PPO, para 6.

[119] Prisons and Probation Ombudsman for England and Wales (2013) *A report by the Prisons and Probation Ombudsman Nigel Newcomen CBE*, London: PPO, para 189.

[120] Prisons and Probation Ombudsman for England and Wales (2013) *A report by the Prisons and Probation Ombudsman Nigel Newcomen CBE*, London: PPO, para 140.

[121] Personal communication from Eric Allison.

[122] House of Lords *Hansard*, 30 October 2013: Column WA273.

[123] National Offender Management Service (2011) *A review of six use of force incidents at HMP/YOI Hindley. Final report*, London: National Offender Management Service, p 7.

[124] National Offender Management Service (2011) *A review of six use of force incidents at HMP/YOI Hindley. Final report*, London: National Offender Management Service, p 13.

[125] National Offender Management Service (2011) *A review of six use of force incidents at HMP/YOI Hindley. Final report*, London: National Offender Management Service, p 5.

[126] National Offender Management Service (2011) *A review of six use of force incidents at HMP/YOI Hindley. Final report*, London: National Offender Management Service, p 10.

[127] HM Prison Service (2005) *Use of force. Prison service order number 1600*, London: HM Prison Service, p 15.

[128] Her Majesty's Chief Inspectorate of Prisons (2014) *Report on an unannounced inspection of HMP & YOI Wetherby 7-18 October 2013 by HM Chief Inspector of Prisons*, London: HMIP, p 29.

[129] Her Majesty's Chief Inspectorate of Prisons (2014) *Report on an unannounced inspection of HMYOI Cookham Wood by HM Chief Inspector of Prisons*, London: HMIP, p 30.

Chapter Seven

[1] Berelowitz, S. with Hibbert, P. (2011) *'I think I must have been born bad.' Emotional wellbeing and mental health of children and young people in the youth justice system*, London: Office of Children's Commissioner for England, p 25.

[2] Her Majesty's Inspectorate of Prisons (2011) *The care of looked after children in custody. A short thematic review*, London: HMIP, p 9. The review was commissioned by the Youth Justice Board.

[3] Her Majesty's Inspectorate of Prisons (2011) *The care of looked after children in custody. A short thematic review*, London: HMIP, p 9.

[4] Kennedy, E. (2013) *Children and young people in custody 2012-13. An analysis of 15–18-year-olds' perceptions of their experiences in young offender institutions*, London: The Stationery Office, pp 27 and 30.

[5] Kennedy, E. (2013) *Children and young people in custody 2012-13. An analysis of 15–18-year-olds' perceptions of their experiences in young offender institutions*, London: The Stationery Office, p 103.

[6] Speech at The Temple Church first choral service of the legal year, 7 October 2012, by Nick Hardwick, Chief Inspector of Prisons, p 5.

[7] Coyle, A. (1994) *The prisons we deserve*, London: HarperCollins, p 43.

[8] Kelso, P. (2000) 'Boys behind bars', *The Guardian*, 17 November.

[9] Tower Hamlets Safeguarding Children Board (2013) *Serious case review executive summary. Services provided for child F June 2004- January 2012*, London: Tower Hamlets Safeguarding Children Board, pp 10 and 15.

[10] Goldson, B. and Coles, D. (2005) *In the care of the state? Child deaths in penal custody in England and Wales*, London: INQUEST, pp 49-50.

[11] Children's Rights Alliance for England (2012) *Ending violence against children in custody. Findings from research with children and young people*, London: CRAE, p 20.

[12] Howard League for Penal Reform (2010) *Life inside 2010. A unique insight into the day to day experiences of 15-17 year old males in prison*, London: Howard League for Penal Reform, p 24.

[13] Her Majesty's Inspectorate of Prisons (2014) *Report on an unannounced inspection of HMYOI Cookham Wood 9-20 June 2014 by HM Chief Inspector of Prisons*, London: HMIP, p 95.

[14] Her Majesty's Inspectorate of Prisons (2014) *Report on an unannounced inspection of HMYOI Werrington 23 September- 4 October 2013 by HM Chief Inspector of Prisons*, London: HMIP, p 94

[15] Her Majesty's Inspectorate of Prisons (2014) *Report on an unannounced inspection of HMP & YOI Wetherby 7-18 October 2013 by HM Chief Inspector of Prisons*, London: HMIP, p 93.

[16] Her Majesty's Inspectorate of Prisons (2014) *Report on an unannounced inspection of HMYOI Hindley 3-14 March 2014 by HM Chief Inspector of Prisons*, London: HMIP, p 100.

[17] Her Majesty's Inspectorate of Prisons (2014) *Report on an unannounced inspection of HMYOI Wetherby Keppel Unit 12-23 August 2013 by HM Chief Inspector of Prisons*, London: HMIP, p 80.

[18] Her Majesty's Inspectorate of Prisons (2013) *Report on an unannounced inspection of the decommissioning of HMYOI Ashfield 11-14 February 2013 by HM Chief Inspector of Prisons*, London: HMIP, pp 20-21.

[19] Her Majesty's Inspectorate of Prisons (2013) *Report on an unannounced inspection of HMP/YOI Feltham (Feltham A – children and young people) 21-25 January 2013 by HM Chief Inspector of Prisons*, London: HMIP, p 85.

[20] Her Majesty's Inspectorate of Prisons (2013) *Report on an announced inspection of HMYOI Warren Hill 4-8 March 2013 by HM Chief Inspector of Prisons*, London: HMIP, p 55.

[21] Her Majesty's Inspectorate of Prisons (2013) *Report on an unannounced inspection of HMYOI Cookham Wood 7-17 May 2013 by HM Chief Inspector of Prisons*, London: HMIP, p 92.

[22] Ofsted, Her Majesty's Inspectorate of Prisons and Care Quality Commission (2013) *The inspection of Hassockfield secure training centre: February/March 2013*, Manchester: Ofsted, p 32.

[23] Ofsted, Her Majesty's Inspectorate of Prisons and Care Quality Commission (2013) *Inspection of Medway secure training centre: June 2013*, Manchester: Ofsted, p 17.

[24] Ofsted, Her Majesty's Inspectorate of Prisons and Care Quality Commission (2013) *The inspection of Oakhill secure training centre: March 2013*, Manchester: Ofsted, p 29.

[25] Ofsted, Her Majesty's Inspectorate of Prisons and Care Quality Commission (2014) *Inspection of Oakhill secure training centre: February 2014*, Manchester: Ofsted, p 25.

[26] Children Act 1989, s 23ZB, as inserted by Children and Young Persons Act 2008, s 16.

[27] House of Lords *Hansard*, 30 October 2013: Column WA277.

[28] HM Government (2010) *The Children Act 1989 guidance and regulations volume 2: Care planning, placement and case review*, London: Department for Children, Schools and Families, para 3.193.

[29] Ministry of Justice (2013) *Independent advocacy services to children and young people. Schedule 1: authority's requirements. Service specification*, London: MoJ.

[30] Tomalin, C. (2011) *Charles Dickens. A life*, London: Viking, p 25.

[31] Prisons and Probation Ombudsman for England and Wales (2008) *Circumstances surrounding the death of a trainee at HMP and YOI Hindley, in September 2005*, London: PPO, p 10.

[32] Prisons and Probation Ombudsman for England and Wales (2008) *Circumstances surrounding the death of a trainee at HMP and YOI Hindley, in September 2005*, London: PPO, p 14.

[33] Prisons and Probation Ombudsman for England and Wales (2006) *Circumstances surrounding the death of a boy at Hassockfield secure training centre on 8 August 2004*, London: PPO, p 114.

[34] Prisons and Probation Ombudsman for England and Wales (2006) *Circumstances surrounding the death of a boy at Hassockfield secure training centre on 8 August 2004*, London: PPO, p 79.

[35] Her Majesty's Inspectorate of Prisons (2014) *Report on an unannounced inspection of HMYOI Wetherby Keppel Unit 12 – 23 August 2013 by HM Chief Inspector of Prisons*, London: HMIP, p 50

[36] Her Majesty's Inspectorate of Prisons (2014) *Report on an unannounced inspection of HMYOI Hindley 3-14 March 2014 by HM Chief Inspector of Prisons*, London: HMIP, p 15.

[37] National Offender Management Service (2011) *PSI 11/2011*, London: MoJ, p 7.

[38] Youth Justice Board for England and Wales (2002) *Rewards and sanctions systems. Guidance (and mandatory requirements) in the juvenile secure estate*, London: YJB, p 29.

[39] Her Majesty's Inspectorate of Prisons (2013) *Report on an unannounced inspection of HMYOI Hindley 19- 23 November 2012 by HM Chief Inspector of Prisons*, London: HMIP, p 5.

[40] Her Majesty's Inspectorate of Prisons (2013) *Report on an unannounced inspection of HMYOI Hindley 19- 23 November 2012 by HM Chief Inspector of Prisons*, London: HMIP, pp 59 and 14.

[41] Her Majesty's Inspectorate of Prisons (2014) *Report on an unannounced inspection of HMYOI Hindley 3-14 March 2014 by HM Chief Inspector of Prisons*, London: HMIP, p 100.

[42] Her Majesty's Inspectorate of Prisons (2013) *HMYOI Hindley. Summary of questionnaires and interviews: Children and young people's self-reported perceptions 13 November 2012*, London: HMIP, Q5 and Q8.

[43] Her Majesty's Inspectorate of Prisons (2013) HMYOI Hindley. *Summary of questionnaires and interviews: Children and young people's self-reported perceptions 13 November 2012*, London: HMIP, Q5 and Q8

[44] Her Majesty's Inspectorate of Prisons (2013) *Report on an unannounced inspection of HMYOI Hindley 19-23 November 2012 by HM Chief Inspector of Prisons*, London: HMIP, p 5.

[45] *HC (A child, by his litigation friend CC) v SSHD and Commissioner of Police of the Metropolis* [2013] EWHC 982 (Admin) [85].

[46] Johnson, M. (2008) *Wasted*, London: Sphere, pp 113-14.

[47] Kennedy, E. (2013) *Children and young people in custody 2012-13. An analysis of 15–18-year-olds' perceptions of their experiences in young offender institutions*, London: The Stationery Office, p 41.

[48] Kennedy, E. (2013) *Children and young people in custody 2012-13. An analysis of 15–18-year-olds' perceptions of their experiences in young offender institutions*, London: The Stationery Office, p 151.

[49] Elwood, C. (2013) *Children and young people in custody 2012-13. An analysis of 12–18-year-olds' perceptions of their experience in secure training centres*, London: HMSO, p 27.

[50] Howard League for Penal Reform (2010) *Life inside. A unique insight into the day to day experiences of 15-17 year old males in prison*, London: Howard League for Penal Reform, p 20.

[51] Carlile, A. (2006) *An independent inquiry into the use of physical restraint, solitary confinement and forcible strip searching of children in prisons, secure training centres and local authority secure children's homes*, London: Howard League for Penal Reform, p 62.

[52] Her Majesty's Inspectorate of Prisons (2013) *Report on an unannounced inspection of HMYOI Cookham Wood by HM Chief Inspector of Prisons 7-17 May 2013 by HM Chief Inspector of Prisons*, London: HMIP, p 27.

[53] Her Majesty's Inspectorate of Prisons (2013) *Report on an unannounced inspection of HMYOI Cookham Wood 7-17 May 2013 by HM Chief Inspector of Prisons*, London: HMIP, p 21.

NOTES

[54] Her Majesty's Inspectorate of Prisons (2013) *Report on an unannounced inspection of HMYOI Cookham Wood 7-17 May 2013 by HM Chief Inspector of Prisons*, London: HMIP, p 12.

[55] Talbot, J. (2008) *Experiences of the criminal justice system by prisoners with learning disabilities and difficulties*, London: Prison Reform Trust, p 50.

[56] Dennis, S. (2000) 'My boy waved goodbye, went to his cell. Then hanged himself; scandal of jail suicides', *Mirror*, 16 August.

[57] *The York Press*, 3 June 1999, 'Farewell note agony of cell tragedy parents'.

[58] Cited in Davies, R. (2010) 'Marking the 50th anniversary of the Platt report: from exclusion to toleration and parental participation in the care of the hospitalized child', *Journal of Child Health Care*, vol 14, no 1, p 12.

[59] Platt, H. (1959) *The welfare of children in hospital. Report of the Committee*, London: Her Majesty's Stationery Office, p 2.

[60] Platt, H. (1959) *The welfare of children in hospital. Report of the Committee*, London: Her Majesty's Stationery Office, p 18.

[61] Oswin, M. (1978) *Children living in long-stay hospitals*, London: William Heinemann Medical Books Ltd, p 8.

[62] Oswin, M. (1978) *Children living in long-stay hospitals*, London: William Heinemann Medical Books Ltd, p vii.

[63] The Visits to Children in Long-Term Residential Care Regulations 2011.

[64] Ministry of Justice (2011) *Breaking the cycle: government response. Presented to Parliament by the Lord Chancellor and Secretary of State for Justice by Command of Her Majesty*, London: The Stationery Office, p 10.

[65] Legal Aid, Sentencing and Punishment of Offenders Act 2012, s 104, came into force in December 2012.

[66] Animal Welfare Act 2006, s 18.

[67] House of Lords *Hansard*, 30 October 2013: Column 276W.

[68] National Offender Management Service (2011) *PSI 16/2011. Providing visits and services to visitors*, London: MoJ, para 3.9.

[69] Office of the Children's Commissioner (2012) *Annual report and financial statements for 2011-2012*, London: The Stationery Office, p 19.

[70] User Voice (2011) *Young people's views on safeguarding in the secure estate. A User Voice report for the Youth Justice Board and the Office of the Children's Commissioner*, London: Youth Justice Board for England and Wales, p 22.

[71] Her Majesty's Inspectorate of Prisons (2014) *Report on an unannounced inspection of HMYOI Werrington 23 September – 4 October 2013 by HM Chief Inspector of Prisons*, London: HMIP, p 26.

[72] Hagell, A., Hazel, N. and Shaw, C. (2000) *Evaluation of Medway secure training centre*, London: Home Office, p 99.

[73] Hagell, A., Hazel, N. and Shaw, C. (2000) *Evaluation of Medway secure training centre*, London: Home Office, p 100.

[74] User Voice (2011) *Young people's views on safeguarding in the secure estate. A User Voice report for the Youth Justice Board and the Office of the Children's Commissioner*, London: Youth Justice Board for England and Wales, p 22.

[75] Ofsted, Her Majesty's Inspectorate of Prisons and Care Quality Commission (2013) *The inspection of Hassockfield Secure Training Centre: February / March 2013*, Manchester: Ofsted, p 32.

[76] Ofsted, Her Majesty's Inspectorate of Prisons and Care Quality Commission (2013) *The inspection of Hassockfield Secure Training Centre: 10-20 September 2013*, Manchester: Ofsted, p 30.

[77] Ofsted, Her Majesty's Inspectorate of Prisons and Care Quality Commission (2013) *The inspection of Hassockfield Secure Training Centre: February / March 2013*, Manchester: Ofsted, p 32.

[78] Ofsted, Her Majesty's Inspectorate of Prisons and Care Quality Commission (2013) *The inspection of Oakhill Secure Training Centre: March 2013*, Manchester: Ofsted, p 29.

[79] Ofsted, Her Majesty's Inspectorate of Prisons and Care Quality Commission (2013) *The inspection of Oakhill Secure Training Centre: March 2013*, Manchester: Ofsted, p 29.

[80] Ofsted, Her Majesty's Inspectorate of Prisons and Care Quality Commission (2014) *Inspection of Oakhill Secure Training Centre: February 2014*, Manchester: Ofsted, p 25.

[81] Ofsted, Her Majesty's Inspectorate of Prisons and Care Quality Commission (2014) *Inspection of Oakhill secure training centre: February 2014*, Manchester: Ofsted, p 25.

[82] Ofsted, Her Majesty's Inspectorate of Prisons and Care Quality Commission (2013) *The inspection of Hassockfield secure training centre: 10-20 September 2013*, Manchester: Ofsted, p 23.

[83] Ofsted, Her Majesty's Inspectorate of Prisons and Care Quality Commission (2014) *Inspection of Oakhill secure training centre: July 2014*, Manchester: Ofsted, p 22.

[84] Ofsted, Her Majesty's Inspectorate of Prisons and Care Quality Commission (2014) *Inspection of Rainsbrook secure training centre: November / December 2013*, Manchester: Ofsted, pp 20-1.

[85] House of Commons *Hansard*, 13 April 1994, volume 241.

[86] Crook, F. (2010), 'Charities, judicial reviews and matters of government policy', blog, 15 September, www.howardleague.org/francescrookblog/charities-judicial-reviews-and-matters-of-government-policy/

[87] House of Commons *Hansard*, 27 June 1995: Columns 581-2W.

[88] Goodchild, S. (1999) 'Child jail to be run by firm in sex abuse case', *The Independent*, 27 June.

[89] Miller, J. (2003) 'Worker rights in private prisons', in A. Coyle, A. Campbell and R. Neufeld (eds) *Capitalist punishment: prison privatisation and human rights*, London: Zed Books, p 141.

[90] US Department of Justice press release, 30 March 2000, 'Justice department sues, files for emergency relief to protect juveniles in Louisiana's Jena Juvenile Justice Center'.

[91] CBS News, 9 May 2000, 'Locked inside a nightmare. Wackenhut's private prisons scrutinised'.

[92] House of Commons *Hansard*, 2 July 1998: Column: 246.

[93] House of Lords *Hansard*, 8 November 2013: Column WA90.

[94] House of Lords *Hansard*, 8 November 2013: Column WA88.

[95] Murray, R. (2012) *Children and young people in custody 2011-12. An analysis of the experiences of 15–18 year-olds in prison*, London: The Stationery Office, pp 101 and 149.

[96] Corston, J. (2007) 'Foreword', in *The Corston report. A report by Baroness Jean Corston of a review of women with particular vulnerabilities in the criminal justice system*, London: Home Office.

[97] Williams, K., Papadopoulou, V and Booth, N. (2012) *Prisoners' childhood and family backgrounds. Results from the surveying prisoner crime reduction (SPCR) longitudinal cohort study of prisoners*, London: Ministry of Justice, p 11.

[98] Youth Justice Board for England and Wales (2007) *Annual report and accounts 2006/07*, London: The Stationery Office, p 14.

[99] Youth Justice Board for England and Wales (2007) *Annual report and accounts 2006/07*, London: The Stationery Office, p 14.

[100] 11 Million (2008) *Prison mother and baby units – do they meet the best interests of the child?*, London: Office of Children's Commissioner for England, p 32.

[101] Robins, L. (2012) *Mother and baby prison units. An investigative study*, Wellington: New Zealand Winston Churchill Memorial Trust, pp 87-8.

[102] House of Commons *Hansard*, 12 May 2014: Column 537.

[103] House of Lords *Hansard*, 22 October 2014: Column 679.

Chapter Eight

[1] Batmanghelidjh, C. (2013) *Mind the child*, London: Penguin Books, p 11.

[2] Children's Food Trust (2013) *Food provision in juvenile young offender institutions in England and Wales*, London: Youth Justice Board for England and Wales, p 34.

[3] Children's Food Trust (2013) *Food provision in juvenile young offender institutions in England and Wales*, London: Youth Justice Board for England and Wales, p 18.

[4] Children's Food Trust (2013) *Food provision in juvenile young offender institutions in England and Wales*, London: Youth Justice Board for England and Wales, p 12.

[5] Children's Food Trust (2013) *Food provision in juvenile young offender institutions in England and Wales*, London: Youth Justice Board for England and Wales, p 13.

[6] Children's Food Trust (2013) *Food provision in juvenile young offender institutions in England and Wales*, London: Youth Justice Board for England and Wales, p 35.

[7] Department for Children, Schools and Families (2007) *The children's plan. Building brighter futures*, Norwich: Her Majesty's Stationery Office, p 3.

[8] Ryan, M. and Tunnard, J. (2008) *Emotional well-being at Wetherby YOI. A review of the young people's journey in custody*, London: RyanTunnardBrown, p 11.

[9] House of Commons Justice Committee (2013) *Youth justice. Seventh report of session 2012-13*, London: The Stationery Office, ev 40.

[10] BBC News, 17 September 2013, 'Starved boy Daniel Pelka "invisible" to professionals'.

[11] Sereny, G. (1995) *The case of Mary Bell. A portrait of a child who murdered* (2nd edn), London: Pimlico, p 280.

[12] The Howard League for Penal Reform (2010) *Life inside 2010. A unique insight into the day to day experiences of 15-17 year old males in prison*, London: Howard League for Penal Reform, p 22.

[13] Voice and Barnardo's (2012) *Developing the secure estate for children and young people in England and Wales – young people's consultation report. A report produced for the Youth Justice Board by Voice and Barnardo's*, London: Youth Justice Board for England and Wales, p 29.

[14] Willow, C. (2002) *It's not fair. Young people's reflections on children's rights*, London: The Children's Society, pp 52 and 44.

[15] House of Commons Justice Committee (2013) *Youth justice. Seventh report of session 2012-13*, London: The Stationery Office, ev 125.

[16] Her Majesty's Inspectorate of Prisons (2011) *The care of looked after children in custody. A short thematic review*, London: HMIP, p 41.

[17] Crook, F. (2001) 'Bread and water', blog, 4 August, www.howardleague.org/francescrookblog/bread-and-water/

[18] Her Majesty's Inspectorate of Prisons (2013) *Report on an unannounced inspection of the decommissioning of HMYOI Ashfield 11-14 February 2013 by HM Chief Inspector of Prisons*, London: HMIP, p 33.

[19] Her Majesty's Inspectorate of Prisons (2013) *Report on an unannounced full follow-up inspection of HMP/YOI Eastwood Park Mary Carpenter Unit. 13-17 August 2012 by HM Chief Inspector of Prisons*, London: HMIP, pp 75-76.

[20] Her Majesty's Inspectorate of Prisons (2013) *Report on an unannounced inspection of HMYOI Cookham Wood 7-17 May 2013 by HM Chief Inspector of Prisons*, London: HMIP, p 85.

[21] Her Majesty's Inspectorate of Prisons (2013) *Report on an unannounced inspection of HMYOI Cookham Wood 7-17 May 2013 by HM Chief Inspector of Prisons*, London: HMIP, p 41.

[22] Her Majesty's Inspectorate of Prisons (2013) *Report on an unannounced inspection of HMYOI Cookham Wood 7-17 May 2013 by HM Chief Inspector of Prisons*, London: HMIP, p 41.

[23] Her Majesty's Inspectorate of Prisons (2014) *Report on an unannounced inspection of HMYOI Cookham Wood 9-20 June 2014 by HM Chief Inspector of Prisons*, London: HMIP, p 46.

[24] Her Majesty's Inspectorate of Prisons (2014) *Report on an unannounced inspection of HMYOI Werrington 23 September-4 October 2013 by HM Chief Inspector of Prisons*, London: HMIP, p 44.

[25] Her Majesty's Inspectorate of Prisons (2013) *Report on an unannounced inspection of HMYOI Cookham Wood 7-17 May 2013 by HM Chief Inspector of Prisons*, London: HMIP, p 41.

[26] Independent Monitoring Board (2012) *HM YOI Cookham Wood. Annual report of the Independent Monitoring Board*, London: HMIP, p 18.

[27] Her Majesty's Inspectorate of Prisons (2013) *Report on an unannounced inspection of HMP/YOI Feltham (Feltham A – children and young people) 21-25 January 2013 by HM Chief Inspector of Prisons*, London: HMIP, p 45.

[28] Ofsted, Her Majesty's Inspectorate of Prisons and Care Quality Commission (2013) *Inspection of Hassockfield secure training centre: September 2013*, Manchester: Ofsted, p 38.

[29] Ofsted, Her Majesty's Inspectorate of Prisons and Care Quality Commission (2014) *Inspection of Rainsbrook secure training centre: November/December 2013*, Manchester: Ofsted, p 38.

[30] Ofsted, Her Majesty's Inspectorate of Prisons and Care Quality Commission (2013) *Inspection of Medway secure training centre: June 2013*, Manchester: Ofsted, p 35.

[31] The Children's Homes Regulations 2001, reg 13.

[32] The Secure Training Centre Rules 1998, rule 16.

[33] The Young Offender Institution Rules 2000, rule 20.

[34] Council of Europe (2009) *Report to the Government of the United Kingdom on the visit to the United Kingdom carried out by the European Committee for the Prevention of Torture and Inhuman or Degrading Treatment or Punishment (CPT) from 18 November to 1 December 2008*, Strasbourg: Council of Europe, p 44.

[35] Council of Europe (2009) *Response of the United Kingdom Government to the report of the European Committee for the Prevention of Torture and Inhuman or Degrading Treatment or Punishment (CPT) following its visit to the United Kingdom from 18 November to 1 December 2008*, Strasbourg: Council of Europe, p 25.

[36] Her Majesty's Inspectorate of Prisons (2009) *Report on an unannounced short follow- up inspection of HMYOI Huntercombe. 9-12 December 2008 by HM Chief Inspector of Prisons*, London: HMIP, p 48.

[37] Her Majesty's Inspectorate of Prisons (2006) *Report on an announced inspection of HMYOI Huntercombe. 8-12 May 2006 by HM Chief Inspector of Prisons*, London: HMIP, p 13.

[38] Mooney. A., Statham, J. and Storey, P. (2007) *The health of children and young people in secure settings. Final report to the Department of Health*, London: Thomas Coram Research Unit, p 30.

[39] Berelowitz, S. with Hibbert, P. (2011) *'I think I must have been born bad.' Emotional wellbeing and mental health of children and young people in the youth justice system*, London: Office of Children's Commissioner for England, p 50.

[40] Children's Food Trust (2013) *Food provision in juvenile young offender institutions in England and Wales*, London: Youth Justice Board for England and Wales, p 17.

[41] Children's Food Trust (2013) *Food provision in juvenile young offender institutions in England and Wales*, London: Youth Justice Board for England and Wales, p 17.

[42] Sykes, G.M. (2007) *The society of captives. A study of maximum security prison* (2nd edn), Princeton, NJ: Princeton University Press, pp 4 and 8.

[43] Department of Health and Ministry of Justice (2011) *Government response to the Office of Children's Commissioner's report: 'I think I must have been born bad' – emotional well-being and mental health of children and young people in the youth justice system*, London: DH and MoJ, pp 10-11.

[44] Letter to Rt Hon Crispin Blunt, MP, from Sue Berelowitz, deputy children's commissioner/chief executive of the Office of Children's Commissioner for England, 5 December 2011.

[45] Children's Food Trust (2013) *Food provision in juvenile young offender institutions in England and Wales*, London: Youth Justice Board for England and Wales, p 11.

[46] Youth Justice Board for England and Wales and Ministry of Justice (2012) *Developing the secure estate for children and young people in England and Wales. Plans until 2015*, London: YJB, p 3.

[47] Youth Justice Board and Ministry of Justice (2013) *Service level agreement for young people's public sector YOIs*, London: YJB, p 7.

[48] Youth Justice Board and Ministry of Justice (2013) *Service level agreement for young people's public sector YOIs*, London: YJB, p 9.

[49] Youth Justice Board for England and Wales and Ministry of Justice (2012) *Developing the secure estate for children and young people in England and Wales. Plans until 2015*, London: YJB, p 5.

[50] Levy, A. and Kahan, B. (1991) *The pindown experience and the protection of children. The report of the Staffordshire child care inquiry 1990*, Stafford: Staffordshire County Council, p 112.

[51] Department of Health (1993) *The Children Act guidance and regulations. Volume 4 residential care* (3rd edn), Norwich: HMSO, pp 17-18.

[52] *MA (formerly a child but now of full age) & Others v Independent Adjudicator & Director, HMYOI Ashfield* [2013] EWHC 438 (Admin) [33].

[53] Ministry of Justice press release, 10 January 2013, 'Changes to the prison estate'.

[54] House of Commons *Hansard*, 12 March 2012: Column 102W.

[55] Berelowitz, S. with Hibbert, P. (2011) *'I think I must have been born bad.' Emotional wellbeing and mental health of children and young people in the youth justice system*, London: Office of Children's Commissioner for England, p 50.

[56] Her Majesty's Inspectorate of Prisons (2014) *Report on an unannounced inspection of HMYOI Werrington 23 September-4 October 2013 by HM Chief Inspector of Prisons*, London: HMIP, p 33; Her Majesty's Inspectorate of Prisons (2014) *Report on an unannounced inspection of HMP &YOI Wetherby 7-18 October 2013 by HM Chief Inspector of Prisons*, London: HMIP, p 13; Her Majesty's Inspectorate of Prisons (2014) *Report on an unannounced inspection of HMYOI Hindley 3-14 March 2014 by HM Chief Inspector of Prisons*, London: HMIP, p 6.

[57] Goffman, E. (1974) *Asylums. Essays on the social situations of mental patients and other inmates*, London: Penguin Books, p 24.

[58] Mooney. A., Statham, J. and Storey, P. (2007) *The health of children and young people in secure settings. Final report to the Department of Health*, London: Thomas Coram Research Unit, p 30.

Chapter Nine

[1] Morrison, B. (1997) *As if*, London: Granta Books, p 27.

[2] Her Majesty's Inspectorate of Prisons (1997) *Young prisoners. A thematic review by HM Chief Inspector of Prisons for England and Wales*, London: Home Office, para 4.07.

[3] Her Majesty's Inspectorate of Prisons (1997) *Young prisoners. A thematic review by HM Chief Inspector of Prisons for England and Wales*, London: Home Office, para 4.07.

[4] Howard League for Penal Reform (2010) *Life inside. A unique insight into the day to day experiences of 15-17 year old males in prison*, London: Howard League for Penal Reform, p 10.

[5] Howard League for Penal Reform (2010) *Life inside. A unique insight into the day to day experiences of 15-17 year old males in prison*, London: Howard League for Penal Reform, p 10.

[6] The Welfare of Animals (Transport) (England) Order 2006, reg 4(1).

[7] Criminal Justice Act 1991, s 82(3)(d).

[8] The Secure Training Centres (Escorts) Rules 1998, rule 3.

[9] Anderson, L. (2013) 'Magistrate furious after damaged cells result in criminals waiting for prison escort in Newton Aycliffe Magistrates Court reception area', *The Northern Echo*, 15 July.

[10] Bryan, K., Freer, J. and Furlong, C. (2007) '*Language and communication difficulties in juvenile offenders*', *International Journal of Language & Communication Disorders*, vol 42, no 5, pp 505-20.

[11] Her Majesty's Inspectorate of Prisons (2013) *Report on an inspection visit to court custody facilities in Cleveland, Durham and Northumbria 6-15 August 2012*, London: HMIP, p 12.

[12] James, E. (2003) *A life inside. A prisoner's notebook*, London: Atlantic Books, p xiii.

13 Bateman, T. (2012) 'Who pulled the plug? Towards an explanation for the fall in child imprisonment in England and Wales', *Youth Justice*, 1, p 39.
14 Criminal Justice Act 1982, s 1(4).
15 *House of Lords Hansard, 22 June 1982: Column 945.*
16 *House of Lords Hansard,* 12 March 1991: Column 102.
17 Criminal Justice Act 2003, s 152.
18 Criminal Justice Act 2003, s 174, inserted by Legal Aid, Sentencing and Punishment of Offenders Act 2012, s 64(8).
19 Gibbs, P. and Hickson, S. (2009) *Children: innocent until proven guilty. A report on the overuse of remand for children in England and Wales and how it can be addressed,* London: Prison Reform Trust, p 18.
20 Grimshaw, R. (ed) with Schwartz, J. and Wingfield, R. (2011) *My story. Young people talk about the trauma and violence in their lives,* London: Centre for Crime and Justice Studies, p 54.
21 Her Majesty's Inspectorate of Prisons (2014) *Report on an inspection visit to court custody facilities in Norfolk and Suffolk by HM Chief Inspector of Prisons 30 September-4 October 2013 by HM Chief Inspector of Prisons,* London: HMIP, p 7.
22 Her Majesty's Inspectorate of Prisons (2013) *Report on an inspection visit to court custody facilities in Lancashire and Cumbria 18-26 February 2013 by HM Chief Inspector of Prisons,* London: HMIP, p 12.
23 Her Majesty's Inspectorate of Prisons (2014) *Report on an inspection visit to court custody facilities in Cambridgeshire and Essex 6-14 January 2014 by HM Chief Inspector of Prisons,* London: HMIP, p 13.
24 Her Majesty's Inspectorate of Prisons (2014) *Report on an inspection visit to court custody facilities in Cambridgeshire and Essex 6-14 January 2014 by HM Chief Inspector of Prisons,* London: HMIP, p 17.
25 Her Majesty's Inspectorate of Prisons (2013) *Report on an inspection visit to court custody facilities in Merseyside and Cheshire 15-19 October 2012 by HM Chief Inspector of Prisons,* London: HMIP, p 17.
26 Her Majesty's Inspectorate of Prisons (2013) *Report on an inspection visit to court custody facilities in Lancashire and Cumbria 18-26 February 2013 by HM Chief Inspector of Prisons,* London: HMIP, p 24.
27 Her Majesty's Inspectorate of Prisons (2013) *Report on an inspection visit to court custody facilities in Cleveland, Durham and Northumbria 6-15 August 2012 by HM Chief Inspector of Prisons,* London: HMIP, p 21.
28 Children and Young Persons Act 1933, s 31.
29 *R (on the application of T (by his mother and litigation friend RT)) v Secretary of State for Justice and another* [2013] EWHC 1119 (Admin) [27].
30 Her Majesty's Inspectorate of Prisons (2013) *Report on an inspection visit to court custody facilities in Merseyside and Cheshire 15-19 October 2012 by HM Chief Inspector of Prisons,* London: HMIP, p 16.

[31] Her Majesty's Inspectorate of Prisons (2013) *Report on an inspection visit to court custody facilities in Nottinghamshire and Derbyshire by HM Chief Inspector of Prisons 8-11 July 2013 by HM Chief Inspector of Prisons*, London: HMIP, p 15.

[32] Her Majesty's Inspectorate of Prisons (2013) *Report on an inspection visit to court custody facilities in Cleveland, Durham and Northumbria 6-15 August 2012 by HM Chief Inspector of Prisons*, London: HMIP, p 23.

[33] Her Majesty's Inspectorate of Prisons (2013) *Report on an inspection visit to court custody facilities in Cleveland, Durham and Northumbria 6-15 August 2012 by HM Chief Inspector of Prisons*, London: HMIP, p 24.

[34] Sereny, G. (1995) *The case of Mary Bell. A portrait of a child who murdered*, London: Pimlico, p 70.

[35] Her Majesty's Inspectorate of Prisons (2014) *Report on an inspection visit to court custody facilities in Cambridgeshire and Essex 6–14 January 2014 by HM Chief Inspector of Prisons*, London: HMIP, p 16.

[36] Her Majesty's Inspectorate of Prisons (2013) *Report on an inspection visit to court custody facilities in Lancashire and Cumbria 18-26 February 2013 by HM Chief Inspector of Prisons*, London: HMIP, p 22.

[37] Howard League for Penal Reform (2002) *Barred rights. An independent submission to the United Nations Committee on the Rights of the Child*, London: HMIP, p 17.

[38] INQUEST press release, 12 April 2013, 'Jury delivers damning narrative verdict after inquest into the death of 18 year old Ben Grimes at HMYOI Portland'.

[39] Goldson, B. and Coles, D. (2005) *In the care of the state? Child deaths in penal custody in England and Wales*, London: INQUEST, pp 48-9.

[40] International Centre for Prison Studies July–August 2013 news digest, www. prisonstudies.org/images/news_events/icpsnewsdigestjulyaug2013.pdf

[41] Ministry of Justice and Youth Justice Board (2012) *Developing the secure estate for children and young people in England and Wales. Government response to the consultation*, London: MoJ, p 13.

[42] Murray, R. (2012) *Children and young people in custody 2011-12. An analysis of the experiences of 15–18-year-olds in prison*, London: HM Inspectorate of Prisons and the Youth Justice Board for England and Wales, p 17.

[43] Gove, M. (2013) 'I'm ending this scandal over children's care', *The Telegraph*, 12 September.

[44] Department for Education (2013) *Children's homes data pack*, London: DfE, p 32.

[45] Independent Monitoring Boards (2013) *HMP/YOI Ashfield annual report July 2011-June 2012*, London: Ministry of Justice, p 9.

[46] House of Commons *Hansard*, 7 June 2004: Column 192W.

[47] HM Chief Inspector of Prisons for England and Wales (2012) *Annual report 2011-12*, Norwich: HMSO, p 25.

[48] Independent Monitoring Board (2014) *Annual report HMP YOI Feltham*, London: Ministry of Justice, p 4; Independent Monitoring Board (2013) *HMYOI Cookham Wood annual report of the Independent Monitoring Board 1 August 2012-31 July 2013*, London: Ministry of Justice, p 5; and Independent Monitoring Board (2013) *Annual report of the Independent Monitoring Board of HMP/YOI Warren Hill 1 June 2012-31 May 2013*, London: Ministry of Justice, p 4.

[49] Her Majesty's Inspectorate of Prisons (2013) *Report on an inspection visit to court custody facilities in Nottinghamshire and Derbyshire 8-11 July 2013 by HM Chief Inspector of Prisons*, London: HMIP, p 14.

[50] Her Majesty's Inspectorate of Prisons (2008) *Prisoners under escort. A short follow-up thematic review*, London: HMIP, p 24.

[51] Independent Monitoring Board (2011) *Annual report of the Independent Monitoring Board of HMP/YOI Warren Hill 1 June 2010-31 May 2011*, London: Ministry of Justice, para 6.9.

[52] Independent Monitoring Board (2014) *Annual report of the Independent Monitoring Board of HMP/YOI Warren Hill 1 June 2013-16 January 2014*, London: Ministry of Justice, page 11.

[53] *R (Howard League for Penal Reform) v Secretary of State for the Home Department and Department of Health* [2002] EWHC 2497 (Admin) [111-112].

[54] Her Majesty's Inspectorate of Prisons (2014) *Report on an unannounced inspection of HMYOI Werrington 23 September-4 October 2013 by HM Chief Inspector of Prisons*, London: HMIP, p 19.

[55] Her Majesty's Inspectorate of Prisons (2010) *Report on an unannounced short follow-up inspection of HMYOI Brinsford (Juvenile) 30 November-3 December 2009 by HM Chief Inspector of Prisons*, London: HMIP, p 13.

[56] Her Majesty's Inspectorate of Prisons (2009) *Report on a full announced inspection of HMYOI Castington 19-23 January 2009 by HM Chief Inspector of Prisons*, London: HMIP, p 10.

[57] Her Majesty's Inspectorate of Prisons (2009) *Report on an announced inspection of HMYOI Stoke Heath Juveniles only 13-17 October 2008 by HM Chief Inspector of Prisons*, London: HMIP, p 17.

[58] Her Majesty's Inspectorate of Prisons (2009) *Report on an unannounced short follow-up inspection of HMYOI Ashfield 26-29 August 2008 by HM Chief Inspector of Prisons*, London: HMIP, p 17.

[59] Her Majesty's Inspectorate of Prisons (2013) *Report on an inspection visit to court custody facilities in Nottinghamshire and Derbyshire 8-11 July 2013 by HM Chief Inspector of Prisons*, London: HMIP, p 14.

[60] Her Majesty's Inspectorate of Prisons (2013) *Report on an inspection visit to court custody facilities in Nottinghamshire and Derbyshire 8-11 July 2013 by HM Chief Inspector of Prisons*, London: HMIP, p 14.

[61] Her Majesty's Inspectorate of Prisons (2013) *Report on an announced inspection of HMYOI Warren Hill 4-8 March 2013 by HM Chief Inspector of Prisons*, London: HMIP, p 17.

[62] Her Majesty's Inspectorate of Prisons (2014) *Report on an announced inspection of HMYOI Hindley 3-14 March 2014 by HM Chief Inspector of Prisons*, London: HMIP, p 90.

[63] Her Majesty's Inspectorate of Prisons (2013) *Report on an unannounced inspection of HMP/YOI Feltham (Feltham A – children and young people) 21-25 January 2013 by HM Chief Inspector of Prisons*. London: HMIP, p 21.

[64] Her Majesty's Inspectorate of Prisons (2013) *Report on an unannounced inspection of HMP/YOI Feltham (Feltham A – children and young people) 21-25 January 2013 by HM Chief Inspector of Prisons*, London: HMIP, p 21.

[65] Her Majesty's Inspectorate of Prisons (2013) *Report on an announced inspection of HMYOI Warren Hill 4-8 March 2013 by HM Chief Inspector of Prisons*, London: HMIP, p 17.

[66] Her Majesty's Inspectorate of Prisons (2013) *Report on an announced inspection of HMYOI Warren Hill 4-8 March 2013 by HM Chief Inspector of Prisons*, London: HMIP, p 17.

[67] Her Majesty's Inspectorate of Prisons (2013) *Report on an announced inspection of HMYOI Warren Hill 4-8 March 2013 by HM Chief Inspector of Prisons*, London: HMIP, pp 75 and 17.

[68] Bowman, P.C. (2004) 'A thousand days of despair', *The Guardian*, 12 August.

[69] Letter from director general of the prison service, Derek Lewis, to Mr George Howarth MP, 29 June 1995, cited in House of Commons *Hansard*, 29 June 1995: Column 769.

[70] Howard League for Penal Reform (2010) *Life inside. A unique insight into the day to day experiences of 15-17 year old males in prison*, London: Howard League for Penal Reform, p 10.

[71] Youth Justice Board for England and Wales (2012) *Annual report and accounts 2011/12*, London: YJB, p 14. The contract value is available here: http://www.publictenders.net/node/1698838.

[72] House of Lords *Hansard*, 20 June 2013: Column WA86.

[73] Ofsted, Her Majesty's Inspectorate of Prisons and Care Quality Commission (2014) *Inspection of Hassockfield secure training centre: July 2014*, Manchester: Ofsted, p 10.

[74] House of Lords *Hansard*, 4 December 2012: Column WA156.

[75] Care Quality Commission, Her Majesty's Inspectorate of Prisons and Ofsted (2014) *Inspection of Oakhill secure training centre: February 2014*, Manchester: Ofsted, p 17.

[76] Howard League for Penal Reform press release, 8 March 2013, 'International Women's Day: Howard League appeals to UN over imprisonment of pregnant 16-year-old girl'.

[77] Mills, H. (1996) 'Howard unchains pregnant prisoners', *The Independent*, 19 January.

[78] Ramsbotham, D. (2005) *Prisongate. The shocking state of Britain's prisons and the need for visionary change*, Cambridge: The Free Press, p 18.

[79] Mills, H. (1996), 'Howard unchains pregnant prisoners', *Independent* newspaper, 19 January 1996.

[80] Department of Health /Her Majesty's Prison Service (2006) *A twelve-month study of prison healthcare escorts and bedwatches*, London: DH, p 41.

[81] Prisons and Probation Ombudsman for England and Wales (2006) *Investigation into the circumstances surrounding the death in custody of a male trainee at a hospital in January 2005*, London: PPO, pp 29-30.

Chapter Ten

[1] Yorkshire Evening Post, 15 October 2013, 'Inquest into death of Leeds teenage prisoner'.

[2] James, E. (2003) *A life inside. A prisoner's notebook*, London: Atlantic Books, p xv.

[3] Berman, G. and Dar, A. (2013) *Prison population statistics*, London: House of Commons Library, p 9.

[4] Ministry of Justice (2014) *Safety in custody statistics quarterly update to 31 December 2013*, Table 3.3: Prisoner assailants, victims and fighters by age and calendar year, England and Wales, 2000-2012, London: MoJ.

[5] POA (undated) 'The role of a prison officer', www.poauk.org.uk/index. php?the-role-of-a-prison-officer

[6] Ministry of Justice (2014) *Safety in custody statistics quarterly update to 31 December 2013*, Table 3.3: Prisoner assailants, victims and fighters by age and calendar year, England and Wales, 2000-2012, and Table 3.11: Assaults on staff by prisoner age group and calendar year, England and Wales, 2000-2012, London: MoJ.

[7] Howard League for Penal Reform (2010) *Life inside 2010. A unique insight into the day to day experiences of 15-17 year old males in prison*, London: Howard League for Penal reform, p 18.

[8] National Preventive Mechanism (2013) *Response to the Ministry of Justice consultation 'Transforming youth custody'*, London: NPM, p 5.

[9] Ministry of Justice (2013) *Safety in custody statistics quarterly update to 31 December 2012*, Table 3.14: Assault incidents (including fights) by establishment, England and Wales, London: MoJ.

[10] Ministry of Justice (2014) *Safety in custody statistics quarterly update to 31 December 2013*, Table 3.14: Assault incidents (including fights) by establishment, England and Wales, London: MoJ.

[11] Ministry of Justice (2014) *Safety in custody statistics quarterly update to 31 December 2013*, Table 3.14: Assault incidents (including fights) by establishment, England and Wales, London: MoJ.

[12] Her Majesty's Chief Inspector of Prisons, Her Majesty's Chief Inspector of Probation and Her Majesty's Chief Inspector of Constabulary (2010) *The management of gang issues among children and young people in prison custody and the community: a joint thematic review*, London: HMIP, p 43.

[13] HM Inspectorate of Prisons (2011) *Thematic report by HM Inspectorate of Prisons. The care of looked after children in custody. A short thematic review*, London: HMIP, p 70.

[14] Russell, F. (1999) 'Youth prison faces brutality claims', *The Guardian*, 17 November.

[15] Her Majesty's Inspectorate of Constabulary (2013) *'Mistakes were made.' HMIC's review into allegations and intelligence material concerning Jimmy Savile between 1964 and 2012*, London: HMIC, p 46.

[16] Bright, M. (2000) 'Prisons chief admits reign of terror by jail staff', *The Observer*, 13 February.

[17] *Dorset Echo*, 6 February 2001, 'Jails' chief in attack on YOI'.

[18] Her Majesty's Inspectorate of Prisons (2001) *Report on an announced follow-up inspection of HM young offender institution Portland 5-8 December 2000 by HM Chief Inspector of Prisons*, London: HMIP, p 3.

[19] Howard League for Penal Reform (2004) *Children in prison: promoting human rights – protecting welfare*, seminar briefing, 6 October, London: Howard League for Penal Reform, p 3.

[20] Howard League for Penal Reform (2004) *Children in prison: promoting human rights – protecting welfare*, seminar briefing, 6 October, London: Howard League for Penal Reform, p 4.

[21] Howard League for Penal Reform (2004) *Children in prison: promoting human rights – protecting welfare*, seminar briefing, 6 October, London: Howard League for Penal Reform, p 4.

[22] Howard League for Penal Reform (2004) *Children in prison: promoting human rights – protecting welfare*, seminar briefing, 6 October, London: Howard League for Penal Reform, p 4.

[23] Howard League for Penal Reform (2004) *Children in prison: promoting human rights – protecting welfare*, seminar briefing, 6 October, London: Howard League for Penal Reform, p 4.

[24] Bright, M. (2001) 'Horrors grow in Britain's violent jails', *The Observer*, 4 March.

[25] Howard League for Penal Reform (2004), *Children in prison: promoting human rights – protecting welfare*, seminar briefing, 6 October, London: Howard League for Penal Reform, p 3.

[26] BBC News, 23 October 2001, 'Prison chaplain settles 'brutality' claim'.

[27] Howard League for Penal Reform (2004), *Children in prison: promoting human rights – protecting welfare*, seminar briefing, 6 October, London: Howard League for Penal Reform, p 4.

[28] Howard League for Penal Reform (2004), *Children in prison: promoting human rights – protecting welfare*, seminar briefing, 6 October, London: Howard League for Penal Reform, p 4.

[29] Howard League for Penal Reform (2004), *Children in prison: promoting human rights – protecting welfare*, seminar briefing, 6 October, London: Howard League for Penal Reform, p 5.

[30] Johnson, M. (2008) *Wasted. Violence, addiction – and hope*, London: Sphere, p 109.

[31] Johnson, M. (2008) *Wasted. Violence, addiction – and hope*, London: Sphere, p 112.

[32] Keith, B. (2006) *Report of the Zahid Mubarek Inquiry. Volume 1*, London: The Stationery Office, pp 418-19.

[33] Keith, B. (2006) *Report of the Zahid Mubarek Inquiry. Volume 1*, London: The Stationery Office, p 419.

[34] Keith, B. (2006) *Report of the Zahid Mubarek Inquiry. Volume 1*, London: The Stationery Office, p 314.

[35] Keith, B. (2006) *Report of the Zahid Mubarek Inquiry. Volume 1*, London: The Stationery Office, p 312.

[36] Keith, B. (2006) *Report of the Zahid Mubarek Inquiry. Volume 1*, London: The Stationery Office, p 61.

[37] Keith, B. (2006) *Report of the Zahid Mubarek Inquiry. Volume 1*, London: The Stationery Office, p 312.

[38] House of Commons *Hansard*, 9 September 2010: Column 684W.

[39] BBC News, 11 August 2000, 'Jail boss resigns over conditions'.

[40] *Regina v Secretary of State for The Home Department (Respondent) ex parte Amin (FC) (Appellant)* (2003) [21].

[41] *Regina v Secretary of State for The Home Department (Respondent) ex parte Amin (FC) (Appellant)*, (2003) [41].

[42] Dodd, V. (2001) 'Malicious racism' in youth prison', *The Guardian*, 22 January.

[43] Narey, M. (undated) 'Prisons, brutality and decency. Reflections on thirty years', www.slideshare.net/martinnarey/prisons-brutality-and-decency-reflections-on-thirty-years#, p 5

[44] Kennedy. E. (2013) *Children and young people in custody 2012-13. An analysis of 15–18-year-olds' perceptions of their experiences in young offender institutions*, London: The Stationery Office, p 11.

[45] Elwood, C. (2013) *Children and young people in custody 2012-13. An analysis of 12–18-year-olds' perceptions of their experience in secure training centres*, London: HM Inspectorate of Prisons, p 7.

[46] Kennedy. E. (2013) *Children and young people in custody 2012-13. An analysis of 15–18-year-olds' perceptions of their experiences in young offender institutions*, London: The Stationery Office, pp 134 and 37.

[47] Kennedy. E. (2013) *Children and young people in custody 2012-13. An analysis of 15–18-year-olds' perceptions of their experiences in young offender institutions*, London: The Stationery Office, p 12.

[48] Office of Children's Rights Director for England (2012) *Children's care monitor 2011. Children on the state of social care in England*, Manchester: Ofsted, p 7.

[49] Her Majesty's Inspectorate of Prisons (2014) *Report on an announced inspection of HMYOI Hindley 3-14 March 2014 by HM Chief Inspector of Prisons*, London: HMIP, p 6.

[50] Her Majesty's Inspectorate of Prisons (2013) *Report on an announced inspection of HMYOI Warren Hill 4-8 March 2013 by HM Chief Inspector of Prisons*, London: HMIP, p 11.

[51] Her Majesty's Inspectorate of Prisons (2013) *Report on an announced inspection of HMYOI Warren Hill 4-8 March 2013 by HM Chief Inspector of Prisons*, London: HMIP, p 26.

[52] Goldson, B. (2002) *Vulnerable inside. Children in secure and penal settings*, London: The Children's Society, p 142.

[53] Goldson, B. (2002) *Vulnerable inside. Children in secure and penal settings*, London: The Children's Society, pp 142-3.

[54] National Children's Bureau (2008) *A review of safeguarding in the secure estate*, London: Youth Justice Board for England and Wales, p 1.

[55] Prisons and Probation Ombudsman for England and Wales (2013) *A report by the Prisons and Probation Ombudsman Nigel Newcomen CBE. Case number 46831/2012*, London: PPO, p 23.

[56] Duncan, G. (2008) *From the inside. Experiences of prison mental health care*, London: Sainsbury Centre for Mental Health, p 33.

[57] de Viggiani, N. (2012) 'Trying to be something you are not: masculine performances within a prison setting', *Men and Masculinities*, vol 15, no 3, pp 276-7.

[58] Children's Rights Alliance for England (2012) *Ending violence against children in custody. Findings from research with children and young people*, London: CRAE, pp 18-24.

[59] Bright, C. (2011) *Keppel Unit process evaluation: Summary*, London: Youth Justice Board for England and Wales, p 4.

[60] Bright, C. (2011) *Keppel Unit process evaluation: Summary*, London: Youth Justice Board for England and Wales, p 4.

[61] Howard League for Penal Reform (2010) *Life inside 2010. A unique insight into the day to day experiences of 15-17 year old males in prison*, London: Howard League for Penal Reform, p 12.

[62] Children's Rights Alliance for England (2012) *Ending violence against children in custody. Findings from research with children and young people*, London: CRAE, p 24.

[63] Murray, R. (2012) *Children and young people in custody 2011-12. An analysis of the experiences of 15–18-year-olds in prison*, London: HM Inspectorate of Prisons, p 39.

[64] Ofsted (2012) *The inspection of Rainsbrook secure training centre: December 2012*, Manchester: Ofsted, p 41.

[65] Ofsted, Her Majesty's Inspectorate of Prisons and Care Quality Commission (2014) *The inspection of Hassockfield secure training centre: July 2014*, Manchester: Ofsted, p 37.

[66] Prisons and Probation Ombudsman for England and Wales (2009) *Investigation into the circumstances surrounding the death of a boy at HMYOI Lancaster Farms in November 2007*, London: PPO, p 8.

[67] Prisons and Probation Ombudsman for England and Wales (2009) *Investigation into the circumstances surrounding the death of a boy at HMYOI Lancaster Farms in November 2007*, London: PPO, p 107.

[68] Prisons and Probation Ombudsman for England and Wales (2009) *Investigation into the circumstances surrounding the death of a boy at HMYOI Lancaster Farms in November 2007*, London: PPO, p 7.

[69] Prisons and Probation Ombudsman for England and Wales (2009) *Investigation into the circumstances surrounding the death of a boy at HMYOI Lancaster Farms in November 2007*, London: PPO, pp 107-8.

[70] Prisons and Probation Ombudsman for England and Wales (2009) *Investigation into the circumstances surrounding the death of a boy at HMYOI Lancaster Farms in November 2007*, London: PPO, p 8.

[71] HM Inspectorate of Prisons (2011) *Thematic report by HM Inspectorate of Prisons. The care of looked after children in custody. A short thematic review*, London: HMIP, pp 36 and 67.

[72] Harrington, R. and Bailey, S. with others (2005) *Mental health needs and effectiveness of provision for young offenders in custody and in the community*, London: Youth Justice Board for England and Wales, p 20.

[73] Berelowitz, S. (2011) *'I think I must have been born bad.' Emotional well-being and mental health of children and young people in the youth justice system*, London: Office of the Children's Commissioner, p 48.

[74] Prestage, M. (1994) 'How to beat bullies from the inside', *TES*, 2 December; and *The Independent*, 30 August 1994, 'Remand prisoners under 21 found hanged this year'.

[75] Dennis, S. (2000) 'My boy waved goodbye, went to his cell. Then hanged himself; scandal of jail suicides', *Mirror*, 16 August.

[76] *Yorkshire Post*, 3 May 2001, 'Lesson hope after cell death inquest'.

[77] Allison, E. (2014) 'Prison officers' failings contributed to vulnerable boy's death, inquest rules', *The Guardian*, 4 April.

[78] Harrington, R. and Bailey, S. with others (2005) *Mental health needs and effectiveness of provision for young offenders in custody and in the community*, London: Youth Justice Board for England and Wales, p 39.

Chapter Eleven

[1] Gibbens, E.B. (1967) *Administration of punishment at Court Lees approved school: report of inquiry*, London: Her Majesty's Stationery Office.

[2] Cited in Parton, N. (1991) *Governing the family, child care, child protection and the state*, London: Macmillan, p 29.

[3] House of Commons Select Committee on Health (1998) *Children looked after by local authorities'*, Table entitled 'Children in care/looked after by local authorities at 31 March, 1965-1996, England', London: The Stationery Office, para 33.

[4] Corby, B., Doig, A. and Roberts, V. (2001) *Public inquiries into abuse of children in residential care*, London: Jessica Kingsley Publishers, pp 77-8.

5   Vatican press release, 5 December 2013, 'The Pope to create a Commission for the Protection of Minors'.

6   BBC Panorama film on Winterbourne View, www.youtube.com/ watch?v=submGwyJOK8

7   Brown, L. and Brooke, C. (2012) '"Culture of cruelty": 11 care home workers sentenced for shocking abuse of vulnerable residents exposed by Panorama probe', *Mail Online*, 26 October.

8   User Voice (2011) *Young people's views on safeguarding in the secure estate*, London: Youth Justice Board for England and Wales, p 20.

9   Gray, D. and Watt, P. (2013) *'Giving victims a voice.' A joint MPS and NSPCC report into allegations of sexual abuse made against Jimmy Savile under Operation Yewtree*, London: Metropolitan Police and NSPCC, pp 20-1.

10 The Right Honourable the Lord Judge, Lord Chief Justice of England and Wales (2013) 'Half a century of change: the evidence of child victims', Toulmin Lecture in Law and Psychiatry, King's College London, 20 March, p 3.

11 BBC Radio 4 Today programme, 6 March 2013.

12 Crown Prosecution Service (2013) *Guidelines on prosecuting cases of child sexual abuse*, London: CPS, para 53.

13 Her Majesty's Inspectorate of Constabulary (2013) *'Mistakes were made.' HMIC's review into allegations and intelligence material concerning Jimmy Savile between 1964 and 2012*, London: HMIC, p 10.

14 Her Majesty's Inspectorate of Constabulary (2013) *'Mistakes were made.' HMIC's review into allegations and intelligence material concerning Jimmy Savile between 1964 and 2012*, London: HMIC, p 46.

15 Levitt, A. (2013) *In the matter of the late Jimmy Savile. Report to the Director of Public Prosecutions by Alison Levitt QC*, London: CPS, p 64.

16 Levitt, A. (2013) *In the matter of the late Jimmy Savile. Report to the Director of Public Prosecutions by Alison Levitt QC*, London: CPS, p 24.

17 Exton, L. and Thandi, K. (2013) *Would they actually have believed me? A focus group exploration of the underreporting of crimes by Jimmy Savile*, London: NSPCC, p 7.

18 Brown, J. (2013) 'Margaret Thatcher made repeated attempts to get Jimmy Savile knighted – despite pleas from concerned aides', *The Independent*, 17 July.

19 Early day motion 2337, 31 October 2011, www.parliament.uk/edm/2010-12/2337

20 Levitt, A. (2013) *In the matter of the late Jimmy Savile. Report to the Director of Public Prosecutions by Alison Levitt QC*, London: CPS, p 25.

21 Pettifor, T. (2012) 'Jimmy Savile scandal: disgraced star was allowed to stay overnight at girls school run by Home Office', *Mirror*, 17 October.

22 *The Residential Care Homes (Amendment) Regulations 1988, regulation 4*, prohibited corporal punishment as a sanction in residential care.

23 House of Commons *Hansard*, 16 November 1967: Columns 653–725. More information about the Court Lees Inquiry can be found at: House of Lords *Hansard*, 2 April 1968: Columns 1196–218.

24 Smith-Squire, A. (2012) 'I feared no-one would believe me', *Bella Magazine*, 16 October.

25 Hyland, J. (1993) *Yesterday's answers. Development and decline of schools for young offenders*, London: Whiting and Birch Ltd, p 49.

26 National Crime Agency (2013) *CEOP Thematic assessment. The foundations of abuse: a thematic assessment of the risk of child sexual abuse by adults in institutions*, London: NCA, p 4.

27 Hope, C. (2012) 'Jimmy Savile: nine BBC staff facing abuse allegations', *The Telegraph*, 23 October.

28 Pettifor, T. (2012) 'Jimmy Savile scandal: disgraced star was allowed to stay overnight at girls school run by Home Office', *Mirror*, 17 October.

29 House of Lords *Hansard*, 26 November 2013: Column WA267.

30 Criminal Justice Act 2003, s 142A(3)(a), as amended by Criminal Justice and Immigration Act 2008, s 9.

31 Lampard, K. (2014) *Independent oversight of NHS and Department of Health investigations into matters relating to Jimmy Savile. An assurance report for the Secretary of State for Health*, London: Department of Health, appendices A and B.

32 Her Majesty's Inspectorate of Prisons (2001) *Report on a full announced inspection of HM YOI /RC Onley 9-13 July 2001 by HM Chief Inspector of Prisons*, London: HMIP, p 14.

33 *R (The Howard League for Penal Reform) v Secretary of State for the Home Department and Department of Health* [2002] EWHC 2497 (Admin) [79].

34 *R (The Howard League for Penal Reform) v Secretary of State for the Home Department and Department of Health* [2002] EWHC 2497 (Admin) [160].

35 *R (The Howard League for Penal Reform) v Secretary of State for the Home Department and Department of Health* [2002] EWHC 2497 (Admin) [165].

36 *R (The Howard League for Penal Reform) v Secretary of State for the Home Department and Department of Health* [2002] EWHC 2497 (Admin) [123].

37 National Children's Bureau (2008) *A review of safeguarding in the secure estate*, London: Youth Justice Board for England and Wales, p 53.

38 The Local Safeguarding Children Boards Regulations 2006, reg 5.

39 Kennedy, E. (2013) *Children and young people in custody 2012-13. An analysis of 15–18-year-olds' perceptions of their experiences in young offender institutions*, London: The Stationery Office, p 98.

40 Kennedy, E. (2013) *Children and young people in custody 2012-13. An analysis of 15–18-year-olds' perceptions of their experiences in young offender institutions*, London: The Stationery Office, p 118.

41 Elwood, C. (2013) *Children and young people in custody 2012-13. An analysis of 12–18-year-olds' perceptions of their experience in secure training centres*, London: HM Inspectorate of Prisons, p 23.

42 Collins, D. (2013) 'Borstal governor was "a leading member" of paedophile ring which preyed on inmates, victims claim', *Mirror*, 31 October.

43 Durham Constabulary (2014) press release 'Operation Seabrook – Medomsley detention centre', 1 May.

44 House of Lords *Hansard*, 17 December 2013: Column 178W.

45 The Young Offender Institution (Amendment) Rules 1989, rule 2.

46 Ministry of Justice and Youth Justice Board for England and Wales (2013) *Service specification for independent advocacy services to children and young people. Schedule 10: confidentiality undertaking*, London: MoJ.

47 Ministry of Justice and Youth Justice Board for England and Wales (2013) *Service specification for independent advocacy services to children and young people. Lots 1 and 2 (North and South)*, London: MoJ, pp 23 and 24.

48 Department of Health (2002) *National standards for the provision of children's advocacy services,* London: DH, p 11.

49 Creighton, S.J. and Russell, N. (1995) *Voices from childhood: a survey of childhood experiences and attitudes to child rearing among adults in the United Kingdom,* NSPCC Policy, Practice, Research series, London: NSPCC, p 46.

50 BBC News, 27 January 2014, 'Medomsley detention centre: victims' lives were "ruined"'.

51 Cited in Day, C., Hibbert, P. and Cadman, S. (2008) *A literature review into children abused and/or neglected prior custody*, London: Youth Justice Board for England and Wales, p 14.

52 Cited in Jütte, S., Bentley, H., Miller, P. and Jetha, N. (2014) *How safe are our children?*, London: NSPCC, p 4.

53 Prisons Ombudsman (2001) *Listening to young prisoners. A review of complaints procedures in young offender institutions by the Prisons Ombudsman*, London: PPO, p 1.

54 Prisons Ombudsman (2001) *Listening to young prisoners. A review of complaints procedures in Young Offender Institutions by the Prisons Ombudsman*, London: PPO, p 10.

55 The Secure Training Centre Rules 1998, rule 8(6).

56 The Criminal Legal Aid (General) (Amendment) Regulations 2013, reg 4.

57 House of Lords *Hansard*, 29 January 2014: Column 1298.

58 McGurk, B.J., Forde, R. and Barnes, A. (2000) *Sexual victimisation among 15–17-year-old offenders in prison*, London: Home Office, p 17.

59 McGurk, B.J., Forde, R. and Barnes, A. (2000) *Sexual victimisation among 15–17-year-old offenders in prison*, London: Home Office, p 17.

60 Barter, C. (1998) *Investigating institutional abuse of children. An exploration of the NSPCC experience*, London: NSPCC, p 15.

61 McGurk, B.J., Forde, R. and Barnes, A. (2000) *Sexual victimisation among 15–17-year-old offenders in prison*, London: Home Office, p 19.

62 Cited in Allison, E. and Hattestone, S. (2012) 'Prisons chief admits failings in service over sexual abuse', *The Guardian*, 13 April.

[63] D'Arcy, M. and Gosling, P. (1998) *Abuse of trust. Frank Beck and the Leicestershire children's homes scandal*, London: Bowerdean Publishing Company Ltd, p 143.

[64] Beck, A.J., Cantor, D., Hartge, J. and Smith, T. (2013) *Sexual victimization in juvenile facilities reported by youth, 2012. National survey of youth in custody, 2012*, Washington, DC: US Department of Justice, p 4.

[65] House of Lords *Hansard*, 15 July 2013: Column: WA100.

[66] Harker, L. and others (2013) *How safe are our children?*, London: NSPCC, p 70.

[67] House of Commons *Hansard*, 20 July 2010: Column 170.

[68] House of Lords *Hansard*, 21 July 2010: Column 973.

[69] Glover, J. and Hibbert, P. (2008) *Locking up or giving up – is custody for children always the right answer?*, London: Barnardo's, p 7.

[70] Goldson, B. (2009) 'Child incarceration: institutional abuse, the violent state and the politics of impunity', in P. Scraton and J. McCulloch (eds) *The violence of incarceration*, London: Routledge.

[71] Tower Hamlets Safeguarding Children Board (2013) *Serious case review executive summary. Services provided for Child F June 2004 – January 2012*, London: Tower Hamlets Safeguarding Children Board, p 11.

[72] Tower Hamlets Safeguarding Children Board (2013) *Serious case review executive summary. Services provided for Child F June 2004-January 2012*, London: Tower Hamlets Safeguarding Children Board, pp 12-13.

[73] Stainton Rogers, W. Hevey, D. and Ash, E. (1989) *Child abuse and neglect. Facing the challenge*, London: The Open University, p 206.

Chapter Twelve

[1] Cohen, S. (2005) *States of denial. Knowing about atrocities and suffering*, Cambridge: Polity Press, pp 7-8.

[2] Carlile, A. (2006) *An independent inquiry into the use of physical restraint, solitary confinement and forcible strip searching of children in prisons, secure training centres and local authority secure children's homes*, London: Howard League for Penal Reform, p 62.

[3] *R (Shoesmith) v Ofsted and others* [2011] EWCA Civ 642.

[4] National Preventive Mechanism (2012) *Monitoring places of detention. Second annual report of the United Kingdom's National Preventive Mechanism 1 April 2010-31 March 2011*, London: The Stationery Office, p 4.

[5] Youth Justice Board for England and Wales (2014) *Deaths of children in custody: action taken, lessons learnt*, London: YJB, p 10.

[6] Laming, W.H. (2003) *The Victoria Climbié Inquiry. Report of an inquiry by Lord Laming*, Norwich: HMSO, p 30.

[7] Laming, W.H. (2003) *The Victoria Climbié Inquiry. Report of an inquiry by Lord Laming*, Norwich: HMSO, p 346.

[8] Youth Justice Board for England and Wales press release, 'YJB to withdraw from Hassockfield STC and Hindley YOI', 23 October 2014.

[9] House of Commons *Hansard*, 12 July 2007: Column 1718.

[10] Sambrook, C. (2013) 'G4S guard fatally restrains 15 year old – gets promoted', OurKingdom website, 22 July, www.opendemocracy.net/ourkingdom/clare-sambrook/g4s-guard-fatally-restrains-15-year-old-gets-promoted.

[11] *Private Eye* (2012) 'To Serco with love', January, issue 1306, p 30.

[12] Prisons and Probation Ombudsman for England and Wales (2006) *Circumstances surrounding the death of a boy at Hassockfield secure training centre on 8 August 2004. Report by the Prisons and Probation Ombudsman for England and Wales*, London: PPO, p 105.

[13] Department for Education (2011) *Children Act 1989 guidance and regulations volume 5: children's homes*, London: DfE, para 2.96.

[14] Stein, M. (2011) *Care less lives. The story of the rights movement of young people in care*, London: Catch 22.

[15] NSPCC (2013) *Real life stories. The NSPCC annual report and accounts 2012/13*, London: NSPCC, p 11.

[16] Méndez, J. (2011) *Interim report prepared by the Special Rapporteur of the Human Rights Council on torture and other cruel, inhuman or degrading treatment or punishment*, New York: UN General Assembly, para 26. The Rapporteur defines solitary confinement as physical and social isolation in cells for 22 or more hours a day.

[17] Méndez, J. (2011) *Interim report prepared by the Special Rapporteur of the Human Rights Council on torture and other cruel, inhuman or degrading treatment or punishment*, New York: UN General Assembly, para 77.

[18] Committee on the Rights of the Child (2007) General comment no. 10. Children's rights in juvenile justice, Geneva: UN, para 89.

[19] Bright, C. (2011) *Keppel Unit process evaluation: summary*, London: Youth Justice Board for England and Wales, p 5.

[20] Stern, V. (2006) 'Crime and punishment in a market society: how just is the criminal justice system?', British Institute of Human Rights lecture, 9 February.

[21] McAra, L. and McVie, S. (2011) 'Youth justice? The impact of system contact on patterns of desistance', in S. Farrall, M. Hough, S. Maruna and R. Sparks (eds) *Escape routes. Contemporary perspectives on life after punishment*, London: Routledge, p 101.

[22] United Nations General Assembly (1985) *United Nations standard minimum rules for the administration of juvenile justice*, New York: UN.

[23] Youth Justice Board press release, 24 October 2006, 'Crisis point reached as the number of young people in custody reaches record high'.

[24] McAra, L. and McVie, S. (2011) 'Youth justice? The impact of system contact on patterns of desistance', in S. Farrall, M. Hough, S. Maruna and R. Sparks (eds) *Escape routes. Contemporary perspectives on life after punishment*, London: Routledge.

[25] McAra, L. and McVie, S. (2011) 'Youth justice? The impact of system contact on patterns of desistance', in S. Farrall, M. Hough, S. Maruna and R. Sparks (eds) *Escape routes. Contemporary perspectives on life after punishment*, London: Routledge, p 102.

[26] Williams, G. and McCreadie, J. (1992) *Ty Mawr community home inquiry*, Gwent: Gwent County Council, pp 35 and 37.

[27] House of Lords *Hansard*, 24 June 1992: Columns 504-38.

[28] Bland, A. (2013) 'Inside Feltham: why London's young offender institution is one of the scariest prisons in Britain', *The Independent*, 31 August.

[29] *The Independent*, 22 January 1993, 'Boy found dead in cell "not a risk"'.

[30] Prestage, M. (1994) 'How to beat bullies from the inside', *TES*, 2 December.

[31] Independent news, 3 October 1995, 'Cell death inquiry'; *Shropshire Star*, 28 October 2009, '"Near-moronic bully" fails in jail term bid'.

[32] INQUEST press release, 26 February 1999, 'Inquest opens into the death of 16 year old Nicholas Whelan in HMYOI Glen Parva'.

[33] *Lancashire Telegraph*, 7 October 1999, 'Family call for policy change after cell death'.

[34] *The York Press*, 24 August 2000, 'Last hours of cell hanging teenager'.

[35] Dennis, S. (2000) 'My boy waved goodbye, went to his cell. Then hanged himself; scandal of jail suicides', *Mirror*, 16 August.

[36] Neustatter, A. (2002) *Locked in. Locked out. The experience of young offenders out of society and in prison*, London: Calouste Gulbenkian Foundation, pp 75-6.

[37] BBC Panorama programme, 11 March 2001, 'Young offenders at risk'.

[38] Goldson, B. and Coles, D. (2005) *In the care of the state? Child deaths in penal custody in England and Wales*, London: INQUEST, p 48.

[39] BBC News, 11 December 2001, 'Teenager "attempted suicide four times"'.

[40] Youth Justice Board for England and Wales (2014) *Deaths of children in custody: action taken, lessons learnt*, London: YJB, p 13.

[41] Davies, N. (2004) 'Wasted lives of the young let down by jail system', *The Guardian*, 8 December.

[42] BBC News, 7 October 2004, 'Teenage inmate hanged in cell'.

[43] Gilroy, D. (2004) *Youth Justice Board serious incident review. Gareth Paul Myatt*, London: Youth Justice Board for England and Wales, pp 10-11.

[44] Prisons and Probation Ombudsman for England and Wales (2006) *Circumstances surrounding the death of a boy at Hassockfield secure training centre on 8 August 2004*, London: PPO, pp 13-14.

[45] Coroner's summing up notes, pp 4-5 and 12.

[46] Prisons and Probation Ombudsman for England and Wales (2008) *Circumstances surrounding the death of a trainee at HMP and YOI Hindley, in September 2005*, London: PPO, p 12.

[47] St Helens Safeguarding Children Board (2009) *Serious case review: L. Executive summary*, St Helens: St Helens Safeguarding Children Board, pp 2 and 5.

[48] INQUEST press release, 28 January 2014, 'Serious failures identified by jury at inquest into death of 17 year old Ryan Clark at HMYOI Wetherby'.

[49] Tower Hamlets Safeguarding Children Board (2013) *Serious case review executive summary. Services provided for Child F June 2004-January 2012*, London: Tower Hamlets Safeguarding Children Board, pp 6 and 13.

[50] Youth Justice Board (2014) *Deaths of children in custody: Action taken, lessons learnt*, London: YJB, p 13. INQUEST collates and publishes a list of children who have died in prison: www.inquest.org.uk/pdf/Deaths_of_Children_in_Penal_Custody_1990-date.pdf

[51] Youth Justice Board for England and Wales and Ministry of Justice (2014) *Youth justice statistics 2012/13 England and Wales*, Table 5.5: Young people sentenced for indictable offences by gender and type of sentence, 2002/03 to 2012/13, London: MoJ.

[52] 'Transforming youth custody' was the title of the government's 2013 Green Paper on child custody.

[53] Goldson, B. (2006) 'Penal custody: intolerance, irrationality and indifference', in Goldson, B. and Muncie, B. (eds) *Youth crime and justice*, London: Sage Publications, p 139.

[54] United Kingdom-London: Justice services, 2014/S 090-157408, contract notice: http://ted.europa.eu/udl?uri=TED:NOTICE:157408-2014:TEXT:EN:HTML

[55] Bland, A. (2013) 'Inside Feltham: why London's young offender institution is one of the scariest prisons in Britain', *The Independent*, 31 August.

[56] Prisons and Probation Ombudsman for England and Wales (2013) *A report by the Prisons and Probation Ombudsman Nigel Newcomen CBE*, London: PPO, paras 133 and 135.

[57] The Youth Justice Board reports that at least 69% of the 16 children who have died in custody since it took on the placement function in 2000 were, at some time in their childhood, subject to care orders: Youth Justice Board (2014) *Deaths of children in custody: Action taken, lessons learnt*, London: YJB, p 33.

[58] Bland, A. (2013) '"Nobody gave a toss": ex prisons boss, Sir Martin Narey, says no one cared about suicides', *The Independent newspaper*, 30 August.

[59] House of Commons *Hansard*, 9 January 1996: Column 20.

[60] Coroner's factual summing-up notes, p 45.

[61] Her Majesty's Inspectorate of Prisons (2013) *Report on an unannounced inspection of HMYOI Hindley 19-23 November 2012 by HM Chief Inspector of Prisons*, London: HMIP, p 5.

[62] *Yvonne Scholes v Secretary of State for the Home Department* [2006] EWCA Civ 1343 [32].

[63] House of Commons Justice Committee (2013) *Youth justice. Seventh report of session 2012-13*, London: The Stationery Office, p 41.

[64] Kennedy, H. (1995) *Banged up. Beaten up. Cuting up. Report of the Howard League commission of inquiry into violence in penal institutions for teenagers under 18*, London: Howard League for Penal Reform, p 101.

[65] Justice Studio (2014) *'They helped me, they supported me.' Achieving outcomes and value for money in secure children's homes*, Secure Accommodation Network, www.cypnow.co.uk/digital_assets/419/SAN_report_final.pdf

[66] Justice Studio (2014) *'They helped me, they supported me.' Achieving outcomes and value for money in secure children's homes*, Secure Accommodation Network, p 42, www.cypnow.co.uk/digital_assets/419/SAN_report_final.pdf

[67] Department for Education (2011) *Children's homes: national minimum standards*, London: DfE, p 4.

[68] Justice Studio (2014) *'They helped me, they supported me.' Achieving outcomes and value for money in secure children's homes*, Secure Accommodation Network, p 56, www.cypnow.co.uk/digital_assets/419/SAN_report_final.pdf

[69] Solomon, E. and Allen, R. (2009) *Reducing child imprisonment in England and Wales – lessons from abroad*, London: Prison Reform Trust, p 22.

[70] 'Pad' is prison slang for cell.

[71] INQUEST press release, 'Jury rules catalogue of shocking failures led to preventable death of 17 year old Jake Hardy at Hindley prison, 4 April 2014'.

[72] Youth Justice Board for England and Wales press release, 'YJB to withdraw from Hassockfield STC and Hindley YOI', 23 October 2014.

[73] INQUEST press release, 'Jury rules catalogue of shocking failures led to preventable death of 17 year old Jake Hardy at Hindley prison', 4 April 2014.

[74] POA: The Professional Trades Union for Prison, Correctional and Secure Psychiatric Workers, 'The role of a prison officer', www.poauk.org.uk/index.php?the-role-of-a-prison-officer

[75] Bateman, T. (2012) 'Who pulled the plug? Towards an explanation of the fall in child imprisonment in England and Wales', *Youth Justice*, 12, p 39. Bateman's figures relate to 10- to 16-year-olds.

[76] Youth Justice Board for England and Wales (2003) *Annual statistics 2002/03*, London: YJB, p 76.

Index

Note: page numbers in bold type refer to tables.